American Popular Music

Rock and Roll

American Popular Music

Blues
Classical
Country
Folk
Jazz
Rhythm & Blues, Rap, and Hip-Hop
Rock and Roll

General Editor: Richard Carlin

Editorial Board:

Barbara Ching, Ph.D., University of Memphis

Ronald D. Cohen, Ph.D., Indiana University-Northwest

William Duckworth, Bucknell University

Kevin J. Holm-Hudson, Ph.D., University of Kentucky

Nadine Hubbs, Ph.D., University of Michigan

Craig Morrison, Ph.D., Concordia University (Montreal)

Albin J. Zak III, Ph.D., University at Albany (SUNY)

American Popular Music

Rock and Roll

Craig Morrison

Foreword by Kevin J. Holm-Hudson, Ph.D.
University of Kentucky

An imprint of Infobase Publishing

American Popular Music: Rock and Roll

Facts On File, Inc.
An imprint of Infobase Publishing
132 West 31st Street
New York NY 10001

ISBN-10: 0-8160-5317-0
ISBN-13: 978-0-8160-5317-9

Library of Congress Cataloging-in-Publication Data

Morrison, Craig, 1952–
    American popular music : rock and roll / Craig Morrison ; foreword by Kevin J. Holm-Hudson.
       p. cm.
    Includes bibliographical references and index.
    ISBN 0-8160-5317-0 (hc : alk. paper)
    1. Popular music—United States—Encyclopedias. I. Holm-Hudson, Kevin. II. Title.
    ML102.R6M67 2005
    781.66'0973'03—dc22   2004025447

Facts On File books are available at special discounts when purchased in bulk quantities for businesses, associations, institutions, or sales promotions. Please call our Special Sales Department in New York at (212) 967-8800 or (800) 322-8755.

You can find Facts On File on the World Wide Web at http://www.factsonfile.com

Text design by James Scotto-Lavino
Cover design by Nora Wertz

Printed in the United States of America

VB FOF 10 9 8 7 6 5 4 3 2

This book is printed on acid-free paper.

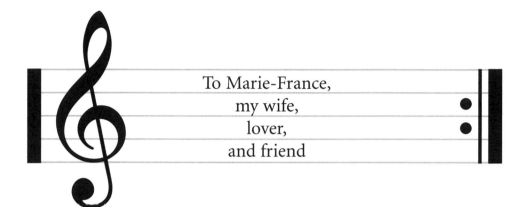

To Marie-France,
my wife,
lover,
and friend

Contents

Foreword

I was so much older then—I'm younger than that now: Rock's rolling odyssey

Rock music is the dominant sound of the modern age. It can be heard on the radio, in television advertisements, movies, restaurants, and shopping malls. A sound that was once regional, confined to a few southern cities and heard in rural juke joints, has matured, absorbing and being influenced by every conceivable style from jazz to Gregorian chant to African drumming. Along the way, rock—and those related styles such as rap and R&B that have fed off and also fused back into rock's continuing development—has gone global. Karaoke clubs around the world offer locals the opportunity to sing—to be—Madonna or Bruce Springsteen for a night. Germany and other European countries have thriving local hip-hop scenes. Japan has a prospering alternative-music scene, from the thrash-progressive group Ruins to the Ramones-style "girl group" Shonen Knife. A Finnish group called "4R" has its own version of U2's signature sound.

Once the sound of youthful defiance, rock now crosses generations; my senior-age mother likes to listen to U2 alongside Frank Sinatra and Enya. Once a medium for rebellion and voicing social change, rock has become a marketing tool for big business. Led Zeppelin's "Rock and Roll" is now used to sell Cadillacs; other car companies regularly bring once-obscure cult favorites, such as Nick Drake's "Pink Moon" (Volkswagen) and T. Rex's "20th Century Boy" (Mitsubishi), into the mainstream. Once regarded by some Christian church leaders as the sound of Satan himself, rock music can now be heard in churches around the world. It is sometimes hard to remember, since rock music is

literally everywhere now (even in deep space, where Chuck Berry's "Johnny B. Goode" was sent up with the *Voyager* space probes in 1977), that rock was once a small-town, small-time affair.

Charles Gillett, in his classic text *The Sound of the City*, points out that by the mid-1950s there were already five distinct strands of rock 'n' roll. There was what he called "Northern band rock 'n' roll," represented by Bill Haley and His Comets. There was Memphis rockabilly, initially centered on Sam Phillips' Sun Records and the artists—Elvis Presley, Carl Perkins, Jerry Lee Lewis, and others—who recorded there, infusing a country sound with a pumped-up rhythm-and-blues energy. Chicago rhythm and blues was similarly centered on a record label, in this case Chess Records, represented by the songs of Chuck Berry and Bo Diddley. Chess also recorded blues artists such as Muddy Waters and Howlin' Wolf, who amplified themselves so they could be heard in noisy clubs (years before Bob Dylan shocked American audiences with his electrification of folk music, Muddy Waters similarly scandalized blues purists in Britain with his amplified sound). Although Chicago urban blues may be regarded as a style distinctly different from rock, the songs of Muddy Waters, Willie Dixon, and Howlin' Wolf brought the passion and sexuality of down-home blues into the urban north and were to become crucial elements of the 1960s British invasion and the hard rock of the late 1960s. The New Orleans dance blues of artists such as Little Richard and Fats Domino brought that city's energetic "second-line" rhythms into rock 'n' roll (listen to Domino's "I'm Walkin'" for a good example). Finally, the doo-wop sound of vocal groups brought a softer side to rock 'n' roll, giving voice to the sentimental nature of teen romance and restoring generational connections by using older Tin Pan Alley songs for much of its material ("Blue Moon," "In the Still of the Night").

The differences between these five major strands of early rock were brought about by differences in culture, landscape, and environment. There were other regional sounds to come as well, from Texas (Buddy Holly, Roy Orbison), Detroit (John Lee Hooker), southern California (the Beach Boys), and elsewhere, all bringing in their own unique contributions to rock's musical melting pot. Unlike Great Britain, for example, with its more uniform geography and culture, the sheer size and cultural diversity of the United States ensured that early rock 'n' roll would be a crazy quilt of styles and influences. By the same token, Britain's smaller size ensured that its musical cross-fertilizations in the mid- to late-1960s "British invasion" could take place that much more rapidly. When the first wave of British groups—the Beatles, the Rolling Stones, Gerry and the Pacemakers, the Dave Clark Five, and others—arrived in America, they brought with them a version of America's music, introducing many young listeners to America's great indigenous tradition of blues and R&B. Many listeners responded enthusiastically to the "new" sounds. For a country that had seemingly suffered a collective amnesia at the hands of the "teen idol" producers and the trauma of the Kennedy assassination, British groups offered a musical Rosetta Stone for America's musical identity.

The first great rock mergers came at about the same time that rock lost its apostrophes. Rock 'n' roll became rock *and* roll, and then simply rock, by which it signaled that it had matured. Folk rock was the first stylistic merger, as Dylan's push for serious and probing lyric writing led to the groundbreaking work of the Byrds and Simon and Garfunkel. In Britain, it was one of the 1960s' greatest ironies that—much as America had learned of its own blues and R&B from the British invasion—the folk and folk rock efforts of Americans such as Bob Dylan, Judy Collins, and Joan Baez educated British musicians about their own folk music traditions, which had been nearly lost to industrialization. A thriving folk rock scene emerged in Britain a few years after the one in America, spearheaded by groups such as Fairport Convention, the Albion Country Band, and Steeleye Span.

Other stylistic fusions followed quickly in America—jazz rock, raga rock, country rock, electronic rock. The 1970s heyday of progressive rock, which originated in Britain, seemed for many a final frontier, as rock sought to fuse its style with classical and symphonic elements. Other styles—such as the introspective, folk-influenced songs of the singer-songwriters and the aggressive, back-to-basics sound of punk rock—were retrenchments from the complexities of previous styles.

Throughout its history, however, rock music can also be seen as a mirror of contemporary social concerns. For example, the desegregation of schools mandated by the landmark *Brown v. Board of Education* Supreme Court case in 1954 is musically paralleled by Elvis's equally landmark Sun session that same year. "That's All Right" was *Brown* played out in a musical format; once Elvis desegregated the airwaves with his musical melding of black and white styles, nothing on the social front could stay the same for long. Similar analogies can be found between the blending of male and female gender roles in the 1970s, in the wake of the women's movement, and the androgynous personas of glam or glitter rock (*Ziggy Stardust*–era David Bowie, the Sweet, T. Rex, and Elton John). The emergence of disco came not long after the Stonewall riots in New York's Greenwich Village catalyzed the gay-rights movement in 1969. In each of these cases, the musical changes followed changes in society. Music could not change the world, as many in the 1960s counterculture believed rock could, but it could comment upon it. Today, many rock songs, even if the lyrics are not political, can almost be read as historical documents with a catchy tune or guitar hook.

Ultimately, rock fragmented at about the same time as the counterculture to which it once gave a unified voice. As rock was beginning to fragment irreparably into various "formats" in the 1970s, a British graphic artist named Pete Frame began creating elaborately detailed "rock family trees" for various bands, showing who played with which group and for how long, what bands they came from, and where they went after they left. Frame's diagrams, shown on several albums (by Fairport Convention, King Crimson, and Soft Machine, among others) and collected in a book entitled *The Complete Rock Family Trees,* bear witness to a time in rock history when musicians mattered, and when fans followed such connections between groups. A new group such as Blind Faith—with the talents of Eric Clapton, Steve Winwood, Ginger Baker and Ric Grech—could sell out concerts across America before even releasing an album, before anyone had heard even a note of their music, simply because of the prestige of individual players' band pedigrees.

Today, rock and roll has arguably lost this sense of connectedness. A seemingly endless parade of new stars is presented on the radio, on TV music channels such as MTV, and on the Internet. Listening habits have shifted back from albums to individual songs, and the popular mp3 format makes the computer a kind of "digital jukebox." As a result, concept albums, once all the rage in the late 1960s and early 1970s, are virtually a thing of the past (albums such as Radiohead's *OK Computer,* Hüsker Du's *Zen Arcade* and Neil Young's *Greendale* are notable—and infrequent—exceptions), but consumers now have the power to compile personalized "concept albums" in the form of themed mix CDs and tapes and mp3 player sequences. True, the presence of samples in rap music helps to reassert historical or stylistic connections for listeners who are really interested in seeking them out (and Chuck D of Public Enemy has repeatedly asserted that the group chooses samples as a kind of connection with the "great tradition" of African-American popular music). However, this kind of historical awareness is largely lost in rock and pop's preoccupations with using the "star-making machinery" to promote the "next big thing" before it fades away.

This book restores some of these connections. In every entry, among the historical facts about a particular artist, band, or style are references to other artists and bands, providing a necessary context for their contributions. Craig Morrison sees to it that the line of connectedness is synchronic (contemporaries influencing each other) as well as diachronic (connecting artists and bands across decades, sometimes in unexpected ways). Readers who can say, with the Rolling Stones, "It's only rock and roll . . . but I like it," can now discover for themselves *why* they like it.

I hope that readers, while researching favorite artists, will explore some of the equally great historical influences on those artists and explore their music. Whether it is labeled "retro" or "old skool," it's really about connecting rock's present with where it has been, with an eye on where rock is going.

Rock keeps moving, but it also leaves many tracks to explore.

Kevin Holm-Hudson,
University of Kentucky

Preface

American popular music reflects the rich cultural diversity of the American people. From classical to folk to jazz, America has contributed a rich legacy of musical styles to the world over its two-plus centuries of existence. The rich cross-fertilization of cultures—African-American, Hispanic, Asian, and European—has resulted in one of the unique musical mixtures in the world.

American Popular Music celebrates this great diversity by presenting to the student, researcher, and individual enthusiast a wealth of information on each musical style in an easily accessible format. The subjects covered are:

Blues
Classical music
Country
Folk music
Jazz
Rock and Roll
Rhythm and Blues, Rap, and Hip-Hop

Each volume presents key information on performers, musical genres, famous compositions, musical instruments, media, and centers of musical activity. The volumes conclude with a chronology, recommended listening, and a complete bibliography or list of sources for further study.

How do we define *popular music?* Literally, any music that attracts a reasonably large audience is "popular" (as opposed to "unpopular"). Over the past few decades, however, as the study of popular music has grown, the term has come to have specific meanings. While some might exclude certain genres covered in this series—American classical music leaps to mind—we felt that it was important to represent the range of musical styles that have been popular in the United States over its entire history. New scholarship has brought to light the interplay among genres that previously were felt to be unrelated—such as the influence of folk forms on classical music, opera's influence on jazz, or the blues' influence on country—so that to truly understand each musical style, it is important to be conversant with at least some aspects of all.

These volumes are intended to be introductory, not comprehensive. Any "A to Z" work is by its very nature selective; it's impossible to include *every* figure, *every* song, or *every* key event. For most users, we hope the selections made here will be more than adequate, giving information on the key composers and performers who shaped each style, while also introducing some lesser-known figures who are worthy of study. The Editorial Board and other outside advisers played a key role in reviewing the entry lists for completeness.

All encyclopedia authors also face the rather daunting task of separating fact from fiction when writing short biographies of performers and composers. Even birth and death dates can be "up for grabs," as artists have been known to subtract years from their lives in their official biographies. "Official" records are often unavailable, particularly for earlier artists who may have been born at home, or for those whose family histories themselves are shrouded in mystery. We have attempted to draw on the latest research and most reliable sources whenever possible, and have also pointed out when key facts are in dispute. And, for many popular performers, the myth can be as important as the reality when it comes to their lives, so we have tried to honor both in writing about their achievements.

Popular music reflects the concerns of the artists who create it and their audience. Each era of our country's history has spawned a variety of popular music styles, and these styles in turn have grown over the decades as new performers and new times have arisen. These volumes try to place the music into its context, acknowledging that the way music is performed and its effect on the greater society is as important as the music itself. We've also tried to highlight the many interchanges between styles and performers, because one of the unique—and important—aspects of American cultural life is the way that various people have come together to create a new culture out of the interplay of their original practices and beliefs.

Race, class, culture, and sex have played roles in the development of American popular music. Regrettably, the playing field has not always been level for performers from different backgrounds, particularly when it comes to the business aspects of the industry: paying royalties, honoring copyrights, and the general treatment of artists. Some figures have been forgotten or ignored who deserved greater attention; the marketplace can be ruthless, and its agents—music publishers, record producers, concert promoters—have and undoubtedly will continue to take advantage of the musicians trying to bring their unique voices to market. These volumes attempt to address many of these issues as they have affected the development of individual musicians' careers as well as from the larger perspective of the growth of popular music. The reader is encouraged to delve further into these topics by referring to the bibliographies in each volume.

Popular music can be a slave itself to crass commercialism, as well as a bevy of hangers-on, fellow travelers, and others who seek only to make a quick buck by following easy-to-identify trends. While we bemoan the lack of new visionary artists today like Bessie Smith, Miles Davis, Pauline Oliveros, or Bob Dylan, it's important to remember that when they first came on the scene the vast majority of popular performers were journeymen musicians at best. Popular music will always include many second-, third-, and fourth-tier performers; some will offer one or two recordings or performances that will have a lasting impact, while many will be celebrated during their 15 minutes of fame, but most will be forgotten. In separating the wheat from the chaff, it is understandably easier for our writers working on earlier styles where the passing of time has helped sort out the important from the just popular. However, all the contributors have tried to supply some distance, giving greatest weight to the true artists, while acknowledging that popular figures who are less talented can nonetheless have a great impact on the genre during their performing career—no matter how brief it might be.

All in all, the range, depth, and quality of popular musical styles that have developed in the United States over its lifetime is truly amazing. These styles could not have arisen anywhere else, but are the unique products of the mixing of cultures, geography, technology, and sheer luck that helped disseminate each style. Who could have forecast the music of Bill Monroe before he assembled his first great bluegrass band? Or predicted the melding of gospel, rhythm and blues, and popular music achieved by Aretha Franklin during her reign as "Queen of Soul"? The tinkering of classical composer John Cage—who admitted to having no talent for creating melodies—was a truly American response to new technologies, a new environment, and a new role for music in our lives. And Patti Smith's particular take on poetry, the punk-rock movement, and the difficulties faced by a woman who leads a rock band make her music particularly compelling and original—and unpredictable to those who dismissed the original rock records as mere "teenage fluff."

We hope that the volumes in this series will open your eyes, minds, and, most important, your ears to a world of musical styles. Some may be familiar, others more obscure, but all are worthy. With today's proliferation of sound on the Web, finding even the most obscure recording is becoming increasingly simple. We urge you to read deeply but also to put these books down to listen. Come to your own conclusions. American popular music is a rich world, one open to many different interpretations. We hope these volumes serve as your windows to these many compelling worlds.

Richard Carlin,
General Editor

Acknowledgments

Thanks to the following for suggestions on portions of the manuscripts: Wade Nelson, Jonathan Nolet-Arthur, Chris Hand, Andy Gryn, Richard Carlin, Kevin Holm-Hudson, and James Chambers and Laura Magzis of Facts On File.

Some of the material on rockabilly and Jerry Lee Lewis has been modified from articles by Craig Morrison that originally appeared in *Encyclopaedia Britannica,* used by permission. Excerpts of Craig Morrison's article on rock and roll from the *Routledge Encyclopedia of the Blues* are printed with permission of Routledge.

Introduction

This book is intended to be a reference for people who are interested in learning more about rock and roll and its development. The Chronology, in Appendix II, provides an overview of rock's evolution and introduces the styles and artists who are presented in greater depth in the A-to-Z entries. The topics of the individual entries have been chosen to cover as many of the vital components and essential and representative performers as possible. Entries are thoroughly cross-referenced (indicated by SMALL CAPITAL LETTERS) to aid in research. Because this *Rock and Roll* volume is part of the *Encyclopedia of American Popular Music* series, there is an emphasis on artists from the United States, though many important international acts and movements are highlighted. In the series are volumes on other types of music, where interested readers can find details of certain performers whose styles are related to rock but are more readily associated with other genres.

In the A-to-Z entries rock and roll's 1950s pioneers are well represented. These entries show how rock evolved from earlier genres and how the music of these artists paved the way for its future developments. Many of them still influence young musicians.

Several pioneers came to rock and roll from blues and rhythm-and-blues traditions, such as BIG JOE TURNER, FATS DOMINO, CHUCK BERRY, BO DIDDLEY, and LITTLE RICHARD. RITCHIE VALENS took these influences and added a Spanish tinge. Blues, R&B, and gospel were the foundations of MOTOWN, a 1960s style synonymous with a Detroit record company that operated like a pop music factory. Also in the 1960s white artists such as the RIGHTEOUS BROTHERS and the RASCALS created original styles inspired by R&B artists.

Other rock pioneers had a country background and came to rock and roll by adding an R&B influence, such as BILL HALEY AND HIS COMETS. ROCKABILLY, a new way to blend white and black traditions, crystallized with the debut of ELVIS PRESLEY. Other artists explored this style, extending it with their own contributions, such as CARL PERKINS, JERRY LEE LEWIS, BRENDA LEE, EDDIE COCHRAN, ROY ORBISON, the EVERLY BROTHERS, BUDDY HOLLY, and RICKY NELSON. In the 1960s DEL SHANNON's energetic rock had an undercurrent of anguish borrowed from Hank Williams' country songs.

Pop music was another forerunner of rock and roll. BOBBY DARIN was one of many singers who got into rock from pop. Pop vocal groups were the predecessors of the DOO-WOP groups, represented here by DION AND THE BELMONTS and the FOUR SEASONS, and the GIRL GROUPS, represented by The SHIRELLES. All types of early rock were brought back to life through the ROCK REVIVAL of the 1970s.

The vogue for INSTRUMENTAL ROCK that occurred in the late 1950s was carried into SURF music. The BEACH BOYS turned surf into a vocal form and competed with the BEATLES once they arrived in North America as the spearhead of the BRITISH INVASION. British acts dominated rock music in the mid-1960s, many of them contributing much to the history of rock, including the ROLLING STONES, the

ANIMALS, the KINKS, DONOVAN, the WHO, and the YARDBIRDS.

In America GARAGE ROCK was one response to the British groups. Another was a kind of rock founded on American folk traditions. FOLK ROCK was ushered in by BOB DYLAN and the BYRDS, and soon included BUFFALO SPRINGFIELD, SIMON AND GARFUNKEL, and the MAMAS AND THE PAPAS. Yet another reaction in the United States to the British invasion was the attempt to manufacture a similar type of group. The MONKEES may have been formed by television producers, but they turned into a real and immensely popular group with a varied repertoire of high quality.

From the mid-1960s to the present, a style of rock called POWER POP has explored the possibilities for the kind of catchy songs with harmony singing that were introduced by the Beatles and their peers.

The next major style to emerge was PSYCHEDELIC ROCK. In Los Angeles the BYRDS were pioneers, and many bands pursued an original direction, including the DOORS. In San Francisco the GRATEFUL DEAD and the JEFFERSON AIRPLANE were among the top bands, and JANIS JOPLIN and CARLOS SANTANA added their own artistry to the scene. In London PINK FLOYD began as a psychedelic band.

In the same period some acts were too idiosyncratic to fit into standard categories. FRANK ZAPPA is an example of a rock musician who followed his own creativity, ignoring trends in music except as targets for his satire. The VELVET UNDERGROUND, rock's quintessential cult band, also charted their own course, becoming one of the genre's most influential units.

By the late 1960s BLUES ROCK was established, inspired by the music of ERIC CLAPTON, and it was developed in America by the ALLMAN BROTHERS BAND and AEROSMITH. Closely related to blues rock was an intense style called hard rock, played by STEPPENWOLF, JIMI HENDRIX, CREAM, and LED ZEPPELIN, among others, all of whom had blues rock and psychedelia within their style. HEAVY METAL was a vibrant offshoot of hard rock, and found its iconic act in the 1980s with METALLICA.

PROGRESSIVE ROCK, vastly popular in North America in the 1970s, was chiefly produced by musicians in the United Kingdom and Europe. GLAM ROCK introduced theatrical spectacle to the genre. In the United Kingdom, as practiced by DAVID BOWIE and QUEEN, glam was concerned with subverting gender expectations. In America, in the work of ALICE COOPER and KISS, it was more about the macabre and the fantastic.

Looking back to 1950s rock and earlier times, ROOTS ROCK went back to basics, as played by the BAND and CREEDENCE CLEARWATER REVIVAL. Looking to folk and early rock and roll for inspiration, SINGER-SONGWRITERS such as NEIL YOUNG brought a poetic sensibility to personal concerns and banded together to support social causes. BRUCE SPRINGSTEEN was part singer-songwriter and part roots rocker. Another movement that took inspiration from earlier music was COUNTRY ROCK, played most successfully by the EAGLES. They soon dropped most of the country elements, becoming what radio programmers later defined as CLASSIC ROCK, which included such top-selling acts as ELECTRIC LIGHT ORCHESTRA, FLEETWOOD MAC, and STEELY DAN.

PUNK ROCK was a reaction against the cult of musicianship and the indulgences that typified progressive and classic rock. The RAMONES were a punk band of great influence. More commercial than punk but sharing some of the same values was NEW WAVE, represented here by BLONDIE and TALKING HEADS. The latter were forerunners of ALTERNATIVE ROCK, a style popularized by R.E.M. and U2.

In the late 1980s GRUNGE emerged in the Pacific Northwest, making stars of NIRVANA and PEARL JAM in the 1990s. At about the same time a resurgence of interest in improvisation lead to the JAM BANDS movement, represented by the DAVE MATTHEWS BAND. British groups who took inspiration from the Beatles and later music were popular in the mid-1990s with a style called Britpop, represented by OASIS. A further extension of alternative rock was developed by RADIOHEAD.

Besides the style and artist entries, some of the behind-the-scenes roles are represented: LEIBER AND STOLLER for the nonperforming songwriters, SAM PHILLIPS and PHIL SPECTOR for the producers, and LESTER BANGS for the rock critics. Additionally, there is an entry for each of the main instruments of rock: BASS, DRUMS, GUITAR, and KEYBOARDS. Many of the key events in rock's history are noted in the Chronology, but there is a separate entry for ROCK FESTIVALS, and because of their cultural importance, two of them receive detailed treatment: the MONTEREY POP FESTIVAL and WOODSTOCK.

A-to-Z Entries

Aerosmith

Aerosmith made one of the most remarkable comebacks in the world of entertainment. They went from being an ambitious, very popular, and influential hard rock band in the 1970s to one that was brought down and torn apart by self-indulgence via substance abuse. Through rededication and perseverance they lifted themselves back up, and from the mid-1980s onward they reached even greater heights.

By any reckoning, Aerosmith is among the top bands in rock. According to the Recording Industry Association of America, in the United States as of 2003, Aerosmith had sold 63.5 million albums. That was as many as the ROLLING STONES, and more than AC/DC, BRUCE SPRINGSTEEN, Madonna, Michael Jackson, METALLICA, or Van Halen. In rock and pop, only the BEATLES, LED ZEPPELIN, ELVIS PRESLEY, the EAGLES, Billy Joel, PINK FLOYD, and Elton John had sold more albums. Aerosmith's *Greatest Hits* alone sold 10 million copies.

They have won multiple awards—Grammys, MTVs, American Music Awards, and more—and are such a part of popular culture they have been portrayed in cartoon form on *The Simpsons* and even have their own video arcade game. In the booklet for the box set of their 1970s period, *Pandora's Box,* they are praised in quotes by musicians as diverse as Slash (of Guns n' Roses), Jimmy Page (of Led Zeppelin), Joni Mitchell, LITTLE RICHARD, and members of Skid Row, Mötley Crüe, and Living Colour.

In the mid-1960s in New Hampshire, lead vocalist Steven Tyler (b. 1948), inspired by BRITISH INVASION groups, started playing in bands. By the end of the decade, one of them, called Chain Reaction, was big enough to open for the BYRDS, the BEACH BOYS, and the YARDBIRDS (the Jimmy Page lineup). But they were not big enough to move beyond playing New York bars and into larger venues and concert halls. One night in 1969, on a return visit to New Hampshire, Tyler dropped into a club he had played many times before to check out a band that included guitarist Joe Perry (b. 1950). The two had met in an ice cream parlor where Tyler was working in the resort town of Sunapee. The band, called the Jam Band, also included bassist Tom Hamilton (b. 1951). Tyler was impressed, particularly by their rhythmic groove on FLEETWOOD MAC's "Rattlesnake Shake."

Tyler, who had already recorded with Chain Reaction and took a disciplined approach to music, and Perry and Hamilton, who had a looser approach that valued the feel of the music, teamed up. With drummer Joey Kramer (b. 1950) and guitarist Ray Tabano they formed Aerosmith in 1970 and moved into communal poverty in an apartment on Commonwealth Avenue in Boston. In 1971 the lineup was settled when Brad Whitford (b. 1952) replaced Tabano. That year, before they had a record contract, Aerosmith did a live 10-minute rendition of "Rattlesnake Shake" that was recorded on a radio broadcast in Cincinnati.

They were inspired by British bands: the Yardbirds, CREAM, Led Zeppelin, the Rolling Stones, the Beatles. In performances at frat parties and high schools, the band developed its individual sound. Throughout Aerosmith's career, it has focused on

Aerosmith (Ron Pownall/Michael Ochs Archives.com)

original songs—mostly written by Tyler, sometimes with help from Perry or Whitford—but cover songs remained in their repertoire and sometimes were recorded. The choice of songs reveals their debt to their forerunners and gives an insight into rock's lines of influence. "All Your Love," by Chicago bluesman Otis Rush, was picked up from Clapton's version with John Mayall. "Train Kept A-Rollin' " no doubt came from the Yardbirds' version (they got it from Johnny Burnette and the Rock 'n Roll Trio's 1956 rockabilly record, and they got it from Tiny Bradshaw's jump blues rendition in 1951). "Milkcow Blues," an old blues standard, may have been learned from the KINKS' version (they got it from ELVIS PRESLEY).

Aerosmith attracted a management team who booked them for a showcase at Max's Kansas City, a famed New York City club. Columbia Records president Clive Davis was impressed and signed the band. When their self-titled debut album, recorded in Boston, came out in 1973, the press dismissed them as Stones imitators, but the fans came in droves to their shows. They had a moderate hit record in "Dream On," and took to the road, opening for more established bands, recorded a second album, and hit the road again.

Their third album, *Toys in the Attic* (1975), was their breakthrough. When "Sweet Emotion" hit the top 40, their management lobbied to rerelease "Dream On," their first hit, and it went into the top

10 this time, as did "Walk This Way." The band's first two albums picked up more sales, and Aerosmith established itself as a headliner and made the cover of *Rolling Stone* magazine. Their next two albums sold well, and each had a hit single or two, but along with the material trappings of fame (mansions and fancy cars) came parties and alcohol and drug abuse, particularly for Tyler and Perry.

The band played some mammoth rock festivals and released a live double LP. They participated in *Sgt. Pepper's Lonely Hearts Club Band* (1978), a movie loosely modeled after the Beatles album of the same name. It did little for their career, except that their revival of the Beatles' "Come Together" was a chart hit. During the difficult recording of the next album and a tour undertaken mainly for financial reasons, the tension between Tyler and Perry drove Perry to leave for a solo career. Tyler collapsed on stage while touring to support the finished album, made with a replacement guitarist, and then had a motorcycle accident. Whitford then left for another project, and another replacement guitarist was brought in. The album, *Rock in a Hard Place* (1982), sold poorly. With the arrival of punk and disco, hard rock excesses were ripe for satire. Perry was now broke, and Tyler got arrested for possession of drugs and drug paraphernalia. He avoided jail by pleading guilty, paying a fine, and going on probation for three years.

In 1984 Perry and Whitford rejoined the group, and the lineup was whole again for the first time in five years. They signed with the Geffen label and did a reunion tour. After another album—not one of their best—Tyler and Perry sought help for their addictions and eventually recovered. Aerosmith's real rebirth came with a version of "Walk This Way" by rap trio Run-D.M.C. recorded in collaboration with Tyler and Perry, who also appeared in the popular video.

Two live albums, recorded in the late 1970s, put the band back on the charts, and *Permanent Vacation* (1987), their ninth studio album, restored their reputation and returned them to the big-time. The hits came with award-winning videos,

such as "Dude (Looks Like a Lady)" and "Angel." That album was produced by Bruce Fairburn, as were *Pump* (1989), featuring "Love in an Elevator" and "Janie's Got a Gun," and *Get a Grip* (1993), with "Livin' on the Edge" and "Cryin'." All sold in astonishing numbers. The tour for *Nine Lives* (1997) was one of the top-grossing tours of the year. That album debuted at number one on the charts, and won two Grammys. That year, the band's memoirs, a best-selling book called *Walk This Way* (cowritten by Stephen Davis), revealed much about their misadventures. In 1998 they had their biggest-selling single to date in "I Don't Want to Miss a Thing" (written by pop songwriter Diane Warren). It was released (with three other Aerosmith songs) on the soundtrack to the film *Armageddon*, which starred Steve Tyler's daughter, Liv Tyler. In 2001, the year *Just Push Play* came out, Aerosmith was inducted into the Rock and Roll Hall of Fame. In 2004 they reconnected to their blues roots with *Honkin' on Bobo*.

Allman Brothers Band, The

They are the architects and most brilliant exponents of southern rock, a powerful blend of rock, blues, R&B, gospel, and western swing. For more than three decades, the Allman Brothers Band has persevered despite tragedy and conflict, drug addiction and personnel changes, breakups and solo careers. Their signature sound is the combination of two drummers, BASS, KEYBOARDS, strong vocals, and the interplay of two lead guitarists, sometimes playing in harmony. Their repertoire includes versions of blues classics, and original songs and instrumentals, often arranged as vehicles for extended solos. The Allman Brothers Band began in 1969, but Duane Allman (1946–71) and his younger brother Gregg (b. 1947) had been playing together in bands since 1961. Duane played lead GUITAR, and Gregg played guitar and organ and did most of the lead singing. Duane, nicknamed Sky Dog, developed into one of rock's greatest guitarists, and Gregg into one of rock's most soulful vocalists.

When the boys were quite young, their father, a sergeant in the U.S. Army who was home on Christmas leave from the Korean War, was murdered by a hitchhiker during a robbery. In 1958 their mother relocated the family to Daytona Beach, Florida. A little later on, inspired by seeing the great blues guitarist B. B. King perform, Duane and Gregg got into music. They started playing in local bands, such as the Escorts, who did R&B, and added BRITISH INVASION styles when they became popular. The blond brothers also started to hang out with black musicians, and Duane got into motorcycle riding. In 1965 and 1966 their band was called the Allman Joys; they worked the roadhouse circuit, doing their own arrangements of R&B and British blues. As the Hour Glass, they made two albums, in 1967 and 1968, for the Liberty label of Los Angeles and then broke up.

Gregg stayed in Los Angeles. Duane, who had started to play slide guitar while in California, inspired by Jesse Ed Davis' playing with Taj Mahal, worked as a session musician in Muscle Shoals, Alabama. He contributed to recordings by Aretha Franklin, Wilson Pickett, King Curtis, John Hammond, and others. Phil Walden, who had been the late Otis Redding's manager, asked Duane to put together a trio to make some records. With drummer Jai Johanny Johanson (b. 1944), also known simply as Jaimoe, who had played with Redding, Duane went to Jacksonville, Florida, to recruit bassist Berry Oakley (1948–72), an old friend who was in a band called the Second Coming. They jammed together, along with guitarist Dickey Betts (b. 1943), also in the Second Coming, and a second drummer, Butch Trucks, another old friend. The musical interplay was so exciting that the trio concept was dropped. To round out the new band, Gregg was summoned from Los Angeles. They felt a spiritual brotherhood, and to mark it, each member had a psychedelic mushroom tattooed on his ankle. Walden signed on as manager and put the band on his newly formed Capricorn label.

They relocated to Macon, Georgia, site of the Capricorn studios, and shared a cramped house.

They lived in communal poverty, jammed every day, wrote songs at the nearby cemetery, and gave free concerts in the local park to try out their material. Their debut album, *The Allman Brothers Band* (1969), is blues rock featuring the twin lead guitars of Duane and Dickey Betts, and Gregg's vocals. With strong songs in "It's Not My Cross to Bear," "Dreams," and "Whipping Post," which became a concert staple, it was well received by critics but was not a big seller. Their second album, *Idlewild South* (1970), showed the band to be tighter, less fixated on blues, more nuanced (including acoustic textures), and more original. Tom Dowd came in as producer. He had previously recorded CREAM, John Coltrane, Aretha Franklin, Ray Charles, and the Rascals. His method was to have the band set up as if they were on stage and record live in the studio. As the stage is their natural element, it was the perfect technique for the band. Betts emerged as a songwriter with the gospelish "Revival (Love Is Everywhere)." His instrumental composition "In Memory of Elizabeth Reed" became one of their signature pieces, as did Gregg Allman's "Midnight Rider."

After seeing the Allman Brothers perform in Miami, ERIC CLAPTON invited Duane to participate in sessions there for what became the celebrated *Layla (and Other Assorted Love Songs)* (1970). Clapton credits Duane Allman as the catalyst for the project. Completed in less than two weeks, the double album was issued as "by Derek and the Dominos," with the Derek moniker referring to Duane and Eric.

In March 1971 the Allman Brothers performed for two nights in New York City as part of a triple bill with Elvin Bishop and Johnny Winter at the Fillmore East, the famous venue run by Bill Graham. Selections from the Allman Brothers shows were released as a double album, *At Fillmore East*. It is a tour de force, considered to be the band's masterpiece and one of the finest recordings of a live band at its peak. (The entire two nights were issued in 1992 as *The Fillmore Concerts*.) The band is shown to be a seasoned, powerful, and creative unit, and the chemistry between the members is in full evidence on the blues covers and virtuosic jams that, despite their length ("Whipping Post" takes up one whole side—almost 23 minutes), waste nothing. Critics showered it with praise—the *Rolling Stone* reviewer declared them "the best damn rock and roll band this country has produced in the past five years"—and it went into the top 20 on the charts.

In October 1971, before the next album was completed, Duane Allman was killed in a motorcycle accident in Macon, Georgia. His death was a severe blow. On the sessions to finish the next record, Dickie Betts handled all the guitar parts. *Eat a Peach* (1972), another double album, with some of the band's best material, was their first to make the top 10. (The bands' fans, who rival those of the GRATEFUL DEAD's "Deadheads" in their

Allman Brothers (Michael Ochs Archives.com)

intense loyalty, are called "peach heads.") The album has three facets: three more live tracks from the Fillmore sessions, including the monumental "Mountain Jam" (a 33-minute set of variations on DONOVAN's "First There Is a Mountain"), three studio tracks that had been done with Duane, including "Blue Sky," which showed Betts' country leanings, and three more that were made after Duane's death, including Gregg's romantic ballad "Melissa."

The band decided not to find another guitarist, adding instead pianist Chuck Leavell, an accomplished musician who could play blues, jazz, and funk. His fluent playing and energy inspired the band, and the easygoing *Brothers and Sisters* (1973) was a fine recording and their only number-one album. However, before it was completed, another tragedy occurred. Bassist Berry Oakley also died in a motorcycle crash, three blocks away from where Duane Allman had been killed just over a year earlier. The band soldiered on, adding Lamar Williams as bassist. Betts took a more prominent role, and his singing, writing, and guitar playing are impressive. The three most notable songs on the album are his: the instrumental "Jessica"; the rhythmic "Southbound" with his furious guitar solos; and the country-based "Ramblin' Man," which featured his clear vocals. The latter concluded with a lengthy harmonized guitar section played by Betts and guest musician Les Dudek. "Ramblin' Man," made number two and is their highest-charting single to date.

The Allman Brothers Band played larger venues and to bigger crowds than ever. In July 1973, along with the BAND and the Grateful Dead, they performed for 600,000 people at Watkins Glen, New York. During the next years, despite some noteworthy recordings mixed with the uneven ones, the band was in decline, frayed by drug abuse and personality conflicts. Gregg Allman and Dickie Betts pursued solo careers. The Allman Brothers Band split up temporarily in 1976 because the rest of the band felt disgusted and betrayed when Gregg acquiesced to pressure and testified against a former roadie who had been charged with drug dealing. Leavell, Williams, and Johanson formed Sea Level. Gregg moved to Los Angeles and had a heavily publicized but unhappy marriage to actor/singer Cher. The band set aside their differences and re-formed in 1978, hitting their stride with *Enlightened Rogues* (1979), with Tom Dowd back as producer. Bassist Dave Goldflies and guitarist Dan Toler came in from Betts's solo band, replacing Leavell and Williams, who refused to join. Newer styles like disco and punk were popular at the time, and the band's fire and inspiration did not last. In 1982 the Allman Brothers Band again split up.

In 1989, spurred by the success of a four-CD box set of classics and archival material called *Dreams,* they re-formed yet again. Williams had died of cancer in 1983, and Leavell was a touring member of the ROLLING STONES. New recruits were guitarist Warren Haynes and bassist Allen Woody. The revitalized band released *Seven Turns* (1990) to excellent if somewhat generous reviews. This was followed by the worthy and energetic *Shades of Two Worlds* (1991) and *Where It All Begins* (1994) and some live CDs and DVDs, and popular tours. They were venerated as pioneers of the JAM BANDS scene.

Other personnel changes occurred. Marc Quinones joined the band as a percussionist in 1992. Haynes and Woody maintained a popular side project band called Gov't Mule until Woody's death in 2000. His place in the Allman Brothers was filled by Oteil Burbridge. Dickey Betts was fired in 2000 and returned to his solo career. Derek Trucks, the young nephew of drummer Butch Trucks and a leader of his own band, came in as second guitarist. *Hittin' the Note* (2003), a band and fan expression for when the music soars, was the first album of new material in almost a decade and the first Allman Brothers Band recording without Betts. The band managed the inconceivable: a record that rivals their best work.

One of the best live ensembles anywhere, with two magnificent guitarists, a great singer, and one of the finest of all of rock's legendary rhythm sections, the Allman Brothers fused the impetus of the British blues bands to a native grasp of the traditions of the American South, creating a unique blend that was highly influential but never matched. They paved the way for other southern rock bands, including the Marshall Tucker Band, Lynyrd Skynyrd, Blackfoot, Molly Hatchet, the Charlie Daniels Band, Black Oak Arkansas, and more recently, the Black Crowes. In the 21st century the Allman Brothers Band can draw more than 20,000 fans to outdoor venues and fill 2,000-seat theaters for a run of several days, even weeks at a time, still capable of "hittin' the note."

alternative rock

Alternative rock, a term popularized in the 1980s, is sometimes called college rock. It groups together diverse strands of underground music that emerged after PUNK ROCK and NEW WAVE. The most successful of the types of music called alternative was GRUNGE. After *grunge* became almost synonymous with *alternative,* the term *indie* (for "independent rock") replaced it somewhat. Therefore, *alternative* refers primarily to artists from the 1980s to the mid-1990s, and indie, despite being an older term, tends to be used more for artists from the 1990s and beyond.

The do-it-yourself attitude of punk carried over into alternative music. It did not matter who or where you were—what mattered was dedication, pragmatism, and frugality. Bands networked, sharing information on venues and record labels. They booked their own shows, gave recordings to disc jockeys and reviewers, created their own posters, loaded their own equipment, drove across the country in vans to get to their gigs, and stayed with fans or other bands while on tour.

All this involvement took some of the mystery out of the music business. Self-expression and having control over one's music meant more than selling records. Obscurity was tied up with the notion of authenticity, and an antimaterialistic attitude was a political statement against mindless consumerism. What was most important was commitment and the ability to play exciting shows and make good records. Sales were less important (though some degree of success was of course necessary for financial reasons and moral encouragement). Discovering or knowing a band that few others were aware of gave a cachet of hipness to the fan, and bands that got big or signed to a major label were often accused of compromising their art, of selling out to the corporate establishment. Indeed, alternative music, by its very name, defines itself by what it is not. It is not polished, formulaic music made by efficient professionals for the purpose of selling millions of records to a mainstream audience. It is the alternative: rebellious, clever, eccentric, somewhat cynical, and made by bands that begin as committed amateurs in a community or "scene."

The term *scene* ascribes a musical practice to a place: any city or region with a thriving local music community. The typical location for a vibrant rock scene is a college city at some distance from the music industry's main centers in New York, Los Angeles, and Nashville. Not only can new types of music develop away from the scrutiny of those who would commercialize it at first bloom, but the rents are generally cheaper, meaning people have more time to devote to music. The population of this type of city contains thousands of young people, many of them students or former students. Most of the young people are music lovers, and among them is a contingent that wants to hear something new, something homegrown or little known, something to get excited about.

When popular bands play for appreciative audiences in nightclubs, music's power to move, to affect, and to gather people together in a shared experience is most easily seen. Beyond and behind the bands, clubs, and consumers is a larger artistic and business community comprising promoters, poster artists, writers, disc jockeys, publishers of underground newspapers and fanzines, and the people who run the independent labels, recording studios, record stores, clothing stores, instrument stores, and sound rental companies. All are important to the scene.

If the scene seems to be happening . . . if some of the records get airplay or press notice . . . if someone from elsewhere visits and reports back that something special is going on . . . if there is some word of mouth about certain bands . . . then reputations are made. With talent, hard work, timing, and luck, some bands break out and become famous. Then what usually happens is like a gold rush, as major labels descend on the city and sign up every likely candidate for the next big thing. Some bands lose their edge when recording for a major label, as their music is subjected to increased expectations and the vision of a producer. Those that do well commercially often are subjected to a backlash from their old fans. Others make fine music that doesn't sell well and feel discouraged. More bands move in or begin. "Scenesters" lament the end of the good old days.

Among the biggest success stories to come out of alternative music are U2 (from Dublin, Ireland), R.E.M. (from Athens, Georgia), and NIRVANA and PEARL JAM (both from the Seattle area). Other notable alternative bands include the B-52s (from Athens, Georgia), the Pixies, Mission of Burma, and the Lemonheads (all from Boston), Dinosaur Jr. (Amherst, Massachusetts), Sonic Youth (New York City), the Replacements and Hüsker Dü (both from Minneapolis), Guided by Voices (Dayton, Ohio), the Butthole Surfers (San Antonio, Texas), and the Meat Puppets (Phoenix, Arizona). The Smiths, Echo and the Bunnymen, the Jesus and Mary Chain, the Cure, and the Wedding Present came from England. Björk came out of a band called the Sugarcubes (from Iceland). In the indie era, solo artists came to the fore, including the eclectic Beck, known for his 1994 hit song "Loser" and the 1996 album *Odelay;* Liz Phair, whose *Exile in Guyville* in 1993 was a sensation for its forthright, confessional lyrics and deadpan delivery; and Juliana Hatfield, whose best album is perhaps *Only Everything* (1995).

Since alternative was so inclusive, there was room for many styles and movements; their chief commonality was their distance from conventional pop. Alternative acts expressed this distance in many ways, such as rough voice quality, low fidelity production, murky textures, eccentric song construction, avoidance of romantic themes, obscene or profane lyrics, or incomprehensible vocals. Alternative music encompassed so many styles because the scenes that supported it allowed for it. Because audiences did not want something marketed by corporate culture, all kinds of odd music could have a place. Among the styles and movements considered alternative were offshoots of punk and new versions of older styles. Punk mixed with HEAVY METAL to make hardcore (Black Flag, Minor Threat, Fugazi), with ROCKABILLY to make psychobilly (the Cramps), with country to make cowpunk (Lone Justice, Jason and the Scorchers), and with mechanical instruments to make industrial (Nine Inch Nails, Ministry, Skinny Puppy). Punk mixed with old blues in the music of the Gun Club, with funk in the music of the Red Hot Chili Peppers, and with REGGAE in the music of Bad Brains. There was ROOTS ROCK (Los Lobos), the rockabilly revival (Stray Cats), and the continued revival of ska, a Jamaican style that predated reggae (the Mighty Mighty Bosstones). POWER POP artists of the time, such as the Bangles and Jules Shear, were considered alternative, as was the so-called paisley underground, actually neopsychedelia (Green on Red, the Rain Parade). There were also alternative forms of folk (Violent Femmes, Michelle Shocked) and a younger generation of SINGER-SONGWRITERS (Suzanne Vega, Ani DiFranco).

The foundations of alternative rock are the GARAGE ROCK and early psychedelic bands of the mid-1960s and afterward. The line of influence, however, begins in New York with the VELVET UNDERGROUND. They had elements of garage and psychedelia as well as an artistic sensibility that showed up in experimental arrangements and intellectual lyrics. They drew from avant-garde classical music, the Beat writers, and from being hired by the iconoclastic pop artist Andy Warhol as the house band for his traveling multimedia show.

Starting in the late 1960s, rock programs on the newly expanded format of FM radio became a hip alternative to top-40 AM radio. The FM stations played album tracks aimed at the college market, while AM played pop singles directed more at adolescents. In the 1970s FM radio lost its freeform quality as programming was tightened up by station managers, and individual disc jockeys had less say in what they played. When punk arrived around 1977 with its do-it-yourself attitude and antisocial message, there was virtually nowhere for it to get airplay. New wave got onto the radio by mixing punk's energy with disco's dance beat. In the early 1980s new wave and related styles found a home on MTV, the sensational new music television channel. Alternative music was also played on MTV and other TV shows, but another new outlet would be its home: college radio. At college radio stations, a phenomenon that began in the early 1980s and became widespread soon afterward, disc jockeys—usually students working as volunteers—had the freedom to conceive their own weekly shows and play whatever they wanted on the air. By the late 1980s some commercial radio stations followed their lead and featured alternative music programs.

Although only a few acts became household names, alternative rock artists made and still are making honest and intriguing music, and individually and collectively they are important and influential. The more alternative is incorporated into the mainstream, the less it will live up to its name.

Animals, The

One of the most important of the BRITISH INVASION bands, the Animals came out of Newcastle, a tough industrial city in the north of England. Theirs was a powerful, energetic sound rooted in American R&B, absorbed from imported records and hearing and meeting visiting artists such as Sonny Boy Williamson and CHUCK BERRY.

Their first hit was their biggest: "House of the Rising Sun," a number-one song in 1964 in the United Kingdom and the United States and yet another indicator of how much the British invasion drew from American sources. It was an American folk song about a house of prostitution and gambling in New Orleans, Louisiana. Vocalist Eric Burdon, a white man who was one of the United Kingdom's most intense and most black-sounding singers, had been singing the song with traditional jazz bands, with additional words he picked up from BOB DYLAN's first album, which documented some of his repertoire as a Greenwich Village folksinger. Dylan got it from Dave Van Ronk who got it from other singers. As "The Rising Sun Blues," it was collected by folklorist Alan Lomax, who noted that it had British antecedents. Lomax published it in *Our Singing Country* (1941); the words are substantially the same as the Animals' hit version, however, the melody is not. The version by blues legend Leadbelly, called "In New Orleans," used yet another melody. The Animals' version has become the definitive one, and to this day, the song is one of the most frequently played by beginning guitarists, for its basic yet satisfying and instantly recognizable chord progression (which begins as: Am/C/D/F). The success of this song reputedly contributed to the demise of the Animals, in that although all members claimed to have contributed to the arrangement, only organist Alan Price received credit for it (and thus the royalties).

The Animals also revived songs by Sam Cooke, BO DIDDLEY, John Lee Hooker, and Ma Rainey, and most were hits, but many of their best-remembered songs were newly composed, such as "We Gotta Get Out of This Place," "Don't Bring Me Down," "It's My Life," and "Don't Let Me Be Misunderstood." All were produced by Mickey Most.

Besides Burdon's vocals and Price on organ and electric piano, the lineup included Chas Chandler on bass, Hilton Valentine on guitar, and John Steel on drums. When the original band broke up—due to overwork from incessant touring, mismanagement, disputes over royalties, and a rift between the members who took psychedelic drugs and the ones who preferred alcohol—Burdon moved to California. Eric Burdon and the New Animals made their debut at the MONTEREY POP FESTIVAL in 1967, and soon had a hit with "Monterey," a song that described the event. "Sky Pilot," "San Franciscan Nights," and "When I Was Young" were also hits. By that time Chandler had become JIMI HENDRIX's manager, and Price pursued a solo career. Burdon went on to perform with War, while Valentine and Steel dropped out of the music business until the original band reunited for an album and a tour in 1977. In 1983 they made a new album and toured again. Burdon wrote an autobiography *I Used to Be an Animal, But I'm All Right Now* and has sustained a presence on the music scene.

Band, The

The Band are the originators of what would later be called ROOTS ROCK, a style that acknowledged early rock and roll and its roots in country, blues, folk, and gospel and drew elements from all of them into a creative mix where the old and new could coexist.

Ronnie Hawkins, a charismatic rockabilly singer from Arkansas who had had two hits in 1959, moved to Toronto with his band because gigs were plentiful there and the Canadians loved his music. His homesick band members left him one by one, until only one remained: drummer Levon Helm (b. 1942). Because Hawkins had an impressive stage show and got lots of work, he was able to recruit replacements who were the best musicians in the area. The lineup of the Hawks, as his band was called, ended up with two keyboard players, Richard Manuel (b. 1945) and Garth Hudson (b. 1937), plus guitarist Robbie Robertson (b. 1944) and bassist Rick Danko (b. 1943), all teenagers at the time. They then played on the bar and club circuit for so long, drilled by Hawkins, who liked his bands to shine, that they became one of the tightest musical units in the business.

The Hawks decided to go out on their own (Hawkins replaced them and kept on going), and made a couple of records that flopped. But when BOB DYLAN decided to play with a backup group, someone recommended the Hawks. They became Dylan's band during the controversial period when he shifted from being an acoustic folksinger to an electrified folk rocker. They toured and survived the jeers and catcalls from those in the audience who didn't like Dylan's new direction.

Dylan's 1966 motorcycle accident took him out of commission, but he continued to pay his musicians. While waiting for their new boss to recover, they lived in a big pink house in Woodstock, New York. In this time off, their first break from gigging and touring in years, they recorded their first album, *Music from Big Pink* (1968), named for the house where they had prepared it, during months filled with composing, rehearsing, and making demo tapes on their own and with Dylan (which came out later as the celebrated *Basement Tapes*). A painting of the Band by Dylan graces the cover of *Music from Big Pink,* and the album contains one song he wrote and two others he coauthored.

All the players contributed, and there was no apparent leader. In the early days Hudson, the most musically advanced, gave the others lessons in music theory. All but he took a turn singing lead, and though Robertson sang the least, he was the principal songwriter; Manuel, Danko, and Helm also wrote. Their music, already rooted in 1950s rock and roll and folk, incorporated elements of gospel and country, and showed no trace of psychedelia. Masterfully played and sung with conviction, their music was earthy and genuine, a point underlined by the photograph inside the album's fold-out cover, which showed the Band surrounded by family and friends. The album sold well, and other musicians were very impressed. The hit song was "The Weight" ("take a load off Fanny . . . put the load right on me"). In the Band's version, each verse was sung by a different member. Their version hit the charts, but charted lower than did the three cover versions, by Aretha Franklin, Jackie DeShannon, and the combined forces of the Supremes and the Temptations. The Band's version was used in the film *Easy Rider* (but because of licensing reasons, the soundtrack album contained yet another cover version, by a band called Smith).

For their first live shows following the release of the album, they played a three-night stand in San Francisco. Robertson's stage fright made him ill and they nearly canceled the first night, but Bill Graham, the promoter, hired a hypnotist, which helped enough to get Robertson through an abbreviated set. By the end of the weekend, their songs, musicianship, versatility, and cohesiveness

had created a sensation. Their impact on the local musicians was powerful. CREEDENCE CLEARWATER REVIVAL started singing about Americana with "Proud Mary." In 1970 the GRATEFUL DEAD temporarily dropped their psychedelic style for two albums of roots-oriented Americana, considered among their very best. ERIC CLAPTON was impressed and left off the power trio format of CREAM for something more earthy. The rhythm of Elton John's "Daniel" (1973) also shows the influence of the Band.

Their untitled second album (1969) was immediately recognized as a masterpiece. It contains their highest-charting single, "Up on Cripple Creek" (which made number 25), as well as "The Night

The Band (Michael Ochs Archives.com)

They Drove Old Dixie Down." In that song, drummer Levon Helm, in his Arkansas accent, sings in the character of a southerner witnessing the fall of the South in the American Civil War. It was a bigger hit when recorded by Joan Baez.

They played some rock festivals, including Woodstock in 1969 and Watkins Glen in 1973 (a CD of that show came out in 1995). Their third and fourth albums, *Stage Fright* (1970) and *Cahoots* (1971), were spotty. *Rock of Ages* (1972) was a live double album that reprised some of their best-known songs in new arrangements with an added horn section. They acknowledged their roots in *Moondog Matinee* (1973), an album of rock and roll oldies done in their own style. The Band reunited with Dylan for *Planet Waves* (1973) and *Before the Flood* (1974) and more touring. The last Band albums were *Northern Lights—Southern Cross* (1975) and *Islands* (1977).

Weary of the road, they agreed to split up in 1976, but not before making their final show a memorable one. Billed as "The Last Waltz," it was staged in San Francisco on Thanksgiving and filmed by Martin Scorsese. As well as performing their own material, the Band backed up their colleagues and mentors: Ronnie Hawkins, Bob Dylan, Muddy Waters, NEIL YOUNG, Van Morrison, Joni Mitchell, and Neil Diamond. The film, edited by Scorsese and Robertson, was released in 1978 to movie theaters and was well received (though it was criticized by some for minimizing the roles of the other band members). The album also came out in 1978.

Most of the members went on to solo projects or producing. In 1983 all of them except Robertson, who was pursuing a solo career, decided to regroup. Any artist who bids a formal farewell and later decides to return to show business will face a backlash of opinion, and will be judged harshly by some for just doing it for the money, whether that is a motivation or not. The Band was no exception. Additionally, because Robertson, by this time perceived by the public as the most important member, did not participate, the new version of the Band had an uphill battle. Nevertheless, they made new

recordings and toured again, to the delight of old and new fans. Manuel committed suicide in 1986 after a gig in Florida. Helm, Hudson, and Danko carried on as the Band, releasing *Jericho* (1993) and *High on the Hog* (1996). In 1999, at age 56, Rick Danko died in his sleep; no cause was determined, though he had recently been jailed for possession of heroin. Helm wrote an autobiography that mentioned "wounds that may never heal," making an unfortunate coda to one of the most musical, influential, and important bands in rock.

Bangs, Lester (1948–1982) *early rock critic*

Bangs wrote prolifically, if sporadically, not about what was fashionable, but about what he believed in. Feverishly typing for hours, sometimes under the influence of drugs or alcohol, Bangs wrote the way some musicians make rock and roll: with passion, obsession, and devotion. Opinionated, articulate, and curious, he could be irreverent and controversial, but was highly regarded, even by some of the musicians of whom he was critical. He was born in California and lived in Detroit and then New York City, writing for *Rolling Stone, Creem,* and dozens of other magazines and newspapers. He also wrote a fan book on BLONDIE, collaborated on a book about Rod Stewart, and recorded two albums of GARAGE ROCK featuring his singing and harmonica playing. He was influenced by the Beat writers, both in their quest for vitality and their stream-of-consciousness writing style. A fanatical listener who collected records beginning in 1958, he sifted through hours of worthless music to find creative, urgent, and idiosyncratic expression of a high order, whether crude or sophisticated. He found it not just in rock—he loved Van Morrison, the VELVET UNDERGROUND, Robert Quine, and early punk and NEW WAVE—but also in jazz, country, R&B, and pop.

He was portrayed in the movie *Almost Famous* (2000), his story was written by a fellow critic (*Let It Blurt: The Life and Times of Lester Bangs* by Jim DeRogatis, 2000), and he has been the subject of songs by R.E.M. ("It's the End of the World As We

Know It (And I Feel Fine)"), and Bob Seger ("Lester Knew"). There are two collections of his work: *Psychotic Reactions and Carburetor Dung* (1987, edited by Greil Marcus) and *Mainlines, Blood Feasts and Bad Taste: A Lester Bangs Reader* (2003, edited by John Morthland). The title essay of the first collection was classic Bangs. It covered the Count Five's prolific recording career, only it was almost totally fiction. The band was real: they had a huge hit with "Psychotic Reaction" (1966), but made only one album (not counting a reunion album made after Bangs' death).

bass

The electric bass guitar is one of the 20th century's most important musical instruments. Though the electric GUITAR was invented in the 1930s, the electric bass did not arrive until the early 1950s, and was not generally adopted until the 1960s. Therefore, the bass instrument used in most 1950s rock and roll is the acoustic, also known as upright bass, double bass, or even, because of its size, doghouse bass. Its large size is one of the main reasons that bass players were eager to try the more compact and more portable electric bass.

In its early years players who took it up who were already playing the upright bass tended to play both in the same manner. This soon changed because of the possibilities of the new instrument. Due to its compactness—it is held like a guitar and the strings are thinner than those of an acoustic bass—the electric was easier to get around on, and so faster and busier bass lines could be readily executed. Also, most electric basses have frets, like a guitar, so guitarists find switching to electric bass to be relatively painless. The four strings of the bass (whether acoustic or electric), are EADG (low to high). In the standard tuning of the guitar (EADGBE) the lower four strings are the same, just one octave higher. Because of these similarities with the guitar, communication of musical ideas between guitarists and bassists is easy, and many musicians are able to play both instruments.

After early attempts to put electric pickups on the acoustic bass were not satisfactory, Leo Fender developed the Fender Precision Bass, the first mass-produced electric bass, which went to market in 1951. The Fender Jazz Bass came out in 1960. Both are still desirable basses to own. Other manufacturers put out their own models, creating variations of the instrument. There have been changes in body shape, materials, finishes, and electronics. To expand the range of the instrument, detuning devices were invented (they quickly and accurately change pitch, usually to drop the low E to a D), and more strings were added: five and even six-string basses are now fairly common. There are unusual, specially commissioned one-of-a-kind instruments made to personal specifications, and signature models that are mass marketed, designed in collaboration with famous players.

Most electric bassists pluck the strings with their fingers, sometimes alternating the index and middle finger, which gives a warm, rounded sound. Some players, often those who started on guitar, use a pick (usually of plastic), which gives a bright, punchy sound. One former guitarist who plays bass with a pick is Carol Kaye, a consummate sight-reader and improviser, who has played on more than 10,000 recording sessions for such notables as the BEACH BOYS, the MONKEES, the Supremes, and ELVIS PRESLEY. Joe Osborn, another pioneering rock bassist who played on countless sessions in Los Angeles, also plays with a pick. His melodic lines can be heard on such hits as "California Dreamin' " by the MAMAS AND THE PAPAS, "Bridge over Troubled Water" by SIMON AND GARFUNKEL, and "Hello Mary Lou" by RICKY NELSON.

The role the bass plays is to be the base, the foundation, of any ensemble. Some players refer to it as the anchor. The bassist provides two things. The first is harmonic information, conveyed by playing notes that outline the song's chord progression: chord notes, in other words, especially the root. The second is rhythm. The rhythm on the bass can be as simple as a new note every half note (every two foot taps, in other words). The root and the fifth of the chord of the moment are the common choices; this is called two-beat bass and is found in polka music and country music. When the bass plays a new note on every beat (every foot tap), this is called walking bass, and it is frequent in jazz. Another common way to play, suitable for slow songs, is to keep up a basic long-short, long-short sequence. Repeating a riff is a standard way to play blues or blues rock.

In the days of big swing bands, the mid-1930s to the mid-1940s, the rhythm section was often guitar, piano, bass, and drums. The horn sections and the featured soloists and vocalists would be in the forefront, and the rhythm section would provide the background support. In rock and roll, bass and drums work together as the rhythm section, while the guitar and the KEYBOARDS (piano, organ, or synthesizer) have been promoted to the front line.

Though the upright bass continued to be used in classical, jazz, and some styles of country such as bluegrass, by the early 1960s nearly all rock players played electric bass. Styles of bass playing evolved quickly. James Jamerson, one of the Funk Brothers, who were the house band that played on MOTOWN records, was a former acoustic bassist who switched to electric. He accurately played unusual and highly rhythmic bass lines that were very influential, even though most people never knew about him as an individual until years later. Paul McCartney of the BEATLES played a very melodic style that was also very influential. John Entwistle of the WHO used the bass at times as a lead instrument, and sometimes played an eight-string bass. Jack Bruce of CREAM, Phil Lesh of the GRATEFUL DEAD, and Jack Casady of the JEFFERSON AIRPLANE all pioneered a melodic, contrapuntal style that was influenced by classical music and brought attention to the role of the bass player. Donald "Duck" Dunn of Booker T and the MGs, who backed up the soul singers at the Stax label, was an influential, groove-oriented player, as were the bassists who played funk with James Brown, such as Bootsy Collins. Larry Graham of Sly and the Family Stone pioneered a style of rapidly slapping the strings with the thumb and then lifting them so they popped when released. His funky playing, heard on "Thank You (Falettinme Be Mice Elf Agin)" (1970) and other songs, was widely imitated. The slap-and-pop style was part of 1990s ALTERNATIVE ROCK in the bass playing of Les Claypool of Primus and Flea of the Red Hot Chili Peppers. In the 1970s and 1980s Jaco Pastorius, with Weather Report and Joni Mitchell, popularized the sliding sound of the fretless electric bass with a melodic, hornlike style of playing. Others have explored alternate tunings, effects devices such as echo loops that are useful during solos, different kinds of pickups, strings, amplifiers, and no end of playing styles.

The electric bass transformed the foundation, literally, of modern music.

Beach Boys, The

The Beach Boys are the most popular, successful, and influential American rock band. They had more than 30 hits in the top-40 charts, and 16 of their albums entered the top 100. The Beach Boys began in 1961 in Hawthorne, California, in the South Bay section of Los Angeles, very near to the Pacific Ocean. Their name, image, and many of their hits have represented a partially real and partially mythological California lifestyle to the world: sun, sand, surf, tanned and gorgeous guys and girls, hot rods, drive-ins, and freedom.

They were formed by the three Wilson brothers, the fragile and creative eldest one, Brian (b. 1942, KEYBOARDS, BASS); the handsome, reckless middle brother, Dennis (b. 1944, DRUMS), and the stable, peaceful youngest one Carl (b. 1946, GUITAR). Joining them was their extroverted cousin Mike Love (b. 1944, sax), who sang lead on most of their hits and was the emcee at their concerts, and a school friend, Al Jardine (b. 1942, guitar), a fan of folk music. Unsure of the band's prospects, Jardine departed to study dentistry. He was replaced by a young neighbor, David Marks, but reclaimed his spot a year later, in 1963. Their first manager was Murry Wilson, the domineering father of the three brothers. The band fired him in 1964.

Brian, the group's leader, was their chief song-writer, and he conceived their vocal and instrumental arrangements. He was inspired by vocal groups like the Hi-Los and the Four Freshmen, who extended barbershop-quartet-style harmonies into jazz territory. He would come home from school and practice piano along with their records until he could play and understand the complicated vocal harmonies.

Though Love mostly sang lead, the Wilsons all took turns as lead vocalist, and all contributed to their trademark close harmony parts. They applied their lush, glorious singing, with artful, at times astonishing, interweaving counterpoint, to a wide range of material: old rock classics ("Barbara Ann," "Rock and Roll Music"), folk songs ("Sloop John B."), a cappella pieces, but mostly their own compositions. They also did some instrumental pieces.

When they began, Dennis, the only surfer in the band, suggested that Brian write a song about the sport. The result was "Surfin'," and it became a regional hit; the oldest in the group, Love, was then 20, and the youngest, Carl, was 15. Surfing had begun in Hawaii where it was, at least at first, the sport of kings. By the early 1960s, with the advent of lightweight surfboards at the same time as an economic boom and the baby boom, the sport was thriving. Instrumental bands such as Dick Dale and the Del-Tones had been playing their version of the popular instrumental SURF ROCK style, but the Beach Boys were the first to sing about the sport. "Surfin' " led to their getting signed to the Capitol label, and spawned similar hits by the Beach Boys, including "Surfin' Safari," "Surfer Girl," and "Surfin' USA" (musically based on CHUCK BERRY's "Sweet Little Sixteen"). Soon other aspects of the California lifestyle were part of surf music, from "California Girls" to songs about hot rods ("409," "Shut Down," "Little Deuce Coupe," "Fun, Fun, Fun," and "I Get Around"). Another act in surf music was Jan and Dean, with whom Brian Wilson collaborated on "Surf City."

Brian, a shy and troubled soul who could be disarmingly childlike in his interactions, soon showed there was more depth to his writing with hits like "In My Room" (1963), "Don't Worry Baby" and "When I Grow Up to Be a Man" (both 1964). His themes were usually optimistic, with wistful, even melancholic overtones on the more romantic songs. He said "We were always spiritually minded and we wrote music to give strength to people."[1] His music was satisfyingly adventurous. He also had a competitive side, a desire to be the best.

Traditionally, record companies have allowed artists only limited input concerning repertoire, arrangements, and recording. Because the Beach Boys were having hits and because of Brian's obvious talent and growing skills as a writer and arranger, by their third album, he was the sole producer on their recordings. They were the first act in rock to gain complete artistic freedom, something that would soon become an issue for many other performers. Brian developed into a producer and composer, occasionally with Mike Love or others as collaborators, without equal in rock or pop music. Sometimes referred to as a genius, he was spurred on by a sense of competition with the BEATLES.

Finding touring too stressful, in 1965 Brian decided to concentrate on studio work and writing (though he would perform occasionally with the group in ensuing years). Bruce Johnston, formerly of the Rip Chords ("Hey Little Cobra"), and of Bruce and Terry ("Summer Means Fun"), joined the band to fill out the sound and remained as a full-time member. Brian Wilson increasingly saw the Beatles as his true competition and it came to be mutual. He certainly had the talent, and the *Pet Sounds* album (the Beach Boys' 13th) is more orchestrated (building on the wall-of-sound techniques of PHIL SPECTOR). It attracted a devoted following that spread beyond their teenage fan base. Though it was the first of their albums not to go gold, it is one of the most treasured albums in all of rock, and was the inspiration for the Beatles' *Sgt. Pepper's Lonely Hearts Club Band* (1967). Devoid of surfing and hot-rodding images, perhaps because of lyricist Tony Asher, *Pet Sounds* is concerned with deeper, reflective themes, as seen in the longing of

The Beach Boys (Michael Ochs Archives.com)

"Wouldn't It Be Nice" and "God Only Knows," on which Carl Wilson's poignant lead vocal is sublime.

Not long after creating "Good Vibrations," their most ambitious piece—Brian called it a "pocket symphony"—and their biggest hit, the countless hours of studio experimentation, eccentric work methods, and drug use, caused Brian to burn out. The album *Smile,* a collaboration with Van Dyke Parks, which was to be his masterpiece, was not completed. For years it was a source of speculation for fans, who took matters into their own hands by compiling the numerous *Smile* tracks that appeared on official and bootleg releases. The speculation ended with the release of the finished album to rave reviews in September 2004 (all songs were newly recorded).

Like the Beatles and other pop stars, the Beach Boys were intrigued by the teachings of Maharishi Mahesh Yogi, and Mike Love delved into Transcendental Meditation. It was spiritually uplifting, though their music that reflected its influence sold poorly. In 1969 the Beach Boys left Capitol Records, releasing recordings on their own Brother label.

The band continued to make good, if not great, records, while Brian's songwriting contributions steadily diminished. Their earlier success with surfing songs, their carefree image, and even their name proved somewhat of an obstacle to remaining vital in a rock scene that was now embracing psychedelic and heavy rock. They withdrew from the lineup of the MONTEREY POP FESTIVAL, and although they did sometimes play the hippie ballroom circuit alongside groups like the Grateful Dead, they seemed unable to find their footing. They still had hits, but fewer placed in the top 20.

Since 1973 the band has played two roles. As a live band, they are a highly polished and crowd-pleasing act playing primarily their 1960s hits. As recording artists, they have made albums that alternate between creative gems that find a small but devoted audience and commercial continuations of their early image, like *Summer in Paradise* (1992).

Brian spent years in bed, doing drugs and eating, and had a disturbing relationship with his therapist. The state of California withdrew the man's license to practice psychology, and then charged him with illegally prescribing drugs to his patient. Bodyguards then ensured that Brian stayed away from drugs and went jogging with him to ensure he would exercise. Carl, the most stable of the brothers, tired of the band's focus on nostalgia and lack of musical growth, and he left in the early 1980s for a solo career. After one moderate solo hit, he returned to the band.

On July 4, 1980, underlining their association as an all-American band, they played a free concert at the Washington Monument, in Washington, D.C., to a crowd of 500,000. In 1986 they did a remake of the MAMAS AND THE PAPAS' "California Dreamin' " with Roger McGuinn of the BYRDS playing his signature 12-string guitar. In 1987 they did a version of the surf rock classic "Wipe Out" with the rap group Fat Boys. In 1988, the year they were inducted into the Rock and Roll Hall of Fame, the Beach Boys had the biggest-selling hit of their career: "Kokomo," coauthored by John Phillips of the Mamas and the Papas.

In the Beach Boys' history there have been many dramas, tragedies, frictions, lawsuits, divorces, and alcohol and drug addictions. Dennis Wilson died by drowning in 1983, not while surfing but while diving below his boat while it was docked, trying to recover a photo of his estranged girlfriend that he had previously thrown overboard. In the mid-1990s Mike Love sued Brian Wilson over the writing credits on 79 Beach Boys songs and won a $5 million judgment. Carl Wilson died of cancer in 1998.

The band then divided into three factions. The band that uses the name Beach Boys today consists of Mike Love and Bruce Johnston (joined for a time by original member David Marks), plus longtime session players and new members. They put on satisfying concerts for their legions of fans. Another group, called Al Jardine's Family and Friends, which included Brian's daughter, received mixed reviews. Brian Wilson, against all expectations, given his notoriously fragile psyche, has toured, fronting a tight band and performing from his vast catalog to ecstatic audiences.

Beatles, The

The most popular and most successful band in rock began in Liverpool, England, as the Quarrymen, a skiffle group made up of John Lennon (b. 1940) and some schoolmates. At a 1957 churchyard social event, Paul McCartney (b. 1942) heard the band, met the leader, and impressed him by knowing how to play and sing from memory a couple of American rock and roll songs. Soon they joined forces, picking up a still younger George Harrison (b. 1943) as third guitarist and passing through a couple of name changes: Johnny and the Moondogs, then the Silver Beatles, soon shortened to just the Beatles. With Pete Best on drums and Stuart Sutcliffe on bass, the band played local coffee clubs and auditioned for better things, which came in the form of backing up vocalists on short tours.

Hamburg, Germany, with its red-light district and soldiers stationed nearby, opened up as a market, and British groups by the dozens were brought over to feed the demand. Most of the musicians were young—George Harrison was deported for being under 18—and were obliged to play long hours and live in squalid quarters, usually behind the club where they performed. The rigors of long sets made everyone a singer, to share the load, and necessitated large and varied repertoires. The Beatles' live set in this period was captured on tape (on a night that Ringo Starr (b. 1940), on loan from a rival band—Rory Storm and the Hurricanes—happened to be filling in for Best) by a fellow musician who wanted a souvenir. It would be released when the band was famous, and included "Red Sails in the Sunset," "Besame Mucho," and many other songs that now seem unusual. From learning these songs, they picked up musical devices and ideas that would soon show up within their own compositions.

The Hamburg experience—they went five times—was invaluable for other reasons too: they picked up a small but devoted following, mostly bohemian artists and students. One of their fans, Astrid Kirchherr, was a photographer. She posed the Beatles in some of their earliest and most effective publicity shots. In them, they dressed in black leather and sported brushed-forward hairdos that she had proposed (in current German bohemian fashion), which became their trademark. She also had a romance with Stuart Sutcliffe, who stayed on in Hamburg to be with her and resume his art studies, though before long he died from complications of a beating that had occurred after a Liverpool gig.

In Hamburg they got to meet and share the stage with some of their idols, including Gene Vincent and LITTLE RICHARD. Another benefit came when British singer Tony Sheridan, a popular Hamburg attraction, was asked to record in Germany and took the Beatles as his backup band. They accompanied him on a rocking version of the Scottish folksong "My Bonnie," and also were able to record a couple of tracks on their own.

When Sheridan's record became a hit in Germany, a fan in Liverpool came into a record store run by Brian Epstein to order a copy. Epstein had not heard of the group, but he went to see them at one of the Beatles' now-legendary lunchtime shows at a sweaty downstairs club called the Cavern. He signed on as their manager and set about trying to secure a record contract for them. This entailed a trip to London, then and now the center of British industry, where the Beatles' audition for Decca was recorded. Decca and other companies passed on them, saying "the day of groups is over." Epstein, convinced of their potential, gave it one more try and met George Martin, a producer at Parlophone who had made comedy records. He was impressed by Epstein's enthusiasm and was interested enough to have the band come in for a session. Their charm, as much as their musical abilities, won him over, and he became their producer and remained so throughout their career. In summer 1962, just after Martin signed them to the Parlophone label (part of EMI), the lineup solidified with Ringo Starr replacing Pete Best.

To boost their commercial chances, Epstein had new uniforms made: collarless suits, which differentiated and distanced them from typical business attire. The Beatles had a string of hits and rapidly rose to fame in Britain. At the Royal Command Performance in 1963, John made a typically cheeky remark to the audience: "Will the people in the cheaper seats clap your hands, and the rest of you, if you'll just rattle your jewelry."

Their debut performance in America was on television, on *The Ed Sullivan Show,* a Sunday night variety program that drew huge audiences for family viewings. It had acrobats, comedians, puppets, Broadway casts, opera singers, and pop singers. At the Beatles' first appearance they played for the studio audience, which included many screaming girls whose ecstatic reactions were also filmed and seen by 73 million TV watchers. The Beatles performed "She Loves You," "All My Loving," and "Till There Was You" (a song from the Broadway musical *The Music Man*). During one song their first names were superimposed over the film (for John it added "Sorry, girls—he's married"), and Americans got to know them as individuals.

Between "I Want to Hold Your Hand" (1963) and "The Long and Winding Road" (1970), both

The Beatles (Michael Ochs Archives.com)

number-one songs, were more than 60 other hit singles. The band's scope expanded several times: when BOB DYLAN incited them to write something with depth, when they discovered marijuana and LSD, when they heard the BEACH BOYS' "Good Vibrations" and the *Pet Sounds* album, and when George brought in an Indian music influence, first heard in "Norwegian Wood."

The song "Yesterday" (1965) is credited to Lennon-McCartney (as usual), though the sole composer is Paul McCartney, who is the only Beatle present on the recording (he sings and plays acoustic guitar), accompanied by a classical string quartet. This is probably the most covered song to come from rock. More than 2,500 artists had made recordings of it by 1980, and there have been many more since. Like many of the most beloved and often-covered songs

of the 20th century, from "Stardust" and "Georgia on My Mind" (both written by Hoagy Carmichael) to "Swanee," the theme of "Yesterday" is nostalgia for when things were better. The theme of paradise lost has echoed throughout the ages in all art and is part of the human condition.

Several films boosted the Beatles' popularity. The innovative *A Hard Day's Night* (1964), filmed in black and white, captured the band's charm and the craziness of Beatlemania. *Help!* (1965), filmed in color and on location in the Swiss Alps and the Bahamas, had a nutty plot and was also fun. *Magical Mystery Tour* (1967) was directed by the band and was critically received as indulgent and misguided. Of all their artistic endeavors, it is considered their only real flop, and it is seldom seen. *Yellow Submarine* (1968) was an animated film in which the Beatles had little direct involvement, but it was beautifully made and very popular. The film *Let It Be* (1970) documented some of their last recording sessions and revealed their fragmentation.

They tired of touring—Europe, North America, Australia, the Far East—and their last public concert was in San Francisco in 1966. Without the need to be able to reproduce the music in concert, they explored their own creativity and exploited newly available technologies in the recording studio to make some of their greatest work, first the "Strawberry Fields Forever"/"Penny Lane" single and then *Sgt. Pepper's Lonely Hearts Club Band* (1967).

This album changed the course of popular music. The Beatles had come an amazing distance in the five years since securing a recording contract. In 1964 they had conquered America as the undisputed rulers of the BRITISH INVASION. With each new Beatles album, they affirmed their position at the top of all pop and served notice that again the rules of the game had changed, the scope had been broadened, and the level of achievement was raised.

The release of *Sgt. Pepper's* was much anticipated. Millions bought it at first opportunity, and liked it, everything about it, right away. From this unified moment, however, pop and rock began its fragmentation. Until then, every style had been embraced on AM radio: GIRL GROUPS, MOTOWN, soul, British invasion, GARAGE ROCK, FOLK ROCK, the emerging psychedelic San Francisco sound, and various holdovers of older styles. Rock music in all its varieties was now so expanded by the Beatles' example that no one umbrella could cover it, no one force could unify it, and no one fan could embrace all of it.

What no one knew at the time was that this album marked the moment when rock and roll became rock. The "roll" in rock and roll is the swing, the lift that gets people up to dance. This had been carried through the big band era into the rhythm-and-blues and rockabilly combos that served as a large part of the Beatles' early inspirations. But with no live audience to perform for, the Beatles' music could disregard the requirements for dance-floor body rhythms. Their music took on an introverted nature that allowed for more intellectualism and spiritualism, inspired as well by "consciousness-expanding" drugs and Indian religious philosophy.

That this music was for the head and not the body was emphasized by its lavish packaging: the listener could interact with the gatefold (double) jacket, a first for a single vinyl disc. The famous cover shot provided hours of amusement, as people tried to identify the various wax figures (what does she have to do with the Beatles?) and deciphering the hidden messages (what kind of plants are those?). The lyrics were printed (another first for a rock record) on the back cover, inviting deeper listening and pondering. The inside photo made the Beatles, all in mustaches, seem almost there, and there was even a cardboard insert with images and a paper mustache to cut out and wear. It was playtime with the Beatles—be a Beatle.

By wearing a costume and assuming another identity, they were in another movie, a movie presented as a record album. They weren't the Beatles on this album, but another band, the Lonely Hearts Club Band led by Sgt. Pepper. Liberated from being pop stars, they could explore new influences in depth. For Paul McCartney it was the music of his father, the soft-shoe style of the British music-hall tradition. For George Harrison it was the music of India. For John Lennon it was the world of dreams and psychedelic imagery. For all of them it was the freedom to mix and match ideas and play with the possibilities of the studio.

The songs and sounds on the album contained the Beatles' expansion of the available vocabulary of rock: sound effects, brass bands, non-Western instruments, circus keyboards, orchestral swirls, and more. The songs spoke of the need of support ("With a Little Help from My Friends"), the ability and need for personal evolution ("Getting Better," "Fixing a Hole"), the generation gap ("She's Leaving Home"), concern about old age ("When I'm Sixty Four"), spiritual unity ("Within You, Without You"), and day-to-day life and romance ("Lovely Rita" and "Good Morning, Good Morning"). With the reprise of the title song, it is clear that the movie ends, but there is one more song. "A Day in the Life" is therefore the Beatles as the Beatles. Its last line is: "I'd love to turn you on." To what? To a change in ideas. They did.

Their performance of their next single, "All You Need Is Love," was augmented by a large cast and televised in the first satellite broadcast. It reached an unprecedented audience, estimated at 350 million people. Shortly afterward, in 1967 their manager, Brian Epstein, died. It was devastating for them. His death was ruled accidental, although he had on previous occasions attempted suicide and even written suicide notes.

Their interest in the spiritual message of Maharishi Mahesh Yogi involved a trip to India. The songs the Beatles wrote there appeared on the 1968 double album called *The Beatles* (but universally referred to as "the White Album" for its total lack of cover image). One of the songs was John's put-down of the Maharishi, called "Sexy Sadie," and among the other notable songs was Paul's "Blackbird," played on acoustic guitar.

While making *Let It Be*, they were distracted by the film crew documenting the process, as well as frictions within the band. The tapes from those sessions—miles of them—were given to legendary producer PHIL SPECTOR, who edited the mess, adding strings to "Across the Universe." Paul, in particular, was not impressed by the additions. A version of the album with all orchestrations removed would be later issued as *Let It Be . . . Naked* (2003).

Their final album was 1969's *Abbey Road* (though *Let It Be* was released after it), and it is one of their best. The last lyric on the last song on this last record is a poignant bit of wisdom: ". . . and in the end, the love you take is equal to the love you make." The Beatles went their separate ways. They had been growing apart, and the disputes over management, and the influence and inclusion of Lennon's new girlfriend Yoko Ono in the recording studio (she can be heard singing on "Birthday" and "The Continuing Story of Bungalow Bill"), were only part of the story.

Paul released an album on which he wrote, sang, and played everything. George had a backlog of so many songs that his solo debut was a triple album with the philosophical title *All Things Must Pass* (1970). It contained the hit single "My Sweet Lord." (Musically, that song was almost identical to the Chiffons' "He's So Fine" of 1963, and Harrison was sued for what the judge decided was "unconscious plagiarism.") Ringo made several albums and had some hits. Some were remakes of old rock songs like "You're 16," while others were good-natured references to his happy-go-lucky persona, like "I'm the Greatest" (written for him by John). John explored his pain with primal therapy and screamed, musically, through songs like "Mother" ("I wanted you but you didn't want me").

Other musicians have reinterpreted their music as jazz, baroque, bluegrass, and other styles. The most successful of the many parodies was by the Rutles, who made a film called *All You Need Is Cash* (1978). Liverpool became a tourist destination for Beatles fans eager to see the places associated with their heroes. Record collectors sought out rarities, driving the prices up, and other relics of Beatles merchandising became collectibles. The market is full of bootlegs, oddities, and albums of press conferences done on tour. Their own albums were reissued several times, and finally on CD in the UK editions, not the chopped-up alterations that were originally for sale in America. There is a veritable industry in books on the Beatles, including memoirs, chronologies, musical transcriptions and analysis, cartoons, pop-ups, biographies, scrapbooks, illustrated lyrics, studio logs, and discussions of the gear they used. In *The Beatles with Lacan: Rock 'N' Roll As Requiem for the Modern Age* by Henry Sullivan (1995), they and their times were given a psychoanalytic reading. Web sites, conferences, and university courses are devoted to them.

Despite many offers and requests to reunite, they never did. The cherished hope that the Beatles would one day make music together again was dashed in 1980 when Mark David Chapman, a deranged fan, asked John for an autograph as John and Yoko were entering their apartment in New York City. Lennon obliged, and Chapman pulled out a gun and shot him dead. Devastated fans grieved around the world. But there were two songs of "new" Beatles music yet to come. "Free As a Bird" and "Real Love" were demos that John had recorded in the late 1970s. They were transformed by Paul, George, and Ringo as part of the *Anthology* project in the 1990s that resulted in three double CDs, a set of videos and DVDs, and a book.

Paul explored classical composition, did duets with Michael Jackson and Elvis Costello, financed the Liverpool Institute for Performing Arts, and toured several times, to rapturous reception. Ringo was in films and on television, and put together various versions of his All Starr Band, joining forces with friends and colleagues from other notable bands, each taking turns as the featured performer. George made many solo albums, of varying quality, and got involved in movie production and sports car racing. He died in 2001, felled by cancer at age 58. His final album, *Brainwashed,* released posthumously, was one of his best.

The Beatles are still loved, their records are heard, their songs are played by beginning guitarists and established acts of every style, and their memories are cherished.

Berry, Chuck (b. 1926) *pioneering guitarist and songwriter*

Chuck Berry is perhaps the most influential person in rock and roll. He made three enormous contributions to the genre: his songs, his GUITAR style, and the way he wrote lyrics. His enduring songs are known around the world. More than two dozen of his recordings, all for the Chess label of Chicago, were hits on the pop charts; all but a couple were his own compositions. Many placed even higher on the R&B charts. Berry's songs have been recorded by the biggest acts in popular music, including ELVIS PRESLEY, BUDDY HOLLY, JERRY LEE LEWIS, the BEACH BOYS, the BEATLES, the ROLLING STONES, JIMI HENDRIX, the GRATEFUL DEAD, BRUCE SPRINGSTEEN, Rod Stewart, and DAVID BOWIE. His songs have also been played by the smallest names in popular music: virtually every bar and garage

Chuck Berry (Michael Ochs Archives.com)

band knows "Johnny B. Goode" and some other of his numbers.

"Johnny B. Goode" is a rock and roll anthem. The lyrics describe a backwoods southern boy whose impressive guitar-playing ability offers a way out of poverty. It has been redone in all kinds of rock styles, from SURF to hard rock and HEAVY METAL, and has been a favorite of PUNK ROCK bands from the Sex Pistols to NOFX. In the 1960s Buck Owens did a honky-tonk version, and in the 1980s Peter Tosh did a REGGAE one. Tosh, who with Bob Marley and Bunny Livingstone was one of the Wailing Wailers, shifted the geographical setting from Berry's Louisiana to Jamaica. In a classic scene in the movie *Back to the Future* (1985), the character played by Michael J. Fox, who has traveled back in time to 1955, plays "Johnny B. Goode" at a dance, thus helping to invent rock and roll (and introducing the song to a new generation of filmgoers).

Berry's trademark guitar style—playing two and three notes at a time while soloing—must be copied in order to do justice to his songs, something that all rock guitarists have learned to do. (If they haven't, they are not really rock guitarists!)

The lyrics of his songs are playful and inventive, full of poetic images, catchy phrases, clever rhymes, and stories. Though he was 29 years old and married with children when he had his first hit, many of Berry's songs insightfully depict teenage experiences—school days, cars, dating, the rush to grow up—and, of course, the liberating power of rock and roll. Others comment wittily on the situations and frustrations of adult life, racial and class issues included. His songs appealed to a wide range of people and helped rock and roll transcend divisions of race. In the 1950s, however, popular culture was still at odds with elite culture: in "Roll Over Beethoven" (1956) he adds "tell Tchaikovsky the news." The news is that rock and roll is here and that classical, highbrow music is for squares.

Chuck Berry was born in St. Louis, Missouri, the third of six children. In his youth he listened to down-home blues, R&B, and big band jazz, and idolized the primal blues power of Muddy Waters and the smooth vocals of Nat King Cole. In 1952 pianist Johnny Johnson hired Berry to join his trio for a New Year's Eve gig at a prominent nightclub. By spring they were filling the place every weekend, largely because of Berry's magnetic, crowd-pleasing showmanship. One of the things he did was later called the "duck walk," a funny way of moving while crouched low to the ground that he had come up with as a child and often was asked to repeat for the amusement of grown-ups. Audiences at the club were racially integrated, and Berry sang to please the clientele: blues songs, hillbilly songs, and pop. He presented each in its respective manner, but as his music developed, elements from each genre blended into his personal style. This is one of the secrets of his universal popularity. Berry took over as the leader of the band, though Johnny Johnson remained as his pianist, one of the finest in rock and roll.

In search of a record contract, Berry went to Chicago in 1955. There he saw Muddy Waters perform and afterward asked his idol who he should approach. Waters suggested Leonard Chess, who soon signed Berry to his label. Chuck Berry's popularity took off when his debut record, "Maybelline," a mix of country and rhythm and blues, became a hit. It was inspired by "Ida Red" and "Ida Red Likes the Boogie," western swing songs by Bob Wills and His Texas Playboys. Berry's lyrics describe a car race, a theme he would return to in later compositions.[2]

To Berry's supreme disappointment, the label on each copy of "Maybelline" indicated that it was written by him plus two coauthors. They did not help him write it, it was just a shady back-room deal done at Chess in exchange for favors. Thirty years later Berry won back the full rights, but by then he had been cheated out of a great amount of money. Ironically, the deal helped make the song a hit, and without it, it is possible he would have not have had any royalty money to lose.

One of the names on the label was Alan Freed, the influential disc jockey. He might have played the song even without coauthor credit because he had good commercial sense and knew what his radio listeners liked, but his vested interest ensured that it got plenty of airplay. The two maintained good relations. Berry performed in three movies that starred Freed (playing, as in real life, a disc jockey trying to save rock and roll): *Rock, Rock, Rock* (1956), *Mister Rock and Roll* (1957), and *Go, Johnny, Go* (1958), in which Berry also had an acting role as Freed's partner. Freed's story was dramatized in *American Hot Wax* (1976), which portrayed the tensions between the rock and roll fans and the authorities. The film's climax was the recreation of a 1950s concert in which both Berry and his old rival Jerry Lee Lewis played themselves. Other films showing Berry in performance include *Jazz on a Summer's Day* (1958), a documentary of the Newport Jazz Festival, *The T.A.M.I. Show* (1964), a terrific concert with a phenomenal lineup, and *Let the Good Times Roll* (1973), a rock revival show. All are recommended.

In the late 1950s Berry toured extensively, and with the money he earned from his first and further hit records, such as "School Days," "Rock & Roll Music," "Johnny B. Goode," and "Sweet Little Sixteen," he bought some land outside St. Louis and constructed an amusement center and country club called Berry Park.

In late 1959, while on the road with his band in Texas, Berry met a young woman and offered her a job at a nightclub he owned in St. Louis. She accepted, but shortly afterward, when it came out that she was underage and had been working as a prostitute on the side, Berry was charged with transporting a woman across state lines for immoral purposes. The first trial's verdict of guilty was overturned because of the judge's racist remarks, but the second one also found him guilty. He was fined and served two years in jail, beginning in 1962. It was not the first time. He had been jailed from age 17 to 21 for a spree of robberies and a car theft he and two friends committed while joyriding across the United States in 1944. During that jail time he sang in a gospel quartet, played in a band, and took up boxing. During his 1960s incarceration he studied business management and earned his high school diploma, but the whole long affair disrupted his career and dispirited him. Accounts by fellow musicians describe how he was no longer easygoing, but guarded, suspicious, and bitter. It was more than being in jail. The indignities and humiliations of racism and the financial exploitations—crooked managers, stolen writer credits, and missing royalties—made him aloof and independent, determined to be self-sufficient.

While Berry was in jail, interest in R&B was on the rise, and Chess continued releasing his old recordings, to some success. Guitarist Lonnie Mack had a hit with an instrumental version of Berry's "Memphis" in 1963. That year the Beach Boys' "Surfin' USA" borrowed the music from Berry's "Sweet Little Sixteen" (he received no writing credit until his publisher sued and won an out-of-court settlement). Berry was released from jail in 1964, the year Johnny Rivers had his first two hits, both Chuck Berry songs ("Memphis" and "Maybelline"), and BRITISH INVASION acts routinely covered his songs. The Beatles revived his "Roll Over Beethoven" and the Rolling Stones did his "Come On" as their first single (both would record more of his songs). In 1964 he made his first appearances in Britain, and during that year and the next he returned to the pop charts with new material, gaining a half a dozen more hits in America, including "Nadine (Is It You?)," "No Particular Place to Go," and "You Never Can Tell" (repopularized in 1994 when used on the *Pulp Fiction* soundtrack).

In 1966 Berry left Chess for Mercury Records, but aside from *Live at the Fillmore* (on which he was backed by the Steve Miller Band), the recordings are lackluster and he produced no hits for Mercury. By the end of the decade, the ROCK AND ROLL REVIVAL was going strong and providing prestigious bookings, and in 1970 he signed again with Chess, recording some fine work. In 1972 he had two more hits, both recorded live in England. The novelty song "My Ding-A-Ling," done originally by Dave Bartholomew (FATS DOMINO's musical partner) in 1952, was Berry's only number-one hit. *The London Chuck Berry Sessions* (1972), made the top 10 and was his best-selling album.

Berry continued to be a popular live act, and his songs were still being covered. Linda Ronstadt hit with her version of "Back in the USA" (1978). The next year, *Rock It,* Berry's last album of new material, was released, and he was briefly jailed for tax evasion. Since then he has continued to perform, received a multitude of awards, and been in the news for other legal matters.

He was inducted into the Rock and Roll Hall of Fame in 1986, and his book *Chuck Berry: The Autobiography* came out in 1987, as did *Chuck Berry: Hail! Hail! Rock 'n' Roll,* a documentary film of a St. Louis concert honoring his 60th birthday. Directed by Taylor Hackford, who said it was a maddening experience to work with Berry, it is a remarkable film full of interviews that celebrate his artistry and indicate how difficult a man he can be. It has great performances by the star and many guests, including Johnny Johnson, ERIC CLAPTON, and Keith Richards (who did much to organize the music and suffered insults from Berry for his efforts).

Berry is a complex character who can be controlling and aggressive. He can also be gracious. He is very private, reserving his warmth for his close ones. For touring engagements, he has strict demands for transportation and musical equipment, insists on payment in advance, and though the performances can be erratic, due to his mood or the inevitably underrehearsed backup bands, he fulfills his obligations to the letter, playing the contracted time to the minute. Since 1996 he has played monthly at a St. Louis club where he feels more at ease, meets the fans, and enjoys having his children play in the band with him. And his music is still played everywhere a rock guitarist plugs into an amplifier.

Blondie

Blondie was one of the most successful bands to be associated with NEW WAVE music. They formed in 1974, broke up in 1982, and reunited in 1997. They shared a sense of irony and exaggerated artiness and style with new wave bands, but their accessible music, which was based on 1960s pop rock

Blondie (Michael Ochs Archives.com)

traditions, was so eclectic in its scope that their style is hard to categorize. They drew from REGGAE ("The Tide Is High"), rap ("Rapture"), disco ("Heart of Glass"), and synthpop ("Call Me"), as well as PUNK ROCK and jazz. The four songs named above were all number-one singles, and Blondie had four million-selling albums in the United States, but Blondie was even more popular in other countries, particularly England, where six consecutive albums charted in the top 10.

The core members of the band are vocalist Debbie Harry (b. 1945), guitarist Chris Stein (b. 1950), who wrote or cowrote most of their songs, drummer Clem Burke (b. 1955), and keyboardist Jimmy Destri (b. 1954). The band's name played on Debbie Harry's stunning cover-girl looks, bleached blonde hair, and the role of blondes as glamour

icons. With sex appeal and a street-smart attitude, she herself was one of the icons of 1980s rock, and an inspiration to future stars like Madonna, Annie Lennox, the Spice Girls, and, indirectly, Britney Spears and Christina Aguilera.

Harry's down-to-earth attitude probably comes from growing up in a conservative environment in Paterson, New Jersey. She sang in a choir and listened avidly to the radio, but felt stifled in Paterson. After finishing college she moved to New York City in 1965. She hung around Greenwich Village, worked as a secretary and a waitress, and went to screenings of Andy Warhol movies. In 1968, still dark-haired, she recorded an album as part of Wind in the Willows, an otherwise unremarkable folk psychedelic group reminiscent of the MAMAS AND THE PAPAS and DONOVAN. The next year she attended and was impressed by WOODSTOCK. In the early 1970s Harry was part of the Stilettos, a camp version of a GIRL GROUP trio, whose band included her then boyfriend Chris Stein. After the Stilettos broke up, Stein and Harry formed Blondie in 1974, with Harry as the featured performer. The other personnel shifted. Clem Burke joined in 1975, as did Jimmy Destri a few months later.

They made their first single, "X-Offender," and album, just called *Blondie,* in 1976 for the small Private Stock label. BRITISH INVASION, SURF, and girl group sounds mixed with elements of salsa, funk, Broadway tunes, and B-movie soundtracks. Their producer was Richard Gottehrer, whose lengthy credits included cowriting the Angels' "My Boyfriend's Back" (1963), producing the McCoys' "Hang On Sloopy" (1965), and being a member of the Strangeloves, who had hits in the mid-1960s. In 1977 Chrysalis Records bought Blondie's contract from Private Stock and reissued their first album and released their second, *Plastic Letters,* also produced by Gottehrer. After it was released, the bassist on the album, Frank Infante, switched to guitar, and Nigel Harrison came in on bass, making the group a six-piece, which it remained until Blondie disbanded. In spring 1978 two songs were top-10 hits in the United Kingdom: a cover of Randy and the Rainbows' 1963 DOO-WOP hit "Denise," renamed "Denis," and "(I'm Always Touched By Your) Presence, Dear" (written by bassist Gary Valentine, who had played on the debut album). On this album Blondie is tighter and more rocking, but the overall tone is less effervescent than on their debut.

For their third album, *Parallel Lines* (1978), they used British producer and songwriter Mike Chapman, who had worked with the Sweet and other GLAM ROCK bands earlier in the 1970s. His disciplined approach refined their sound, and it brought them international stardom. "Picture This" and "Hanging on the Telephone" were hits in the United Kingdom, as were "Heart of Glass" and "Sunday Girl" (both number ones). "Heart of Glass" was their first number-one hit in the United States, and "One Way or Another" made number 24.

Eat to the Beat (1979) contained some of their best rock and roll, and though it sold well it was less artistically and commercially successful. "Dreaming" and "Atomic" were big hits in the United Kingdom and moderate hits in the United States. Each market put one more album song, but not the same one, onto the charts. *Autoamerican* (1980) was an uneven album that explored even more styles. Its hits were huge, though: "The Tide Is High," a cover of a reggae song originally by a Jamaican group called the Paragons, was another international number one. "Rapture" was number one in the United States, the first number-one hit to feature rap. It introduced rap to a wider audience, including some future rappers, and gave Blondie credibility in the hip-hop world (which led in the 1990s to remixes of their classic material and new collaborations with rappers). A single not on the album was yet another number-one hit in both the United States and United Kingdom: "Call Me," the theme from the movie *American Gigolo.* It was a collaboration with German disco producer Giorgio Moroder (who had produced Donna Summer's disco smash "I Feel Love").

By this time tensions and fatigue had set in, and the members worked on individual projects. Debbie Harry's first solo album was *KooKoo* (1981), produced by Nile Rodgers and Bernard Edwards of Chic. It sold well, but some of the material did not suit her style, and the hits were moderate. Jimmy Destri's Bowie-influenced *Heart on a Wall* (1982) had little impact.

Following *The Best of Blondie* (1981), the band, despite dissension, made their sixth and last album (until their reunion): *The Hunter* (1982). "Island of Lost Souls" was a hit in the United States and did better in the United Kingdom. The album as a whole, however, was polished but aimless, an artistic and commercial disappointment. At about this time Stein became seriously ill and was diagnosed with the genetic disease pemphigus, which causes the skin to blister. As a result, Blondie quietly disbanded at the end of 1982. For the four years that Stein battled the disease—he eventually fully recovered—Harry helped care for him. Though they split up as a couple, they remained close.

Destri left music for awhile to become a family man and contractor. Burke continued to record and tour with top acts. Stein, once he recovered, produced various bands and wrote soundtrack music for movies and television shows and assisted Harry on her solo projects. Harry did some acting in TV shows, independent films, and a Woody Allen movie, and made more solo records. *Rockbird* (1986) was undistinguished, aside from the hit single "French Kissin'," which topped the charts in Australia and the United Kingdom. *Def, Dumb & Blonde* (1989) was better received by the critics but did not move the public. *Debravation* (1993) received mixed reviews and did not chart, which the other albums had at least done. From the mid-1990s onward, Harry sometimes sang with the Jazz Passengers as one of a number of featured vocalists. With them she recorded an album live in Spain.

Blondie's legacy was marketed throughout the 1990s in various forms. *Blonde and Beyond* (1993) collected favorite album cuts, B-sides of singles, live tracks, and foreign-language versions of songs. *The Platinum Collection* (1994) gathered all of their singles, some B-sides, and their early demos. On *Remixed Remade Remodeled: The Remix Project* (1995), hip-hop and techno artists updated Blondie's recordings with varied results. Their first live album was *Picture This Live* (1997), recorded in Philadelphia and Dallas in 1978 and 1980.

In 1998 the lineup of Harry, Stein, Destri, and Burke reunited to tour Europe. Former bassist Nigel Harrison and lead guitarist Frank Infante (who was fired in 1982 but reinstated in time to play on *The Hunter* after a court challenge based on a band agreement written in 1979), were left out of the reunion and attempted to sue the others.

For their comeback record, the band aimed to do something fresh, not nostalgic. *No Exit* (1999), their first new album in 17 years, had all their trademark elements and was enthusiastically received, particularly the catchy "Maria," written by Destri. It entered the UK charts at number one, making them the only act to have a British number-one hit in the 1970s, 1980s, and 1990s. *Blondie Live* (1999) documented the reunited group's still inspiring show, with some new songs added to the concert repertoire. *The Curse of Blondie* (released in Europe in 2003 and the United States in 2004) was rated even better than *No Exit*. In 2004 Blondie was again touring internationally.

blues rock

In the mid-1950s in the United Kingdom, there was a craze for a style called skiffle, basically American folk blues interpreted by acoustic guitar strummers and homemade one-string-bass pluckers and washboard scratchers. The BEATLES, under their earlier name the Quarrymen, played skiffle.

By the early 1960s a host of young musicians in the United Kingdom used American music, particularly blues, R&B, blues-based rock and roll, and the gutsy early MOTOWN repertoire for inspiration. What the ROLLING STONES, YARDBIRDS, ANIMALS, Downliners Sect, Paramounts (who became Procol Harum), Them (led by Van Morrison), and others did through their energetic and often inspired renditions was to educate the white pop audience to black music, first through repertoire and then through personal connections. Both the Animals and the Yardbirds backed up blues legend Sonny Boy Williamson in concert and on record. In 1969 FLEETWOOD MAC, while touring the United States, recorded *In Chicago* on location at Chess Studios, joined by blues veterans Willie Dixon, Honeyboy Edwards, Otis Spann, and Walter "Shakey" Horton. On *The London Howlin' Wolf Sessions* (1971), Wolf and his guitarist Hubert Sumlin were backed by the rhythm section of the Rolling Stones, along with ERIC CLAPTON and Steve Winwood. Carrying on the tradition, in 1988 U2 invited B. B. King to sit in for "When Love Comes to Town."

In the 1960s and 1970s British bands resurrected many old blues songs. Big Joe Williams' "Baby Please Don't Go" (1935) was arranged by Van Morrison's Them. CREAM, featuring Eric Clapton, covered Skip James's "I'm So Glad" (1931) and Blind Joe Reynolds' "Outside Woman Blues" (1930). Cream also did "Rollin' and Tumblin'," recorded first by Blind Willie Newbern (1929), and popularized by Little Walter and Muddy Waters. LED ZEPPELIN arranged Memphis Minnie's "When the Levee Breaks" (1929). They also covered "You Shook Me" and "I Can't Quit You Baby," both composed by Willie Dixon. Jeff Beck did Dixon's "I Ain't Superstitious."

The impact on American youth of the BRITISH INVASION groups and their reverence for black music contributed to the explosion of GARAGE ROCK groups, which not only covered the repertoires of the U.K. bands but also caused some musicians and fans to research roots music themselves. Most American rock bands, from the local stars to the hit makers, had at least a couple of blues items on their song list. The band down the street likely knew something by BO DIDDLEY, or just copied, say, the DOORS' version of "Back Door Man" (by Willie Dixon and Howlin' Wolf).

In America blues rock was pioneered in the mid-1960s by the Paul Butterfield Blues Band, an integrated unit from Chicago. Other important early blues rock bands were the Blues Project from New York, whose lengthy version of Muddy Waters' "Two Trains Running" was a concert highlight, the ALLMAN BROTHERS BAND, based in Georgia, who remade Blind Willie McTell's "Statesboro Blues" (1928), and Canned Heat, from Los Angeles, who put their version of "Bull Doze Blues" by Henry Thomas (1928) on the pop charts (as "Going Up the Country," 1968). Bands from San Francisco's psychedelic scene drew heavily from the blues repertoire, including the GRATEFUL DEAD, who had numerous blues and jug band pieces in their repertoire, often stretched by improvisations, and Big Brother and the Holding Company, featuring JANIS JOPLIN, who did a version of Big Mama Thornton's "Ball and Chain."

HEAVY METAL carried on the project of creating blues-influenced riffs. That teenage players in the 21st century are still eager to learn the songs and

styles of Robert Johnson and Muddy Waters and the great riffs from the 1950s and 1960s bodes well for the futures of both blues and rock.

Bowie, David (b. 1947) *British singer and songwriter*

Bowie's first hit in America was "Changes" (1972), an apt title for a man who has passed through so many artistic phases and images in his career that he is commonly referred to as a chameleon. David Bowie is gifted, charismatic, enigmatic, and unpredictable. His risk-taking creativity has enticed and confounded fans and critics from the late 1960s to the present, though much of the time the public does not know what to make of him. In the 1970s he was the most important figure in rock, and he continues as a major star.

His output has varied from accessible commercial pop to inscrutable avant-garde experiments. A partial list of the kinds of music in Bowie's catalog would include folk; various forms of rock from pop to hard rock to alternative; soul; post-disco dance music; techno; and drum 'n' bass sounds. His influences cover a wide range as well, from Frank Sinatra and BOB DYLAN to Andy Warhol and the VELVET UNDERGROUND.

Bowie is a manipulator of the media, often fabricating stories and making misleading statements. He has declared that he is gay and then admitted he is predominantly heterosexual, made outlandish remarks about politics, and made pronouncements about career moves that never transpire. Some of these are just publicity stunts—when it comes to self-promotion he is a master—others, perhaps, are wishful thinking. They have been attributed to periods of drug abuse and to the mental illness, in the form of schizophrenia, that affects his mother's side of the family. He is rarely self-revealing in his lyrics, and his comments on modern life and portraits of known and fictional people are purposefully disjointed in an artistic, sometimes playful, way. Among Bowie's common themes are alienation, isolation, and nightmarish visions of the future. Embedded in some of his lyrics are keywords derived from his involvement with occult mysticism.

In the 1970s Bowie helped introduce theatrical elements to rock, becoming a GLAM ROCK superstar with his most famous stage persona: Ziggy Stardust, a messianic alien rock star. He explored the theatrical side of his nature early in his career in the form of mime, but he has expressed it as a rock star in various other personae, in spectacularly staged concerts with Bowie in costume making dramatic gestures, in the varied nature of his music, and in imaginative promotional videos. He has worked as a theatrical actor, notably the title role in the Broadway production of *The Elephant Man* (1980), which brought him rave reviews, and has appeared in numerous films.

There are several recognizable phases of his career, the earliest predating his first hit in 1969. In the mid-1960s he was part of the R&B scene in London (his birthplace), playing saxophone and singing in bands that, starting in 1964, released unsuccessful singles. They were the King Bees (named after a song by bluesman Slim Harpo), the Mannish Boys (named after a song by bluesman Muddy Waters), and Davy Jones and the Lower Third. Jones is his real last name, but to avoid confusion with Davy Jones of the MONKEES he changed it in 1966 to Bowie. (It is a reference to the famous Bowie knife, whose invention is credited to Jim Bowie, an American pioneer hero who was killed at the battle of the Alamo in Texas in 1836.) Though he recorded, as Davy Jones, some blues songs, the singles released in 1966 were more influenced by soul music. Little of David Bowie's music has direct blues coloration, but the later developments of black music—soul, funk, and disco—often inform his songs.

Between his first album in 1967 and the move to glam rock, his music followed contemporary pop rock styles, touching on cabaret, singer-songwriter folk, and hard rock. He came to public attention in 1969 with the folkish "Space Oddity," released just before the United States put a man on the Moon. It was inspired by Stanley Kubrick's film *2001: A Space Odyssey* (1968), and it was a top-10 hit in the United Kingdom (it charted in the United States only when reissued in 1973). "Space Oddity" introduced the character of Major Tom, an astronaut who leaves his capsule for a walk in space and loses contact with ground control. In one of his biggest hits, "Ashes to Ashes" (1980), Bowie revisited the theme, stating, "Major Tom's a junkie, strung out on heaven's high, hitting an all-time low." Peter Schilling, a German pop singer, had a big hit with a techno dance sequel: "Major Tom (Coming Home)" in 1983.

David Bowie (Michael Ochs Archives.com)

In rock's self-consciously decadent glam period of the early 1970s, Bowie emerged as a trendsetting international star. In the U.K. charts in 1972 and 1973, he had four top-10 albums and eight top-10 singles. In America, as in other markets, most of them also charted, though not as high. On *The Rise and Fall of Ziggy Stardust and the Spiders from Mars* (1972), Bowie's fifth album, he not only made a creative leap from his previous work, but he became a superstar by pretending he was one. It is a rock and roll landmark, one of the best concept albums ever made. It was inspired by the life of unstable rockabilly singer Vince Taylor, who became a star in France, and the brutal social critique of Stanley Kubrick's science fiction film *A Clockwork Orange* (1971), adapted from the novel by Anthony Burgess. Another inspiration, published the same year as Kubrick's film, was *Wild Boys: A Book of the Dead* by William S. Burroughs, the story of an amoral future populated by gangs of marauding boys who rebel against an oppressive establishment. Bowie's story is about Ziggy Stardust, a sexually ambiguous extraterrestrial singer who comes to Earth to bring the gospel of rock and roll. He gets famous, only to be destroyed by the fanaticism he created. Bowie's backing band, featuring Mick Ronson's aggressive guitar playing, was superb, and the lavish, innovative live show was documented by filmmaker D. A. Pennebaker, who shot the final date of the group's 1973 tour. At that show Bowie dramatically and abruptly announced his retirement. It turned out to be the retirement of the Stardust character, but Bowie intentionally blurred the distinction between himself and his creation, playing the part to the hilt by dyeing his hair orange and giving press conferences as Ziggy, wearing makeup and women's clothes. Bowie said "I wasn't at all surprised that 'Ziggy Stardust' made my career. I packaged a totally credible plastic rock star—much better than any sort of 'Monkees' fabrication. My plastic rocker was much more plastic than anybody's."[3]

Around the same time, Bowie produced records for others: Lou Reed (of the Velvet Underground), the Stooges and their lead singer, Iggy Pop, and Mott the Hoople (for whom he wrote "All the Young Dudes," their biggest hit). *Aladdin Sane* (1973, a pun on the phrase "a lad insane"), was another conceptual work about the disintegration of society, inspired by his experiences in America while touring.

Following that, Bowie did what he dubbed "plastic soul": music influenced by Philadelphia soul music. It was fully realized on *Young Americans* (1975), which contained "Fame," his first number-one single in America. The song was coauthored by John Lennon, who sang backup on the record. *Station to Station* (1976), Bowie's top-selling album, buoyed by the hit "Golden Years," took plastic soul into darker directions. On that album Bowie came out with another persona, the elegant "Thin White Duke," a sophisticated and stylish but emotionless and menacing character who reflected Bowie's reportedly cocaine-induced paranoia.

That year, he had his first movie role, starring in Nicolas Roeg's *The Man Who Fell to Earth*. Bowie played a part that seemed custom-made: a homesick alien who becomes a famous industrialist but gets contaminated by his activities and distracted in his aim to return to give aid to his planet. It was too offbeat to do more than modestly well at the box office, but his performance was praised. Since then his acting career has been sporadic. In *Merry Christmas, Mr. Lawrence* (1983) Bowie played a prisoner of war in a Japanese internment camp. In Martin Scorsese's *The Last Temptation of Christ* (1988) he played the role of Pontius Pilate. Bowie has also contributed music to films, notably the theme song to *Cat People* (1982), and is seen in a Berlin concert sequence in *Christiane F.* (1981). For a television special in 1977, he recorded a medley of "Peace on Earth/Little Drummer Boy" in a duet with Bing Crosby, one of the 20th century's greatest artists, the top one in the years preceding rock and roll. (The medley charted in 2000, 2001, and 2002.)

Bowie lived in Berlin in the late 1970s, making three experimental and surreal albums with producer Brian Eno (formerly of Roxy Music) that showed his fascination with German techno music, dubbed "Krautrock," as exemplified by Kraftwerk and others. In turn, his presence there was an influence on German artists. During the next two years he primarily concentrated on film work, though he did record "Under Pressure" (1981) in collaboration with QUEEN.

Let's Dance (1983) was a huge success. It featured blues guitar great Stevie Ray Vaughn just before he came into his own fame. The title track was Bowie's second American number-one hit, and also charting high in this period were the Motown-styled "Modern Love" and the sensuous "China Girl," cowritten with Iggy Pop. In 1985, to support the Live Aid charity project, he remade "Dancing in the Street," originally done by Motown act Martha and the Vandellas in 1964, in a duet with Mick Jagger.

After the Tin Machine, an alternative guitar rock band project of Bowie's that baffled his fans, he performed new and classic material from his solo career extensively throughout the 1990s and into the 21st century. In 2004, at age 57, a pain in his shoulder caused Bowie to curtail a performance in Germany. Doctors discovered it was not, as initially believed, a pinched nerve, but an acutely blocked artery requiring emergency heart surgery. He went home to New York to recover and the remainder of the tour was canceled. A complex, singular character, Bowie's artistic curiosity enriched the culture of the late 20th century and will no doubt prove to have lasting influence.

British invasion

This term was coined to refer to a period of unprecedented popularity of British artists in America. It began with the arrival of the BEATLES—specifically, their appearance on *The Ed Sullivan Show* in February 1964. In previous years, aside from a handful of hit records, most of them novelty songs, British music was absent on American pop radio. The Beatles' music, already popular in Britain and on the Continent, had begun to be heard in North America in 1963. Less than a week before the Sullivan show, the Beatles received their first gold

album and their first gold single, for *Meet the Beatles!* and "I Want to Hold Your Hand," respectively. The anticipation to see them on the Sullivan show, a Sunday night ritual for countless families, was extremely high. The show with the Beatles had a huge viewing audience, estimated at 73 million. Their performance (and reappearance on the next two shows), brought Beatlemania—the term for the mass hysteria of fan worship that they caused—to America. By April the Beatles held the top five places on the national singles chart.

Beatlemania already existed overseas, and would spread to the far corners of the world, but the love affair that Americans had for the Beatles may have been even more intense because its euphoria seemed to replace the mood of mourning and bewilderment that lingered over the assassination, less than three months earlier, of President John F. Kennedy. The Beatles, with their cheery songs, unified and unusual look, charm, and humor, were a most welcome distraction. In their wake, all things British were in vogue, especially British artists. The British invasion, with the Beatles at the helm, shook things up so much on a cultural level that it can be seen as the start of the 1960s as a concept, an era of cultural transformation (as opposed to the 1960s as a decade in time).

British acts hitherto unknown in North America were heard on radio, and many crossed the Atlantic to be seen on Ed Sullivan's and other TV shows, and to tour. In 1964 alone an avalanche of British invasion acts hit the charts. The ones that were influenced by American R&B had a harder sound and lasted longer: the ROLLING STONES, the KINKS, the ANIMALS, Manfred Mann, and the Dave Clark Five. The Hollies were also R&B influenced, but they specialized in group harmony singing, as did the Bachelors, who revived old pop songs. Two harmony duos, Peter and Gordon and Chad and Jeremy, sang appealing pop songs, as did the solo female vocalists Cilla Black, Petula Clark, Lulu, Marianne Faithfull, and Dusty Springfield, whose soulful voice was much admired. The Beatles had put Liverpool on the map, and they created a demand for others who did the "Mersey beat" or the "Mersey sound" (a reference to the river that runs through Liverpool): the Searchers, the Swinging Blue Jeans, Billy J. Kramer and the Dakotas, and Gerry and the Pacemakers. Herman's Hermits revived R&B songs but also British music hall numbers, the Honeycombs had a female drummer, and the Zombies had sophisticated songs with a jazzy side.

The British invasion carried on in full force in 1965, with more acts getting their first U.S. hits. Some of them became icons: the WHO, the YARDBIRDS, Them (with Van Morrison), the Moody Blues, DONOVAN, and the durable pop vocalist Tom Jones. Other acts had less spectacular careers: Georgie Fame and the Blue Flames (keyboardist Fame later carried on his R&B sound as a support player with Van Morrison), Wayne Fontana and the Mindbenders (who hit again in 1966 without Fontana), Freddie and the Dreamers (who had five hits in six months and no others), Ian Whitcomb (who became a music historian), the Silkie (whose one hit was a Beatles song recorded with the assistance of John Lennon, Paul McCartney, and George Harrison), and the Walker Brothers (three singers, none actually called Walker and not really brothers, who moved to England from the United States).

Through the rest of the 1960s, additional U.K. acts were introduced each year. Hitting the charts for the first time in 1966 were the Troggs with "Wild Thing," the New Vaudeville Band with the good-timey "Winchester Cathedral," and the driving R&B sound of the Spencer Davis Group. By 1967 some of the first-wave bands were no longer making hits. To the R&B covers and crafted, lightweight pop songs of the previous years was added a psychedelic and BLUES ROCK sound. That year Procol Harum, Traffic, the Bee Gees, FLEETWOOD MAC, the Small Faces, and the Jeff Beck Group (including Rod Stewart) all had their debut hits in America. The trend for heavier sounds continued in 1968 and 1969, with the introduction of CREAM, Joe Cocker, Deep Purple, LED ZEPPELIN, King Crimson, and Blind Faith.

From the start, these artists had a deep influence on all aspects of North American popular music. The Beatles set the pace at almost every turn, with their innovative music and attitude. Their influence was immense. Just the fact that the Beatles wrote most of their songs shifted the emphasis from covers to original compositions. They and other groups, such as the Rolling Stones, inspired many to acquire instruments. Most of the already active rock musicians, plus many of the urban folk players, revised their approach. In a spirit of adventure, small groups of four and five friends—male with few exceptions—experimented with musical styles, technology, artificial stimulants, and social alternatives.

The American reaction to the British invasion took many forms. Thousands of acts copied British styles and affected British sounds, clothes, images, and even accents. Despite seeming to be an overnight sensation, the Beatles had years of apprenticeship behind them in the nightclubs of Liverpool and Hamburg, Germany. Their repertoire was vast and varied, and they had absorbed its lessons. While many young musicians found the Beatles' pop-influenced chord progressions and rich harmony singing beyond their capabilities, some experienced musicians were capable of following in the Beatles' musical footsteps or found their own sound using similar materials.

Some bands, such as the Dave Clark Five, stuck to their original sound until it no longer found favor. Others continued to evolve musically and remain viable by staying connected to American music. The Searchers found themselves cited as a seminal influence on FOLK ROCK, POWER POP, and ROOTS ROCK (though the latter two styles were not named until later) and in 1979 and 1981 made albums of new material that touched those styles as well as new wave. Among the writers whose songs the band covered on those albums were Tom Petty, BOB DYLAN, Alex Chilton (of Big Star), and John Fogerty (of CREEDENCE CLEARWATER REVIVAL).

Manfred Mann was another band that was able to evolve, and it had much success in later incarnations. Manfred Mann formed in 1962 as a blues band playing clubs in London clubs and on the South Coast of England. The next year, on getting signed to record, they settled on the name of their keyboard player as the name of the whole band. Crucial to their sound and popularity was vocalist Paul Jones, who also played harmonica. The hits started in 1964 with "5-4-3-2-1," an original composition and a hit in England where it was the theme song of the TV music show *Ready Steady Go!* Their best remembered song is the infectious "Do Wah Diddy Diddy," a cover of a moderate hit by the American R&B group the Exciters and written by the Brill Building team of Jeff Barry and Ellie Greenwich. It made number one on both sides of the Atlantic and later became a staple on oldies radio. Another hit was "Mighty Quinn (Quinn the Eskimo)" (1968), one of many Bob Dylan songs the band was to cover. By then Paul Jones had left for a solo career, and some other personnel shifts occurred. A new version of the band, called Manfred Mann Chapter Three, with Mann, original drummer Mike Hugg, and new members, made albums but not hit singles. Subsequently Mann, with an all-new lineup called Manfred Mann's Earth Band, had hits in the 1970s and 1980s. "Blinded By the Light" (1976) was their biggest, a number-one hit and one of the earliest covers of a BRUCE SPRINGSTEEN song.

Buffalo Springfield

Though they existed only from 1966 to 1968, released only three albums, and had only one big hit, Buffalo Springfield is one of the most important bands in rock. The band launched the careers of NEIL YOUNG and Stephen Stills, pioneered the California COUNTRY ROCK movement, and made some wonderful music. Buffalo Springfield's sound was a rich mix of interweaving guitar parts and harmony vocals. The band was imaginative in both songwriting and arrangements, and though they were considered a FOLK ROCK group, they actually encompassed a range of styles from country to soul to orchestrated ballads and beyond.

Before Buffalo Springfield (named after a brand of steamroller) formed in Los Angeles in 1966, most of the members knew each other from working in folk revival groups. The band consisted of guitarist Stephen Stills (b. 1945), from Texas; guitarist Richie Furay (b. 1944), from Ohio; and three Canadians: guitarist Neil Young (b. 1945), drummer Dewey Martin (b. 1942), and bassist Bruce Palmer (b. 1946). All three guitarists wrote songs, and all sang lead, as did Martin.

"For What It's Worth (Stop, Hey What's That Sound)," written by Stills, is a protest song about conflicts between youth and police on the Sunset Strip in Los Angeles. It hit the top 10 in early 1967, their first and biggest hit. With lines like "there's something happening here, what it is ain't exactly clear," it came to symbolize the generational and ideological gaps of the 1960s. The song has repeatedly been used on soundtracks, such as the film *Forrest Gump* and the TV show *West Wing*, to portray its time. The guitar riffs from "For What It's Worth" show up again in "He Got Game" by Public Enemy from the 1998 Spike Lee movie of the same name. Stills not only played the riffs and sang at the Public Enemy recording session, he also appeared in the video for the song.

Though their talent was enormous and their recordings are of high quality, Buffalo Springfield's albums sold only moderately well. Four other singles made the top 100, but none were big hits. They are: Stills' folky "Bluebird" and soulful "Rock 'n' Roll Woman," and Young's orchestrated "Expecting to Fly" and countryish "On the Way Home" (sung by Furay). Lack of substantial success, dissatisfaction with management, and the stress of touring all caused tension, as did ego clashes and feuding. Neil Young left the band on more than one occasion; at the MONTEREY POP FESTIVAL, David Crosby of the BYRDS joined in. The loss of Palmer—he was deported back to Canada for possession of marijuana—also destabilized the band, as various replacements were used until he returned. When he was deported a second time, Jim Messina took his place for the third and final album. By then, the band was so fragmented that recordings seldom included all members: they worked in various combinations with session musicians filling in. The album was called *Last Time Around* because the band had already split up by the time it was released.

Post-breakup success came to Furay in Poco, one of the earliest and most influential country rock bands. Messina, after passing through the group Poco, teamed with Kenny Loggins. As Loggins and Messina, the duo had a run of hits in the 1970s. Young had a prodigious solo career that made him a superstar. Stills formed Crosby, Stills and Nash, which at times included Young.

Royalty disputes and lingering hurts precluded a full Buffalo Springfield reunion, though rumors circulated for years based on sporadic attempts. In the mid-1980s Palmer and Martin assembled a band called Buffalo Springfield Revisited, which toured North America for a few years. They were sometimes joined on stage by Stills. Young revisited the band himself in a song called "Buffalo Springfield Again" on his CD *Silver and Gold* (2000). They were inducted into the Rock and Roll Hall of Fame in 1997, and a box set that included unreleased recordings was issued in 2001. Bruce Palmer died of a heart attack age 58 in 2004.

Byrds, The

The Byrds, from Los Angeles, are among the handful of most important bands of the 1960s. They pioneered FOLK ROCK with "Mr. Tambourine Man" and "Turn! Turn! Turn!" (both 1965), had the first PSYCHEDELIC ROCK hit record with "Eight Miles High" (1966), were one of the first rock bands to use a synthesizer (1967), and pioneered COUNTRY ROCK with *Sweetheart of the Rodeo* (1968). They were also early and influential in bringing Indian and jazz inflections into rock, and were among the first to incorporate, beyond a novelty level, themes of outer space in their lyrics and portray it in their music (though "Mr. Spaceman" stays on the novelty side).

Their trademark sound was the jingle jangle of Jim McGuinn's electric 12-string guitar and the glorious vocals of McGuinn (b. 1942), Gene Clark (1941–91), and David Crosby (b. 1941), who had an intuitive gift for innovative harmonies. (McGuinn changed his name to Roger in 1968 while briefly involved with an Indonesian religion called Subud.) All three of them had been involved in professional folk acts.

They formed in 1964 as a trio and were aided by a record producer friend of Crosby's, Jim Dickson, who let them rehearse after hours in a studio, recording as they went. Their first moniker was the Jet Set, but when Elektra released a single, they changed it to the Beefeaters (for its British connotations). When the single flopped, Dickson, now their manager, suggested they add bass and drums. He brought in Chris Hillman (b. 1942), a bluegrass mandolin player and a fine singer who quickly picked up the bass. Michael Clarke (1944–93) came to their attention because he looked like Brian Jones of the ROLLING STONES, and he picked up the drums, having played congas.

To create folk rock, the Byrds blended BOB DYLAN's approach with that of the BEATLES. McGuinn had already been playing the acoustic 12-string guitar since around 1957, inspired by Leadbelly, Bob Gibson, and Pete Seeger. Seeing the Beatles in *A Hard Day's Night* in 1964, a moment of inspiration for the whole band, made him want a Rickenbacker electric 12-string like George Harrison's. To get one, plus some other gear, the Byrds borrowed money and McGuinn traded in his acoustic guitar and banjo.

"Mr. Tambourine Man" was written by Bob Dylan. As heard on *Bringing It All Back Home,* Dylan strums acoustic guitar and sings, accompanied by an electric guitarist playing light fills. With its chorus and four lengthy verses, plus a harmonica solo for variety, it is five and a half minutes long. Despite the title, there is no tambourine. The Byrds, working from a demo Dickson had obtained before Dylan redid it for his album, put the song to a Beatles-type beat, added a catchy, Bach-like introduction that featured McGuinn's electric 12-string and the electric bass, kept only the second verse, and sang the chorus in harmony accompanied by a band of session musicians that included drums and tambourine. Their version, at two minutes and 20 seconds, was now pop music, and it went to number one.[4] Though they never worked together, Dylan approved of the Byrds doing his compositions. He did sing a few songs with them in an L.A. club in 1965, as seen in the photo on the back cover of their first album.

Folk rock, perceived as an American answer to the BRITISH INVASION, became the rage. Another Dylan composition, "All I Really Want to Do," was the Byrds' next hit, but Cher (then in the duo Sonny and Cher) saw the Byrds do it in concert and put out a competing version which sold more. The Byrds then had their only other number-one hit: "Turn! Turn! Turn!" Its text was adapted by Pete Seeger (a folk music icon and former member of the Weavers) from the Bible. The wisdom in the song's lyrics, and the plea for peace (the one addition to the words that Seeger contributed), was in contrast to the typical lightweight fare on the radio, and was also in step with the mounting antiwar sentiment of the 1960s.

After two albums, named for their big hits, Gene Clark, whose compositions were one of the band's strengths, left due to a fear of flying. The group continued as a quartet for *Fifth Dimension* (1966)

The Byrds (Michael Ochs Archives.com)

and *Younger Than Yesterday* (1967). Both albums showed the band growing musically, balancing the grounding effects of country rock with the mind expansion of psychedelic music. On "Mr. Spaceman" they looked both earthward and to the heavens: the music was country, but the lyrics were about wanting to ride in a spaceship.

"Eight Miles High," the first psychedelic song to become a hit, made the top 20 in 1966. It was widely taken to be a drug song (as was any with the word *high* in it), but the writers (McGuinn, Clark, and Crosby) claimed it was about an airplane flight to London. That makes sense, despite the trippiness of the music and the lyrics that find strangeness and omens in commonplace images. Transatlantic airplanes do fly at that altitude, and "rain grey town, known for its sound" suggests London, especially as the next phrase is "small faces unbound." (The Small Faces were a popular London band.) The influence of jazz and Indian music is heard in Hillman's dronelike bass part and the modal chords, and McGuinn's highly-praised 12-string guitar solos, inspired by jazz saxophonist John Coltrane's "India."

In summer 1967 they played the MONTEREY POP FESTIVAL. During the recording of *Notorious Byrd Brothers* (1968), a more experimental album and one of their best, two more founding members left. David Crosby soon formed Crosby, Stills and Nash with Stephen Stills (of BUFFALO SPRINGFIELD), and Graham Nash (of the Hollies). Michael Clarke joined up again with Gene Clark in the Dillard and Clark Expedition. That left only McGuinn and Hillman, who brought in his cousin Kevin Kelley to play drums.

The next new recruit was Gram Parsons, now legendary as the catalyst in the country rock movement. He stayed in the band less than a year, but left an indelible mark. *Sweetheart of the Rodeo*, recorded in Nashville, contains bluegrass, honky-tonk, and country rock. From their audience's point of view, it was a major departure, though "You Ain't Goin' Nowhere" (another Dylan composition) made the

charts. It was not one of their best-selling records, but it is one of their most influential.

The new direction suited Chris Hillman, with his bluegrass background, and he and Gram Parsons both left the Byrds to form the Flying Burrito Brothers, which would later include Michael Clarke. The Byrds, that is to say, Roger McGuinn and the musicians he hired, kept country rock as an aspect of their style. McGuinn recruited a new drummer (Gene Parsons, no relation to Gram), a new bassist (John York), and one of the finest country rock lead players in the land, Clarence White. Like Hillman, White not only had a bluegrass background but was also a great electric player. This lineup made the uneven *Dr. Byrds and Mr. Hyde* (1969) and the better *The Ballad of Easy Rider* (1970). The latter had their final hit singles: the title track (from the Peter Fonda movie *Easy Rider*), and "Jesus Is Just Alright," which barely entered the charts (though the Doobie Brothers' remake two years later made the top 40).

With another change of bass players (to Skip Battin), the Byrds made *(Untitled),* a double album with one studio record and one live record (1970), and two more weaker albums, *Byrdmaniax* (1971), and *Farther Along* (1972).

A 1973 reunion of all five original members, instigated by Crosby, did not live up to expectations, and the one album that resulted, *Byrds,* was disappointing. Neither the McGuinn-led Byrds nor the reunited band carried on. Both Gram Parsons and Clarence White died in 1973.

McGuinn did five albums under his own name, then three more with Clark and Hillman, and then returned to his solo career. Crosby was still involved in various combinations of Crosby, Stills and Nash, and Michael Clarke was in Firefall. Hillman was in a short-lived outfit called the Souther-Hillman-Furay Band, and later founded the Desert Rose Band, which did well in the country market.

In 1984 Michael Clarke reactivated the Byrds name for touring, sometimes with Gene Clark or other, later, members. McGuinn, Crosby, and Hillman were offended. They asserted their own claim on the name and did a couple of shows to emphasize it, recording four songs for inclusion in a box set. In 1991, shortly after the Byrds were inducted into the Rock and Roll Hall of Fame, Gene Clark died, deteriorated by drug and alcohol abuse. Michael Clarke died in 1993 of liver failure, the result of alcohol addiction.

The Byrds' sound is clearly an influence on many others, particularly Tom Petty and the Heartbreakers, who redid the Byrds' "So You Want to Be a Rock and Roll Star" and wrote a couple of songs with McGuinn, and on R.E.M., who made the electric 12-string an integral part of their sound.

Clapton, Eric (b. 1945) *masterful British guitarist* Clapton's style is steeped in American blues, and he is a beloved figure. From his tenure in the YARDBIRDS and CREAM and in his solo career, with many important short-lived bands, side projects, and collaborations along the way, Eric Clapton, at his best, has made some spectacular music.

His discomfort at being adulated for his guitar playing abilities, his addictions to heroin and then to alcohol (which he managed to overcome), and the tragedies in his life have all affected his art. At times it has been for the worse, making for some lackluster or perfunctory music, as when he hides his light or seriously takes himself to be a journeyman musician. He actually made an album entitled *Journeyman* in 1989: the term refers to a competent but unexceptional craftsman. The times his music has reached a transcendental quality have come, some of them, from deeply felt reactions to adversity, such as the anguish of being in love with a close friend's wife—expressed in "Layla" (1972), his first top-10 hit—or the tragic accidental death of his young son—in "Tears in Heaven" (1992), from *Unplugged,* his best-selling album. Other times, some of his finest music has occurred when inspired by particular musical figures or spurred on by collaborators.

A sensitive, introspective person, Eric Clapton was raised by his grandparents, whom he was led to believe were his parents, until the truth was revealed to him when he was about nine. His father was absent, and his mother pretended to be his older sister on her occasional visits. This deception was perpetrated to avoid the stigma of the illegitimate child. The person he thought was his brother was actually his uncle; his passing inspired Clapton's *Reptile* album of 2001 (the cover photo shows the artist at age nine). Clapton started to play guitar as an adolescent and later attended art school, but he dropped out to be a professional musician.

In the early 1960s, like many young musicians in their fascination with then-obscure blues recordings, Clapton applied himself to the study of the styles of B. B. King, Albert King, and Freddie King (biologically unrelated to one another), as well as Buddy Guy, Otis Rush, Muddy Waters, and the earlier down-home sounds of Big Bill Broonzy and especially Robert Johnson, with whom he identified. Early in his career Clapton backed up blues pianists Otis Spann and Champion Jack Dupree in the studio and, when Clapton was in the Yardbirds, Sonny Boy Williamson II (Rice Miller) live. Between his tenure in the Yardbirds and Cream, Clapton played with blues crusader John Mayall, and his playing on the classic *Bluesbreakers* (1965) is superb. Around this time, legend has it, fans in London were writing graffiti that said "Clapton is God." On the Mayall album, he recorded his first track as a vocalist, Robert Johnson's "Ramblin' on My Mind."

A project called the Powerhouse that included Stevie Winwood (vocals, organ) from the Spencer Davis Group and Jack Bruce (bass) recorded three songs for the *What's Shakin'* (1966) anthology on the American Elektra label. The album also featured other leading lights of the burgeoning movement to connect rock to its roots: the Lovin' Spoonful, the Paul Butterfield Blues Band, and Al Kooper (of the Blues Project). The album was not a top seller, but was an influence on such groups as the ALLMAN BROTHERS BAND. Jack Bruce would become part of Cream, and the Robert Johnson song "Crossroads" that Powerhouse recorded would be redone to great acclaim by that band. When Cream disbanded, Clapton formed Blind Faith with Winwood, Cream's drummer Ginger Baker, and bassist Ric Grech of the band Family. Blind Faith made only one album. On it is Clapton's first original composition, the spiritual "Presence of the Lord."

He then participated in a one-time-only ensemble led by John Lennon and Yoko Ono called the Plastic Ono Band. Their performance of mostly rock and roll oldies was released as *Live Peace in Toronto 1969*. Weary of the expectations on him as one of the world's most adored guitarists and enjoying the role of a sideman, Clapton participated in numerous studio sessions for various artists. He also briefly joined Delaney and Bonnie and Friends on tour and on record, along with Dave Mason (formerly of Traffic) and George Harrison.

Clapton and Harrison were close friends. Clapton had contributed to Harrison's *Wonderwall* (1968), the first solo album by a member of the BEATLES, and played the solo on Harrison's "While My Guitar Gently Weeps" on the Beatles' *White Album* (1968). Together they wrote "Badge" on Cream's *Goodbye* (1969). Their friendship survived a love triangle: Clapton fell in love with Harrison's wife Patti Boyd, the subject of "Layla." She rejected him at first, but in 1977, after she divorced Harrison, they were wed (they divorced in 1988). The song comes from *Layla and Other Love Songs* (1970) by Derek and the Dominos, a band that included Duane Allman. Clapton played on George Harrison's *All Things Must Pass* in 1970, took part in his concert to raise funds for Bangladesh famine relief in 1971, and toured Japan with him in 1991. In 2002, on the first anniversary of Harrison's death, Clapton was the musical director of the memorial event issued as *Concert for George* (2003).

In 1974, having conquered his heroin addiction, Clapton rebounded with *461 Ocean Boulevard*, his first number-one album. It contained his version of Bob Marley's "I Shot the Sheriff," which gave him his first number-one single and in the process introduced many people to REGGAE music. A host of other recordings (and tours) followed, so many that his fans had trouble keeping up. They were able to do so in 1988 when his record company released *Crossroads*, a six-LP box set retrospective of his career. The *Unplugged* album of 1992, recorded during a performance at MTV, was followed by *From the Cradle* (1994), a set of blues classics. Both were number-one albums. Clapton continues to draw inspiration from the blues. He did an album with B. B. King, issued under both their names, called *Riding with the King* (2000) and an album of nothing but Robert Johnson songs, *Me and Mr. Johnson* (2004).

He is one of the founders of an addiction recovery facility called the Crossroads Centre, located on the Caribbean island of Antigua. It opened in 1998. The next year, to raise funds for it, Clapton put 100 guitars from his personal collection up for auction. Their sale brought in more than $5 million.

classic rock

There are two common meanings ascribed to the term *classic rock*, depending on the intended sense of the first word. When it is used to refer to classical music, classic rock stands for rock music played with or by symphonies. More commonly, the word *classic* is used in the sense of something that has stood the test of time for its excellence. In that sense *classic rock* describes a format for FM radio stations that started in the mid-1980s to capture the ears of aging baby boomers. It refers to the era from the late 1960s to the 1990s, in other words, from JIMI HENDRIX to NIRVANA. Bands that get a lot of airplay in this format include the ROLLING STONES, the WHO, LED ZEPPELIN, AC/DC, the DOORS, the EAGLES, Lynyrd Skynyrd, AEROSMITH, CREEDENCE CLEARWATER REVIVAL, PINK FLOYD, Van Halen, Bad

Company, Boston, ZZ Top, FLEETWOOD MAC, Steve Miller, and Rush.

Classic rock began as hard rock, which got underway in the late 1960s in America and in the United Kingdom. HEAVY METAL branched off from hard rock in the early 1970s. The roots of hard rock go back to 1950s instrumentals by guitarists such as Link Wray, but the way was paved by the mid-1960s BRITISH INVASION bands, whose affinity to American rock and roll was a founding principle of their style. The shifting power chords of the KINKS, as in "You Really Got Me" (1965), are an obvious precedent, but there was also the thump of the Dave Clark Five, the bluesy swagger of the ANIMALS, the guitar heroics and eclecticism of the YARDBIRDS, and the sonic and visual barrage of the WHO. The Who's instrumentation of guitar, bass, and drums would soon be further exploited in the power trio format that came to prominence in late 1966 with CREAM and the Jimi Hendrix Experience. Hendrix had relocated from New York City to London on the urgings of Chas Chandler, formerly the bassist for the Animals.

In America the GARAGE ROCK bands, a response to the British invasion, were also forerunners of hard rock. The hard-hitting Sonics, from Seattle, are a prime example. In 1967 the Vanilla Fudge, from New York City, began a three-year run of hit singles with the specialty of slowing down recent pop songs and playing them in a musical and highly arranged heavy style. Their biggest hit was "You Keep Me Hanging On" (formerly by the Supremes), which charted in summer 1967, when it fit into the vogue for psychedelic music, and again, exactly one year later, this time into the top 10, when it fit into the trend for heavy rock.

Hard rock was an established style in 1968. Like Vanilla Fudge, Blue Cheer and Deep Purple had hits with heavy versions of known songs. Blue Cheer, from San Francisco, reworked Eddie Cochran's rockabilly classic "Summertime Blues" from 10 years earlier. Deep Purple, from England, redid Billy Joe Royal's "Hush" and Neil Diamond's "Kentucky Woman" (the original songs are both

from 1967). Deep Purple did one more heavy cover version (Ike and Tina Turner's "River Deep—Mountain High") but almost all the rest of their output, including their five other chart hits, were composed by the band. Their biggest was "Smoke on the Water," inspired by a fire at a casino in Montreaux, Switzerland, and powered by one of the most famous of all guitar riffs. STEPPENWOLF hit with "Born to Be Wild" (which contained the phrase "heavy metal thunder" in connection with its motorcycling theme), and "Magic Carpet Ride." Iron Butterfly, from San Diego, whose debut album was called *Heavy*, hit with "In-A-Gadda-Da-Vida." Its famous riff was similar to the one in Cream's "Sunshine of Your Love" from earlier in the year. The Beatles had some heavy songs too, like "Helter Skelter" from their "White Album."

Hard rock developed in this period as a reaction to the turbulent state of society. Race riots, student revolutions, protests against the war in Vietnam, and political assassinations caused ruptures that still reverberate. The MC5, from Detroit, incorporated political issues in their music. Another Michigan band, Grand Funk Railroad, from Flint, built up their reputation from energized live shows at massive rock festivals. In England Led Zeppelin took American blues into new directions. By the early 1970s hard rock was thriving. Black Sabbath was pivotal in establishing heavy metal as an offshoot, but hard rock remained strong as a style, with hundreds of bands working in it, such as the ALLMAN BROTHERS BAND, from Florida, whose influences were blues, country, and jazz.

Classic rock is basically the hits and durable songs of hard rock music. For older listeners it acts as nostalgia, but for all listeners, regardless of age, it is also a form of validation for this type of music and a way of keeping it alive while rejecting more current styles. The popularity of classic rock radio stations has helped support many classic rock acts that are still performing. For the radio stations, it is about profits, not music. Playlists are chosen by market research—which can make for some odd choices and frustrating restrictions—and disc jockeys typically know little about the music they are hired to present.

Cochran, Eddie (1938–1960) *influential rockabilly singer and songwriter*

Although he had only a handful of hits in the late 1950s, Cochran was an important trendsetter in ROCKABILLY music. In 1960, at age 21, he died in a car crash. His most popular songs contain infectious dance rhythms and lyrics that articulate teenage concerns, such as throwing a party while parents are gone, wanting to get a car, and going on dates.

His biggest hit was "Summertime Blues" (1958), a lament about having to spend the summer working instead of having fun, a subject that teenagers know well. Some of its drive comes from the punchy, repetitive notes played on the electric BASS: it was one of the first rock songs to use the electric bass instead of the acoustic upright bass. "Summertime Blues" was a hit two more times: in 1968 by a San Francisco power trio called Blue Cheer (whose motto was "louder than God"), and by the WHO on a single from their renowned *Live at Leeds* album (1970).

Cochran began his career singing country music in a duo with Hank Cochran. They were not related but passed themselves off as a brother duet. Eddie Cochran was among the first wave of American rockers to tour overseas. In 1957 he had performed in Australia with LITTLE RICHARD and Gene Vincent. In 1960 he and Vincent toured in England. Before the second part of the tour was to commence, they planned for a brief return to the United States. On the way to the airport, the car they were riding in crashed, killing Cochran and injuring Vincent.

Like BUDDY HOLLY, who died two years before him, Cochran had been moving away f rockabilly, expanding his role in the music business and broadening his style. Yet it is his rockabilly that had the biggest impact. When the rockabilly revival got underway in the late 1970s, Cochran was a major influence, and his presence is particularly felt in the sound and repertoire of the Stray Cats, the most successful of all the revival bands. They reprised "C'mon Everybody," "Jeanie Jeanie Jeanie," and "Somethin' Else." The Stray Cats' guitarist and vocalist Brian Setzer even played the part of Eddie Cochran in the 1987 movie *La Bamba* (about the life of RITCHIE VALENS). Rod Stewart did "Cut Across Shorty," the ROLLING STONES did "Twenty Flight Rock," and LED ZEPPELIN did "Somethin' Else," as did the Sex Pistols.

Eddie Cochran (Michael Ochs Archives.com)

Cooper, Alice

Alice Cooper, the name of an all-male band as well as its singer, achieved fame in the 1970s for their overblown and controversial stage shows. As was typical of other GLAM ROCK bands, their emphasis was on theatrics, sexuality, and androgyny (from their name to their gender-crossing clothes and makeup), and a thumping hard rock sound.

Occasionally the BLUES ROCK riffs that powered hits like "School's Out" (1972) would give way to a ballad such as "Only Women" (1975, also known as "Only Women Bleed").

Alice Cooper the individual was a villainous role played by singer Vincent Furnier (b. 1948). As in *Dr. Jekyll and Mr. Hyde,* the gothic tale by Robert Louis Stevenson of how good and evil exist within the same person, Furnier, a calm, good-natured, and articulate man, transformed onstage into the crazed and unpredictable Alice Cooper. With long, black stringy hair, hideous makeup, and ripped clothes, he would sing and sneer and prance the stage. Props such as a suitcase, a life-sized doll, or a boa constrictor, were part of the act, and Cooper's naughty and violent deeds would be punished by a simulated but realistic-looking execution: by hanging, electrocution, or beheading. The gore was fake, and the character, as in a cartoon, would rise again, unstoppable. The audience would cheer mightily, arms thrusting in time to the music. The idea was to make a provocative show that would assault the senses; there was no special message. Audiences read what they wanted into it, knowing the band did not take any of it seriously. It was horror theater, the playing out of forbidden fantasies born of teenage anxiety.

Also in the band were drummer Neal Smith, bassist Dennis Dunaway, lead guitarist Glen Buxton, and keyboardist Michael Bruce. They began as a garage band in Phoenix, Arizona, in 1965. In 1968 they relocated to Los Angeles, where they got a record deal with FRANK ZAPPA's label. Two years and two albums later, having failed to distinguish themselves, they moved to Detroit, Furnier's birthplace. There they signed to Warner Brothers, whose producer polished their music a little. In 1971 their album *Love It to Death* and its single "Eighteen" became hits, and their stage shows got more elaborate. They become a top concert draw.

Between 1972 and 1975 Alice Cooper had five albums in a row hit the top 10. Before the fifth one, *Welcome to My Nightmare* (1975), Furnier fired the rest of the band and brought in a new crew, all of whom had played with Lou Reed. Alice Cooper was now identified only as Vincent Furnier's alter ego. Furnier was sidelined for a while during treatment for alcoholism. The band's string of hits ended with the new-wave-styled "Clones (We're All)," in 1980. Alice Cooper kept making and selling albums through the 1980s, and finally got another top-10 single in 1989 with "Poison." To date, the last charting song was 1991's antisuicide "Hey Stoopid," with Ozzy Osborne of Black Sabbath on backing vocals and Slash of Guns n' Roses on lead guitar. Cooper has remained active, releasing new records and touring from time to time.

country rock

Traces of country music can be found all through rock. BILL HALEY, BUDDY HOLLY, and the EVERLY BROTHERS were formed by it (as were many other artists), DEL SHANNON was imprinted by it, and Jerry Garcia apprenticed himself to it. The BEATLES, the ROLLING STONES, BOB DYLAN, ELVIS PRESLEY, and Elvis Costello, to name a few, have drawn inspiration from country music. Rock's reliance on stringed instruments aligns it with country, for the string band is one of country's specialties. Country rock is a mix of country styles (Nashville, bluegrass, and honky-tonk) with 1960s rock sensibilities. For rock, country rock's twangy, conventional, and comforting sound meant a return to earthiness, simplicity, and tradition.

It was created in 1966 by the BYRDS, but their country rock songs such as "Time Between" were on albums that were stylistically eclectic. Country rock was not recognized as something distinct until 1968 with the release of their *Sweetheart of the Rodeo.* "You Ain't Going Nowhere," a BOB DYLAN song from that album, is the best candidate for the first hit in country rock. Its momentum was boosted by Dylan's move toward country in *John Wesley Harding* (1968) and his adoption of it in *Nashville Skyline* (1969).

The country side of country rock is heard in the choice of songs and the harmony singing, the two-beat bass playing and the loping rhythms, the emphasis on acoustic guitar, and the use of the banjo, mandolin, Dobro, and pedal steel guitar. Country rock makes little use of the fiddle, however. The rock side of country rock is heard in the subject matter of some lyrics, the reliance on electric bass (by then part of country music, though upright bass was still popular), the willingness to incorporate Beatles-influenced chord progressions, the tradition-breaking use of new instrumental combinations (such as organ and drums in an acoustic string band setting), and the occasional use of timbre-altering devices such as fuzz tone on the pedal steel or phase shifting on the banjo. In other words, country rock was more sonically varied than traditional or commercial country music. It was also more varied than FOLK ROCK and more accessible to the general public (aside from the musicians' long hair and garish drugstore-cowboy clothes) than PSYCHEDELIC ROCK.

Even though country rock was for some participants only one phase in their career, the founders and developers of the style were all part of an extensive community based in Los Angeles. The most prominent were the Byrds and the Flying Burrito Brothers (with and without Gram Parsons), Rick Nelson and the Stone Canyon Band, Dillard and Clark, Linda Ronstadt, the Nitty Gritty Dirt Band, Poco, and the EAGLES, who were the most successful of them all. Mike Nesmith pursued a country rock direction after leaving the MONKEES, who did some country rock themselves. The Byrds were the first established group to commit to the style, and from their ranks sprang many offshoots. The interactions among these musicians are so intricate that trying to understand who joined which band or played on which recording is one of the chief pastimes of country rock fans. In San Francisco the style was taken up by the New Riders of the Purple Sage, the GRATEFUL DEAD, and Commander Cody and His Lost Planet Airmen (transplants from Michigan), whose "Hot Rod Lincoln," a remake of a 1950s country boogie song, was a top-10 hit in 1972. San Francisco and Los Angeles groups interacted as well. For example, Jerry Garcia of the Grateful Dead

played pedal steel on "Teach Your Children" by Crosby, Stills and Nash (1970).

Before country rock was recognized as such, several recordings paved the way. On the flip side of the Beatles' single "Yesterday" (1965) was "Act Naturally," a hit in its own right, sung by Ringo Starr. Country was not what Beatles fans expected, but it was fun and made a lighthearted contrast to the regret expressed in "Yesterday." The lines about "the movies gonna make me a big star" were tongue-in-cheek, because the Beatles were music and movie stars: both *A Hard Day's Night* and *Help!* were already out. "Act Naturally" was a cover song and was considered a novelty. The Beatles did not pursue the country direction.

In 1963 "Act Naturally" had been a number-one country hit for Buck Owens and His Buckaroos. While Nashville was occupied with injecting country with pop, he and Merle Haggard were part of a renaissance of honky-tonk music in Bakersfield, California. The music of both men was an important influence on country rock, as was their preference for Fender guitars. As a destination for masses of migrants from the Midwest, California, particularly Los Angeles, has long been a stronghold for country music. Bob Wills and His Texas Playboys, for example, were based there in the 1950s and found a ready audience.

With so much country music in the air, it was not out of character for Los Angeles rock bands, whose ranks themselves included migrants, to put country tunes on their albums. In 1965 the Byrds' "Satisfied Mind" (a hit 10 years earlier for Porter Wagoner but done by the Byrds in folk rock style) was on *Turn! Turn! Turn!*. In 1966 "Mr. Spaceman" (whose folk rock tambourine, novelty lyrics about aliens, and Beatles-like chorus augment the country elements) was on *Fifth Dimension,* while "Time Between" (with Clarence White guesting on lead guitar) was on *Younger than Yesterday.* Both were original compositions. That year, Rick Nelson's country phase began with the album *Bright Lights and County Music.* BUFFALO SPRINGFIELD showed a country side on their debut album with "Go and

Say Goodbye," whose guitar figure was based on an old fiddle tune called "Salt Creek," and "A Child's Claim to Fame" on *Again* (both 1967).

Country rock's iconic figure is Gram Parsons, a man of incredible influence, who died at age 26 in 1973. His mystique and the veneration accorded to him make him the style's patron saint. Parsons was a southerner, raised in Georgia and Florida. He played rock and folk before immersing himself in mainstream country in Massachusetts, where he briefly attended Harvard University. With the International Submarine Band he went to Los Angeles, and their *Safe at Home* (recorded in 1967) is considered the first country rock album. Parsons then worked with the Byrds for their seminal *Sweetheart of the Rodeo*. Following that, he helped to found the Flying Burrito Brothers, leaving them to make, just before his death, two solo albums with Emmylou Harris as his singing partner. She sang country rock with a traditionalist approach and became one of the biggest stars in country music. She always acknowledged her connection to Parsons, recording many of his songs. Though the ROLLING STONES had already recorded their version of Hank Snow's "I'm Moving On" before they met Gram Parsons, they did not know or feel much about country music. Parsons, as he did with many other people, enabled them to connect with it, and their late 1960s sound included a country influence in songs like "Honky Tonk Women" (and the version of it they called "Country Honk") and "Dead Flowers." The Eagles eulogized him in "My Man" (*On the Border*, 1974).

With the success of the Eagles, country rock reached its peak, but as their career progressed, they left the country touch behind. Poco, one of the earliest and most influential of all country rock bands, was one of the groups that carried the torch. Many artists, such as Bob Dylan and NEIL YOUNG, retained their connection to country music. The country rock bands, ignored for the most part by the country music establishment, were influential on the "new country" movement in the 1980s and the alternative country (also known as "alt-country" or "no depression") of the 1990s.

Cream

From their first recording in 1966 to their farewell concerts in 1968, Cream was a trend-setting band. They were the first of the supergroups—all-star rock bands—and the first of the power trios: heavy rock combos of one guitarist, bassist, and drummer making blues-based music at high volume. Like the Jimi Hendrix Experience, which formed just after they did, Cream explored a creative fusion of pop, rock, blues, and psychedelia, and paved the way for future developments such as heavy metal.

Originating in London, they performed mostly in big stadiums in America. Cream, named to indicate "the cream of the crop," was guitarist ERIC CLAPTON (b. 1945), bassist Jack Bruce (b. 1943), and drummer Ginger Baker (b. 1940). Clapton was by then a veteran of the YARDBIRDS and John Mayall's Bluesbreakers and brought a deep knowledge of the blues. Bruce was classically trained on bass and cello, and he and Baker had not only played together for years in free jazz groups, they had also played R&B for years as the rhythm section of the Graham Bond Organization. They brought in a talent for improvisation.

Each player expanded the possibilities of his instrument. Clapton was pushed to improvise more and did so brilliantly; he was also one of the first to use the wah-wah pedal. Bruce's bass playing was fluid and imaginative, and Baker's drumming, on a kit that included double bass drums, and his extended drum solos were impressive and influential. Bruce was an especially powerful and effective vocalist, and Clapton came into his own as a singer while in Cream, having sung but little with Mayall and not at all with the Yardbirds.

Cream found their style through revamping old blues and writing new songs. Many of those, including "Sunshine of Your Love" and "White Room," their two biggest hits, were written in collaboration with lyricist Pete Brown, a Beat poet who was a jazz and blues fan. Within a year or two, Procol Harum, the GRATEFUL DEAD, and King Crimson were also working regularly with their own nonperforming lyricists.

Following their debut album, *Fresh Cream* (1966), which contained "I Feel Free," a hit in the

Cream (Michael Ochs Archives.com)

live disc. "White Room," with an introduction in 5/4 time, came from the studio disc, while "Crossroads," Robert Johnson's blues classic sung by Clapton, came from the live disc, recorded at the Fillmore in San Francisco. It was also a hit and remains a stellar example of what Cream could achieve in concert.

Tired of touring, and feeling they had achieved their goals and done what they could, Cream disbanded after two sold-out shows at London's Royal Albert Hall. Their final album, *Goodbye* (1969), mixed live and studio tracks. One of the latter, "Badge," was their last hit. It was written by Clapton and George Harrison, who played guitar on it. (Clapton had previously played guitar on the BEATLES' "While My Guitar Gently Weeps.") Cream released two more live albums in the early 1970s.

After Cream split up, Clapton and Baker formed Blind Faith, which lasted for only one album, then moved to solo careers. Bruce made several solo albums. Cream reunited in 1993 for a single performance on the night they were inducted into the Rock and Roll Hall of Fame. In 2005, Cream reunited for four sold-out nights at the Royal Albert Hall. The band brilliantly revisited their old repertoire, the fans were ecstatic, and all but the most severe critics were won over.

United Kingdom, the band toured in the United States to growing acclaim for their instrumental prowess and improvisational abilities. Their second album, *Disraeli Gears* (1967), was their commercial breakthrough. It included "Sunshine of Your Love," a million-seller and their best-known song, with its a distinctive guitar riff that is one of the most famous in rock. That album began their association with producer Felix Pappalardi, and he produced all of their subsequent studio recordings and contributed musically by playing a variety of instruments which augmented their sound, such as the viola on "Anyone for Tennis," a non-album hit single. Pappalardi later was the bassist for Mountain, a power trio that scored with "Mississippi Queen."

Cream's third album was the double *Wheels of Fire* (1968), consisting of one studio disc and one

Creedence Clearwater Revival

Neither the Mississippi Delta nor the Louisiana bayous were their home, as one might assume after hearing "Proud Mary" (about a paddle wheeler) or "Born on the Bayou" or any of their other southern-style songs that some people refer to as swamp rock. Their home was El Cerrito, California, a suburban, working-class town in the East Bay region, near San Francisco.

They formed as a trio of high school friends in 1959: John Fogerty (b. 1945, vocals, guitar), Stu Cook (b. 1945, piano), and Doug Clifford (b. 1945, drums). John's older brother Tom (b. 1941) soon joined as a vocalist. Later, he switched to rhythm guitar, Cook switched to bass, and John sang the lead. By the time of their first hits in 1968, they had put in almost a decade of apprenticeship, having gigged up and down the coast under several names (Tommy Fogerty and the Blue Velvets, the Visions, the Golliwogs) and made some records, one of which became a local hit. After a layoff in which two members served time in the army reserves, they dropped their British influences for a tougher, purely American approach. They also took a new name that foreshadowed how they would revitalize rock by reconnecting it to its roots (*Creedence,* from "credible," *Clearwater,* indicating "pure and essential," and *Revival,* meaning "to bring back to life").

While COUNTRY ROCK was emerging in Los Angeles, Creedence was forging an aggressive, rocking sound that blended country and R&B in a new way. When ELVIS PRESLEY did a similar mix 15 years earlier, it got called ROCKABILLY. Creedence Clearwater Revival, along with the Band (a major inspiration), are the founders of what would eventually be named ROOTS ROCK. Their influences were southern rockers (especially Elvis Presley and LITTLE RICHARD), groups and the guitarists who played memorable instrumentals (Ventures, Booker T and the MGs, Duane Eddy, Freddie King), and folk singers (particularly Leadbelly).

Creedence's first album was released, like all their subsequent ones, on the independent label Fantasy. The album showed affinity with their PSYCHEDELIC ROCK counterparts in San Francisco in its use of feedback, backwards guitar, and extended renditions

Creedence Clearwater Revival (Michael Ochs Archives.com)

of older songs. Though they did occasionally stretch out, their forte was the concise single. Unlike other bands, they did not play love songs, make concept albums, or use orchestration. Their music was at once artistic and straightforward, a rare and winning combination. So were their album covers: each featured a full-sized single color photo of the band looking unpretentious, usually in casual clothes. They also managed their own career and handled their own bookings.

After their first national hits—"Suzy Q" and "I Put a Spell on You," both intriguing remakes of 1950s songs that had been in their repertoire for years—they found greater success with their own songs, almost all written, sung, produced, and arranged by John Fogerty. These retained the immediacy and drive of 1950s rock while extending its vocabulary. Full of interesting lyrics and musical ideas, their music was nonetheless easy to grasp for listeners, dancers, and musicians. John Fogerty played economical riffs and guitar figures that were appealing to listeners and that other guitar players could copy.

At their peak, they were the most successful rock band in the world, performing for gigantic audiences at ROCK FESTIVALS, including WOODSTOCK, and selling millions of records. "Proud Mary" was their first to sell a million copies and remains their most popular song. Ike and Tina Turner's version was also a big hit. The following is only a partial list of their top-10 chart hits from 1969 to 1971: "Bad Moon Rising," "Green River," "Down on the Corner," "Fortunate Son," "Travelin' Band," "Who'll Stop the Rain," "Up around the Bend," "Lookin' Out My Back Door," and "Have You Ever Seen the Rain." These, as well as lesser hits, like "Lodi" and their arrangement of the MOTOWN classic "I Heard It through the Grapevine," and even album tracks such as Leadbelly's "Midnight Special," are still widely known and regularly played by bar bands and solo singers wherever rock music is appreciated.

Though he wrote antiwar songs and songs about the ups and downs of making music, a number of John Fogerty's songs depicted a rural, romanticized South of swamps and catfish, railroads and steam-boats, hoodoos and gypsies. In these songs the band articulated the late 1960s' sense of dread and search for grounding. The songs invoked mythical locales and archetypal characters in imagined scenarios that were set in the past or at least in a very rustic environment. With his raspy and soulful, gospel-style voice, Fogerty sang them in the first person, with a southern accent, as if they were current, lived situations. In "Green River," for example, he mentions bullfrogs, a rope for swinging into the water, railroad hoboes, and barefoot girls dancing in the moonlight. The key line, however, is when Old Cody Junior says "you're gonna find the world is smolderin' an' if you get lost come on home to Green River." Cody is a symbolic name: Buffalo Bill Cody was, around the turn of the 20th century, a famous western sharpshooter, who in presenting his Wild West Show—a performance spectacle with real cowboys and Indians—was presenting, like Fogerty, a romanticized and vanishing way of life, one that was linked to the land.

The band made six top-selling and well-received albums. When Tom Fogerty, tired of being in the shadow of his younger brother, left in 1971 to do solo work, the band continued recording and touring as a trio. Cook and Clifford, feeling stifled creatively by John Fogerty's dominance, then lobbied for greater input. The more democratic album that resulted (*Mardi Gras*, the band's seventh) was not only their weakest, it was their last. They split up in 1972.

The next year John Fogerty released an album of country covers under the name Blue Ridge Rangers, and in 1975 he put out another solo album. On both he played all the instruments, and each album spawned hits. The other members worked in and out of the music business in various projects. Creedence reunited only twice: once as the quartet to play for Tom Fogerty's second marriage (1980), and once as a trio, at a reunion at their old high school (1983).

John Fogerty was out of the public eye for a decade, years filled with legal hassles over contract issues and lost monies, but he staged a major comeback with 1985's *Centerfield* album. Its hits included "Old Man Down the Road," a song whose appeal was boosted by an imaginative video. The long court battles made him refuse to ever again perform his old hits: he did not want to benefit his old label, which now had rights to his artist royalties (which he had given up in exchange for getting released from his contract). He relented in 1987 to play a benefit for Vietnam War veterans, and on other occasions, such as the band's induction to the Rock And Roll Hall of Fame in 1993. At that ceremony, John Fogerty, still distanced from his bandmates for feeling they had tried to sabotage his solo career, played without them. (Tom had died of tuberculosis in 1990.)

In 1997 John's *Blue Moon Special* won a Grammy Award, and also in 1997 Cook and Clifford began touring as Creedence Clearwater Revisited, though they had to fight Fogerty for use of the name (they won). A live album followed. In 1998 John Fogerty released *Premonition,* a superb live album and concert DVD of Creedence hits and newer material. There are two tribute albums of his compositions: *John Fogerty: Wrote a Song for Everyone* (1996) and *Chooglin': A Tribute to the Songs of John Fogerty* (2002).

Darin, Bobby (1936–1973) *pop and rock singer*
Although only occasionally a rock singer—that is why he is in the Rock and Roll Hall of Fame—Darin, an Italian American from the Bronx, was really a versatile pop singer. In its early days rock was for teens and was considered lowbrow music that would soon fade away. Pop was for adults; it earned more respect, and, most of the time, more money. For singers, there was another point of pride in doing pop songs: being more sophisticated musically, they were an artistic challenge. Darin, like ELVIS PRESLEY, EDDIE COCHRAN, the Supremes, and others, spent part of his career recording pop suitable for Las Vegas lounges. Darin made it there (as did Presley and the Supremes).

As a child, Bobby Darin received a medical diagnosis that indicated, correctly as it turned out, that a heart defect would lead to a short life. He became very determined, and his considerable talents found many outlets. Not only a top vocalist who wrote songs and formed his own record company, he was also a film actor, often costarring with his wife, Sandra Dee.

Darin had 41 hits (10 in the top 10) and was in the charts almost constantly from his first hit in 1958 to his last in 1973, the year he died of heart failure in Los Angeles. On Dick Clark's TV and live shows, Darin performed "Splish Splash" (his debut hit, and the first by a white artist for Atlantic Records), plus "Queen of the Hop" and "Dream Lover." In 1959 "Mack the Knife" (the theme from Bertolt Brecht and Kurt Weill's *The Threepenny Opera* of 1928), became his sixth and biggest hit,

winning the Grammy for Song of the Year. It was a big band track that Darin sung in the swinging crooner tradition of Frank Sinatra and other nightclub hipsters. Darin then concentrated on being a pop singer and a Hollywood actor.

Bobby Darin (Michael Ochs Archives.com)

His repertoire covered a wide range. Several of his songs came from films or Broadway musicals, while others revived songs from the 1920s and 1930s. He had a hit with a 19th-century folk song, a turn-of-the-century vaudeville song, a song translated from French, and one sung in French. On one minor hit, he played a piano instrumental.

He returned to rock, specifically folk rock, for some of his last hits, including "If I Were a Carpenter," written by Tim Hardin (who had a hit with Darin's composition "Simple Song of Freedom"). Darin was a great talent, who, while sometimes at a loss for direction, achieved his ambitions and made an indelible mark.

Dave Matthews Band, The

The Dave Matthews Band formed in 1991 and by mid-decade were well established as one of the top ALTERNATIVE ROCK acts, part of the JAM BANDS movement. Their millions of fans have given them number-one albums and years of sold-out shows. Guitarist Dave Matthews (b. 1967) was born in Johannesburg, South Africa. At home he heard a lot of classical, rock, and folk music, and was very taken by the pop perfection of the BEATLES and the spirit and rhythms of Bob Marley. He also was impressed by African music, especially African jazz. He came to the United States in his late teens to avoid serving in the South African army.

Matthews formed his band in Charlottesville, Virginia, to showcase his original songs, written on acoustic guitar. The band consisted of drummer Carter Beauford and saxophonist Leroi Moore from the local jazz scene; plus bassist Stefan Lessard, a 16-year-old prodigy; Boyd Tinsley, a classically trained violinist; and Peter Griesar, who played KEYBOARDS. All but Griesar, who left after a couple of years, stayed in the band, experiencing its rapid rise to fame. The term *grass roots* is often applied to the band's mentality, their following, and the phenomenon of their success. In this case, it means something that grew organically, not by any force of hype or manipulation of the marketplace.

The catchy sound of the Dave Matthews Band (which fans refer to as DMB), has as its core Matthews' adept and idiosyncratic acoustic guitar playing. Playing in standard tuning without a capo, he eschews regular first-position chord shapes, finding interesting melodic ideas and edgy rhythmic patterns up the guitar neck. He has a very percussive way of playing, and is fond of keeping a pattern going on the low strings while simultaneously droning on the higher strings. He formed his playing style as a solo musician looking to make a full sound. In the band his guitar takes on a role similar to that of a piano, creating a rhythmic space over which Moore's sax and Tinsley's violin can add color, supported by Lessard's busy and melodic bass lines (in the role usually reserved for guitar), and Beauford's creative drumming. It was an unusual formation. Matthew's elastic and expressive vocal style, with a wide emotional and dynamic range, was also something new, and he conveys feelings through sensitive, thoughtful lyrics. The band's improvisational abilities and groove orientation, which place them in the camp of jam bands, are brought to the fore in Matthews' compositions.

Acclaimed in local clubs for their refreshing sound, the band's reputation soon spread as they toured in Virginia and the region, gaining new fans everywhere they went. During this period the Dave Matthews Band independently released *Remember Two Things* (1993), recorded live in a club. The album was very popular on college radio, and a few songs on it would show up again on later releases.

Another set of music from this era is *Recently* (1997), an EP. It shows in its five songs the contrasts in Matthews' music, from mellow to harsh. There is a cover of BOB DYLAN's "All along the Watchtower," a song JIMI HENDRIX recast into a definitive version; the DMB did it their own way, with a mighty jam at the end. On two of the songs, recorded in 1994, Matthews plays in a duo with Tim Reynolds, a phenomenal acoustic guitarist. He would be a guest player on all of the band's albums.

The RCA label took note of the band's rising popularity and musicianship and signed them.

Under the Table and Dreaming (1994) had "What Would You Say" and "Satellite" as featured tracks, along with "Ants Marching," one of their signature songs. For more than a year they toured nationally and in Europe, and for two summers they played on the main stage at the H.O.R.D.E. festival.[5]

Crash (1996), DMB's second major-label album, is a studio recording that has the energy of a live show. Beloved by fans, it is an essential item in the band's catalog. It entered the *Billboard* charts at number two and stayed on the charts for two years. "Too Much" and "So Much to Say" got a lot of airplay, but it was "Crash into Me" that propelled them into the mainstream of contemporary rock. It remains their most popular song. As new pop stars, they carried on touring, headlining sold-out shows. At their live dates, they encourage fans, as is the norm for bands in the jam band circuit, to tape the shows.

Tape trading spread their fame but did not dull the appetite for official live releases. *Live at Red Rocks 8.15.95* (1997), a double CD, charted in the top five. Other live CDs, also available on DVD, are *Listener Supported* (1999), *Live in Chicago at the United Center 12.19.98*, *Live at Folsom Field— Boulder, Colorado,* and *The Central Park Concert.* These live recordings reprise songs from studio albums, feature different arrangements, and include some rarely heard numbers.

Before These Crowded Streets (1998), the Dave Matthews Band's eclectic, upbeat third studio album, was acclaimed by fans and critics, and entered the charts at number one. Magazines such as *Spin* put Matthews on their cover page, and described him as the new king of rock. The band hit the road for the next year and a half, playing and selling out stadiums, arenas, and amphitheaters, becoming one of the top-grossing acts in the business. In 2000 their ticket sales brought in $68 million, topped only by Tina Turner's $80 million and 'NSYNC's $74 million. In 2001 DMB were fourth, with $60 million worth of tickets sold, behind U2 ($109 million), 'NSYNC ($86 million), and the Backstreet Boys ($82 million).

Matthews and Tim Reynolds did some touring as a duo, and a 1996 show in Iowa is preserved on the highly regarded double CD *Live at Luther College: An Acoustic Performance by Dave Matthews and Tim Reynolds.* When released in 1999, it debuted, like most DMB albums, near the top of the *Billboard* album charts.

For the band's fourth studio album, *Everyday* (2001), Matthews cowrote the songs in a flurry of creativity with producer Glen Ballard, who had worked with Alanis Morissette on her *Jagged Little Pill. Everyday* was controversial in that it was not the usual jam band approach. Matthews played electric guitar, and the songs were shorter and more polished. "The Space Between" was a hit, and so was "I Did It."

Busted Stuff (2002) is more subdued and has darker lyrics. An earlier version of the album was scrapped, then leaked to the *Internet* and heavily bootlegged, so Matthews revived most of the songs for this edition. Fans are divided in their evaluations: it is either classic and great, or bland and disappointing. *Some Devil* (2003) is a Dave Matthews solo album augmented by guests such as Tim Reynolds (as ever) and Trey Anastasio from Phish. The honest and reflective songs include the pensive "Gravedigger." DMB's adventurous *Stand Up* was released in 2005.

The Dave Matthews Band's fusion of folk, jazz, rock, funk, and world rhythms made them stand out from the pop rock and rap on the radio. They are a unique act whose powerful music managed to make, and will likely continue to make, an intense connection with masses of people.

Diddley, Bo (b. 1928) *rock and roll pioneer*

Bo Diddley is a towering figure, typically wearing horn-rimmed glasses and a black hat and playing hypnotic rhythms on an electric GUITAR with a rectangular body. He has been such an influence on rock that he is called "The Originator." His first record, the self-referential "Bo Diddley" backed with the swaggering "I'm a Man," was a double-sided number-one R&B hit in 1955. It was recorded in

Bo Diddley (far right) (Michael Ochs Archives.com)

Chicago for Checker, a subsidiary of Chess Records, one of the great independent record labels. Diddley's hits made him a star and got him on tour and on television and later in a number of films. Several of his songs have become staples in the repertoires of rock bands, notably "Who Do You Love," "Road Runner," "You Can't Judge a Book by the Cover," "Before You Accuse Me," and "Mona." His bigger influence however comes from his infectious trademark dance rhythm, called the "Bo Diddley beat."

Simplistically described by the phrase "shave and a haircut . . . two bits," the Bo Diddley beat is a syncopated rhythm, usually played by a drummer on his drum kit's tom toms and often augmented by another person shaking the maracas, a percussion instrument comprised of hand-held rattles. With the emphasis on rhythm, there is little or no chord progression: sometimes two chords shift back and forth, or simply one chord is all there is, with the pulsating rhythm and a moving vocal line to keep the listener's attention. Diddley did not invent the beat, but he popularized it in rock and exploited it in creative ways. The compilation album *Bo Diddley Beats* (1992), shows that the rhythm predates him but that most applications of it after him show his influence.

The Bo Diddley beat has its roots in Africa and the Afro-American "patting juba" also known as "hambone": a technique of rhythmically slapping the chest, legs, arms, and cheeks while chanting rhymes. The rhythm associated with it can be traced in popular songs back to the 1800s. An R&B recording called "Hambone" was a novelty hit in 1952 for Red Saunders and His Orchestra, with Delores Hawkins and the Hambone Kids. One of the kids was 13-year-old Delecta Clark. In the late 1950s, as Dee Clark, he had several hits, and one of them, "Hey Little Girl" (1959), used the same beat. But by then it was known as the Bo Diddley beat and it was a fad. Also in the late 1950s it was used by BUDDY HOLLY ("Not Fade Away"), Johnny Otis ("Willie and the Hand Jive"), and BILL HALEY ("Skinny Minnie").

BRITISH INVASION bands were heavily influenced by Bo Diddley's beat, songs, and attitude, among them the ROLLING STONES, the YARDBIRDS, the ANIMALS, the Pretty Things (who took their name from one of his songs) and the WHO (particularly their "Magic Bus"). In "The Story of Bo Diddley" (1964) by the Animals, Eric Burdon narrates a real or imagined incident in which Diddley hears the band performing some of his material and says to Burdon "Man, that sure is the biggest load of rubbish I ever heard in my life." Other 1960s uses of the Bo Diddley beat are found in the Strangeloves' "I Want Candy," the Electric Prunes' "Get Me to the World on Time," and Quicksilver Messenger Service's variations of "Who Do You Love," which take up one side of their celebrated *Happy Trails* LP. In the 1970s it was used in Shirley and Company's "Shame, Shame, Shame" and BRUCE SPRINGSTEEN's "She's the One" (on *Born to Run*), and in the 1980s, in George Michael's "Faith" and U2's "Desire." His influence can be heard also in the music of Ronnie

Hawkins, the DOORS, and George Thorogood. These examples only scratch the surface of how much the beat is found in rock.

Diddley was born Ellas Bates in McComb, Mississippi, but was adopted as an infant by his mother's cousin Gussie McDaniel and so became Ellas McDaniel. The family moved to Chicago when he was five. He took lessons on the violin but was also attracted to the guitar. As a schoolboy he started performing on street corners, and as a teen he went into boxing. By then he was known as Bo Diddley, a nickname given—he does not know why—to him by his grammar school mates. One plausible but incorrect explanation for the nickname is that it refers to the diddley bow. This is a homemade one-stringed instrument (played with a bottle or other device to slide up and down the string) that people in the South, including many famous Mississippi bluesmen when they were young, used to make to amuse themselves. The theory would nicely link Diddley to blues traditions, but he has discounted it, stating that he never played a diddley bow (nor knew of it until people asked him about it in recent years) nor any kind of slide. One thing that does connect him to delta blues traditions is his use of open tunings (retuning the guitar to sound a chord when the open strings are played).

Diddley is a slang word synonymous with "nothing," so it appears that his classmates were putting him down in a humorous way. The same type of humor is what made "Say Man" (1959) into Bo Diddley's biggest pop hit (his records did better on the R&B charts). In it, he and his sidekick, maraca player Jerome Green, trade insults in the Afro-American tradition known as the "dirty dozens" or simply "the dozens." They accuse each other of being ugly. Green says: "The stork that brought you in the world ought to be arrested!" to which Diddley replies "[At least] my mama didn't have to put a sheet over my head so sleep could slip up on me!" Reworked folk themes and a witty sense of humor permeate his recordings, offsetting his imposing, almost menacing, physique. In his galvanizing live performances, he moves with the grace of a boxer. Jerome Green and Diddley's guitar-playing half-sister, known as "The Duchess," were part of his regular backup band through the 1950s and 1960s.

Diddley's talent has other facets. Like Jimmie Rodgers with his blue yodel or Buddy Holly with his hiccupping vocals, Bo Diddley did not always use the musical trademark associated with him. Sometimes he sang pop ballads, was backed by vocal groups in a DOO-WOP style, played SURF, calypso, or did the blues with a straight backbeat. His songs were quite varied, and one of the most popular, "Love Is Strange," a 1957 hit for Mickey and Sylvia, is seldom recognized as one of his compositions, for it was published under a pseudonym. Diddley's guitar style was unusual and innovative and his incorporation of tremolo, reverb, and distortion was highly influential.

He was active through the 1970s, performing on oldies shows and making some records, such as *The London Bo Diddley Sessions*. In the 1980s he became even more of a household name, as millions of people watched his 1985 televised performance at the Live Aid charity concert in Philadelphia, accompanied by George Thorogood and the Destroyers. A 1989 television commercial for Nike shoes paired Bo Diddley with football and baseball star Bo Jackson. The successful promotional campaign included T-shirts with Diddley's name, likeness and the slogan "You Don't Know Diddley."

His impact has been acknowledged by a host of honors, such as his induction into the Rock and Roll Hall of Fame in 1987, and lifetime achievement awards from the Rhythm and Blues Foundation in 1996 and the Grammys in 1998, and an Icon Award from Broadcast Music International (the performing rights organization better known as BMI) in 2002. While he appreciates the acknowledgement, Diddley is vocal in decrying the lack of financial harvest from his music, having been underpaid and cheated out of what is due to him.

He released *A Man amongst Men* in 1996, an album of all new compositions with guests that included the SHIRELLES and members of the Rolling Stones and Bon Jovi. In 1997 an excellent 20-track compilation called *His Best* was issued as part of a series that celebrated the 50th anniversary of Chess Records. *Hey Bo Diddley! A Tribute* (2000) has a roster of blues artists doing his songs. In his 70s Diddley continues to perform, both for financial and musical reasons, and he is still writing and creating new sounds.

Dion (Dion Di Mucci) (also Dion and the Belmonts) (b. 1939) *doo-wop singer*

Dion and the Belmonts, named for Belmont Avenue in their home of the Bronx, were one of the most successful white groups to sing DOO-WOP. "I Wonder Why" (their first hit, 1958) and "Teenager in Love" (1959) are classics of the style. Their biggest was a version of "Where or When," a pop song from 1937 written by Rodgers and Hart. The act split up in 1960 when the Belmonts wanted to carry on with doo-wop and pop songs and Dion wanted to move to a rock sound, which he achieved on his solo hits "Lonely Teenager," "Runaround Sue," "The Wanderer," "Lovers Who Wander," and others. Dion did reunite on occasion with the Belmonts; one special time was documented on *Live at Madison Square Garden 1972*.

His records, some written by Dion and inspired by his experiences and people he knew, succeeded in expressing some difficult emotions. As a teenager, Dion had been in a gang in his tough Italian neighborhood, and learned in that macho environment that introspection and sensitivity were unacceptable. But certain feelings that could not be said could be sung. Dion's wonderful voice expressed hipness and soul, honesty and courage, vulnerability, and, above all, humanity.

Dion always had an R&B influence and loved blues and country music. He scored two hits in 1963 with versions of two Drifters songs, "Ruby Baby" and "Drip Drop." Right after that, the BRITISH INVASION landed, and the hits stopped for Dion. In the mid-1960s he moved to Manhattan and explored the Greenwich Village folk scene, becoming

Dion (Michael Ochs Archives.com)

friends with BOB DYLAN and other singers. Problems with drugs sidelined him for years, but in 1968, aided by a return to the Christianity of his Catholic upbringing, he kicked his heroin addiction for good and never again took drugs or alcohol.

In 1968 the folk-protest "Abraham, Martin, and John" (a lament for Lincoln, King, and Kennedy, who had all been assassinated) marked a return to the charts and a new direction: autobiographical and confessional singer-songwriter material. These were artistically rewarding for him, but not commercial, aside from the revealing "Your Own Back Yard" (1970), his last hit. He did albums of Christian music, performed on the oldies circuit, and attempted several comebacks, which were unsuccessful until a late 1980s album, with guests Lou Reed and Paul Simon, brought notice. Dion

also influenced Billy Joel and BRUCE SPRINGSTEEN, and their music revitalized his own (Springsteen felt honored when Dion recorded a couple of his compositions). Dion's autobiography, *The Wanderer,* was published in 1988, telling of the ups and downs and how he made peace with himself. In the 1990s he returned to the doo-wop style.

Domino, Fats (b. 1928) *rock and roll singer and pianist*

Of the great rock and roll icons of the 1950s, Antoine "Fats" Domino was one of the first to record. Only BILL HALEY predates him on record. His style is New Orleans rhythm and blues, and of all the artists who came to rock and roll from R&B, he was the most successful. His specialty was catchy, danceable songs sung in his warm voice with appealing Creole pronunciation (his first language was French). Domino was usually pictured smiling, dressed in a suit and tie, with curly hair and a mustache. No wild man on (or off) stage, he expressed his flamboyance only in flashy rings and sparkly suits; he was never part of any scandal. Domino's jovial charm and lively music made people happy and led to a long career and amazing accomplishments—23 gold records and total sales of more than 100 million. Though he performed in four early rock and roll movies, he never courted publicity, rarely appearing on television or doing interviews.

A native of New Orleans, he represents a long line of great piano players from that city, including barrelhouse specialist Champion Jack Dupree, whose "Junker Blues" (1941) was the model for Domino's first hit, "The Fat Man." Recorded in 1949 at his first session, it had new words written by Domino and trumpet player Dave Bartholomew, in whose band Domino had been playing. Their lyrics, rather than talking about needles, reefer, and cocaine as in the original version, are about how the singer is 200 pounds, that people call him the Fat Man, and the girls love him because he knows his way around.

"The Fat Man" was on Imperial, a label that Domino would stay with for 13 years. The song hit the R&B charts and sold a million copies. It also established Domino and Bartholomew as a team: together they wrote most of Domino's hits, and Bartholomew not only produced and arranged the recordings but also led the band in the studio and on the road. The band included great musicians, such as the legendary drummer Earl Palmer, and the saxophonists Lee Allen and Herb Hardesty, who played with Domino for decades.

Domino had more hits on the R&B charts, and nine of them went to number one—he also played on Lloyd Price's "Lawdy Miss Clawdy" in 1952—but it was "Ain't That a Shame" (1955) that first put him on the pop charts. Pat Boone covered it, and both versions hit the top 10, Boone's going to number one. (Two later versions were also hits, one by the FOUR SEASONS, in 1963, and one by Cheap Trick, in 1979.)

Another of Domino's hits, also written by him and Bartholomew, was "I'm Walkin'" (1957), and it

Fats Domino (Michael Ochs Archives.com)

was covered by Ricky Nelson. Both versions made the top 20, but this time Domino's went higher. By 1957 the phenomenon of cover versions—immediate competitive recordings that were modeled closely on the original—was losing some steam, as record buyers tended to favor the original recordings, usually because they were of better quality.

Aside from the Domino and Bartholomew compositions, which accounted for many of Domino's biggest sellers, many of his other hits and album tracks were remakes of old songs. This practice was also widespread in early rock and roll, and the music business in general, and is not the same as the cover version phenomenon mentioned above. Because the old songs were no longer on the market, no current artist's career was threatened by another stealing their thunder. The challenging aspect of remaking an old song is to see if it works with a new style. Domino's renditions—from old standards to Hank Williams songs—were all set to his loping R&B beat. The best example of a Domino remake is "Blueberry Hill," his most famous recording.

"Blueberry Hill" was not originally a rock song. It was a pop song written by three men. One of them, bandleader Vincent Rose, had contributed to the 1920s hits "Whispering" and "Avalon." "Blueberry Hill" was first recorded by the famous singing cowboy Gene Autry in 1940. That year at least three big band versions were recorded, and the one by the Glenn Miller Orchestra was a top hit. In 1941 Autry sang "Blueberry Hill" in the movie *The Singing Hill*. In 1949 Louis Armstrong reprised the song, and in 1956 his version was reissued to compete with Domino's. Domino's made number two while Armstrong's made number 29.

The point is that rock and roll came from many sources. Domino's playing in general was influenced by jazz pianist Fats Waller, boogie woogie players like Amos Milburn and Albert Ammons, and the smooth R&B style of Charles Brown. The triplets (three notes played in the time usually allotted for two) that made Fats Domino's version of "Blueberry Hill" so memorable were an aspect of the style of Texas blues pianist Little Willie Littlefield that Domino had adopted. So with a rhythmic idea from blues and a 16-year-old pop song that had been done in western and jazz styles, Fats Domino made his biggest hit, and it crossed over to be popular with rock, pop, and country audiences. He reused that style in many other songs, and it became a way for older songs to be redone for the rock and pop market of the 1950s, as in Pat Boone's "Love Letters in the Sand" (a hit in 1957, written in 1931), Tommy Edwards' "It's All in the Game" (a hit in 1958, written in 1912), and Wilbert Harrison's "Kansas City" (a hit in 1959, written in 1952).

Domino's use of nonsense lyrics was another influential aspect of his style. In one section of "The Fat Man," he sang "wah wah" instead of words, perhaps imitating a trumpet, and it was copied by other singers, as was the "woo woo woo" he sang at the start of "Please Don't Leave Me" (1953). In "I'm in Love Again" (1956), one of Domino's biggest hits, the "ooh whee baby" he sang was reused by others, such as Frankie Ford in "Sea Cruise" (1959).

Among the many artists whom Fats Domino influenced were Little Richard, Ray Charles, Chubby Checker (whose name is a twist on Fats Domino's), and the Beatles. Even before they were called the Beatles, as the Quarrymen they had half a dozen Domino songs in their repertoire. When the Beatles played in New Orleans in 1964, Fats Domino came backstage and they serenaded him with his own "I'm in Love Again." In 1967 Brian Epstein, the Beatles' manager, brought Domino and his band to England for their first tour there, and they enraptured audiences. The next year, Domino's last pop hit was his version of the Beatles' "Lady Madonna." It was on an album called *Fats Is Back* which also included his version of the Beatles' "Lovely Rita." Domino-style triplets can be heard in the Beatles' "Oh, Darling" and John Lennon's 1980 hit "(Just Like) Starting Over." In his solo career Paul McCartney recorded "Ain't That a Shame" and other Domino songs.

Domino left Imperial in the early 1960s and recorded for other labels that tended to add more orchestration and vocal choruses to his songs. He continued to have hits, though they usually charted less high. After "Lady Madonna" in 1968, he no longer recorded for major labels, but Domino continued to perform, frequently in Las Vegas and occasionally overseas, though in later years he preferred not to stray far from his home in New Orleans. He and his wife Rosemary had eight children, every one with a name that begins with the letter "A" (like their father, Antoine). With a comfortable income from royalties, he is content to stay home, where he can enjoy the local food, socialize, drive around in his pink Cadillac, and perform at the New Orleans Jazz and Heritage Festival.

His music shows up on movie and television soundtracks, and his performances are easily found on video and DVD, such as a concert with RICKY NELSON in 1985. Among his many awards are induction into the Rock and Roll Hall of Fame (1986), and a Lifetime Achievement Award at the Grammys (1987). Twenty-five years after his last major-label album, he made another one: *Christmas Is a Special Day* (1993). Numerous collections of his music are available, including a box set of eight CDs, called *Out of New Orleans,* which collects almost all his recordings for the Imperial label.

Donovan (b. 1946) *singer and songwriter*

Born Donovan Leitch, near Glasgow, Scotland, of Irish and Scottish ancestry and raised in England, Donovan is an innovative and influential troubadour. His folk songs and PSYCHEDELIC ROCK records brought him great acclaim in the latter half of the 1960s. He wrote poetically and sang melodiously in an idiosyncratic voice that conveyed gentleness even as it played with phrasing and exaggerated pronunciation and vibrato. He observed relationships, the contradictions and struggles of modern urban life, the beauty of nature, and the realm of childhood wonder. His sincerity and spirituality made him a respected and inspirational representative of hippie philosophy. Cynical later generations who found the "flower power" point of view ridicu-

lously unrealistic would place Donovan as an anachronism, but the tuneful creativity of his music and the wisdom in his lyrics continue to appeal, as does the bohemian view of life that was his foundation. The philosophy expressed in his songs, as he said in a radio interview, was one of "brotherhood, expansion of consciousness, the saving of the planet, awareness of nuclear war, ecology and the re-education of the school system."

He was a central figure in the 1960s rock community and his friendships and associations with other stars were mutually influential. The Jeff Beck Group backed Donovan on "Goo Goo Barabajagal (Love Is Hot)." John Paul Jones and Jimmy Page, before they were in LED ZEPPELIN, contributed to Donovan's biggest hits, and his mix of acoustic and electric instruments and incorporations of Indian music seem to have influenced that band. Jones played BASS and arranged Donovan's "Mellow Yellow" and "Hurdy Gurdy Man." Page is also on "Hurdy Gurdy Man" (and so is future Led Zeppelin drummer John Bonham) as well as on "Sunshine Superman."

The subtitle of "Sunshine Superman" was "For John and Paul," and Donovan was friends with the BEATLES. Paul McCartney sang, or rather whispered, on "Mellow Yellow," and Donovan contributed to the Beatles' "Yellow Submarine" and was among the chorus singing on "All You Need Is Love." In India, while visiting the Maharishi Mahesh Yogi (pictured with Donovan on the cover of his *A Gift from a Flower to a Garden*) to learn about Transcendental Meditation, Donovan showed John Lennon how to play a folk GUITAR finger-picking style. Lennon used it for "Dear Prudence" and passed it on to George Harrison.

His songs have been often covered. McCartney produced Mary Hopkins' *Post Card* (1969), which included three Donovan songs. Herman's Hermits had a hit with "Museum." "Season of the Witch," with its influential two chord vamp, was recorded by Julie Driscoll and Brian Auger and the Trinity, the Vanilla Fudge, and by Al Kooper and Stephen Stills (on *Super Session*). The GRATEFUL DEAD developed an improvisatory piece called "Mountain Jam"

Donovan (Michael Ochs Archives.com)

tled in Europe and whose playing influenced Donovan's guitar style. He was inspired by the Beat writers to travel and, while on the road as a teenager with a friend named Gypsy Dave (immortalized in "To Try for the Sun"), found his love of nature.

Donovan's earliest recordings were folk with acoustic guitar and harmonica, and he scored with his first single, "Catch the Wind," when he was 19. Though initially seen as a younger, British BOB DYLAN, Donovan began working with top producer Mickie Most and arranger John Cameron, and those comparisons disappeared. (Dylan and Donovan met in 1965, as documented in the film *Don't Look Back*.)

Donovan's style evolved to be very eclectic, experimenting with and fusing elements of jazz, folk, blues, Celtic, ethnic, and renaissance and baroque music. On his records one might hear acoustic guitar, electric guitar, acoustic bass, electric bass, DRUMS, sitar and tablas, cello, string quartet, saxophone, clarinet, harpsichord, harmonium, or organ. Some of his music is for children (of all ages), some of it is meditative, and some is very psychedelic. After Donovan gained notoriety from a drug bust, radio programmers began to search his lyrics for drug references (they found a few and imagined others), but Donovan turned away from drugs and got into meditation, and urged others to do the same. Problems with contracts slowed down releases in the United Kingdom, but not in America, where he was already a star.

Though Donovan had a string of successful singles and albums and work in films, he also had business difficulties. He was disillusioned in general and disgusted with the music business in particular. He and his wife Linda (formerly with Brian Jones of the ROLLING STONES), concentrated on raising their family in the California desert. After some time off, he returned to concert stages, and in the 1990s moved to Ireland. At that time there was a revival of interest in 1960s artists, and his back catalog was reissued on CD: both revitalized his career. *Sutras* (1996), produced by Rick Rubin (who also did Johnny Cash's final albums), was a return to form: another

out of Donovan's "There Is a Mountain." The ALLMAN BROTHERS BAND, after Duane Allman sat in with the Dead, did their own "Mountain Jam," and their recorded version was more than 33 minutes long. In "Fat Angel," named for Cass Elliot of the MAMAS AND THE PAPAS, Donovan sang "fly Jefferson Airplane, get you there on time" and JEFFERSON AIRPLANE returned the favor by performing it on their album *Bless Its Pointed Little Head*. Donovan's influence is evident in the music of T.Rex.

Donovan was influenced by Celtic ballads and American music: jazz, country, rock and roll, and folk. In songs that named them, Donovan paid tribute to two of his main inspirations: "House of Jansch" and "Bert's Blues" for Bert Jansch, the British folk guitarist, and "Epistle to Derroll" for Derroll Adams, an American banjo player who set-

set of wistful, haunting, delicate, and evocative songs. His *Beat Cafe* (2004) is a welcome set of jazzy acoustic folk recalling beatnik coffee house days. Donovan continues to charm audiences.

Doors, The

The Doors are a major, some would say the quintessential, 1960s band whose iconic front man, Jim Morrison, died in 1971. They remain an enduring, enticing cultural force. The band has exerted an influence, not so much for their moody acid-rock music—few bands sound like them, except the numerous Doors tribute bands who have, for decades, found a ready market—as for being an archetype. As a model of musicians who banded together to see where their creativity would take them, and who found an international audience in doing so, they still inspire.

Like the BEATLES, the ROLLING STONES, JIMI HENDRIX, and LED ZEPPELIN (and very few other contemporaries), the music of the Doors resonated with successive generations. Though it is ultimately Jim Morrison's persona—the self-destructive, charismatic singer, the genius poet, the agent provocateur, the rebel, the Lizard King, the sex symbol in tight black leather pants—that drives the intense fascination with this band, their music is strong enough to merit its own devotion. It drew from blues, classical, pop, flamenco, and from avant-garde films, literature, and the subconscious mind. In concert the band was exhilarating and unpredictable. They courted chaos, expressed outrage, revealed dark sides of the hippie dream, and—to their detriment—acted out the clash between youth and authority. Their critics dismissed them as pretentious, playing up to the sexual fantasies and rebellious impulses of their audiences, who themselves were often dismissed as teenyboppers. Morrison reveled in hedonistic excess, and his own family—his father was an admiral in the U.S. Navy—came to disown him.

Morrison was keen to push things to the limit just to see what would happen. He could be outrageous, for example berating the audience for their docility. Some saw his behavior as the defiant, even revolutionary acts of a brilliant artist, while others took it to be drunken, rude, obnoxious behavior from a narcissistic lout. Morrison's onstage antics and confrontational attitude led to concert skirmishes, melees, riots, and police busts for allegedly exposing himself, and jail. Legal action against him crippled the band.

Between their demo recordings in 1965 and their final show in 1970, the Doors opened new doors for rock music. Their music was fresh, dramatic, and highly arranged, and they had the chops to pull it off. Musically imprinted by the 1950s rock and rollers, Morrison's husky baritone showed the influence of his two favorite singers: Frank Sinatra and ELVIS PRESLEY. His spontaneous verbal improvisations and worked-out set pieces, which could be humorous, absurd, topical, or scary, were backed at every turn by the rest of the band in a kind of synergy.

They formed in Los Angeles in 1965 after Jim Morrison (b. 1943) and Ray Manzarek (b. 1939), an accomplished classical and blues KEYBOARD player who had grown up in Chicago, met in film school. One day at the beach Morrison sang "Moonlight Drive" and some other of his songs for Manzarek, and they decided to form a band that would set Morrison's poetry to music and mix theater with rock. They were joined by drummer John Densmore (b. 1945) and guitarist Robbie Krieger (b. 1946), one of the few rock musicians to play the electric GUITAR finger style. He also played slide guitar in a blues-influenced style. The band did not have a BASS player: either Manzarek played the bass lines with his left hand on a keyboard designed for that purpose, or a session bassist was added as needed.

They took their name from Aldous Huxley's book about a mescaline trip, *The Doors of Perception* (1954), particularly the William Blake quotation that inspired the title: "If the doors of perception were cleansed, man would see things as they truly are—infinite." There is a spiritual, mystical side to the Doors' music; Morrison was attracted to Native American shamanism, and the others were involved in Transcendental Meditation. Manzarek said: "What the Doors were all about [was] peyote, acid, and infinity; raising your consciousness . . . opening the doors in your head."[6] There are other sides as well to the band's lyrics, mostly but not exclusively by Morrison: outcries against hypocrisy and war and the establishment, a fascination with death and violence, the elements, reptiles, love, and references from blues classics.

Initially the Doors played in nightclubs on the Sunset Strip alongside other Los Angeles bands such as Love and touring acts such as Them (whose "Gloria" the Doors added to their repertoire). There they developed their act and long, partly improvisatory, pieces full of dramatic crescendos and whispered passages. One was the infamous Oedipal fantasy "The End," which got them fired, but not before someone from Elektra Records caught their act, which led to getting signed to the label.

Their first album, *The Doors* (1967), produced, like all their subsequent albums except the last, by Paul A. Rothchild, was a sensation. It included "Break On Through" ("to the other side"), which articulated the band's desire to transcend limitations, "Alabama Song (Whiskey Bar)" written in 1927 in Germany by Kurt Weill and Bertolt Brecht, and most importantly, "Light My Fire," written by Kreiger, which became their signature song. It has four distinct sections, each in a different style. The intro is classical counterpoint, the verse uses a

The Doors (Michael Ochs Archives.com)

simple but unusual minor chord vamp over a Latin rhythm, the chorus shifts to a major key and a rock rhythm, and the solos are a hypnotic minor chord vamp derived from modern jazz. For the single, which hit number one, the long guitar and organ solos were all but removed. The album contained the full-length six-minute version. It became a staple on the emerging FM underground radio shows. José Feliciano's popular cover version emphasized the Latin flavor and dropped the classical intro entirely.

The Doors played "Light My Fire" on the Ed Sullivan television program, where Morrison's good looks and charismatic sexuality resulted in comparisons to Elvis Presley. Having a top single but maintaining a status as an underground band sometimes created tension, partially solved by using "Light My Fire" as a vehicle for further experimentation, especially in the improvisational solos, but also with Morrison taking liberties with the melody and even the lyrics.

They had other radio hits throughout their career, and all of their subsequent studio albums also included at least one. *Strange Days* (1967) has "People Are Strange," "Love Me Two Times," and "The Unknown Soldier." *Waiting for the Sun* (1968) was their biggest-selling album and had their other number-one hit, "Hello, I Love You." *The Soft Parade* (1969), with much orchestration, especially horns, had "Touch Me," their next highest chart success, and three other hits. *Morrison Hotel* (1970), more R&B sounding, featured "Roadhouse Blues," while *L.A. Woman* (1971) contained "Love Her Madly" and "Riders on the Storm," the last song on the last album and the last piece recorded by the original band. *Absolutely Live* (1970), like all six of the studio albums, charted within the top 10.

Morrison's book of poetry, *The Lords and the New Creatures* (1969), sold well, and in 1971 he moved to Paris, living out the image of the wasted romantic poet. He was found dead of a heart attack in a bathtub under circumstances never totally explained. He was 27. He is buried in Père Lachaise cemetery, where his grave has become a shrine, causing no end of grief for the cemetery's management due to visits from fans who write graffiti, throw parties, and leave trinkets and bottles.

The surviving Doors made two albums, *Other Voices* (1971) and *Full Circle* (1972), and from them came two charting songs. They also did solo albums, collaborations with others, session work, and producing. The Doors' legacy has been kept alive by compilations and live albums, box sets, videos and DVDs, fanzines, and novels about the band. The popularity of director Oliver Stone's film *The Doors* (1991), with Val Kilmer in the role of Morrison, brought them further attention. Densmore wrote *Riders on the Storm: My Life with Jim Morrison and the Doors* (1990) and Manzarek wrote *Light My Fire: My Life with the Doors* (1998).

The three survivors were reunited for a TV special, *VH-1 Storytellers: The Doors (A Celebration)* (2001), which featured different lead vocalists, including Eddie Vedder (of PEARL JAM), Scott Weiland (of Stone Temple Pilots), Scott Stapp (of Creed), and Ian Astbury (of the Cult) taking turns accompanied by the veterans. When Astbury, Ray Manzarek, and Robbie Kreiger went on tour as "The Doors of the 21st Century," John Densmore sued for not being included. His spot was filled by Stuart Copeland of the Police, but he soon had to drop out because of an injury. This version of the band still tours.

doo-wop

Doo-wop is vocal groups singing in harmony. It has come to represent the 1950s: sock hops, malt shops, young love, teenage angst, and the delights of early rock and roll. Its name comes from the nonsense syllables that background singers used to fill out the sound; doo-wop could have been called "bop bop diddley bop" or "shang a lang."

Some of the top doo-wop songs are "Earth Angel (Will You Be Mine)" (1954) by the Penguins, from Los Angeles; "Why Do Fools Fall in Love" (1956) by Frankie Lymon and the Teenagers, from New York City; "In the Still of the Nite" (1956) by the Five Satins, from New Haven, Connecticut; and "Blue

Moon" (1961) by the Marcels, from Pittsburgh. These were popular in their day and have remained so. They are pure doo-wop in their theme—romantic love—and in their music—the simple, ubiquitous four-chord "Blue Moon" progression.

Doo-wop's roots are in the black male pop singing groups of the 1940s, particularly the Ink Spots, ballad specialists featuring the high vocals of Bill Kenny, and the Ravens, with bass vocalist Jimmy Ricks in the forefront. The Orioles recorded what is considered the first doo-wop song: "It's Too Soon to Know" (1948), written by their manager, Deborah Chessler. The emotional delivery of lead vocalist Sonny Til, the very slow tempo of the performance, and the unfolding nature of the composition created a sensation and inspired other groups to form. Following the lead of the Ravens and the Orioles, many doo-wop groups named themselves after birds.

The Crows, one of the "bird groups," a quartet from New York City, had a top-20 hit with "Gee" (1954). It was one of the first R&B records on an independent label to cross over to the pop charts, and was the first doo-wop record to sell a million copies. The Crows record sold primarily to teenagers, and its success encouraged independent labels and vocal groups across the nation.

Competing versions of "Sh-Boom" hit the top 10. The Chords, a black group from New York City, who did the original version, and the Crew-Cuts, a white group from Toronto, Ontario, had the hits. Cover versions had been the norm for decades, and any artist or their record company that thought they had a better version, or had a better chance because of contacts, reputation, or payola, did not hesitate to put out their own. The issue of white artists covering the songs of black artists who originated them, usually but not always with inferior versions, would increasingly be seen. Two other versions of "Sh-Boom" made the charts not far behind the Chords and the Crew-Cuts: another version by a black group, the Billy Williams Quartet, showing that cover versions were more about trying to make money than any racial issue, and a parody by Stan Freberg, who thought that the lyrics were not just silly but a trend to be combated with ridicule. The Penguins' "Earth Angel (Will You Be Mine)," like the Crows' "Gee," crossed over from the R&B charts to make the pop top 10. Again the Crew-Cuts cover also made the top 10.

The Bobbettes, ages 11 to 15 at the time they recorded their first and biggest hit, "Mr. Lee" (1957), were unusual in having an all-female line-up. Some groups, like Lillian Leach and the Mellows, were fronted by females, and others, like the Harptones ("Sunday Kind of Love"), the Crests ("16 Candles") and the Platters, whose "Only You (and You Alone)" was the first of their 40 chart hits, had a female vocalist in the ensemble. Some groups were racially integrated, like the Dell-Vikings, who did "Come Go with Me" and "Whispering Bells" in 1957.

Nonetheless, the clichéd image of a doo-wop group is one of four or five guys, blacks or Italians from tough neighborhoods, standing under a streetlight on a corner singing. They have no instruments, so the only sounds other than their voices are finger snaps or hand claps. They can't sing at home because the apartments are small and crowded, but they can in the stairwell at their high school, because the natural reverb there makes everything sound better. They take it seriously, figuring out the harmony parts and getting the syllables, the "oohs" and "aahs," and the falsetto bits just right, and deciding who should sing lead on which song. There are other groups in the city, and some have already made a record or two, sung on stage, and been on the radio, so their ambition and sense of competition is strong. In their repertoire are some recent hits, a couple of reworked old standards, and a few original songs. The members sing in church and maybe in a choir at school, so they know a little about chords and melodies and rhythms, but rehearsals are guided as much by instinct, by whatever sounds and feels good. The reaction of their peers, especially the girls, helps them decide where their strengths lie. They are teenagers, so they sing about young love. For a group name they choose something that sounds classy.

If they are lucky, someone in the record business lets them audition, and if he sees potential to make money, they go in the recording studio. The session musicians are jazz cats who find the music so simple that they are ready to record after a couple of run-throughs. The tenor sax player puts in a hot solo in the middle. The record comes out in a week or so, and in a month or two it's clear if its going to be a hit or not. To promote it, the group, now dressed in matching clothes that their new manager got for them—they do whatever he says—sings a few songs at a theater, along with other groups. Everybody studies everybody else's act, and they decide they need to work out some coordinated stage moves like the Cadillacs.

What happens next depends on hard work, payola, timing, fate, luck. Some groups hit it big, but not for long. Most faded away. Recent research and published interviews reveal stories of glory, exploitation, and tragedy.

The last doo-wop song to make the top 10 was "Denise" by Randy and the Rainbows in 1963. There were few hits after the BRITISH INVASION arrived the next year, though the FOUR SEASONS carried on with some elements of the doo-wop sound through the 1960s.

Then it became nostalgia. Record collectors, crazy about the youthful energy and yearning emotions on doo-wop records, created a big demand. Since most of the records were not hits and were pressed in small quantities on independent labels, prices rose until doo-wop records became among the priciest to collect. Thankfully, most of the best songs were reissued on vinyl and CD. *The Doo Wop Box,* a four-CD set put out by Rhino in 1993, did so well for the company that two more box sets followed.

The popularity of Rhino's doo-wop reissues inspired a celebration of five decades of doo-wop. Two nights of gala concerts of veteran groups were filmed in Pittsburgh for a TV special (later released on DVD) called *Doo Wop 50* (1999). Its popularity led to two sequels, *Doo Wop 51* and *Rock, Rhythm and Doo Wop: The Greatest Songs from Early Rock*

'N' Roll. All are available on DVD. Around the United States, several doo-wop societies, such as the United in Group Harmony Association (UGHA) of New Jersey, founded in 1976, continue to present veteran and new doo-wop groups in concert.

drums

Percussion instruments are the oldest of all instruments. They are found in all cultures, from prehistoric times onward. The hollow part of a drum, the body, serves as a resonating chamber for the sound vibrations produced when the membrane stretched over its end is struck with the hands, a stick, or a mallet. Keys, pegs, or other devices are used tighten or loosen the membrane in order to tune it to different pitch levels. In the 20th century natural materials such as wood for the drums and calfskin for the head were replaced by plastic and other synthetics.

In marching and parade bands, the bass drum, snare, and cymbals are all played by different individuals. The drum set came about in the 19th century, after the invention of the bass drum pedal. The standard drum set comprises a bass drum for keeping a basic pulse with the foot, a snare drum to set the beat in conjunction with the bass drum, one or more tom-toms for different sounds and effects, and various cymbals: paired hi-hats controlled by a foot pedal, a ride cymbal for steady rhythms, and a crash cymbal to be hit occasionally for emphasis. Additions such as cowbells, wood blocks, or chimes are optional. Many rock drummers have a more elaborate kit with additional tom-toms and cymbals, and a few have double bass drums or large hanging gongs. In recent decades some drummers have favored kits with electronic pads. When they are hit, they trigger natural and synthesized sounds stored in data banks.

Modern drum set technique evolved through jazz players. Early drummers, such as Baby Dodds, who played with Louis Armstrong, played New Orleans style. Swing-era drummers, such as Gene Krupa and Buddy Rich, took drumming to new levels and gained attention for their prowess. Louis

Belson pioneered double bass drums. Joe Morello, who played with the Dave Brubeck Quartet, showed how to play in odd time signatures: their "Take Five" is in 5/4 time, that is, the music is grouped in units of five. The standard is units of four (referred to as 4/4, or common time), which is ubiquitous in rock and all forms of popular music. The few exceptions are the old-fashioned waltz (in three) and some slow songs that are in six (such as the "House of the Rising Sun" by the ANIMALS).

The use of drums in the other genres that are the sources of rock and roll can be connected to their proximity to jazz. Drums were part of blues right from the dawn of its recorded history, but only in the first style that was recorded, the classic blues: female vocalists backed by jazz musicians. The drum kit was not part of down-home (rural) blues. When R&B—a mix of blues and jazz—began in the mid-1940s, it included drums. Later forms of blues followed suit.

Earl Palmer is one of the greatest drummers to come out of New Orleans, a city famous for its rhythm. In his boyhood he developed his timing from being a tap dancer, and was a jazz drummer before he got involved with R&B. In the late 1940s he joined trumpeter Dave Bartholomew's band and backed up FATS DOMINO on his first hit, "The Fat Man" (1949). In the early 1950s Palmer recorded with Professor Longhair ("Tipitina") and Lloyd Price ("Lawdy Miss Clawdy"). He then played on many hits by LITTLE RICHARD, such as "Good Golly Miss Molly" and "Tutti Frutti." Palmer drummed on other hits by Fats Domino, including "I'm Walkin'" (1957), and when he moved to Los Angeles later that year he drummed on RICKY NELSON's version of the same song; both were hits. He became a top session player. He played on a few recordings with the BEACH BOYS, and by the mid-1960s was working for producer PHIL SPECTOR and played on such songs as the RIGHTEOUS BROTHERS' "You've Lost That Lovin' Feelin' " and Ike and Tina Turner's "River Deep— Mountain High."

Country music is the other great source of rock and roll, and the use of drums in certain country styles is also related to their proximity to jazz. The first use of drums in the country genre was in western swing, which began in the 1930s as country's response to the new swing style in jazz. Drums were picked up next in country by the hillbilly boogie players of the late 1940s—swing bands had picked up on boogie woogie a decade earlier—but their use was not widespread in honky-tonk until the 1950s and they were never part of bluegrass. The earliest rock and roll songs not to come through R&B came through the influence of western swing, which is the case with BILL HALEY AND HIS COMETS.

When ROCKABILLY began in 1954 at the Sun studio in Memphis with the debut recordings of ELVIS PRESLEY, drums were not present. That was not just because the sessions were exploratory, to see what Presley could do as a vocalist, but probably because the concept never occurred to any of the participants. The few white acts that had already recorded at the studio were hillbilly bands that did not use drums, including the one from which Presley's backup musicians came. When his band went on the road, the trio (acoustic guitar, electric guitar, and upright bass) was augmented by a drummer because the full sound of Presley's early records, enveloped as they were in the "slap back" echo effect invented by SAM PHILLIPS, was not present on stage and the band sounded thin without it. The drummer that joined Presley's band was D. J. Fontana, who had learned drums in his high school band and marching bands. He stayed with Presley from 1954 until Presley's 1968 comeback special, and played on such classic songs as "Hound Dog," "Jailhouse Rock" and "Return to Sender."

Two other rockabilly drummers were also very influential. J. M. Van Eaton was the house drummer at Sun. Like Fontana, he trained in his high school band program. After playing on JERRY LEE LEWIS's debut single, Van Eaton stayed on with Lewis for "Great Balls of Fire" and most of his other recordings for Sun and also backed up dozens of different Sun singers until the early 1960s. An extremely versatile and tasteful musician, he has a readily recognizable style—a simple but influential one that proved difficult to copy. Jerry Allison, one of BUDDY HOLLY's Crickets, was an extremely imaginative drummer, playing with taste and dynamics and doing what the songs called for. He exploited the sound colors of cowbell, cymbals, tom-toms, or whatever was available, including playing on his pant legs (on "Everyday") or a cardboard box (on "Not Fade Away"). He's even been known to scratch his beard into a microphone for a unique percussion sound. Allison's drumming skills later brought him session work with Johnny Burnette, EDDIE COCHRAN, the EVERLY BROTHERS, Johnny Rivers, Buddy Knox, and Bobby Vee.

As Los Angeles' top studio drummer, Hal Blaine observed the rapid changes of styles in the early 1960s: GIRL GROUPS, SURF, FOLK ROCK, and POP ROCK. As part of Phil Spector's studio musicians, known as the Wrecking Crew, Blaine played on some of the great girl group classics, such as the Ronettes' "Be My Baby" (1963) and the Crystals' "Da Doo Ron Ron" (1964). His drumming powered many Beach Boys hits, such as "Surfin' U.S.A." (1963) and "Good Vibrations" (1966). He played on "California Dreamin' " by the MAMAS AND THE PAPAS, "Mr. Tambourine Man" by the BYRDS, and "I Got You Babe" by Sonny and Cher. He also recorded with Elvis Presley, Johnny Rivers, Paul Revere and the Raiders, the Grass Roots, and the Association.

In the early 1960s the soulful feeling and the grooves of the drummers at MOTOWN were very influential, as were the surf drummers. The solos that Ron Wilson of the Surfaris played in "Wipeout" were copied by all virtually all rock drummers. The next major event in the development of rock drumming came with the BRITISH INVASION. Because the top bands all played on *The Ed Sullivan Show,* seeing drummers in action was a catalyst for countless people to want to play themselves. Ringo Starr of the BEATLES was the most important, but Dave Clark, the drummer-leader of the Dave Clark Five, also had a lot of impact.

Ringo Starr is underrated by the public, but not by the leading players and educators in the rock drumming community, who are effusive in their praise. He is a brilliant drummer, one of the most innovative, most consistent, and most influential. A spirited, joyful player with great time and feel, a terrific backbeat, and endless stamina, he is not flashy in his playing, but efficient and highly musical. Starr is versatile but never overplays. He applied his inventiveness to serving the song, and the textures he came up with were tricky and subtle, as any drummer in a Beatles cover band soon discovers. The way he tuned his drums gave them a distinctive sound, and the fact that he was a left-handed player on a kit designed for right-handed people made for some unorthodox but magical fills.

Charlie Watts of the ROLLING STONES played with style and dynamics. His influences were jazz players. Keith Moon of the WHO seemed to have limitless energy, playing with furious motion and a sassy attitude. On "Happy Jack" and "Won't Get Fooled Again" the drums seem to lead the band.

In 1967 two more dexterous and intense British drummers came to the forefront and had great influence of their own. The bands they propelled were power trios and so, like Keith Moon, they took their share of the sonic space. Mitch Mitchell, who played with JIMI HENDRIX, shone on such songs as "Hey Joe," "Purple Haze," and "All Along the Watchtower." Ginger Baker, with CREAM, can be appreciated on such numbers as "Sunshine of Your Love," "White Room," and the drum feature "Toad." Baker was probably the first in rock to use double bass drums.

Another drummer of extraordinary influence is John Bonham of LED ZEPPELIN. His style was deceptively simple. He played hard and precisely, sounding stately and thunderous simultaneously. The sound of his snare and bass drum, as produced by Jimmy Page, has no equal. Great examples of his playing are found on "Moby Dick," "Rock and Roll," and "When the Levee Breaks."

American drummers in the 1960s and 1970s had much to offer as well. Dino Danelli of the Rascals was a confident, showy player, as heard on "Good Lovin' " (when they were still known as the Young Rascals). Levon Helm of the BAND had a loose, southern feel evident in "The Weight." Ron Bushy of

Iron Butterfly played the first extended rock drum solo on a hit record: the title track of *In-A-Gadda-Da-Vida.* The solo played by Mike Shrieve of SANTANA in "Soul Sacrifice" was a highlight of the movie of the WOODSTOCK festival. Sometimes two drummers were employed, such as on some of Elvis Presley's early 1960s recordings. Bands that made that configuration part of their regular ensemble included the GRATEFUL DEAD (with Bill Kreutzmann and Mickey Hart) and the ALLMAN BROTHERS BAND (with Butch Trucks and Jai Johanny Johanson).

British PROGRESSIVE ROCK drummers broke new ground. Bill Bruford of Yes had an unpredictable, unique style and a light touch derived from early jazz playing. He was able to navigate odd meters with ease. Carl Palmer of Emerson, Lake and Palmer had great stamina and a martial style, playing driving rhythms and super fast rolls, as heard on "Tarkus," "Trilogy," and "Brain Salad Surgery." Phil Collins' drumming with Genesis has been somewhat overshadowed by his success as a vocalist. Neil Peart of Rush plays an extremely large kit with enormous energy and has had great influence.

Many other drummers have made noteworthy contributions. To mention a few more, in HEAVY METAL there is Alex Van Halen of Van Halen and Lars Ulrich of METALLICA. Another influential studio drummer is Steve Gadd (who played on "Aja" with STEELY DAN and "Fifty Ways to Leave Your Lover" and "Late in the Evening" with PAUL SIMON). Out of NEW WAVE came Steward Copeland of the Police and from the JAM BANDS came Carter Beauford of the DAVE MATTHEWS BAND.

Drummers will keep developing their instrument and finding new variations on rock's rhythmic vocabulary. As CHUCK BERRY said in "Rock and Roll Music": "It's got a backbeat, you can't lose it."

Dylan, Bob (b. 1941) *influential singer and songwriter*

Dylan is an icon in both folk and rock music. His music is such an individual expression, has gone through so many phases, and has embraced so many genres—from folk and country to blues and rhythm and blues to gospel—that he transcends categories. In keeping with the subject of this volume, this entry highlights his connections with rock music.

One of Bob Dylan's most important contributions to music is the elevation of the role of song lyrics to a more poetic realm. His real name is Zimmerman; by changing it to Dylan, he connected himself to literary tradition, if the widely held belief that he did it in homage to the Welsh writer Dylan Thomas is to be believed. In any case, his lyrics have been inspired by such poets as Allen Ginsberg, T. S. Eliot, and Arthur Rimbaud. There will always be songs about boys and girls in love, but in the 1960s Dylan, by his example, raised the standards. He showed that other topics could be treated and that, even in love songs, lyrics could evoke more complex thoughts and sentiments. He once challenged John Lennon by asking him why BEATLES songs said nothing. Lennon's response was to take songwriting more seriously and he began, from "Help" onward, to write more honestly and introspectively. Dylan had a similar effect on legions of other writers.

Bob Dylan became aware of the guitar through Hank Williams records, and he started to play the instrument himself, mostly self-taught, when he was about 12. He took up piano around the same time. As a teenager in the 1950s, Dylan was a fan of rock and roll, then just emerging. In his adolescence he played rock and roll and R&B in short-lived bands. In his senior year in high school he stated in the yearbook that his goal was "joining Little Richard."

In January 1959, when Dylan was 17, he saw BUDDY HOLLY, RITCHIE VALENS, the Big Bopper, and DION AND THE BELMONTS perform in the town of his birth, Duluth, Minnesota, on the ill-fated Winter Dance Party tour. Two nights later Holly, Valens, and the Big Bopper were dead in a plane crash. In 1998, in his Grammy acceptance speech when *Time out of Mind,* an album with a ROCKABILLY feel on some tracks, won three awards, Dylan recalled: "I went to see Buddy Holly play at the Duluth National Guard Armory and I was three feet away from him . . . and he looked at me. And I just have

Bob Dylan (Michael Ochs Archives.com)

some sort of feeling that he was—I don't know how or why—but I know he was with us all the time we were making this record in some kind of way."[7] The first posthumous hit for Holly was "It Doesn't Matter Anymore" (written by Paul Anka). It contains the line "you go your way and I'll go mine," which may have been the inspiration for Dylan's own "Most Likely You Go Your Way and I'll Go Mine" on *Blonde on Blonde* (1966).

Despite the deaths of three of the headliners, the Winter Dance Party carried on. At the next tour stop, a local band called the Shadows was booked to fill in. A few months later, under the name Bobby Vee, their singer made his debut record. While promoting "Suzie Baby" (the first of 38 songs he put on the charts), Vee hired Bob Dylan, then going by the name Elston Gunn, as a piano player and did two

gigs with him in Fargo, North Dakota (Vee's birthplace). Dylan could play a little like JERRY LEE LEWIS, at least in the key of C, but the economics of buying and hauling a piano around precluded any further gigs with Vee.

Not long afterward, Dylan discovered folk music and moved to New York City to become involved in the Greenwich Village scene and to be around Woody Guthrie. Dylan's early records were acoustic folk music, but in 1962, as part of the sessions for his second album, *The Freewheelin' Bob Dylan,* he recorded several tracks with a band. One of them, "Rocks and Gravel," was not issued at the time, but shows the new style that Dylan would soon develop. It is a hypnotic blues with piano, electric BASS, DRUMS, and acoustic lead GUITAR. That album contained "Blowin' in the Wind," which, through the hit version by Peter, Paul, and Mary, secured Dylan's reputation as the brightest light in folk music.

The legendary moment known as "Dylan goes electric" is when he performed, playing electric guitar and backed by members of the Paul Butterfield Blues Band, at the Newport Folk Festival in July 1965. Stories of this event usually describe the audience booing angrily at Dylan's betrayal of the purity of acoustic folk and its ideals. Bruce Jackson, one of the festival directors, onstage at the time, claims convincingly that the booing occurred not because of the music that was played, but because Dylan and his band left the stage after only three songs. The announcer had warned the audience that the performers that night would be allowed only a limited amount of time. The audience chanted "We want Dylan," and he came out and played two more songs alone with acoustic guitar. That has been interpreted as giving in to the audience's disgust with the electric band, but Jackson states they had prepared only their allotted three songs.[8] The other, more entrenched interpretation, whether true or false, is plausible. The folk revival, the point of entry for Bob Dylan, Joan Baez, and so many other musicians who became prominent, had been going strong since the 1950s, but around the summer of 1965, it fractured into several projects. One of them was FOLK ROCK.

Dylan had been backed by a rock band before, just not in public. On Dylan's fifth album, *Bringing It All Back Home,* released in spring 1965, months before Newport, half of the tracks are with a full ensemble. One of them, "Subterranean Homesick Blues," became his first hit, entering the charts in April. The BYRDS' version of Dylan's song "Mr. Tambourine Man," a number-one hit that summer, ushered in folk rock. Dylan approved, and when acts such as Cher and the Turtles had folk rock hits with

other of his songs, he was encouraged. Subsequent Dylan hits carried on with rock accompaniment. The next three were: "Like a Rolling Stone" (his first major hit), "Positively Fourth Street" (interpreted as a farewell to the Greenwich Village folk crowd and their expectations of him), and "Can You Please Crawl Out Your Window" (in GARAGE ROCK style). *Highway 61 Revisited* (1965) and *Blonde on Blonde* (1966) continued with rock, though the chief influence on these records is R&B.

On tour Dylan used the band later known as the BAND (on their own records) as his backup. Their apprenticeship had been served supporting Arkansas rockabilly singer Ronnie Hawkins. On Dylan's tours some audience members were vocal in expressing resistance to his new direction. That remained true whenever Dylan made a shift, though multitudes of fans followed him anywhere he decided to go.

Folk rock took Dylan away from straight folk. Following a motorcycle accident that removed him from the limelight, he returned with a more country direction, which took him temporarily away from rock. He then returned for more tours with the Band, and with studio musicians made *Blood on the Tracks* (1975) and *Desire* (1976), two of the most acclaimed albums of his career. For a period starting in the late 1970s, he embraced gospel as an expression of a religious conversion. In the 1990s Dylan revisited his folk days, releasing two albums of himself alone with his guitar. For years he has been on what fans call "the never-ending tour," and in concert Dylan has increasingly been playing his own electric lead guitar and, more recently, the piano. His backup band is a relatively stable group of ROOTS ROCK musicians with whom he makes new recordings and who can follow the sometimes radical reinterpretations of old material he presents on stage.

Eagles, The

The Eagles started in COUNTRY ROCK and are the most successful of all the bands to play that style, but their pop instincts led them to develop their own arena rock style, custom made for radio play. Only the BEATLES and LED ZEPPELIN have sold more albums in the United States. After only four albums, the Eagles could justify calling a record *Their Greatest Hits 1971–1975,* and it has sold in higher numbers—28 million copies as of 2003—than any other album (surpassing the former top seller, Michael Jackson's *Thriller*). Because it came out later, "Hotel California," one of the band's biggest hits, is not even on it.

"Hotel California" is one of the iconic songs of the 1970s. None of the members of the Eagles were actually from California; they moved there. The founding four had all come to Los Angeles in the 1960s to be part of the rock music scene that had been expanded by the BEACH BOYS and the BYRDS. Like these trendsetters, and most of the other hit-making groups from that city, harmony singing was one of the Eagles' main attractions.

Their biggest hits—10 of them made the top 10, half of those to number one—are played on CLASSIC ROCK radio to this day. Their recordings were well crafted at every angle and polished to a sheen suitable for Hollywood. Their perfectionist approach to studio recording set a high standard and gave them lots of appeal in the marketplace, but was also criticized for being cold. It also meant that their albums took a long time to make.

Besides their romantic themes, there were other lyrics that self-consciously tapped into the disillu-sioned and hedonistic spirit of the mid-1970s. A sincere ballad, "Desperado," advised hard-hearted Wild West outlaws, such as themselves and their audience (at least by identification), to choose love over money and do it before it was too late. "Hotel California" was like a movie about decadence and paranoia set in the desert and fueled by peyote and tequila. It seemed contemporary. "Life in the Fast Lane" illustrated its sense of living dangerously with a stuttering riff that hinted at roadblocks ahead. Fame, money, and cocaine were on the map. There were Lear jets and egos and all the trappings and traps of the rock star lifestyle—exactly the kind of thing punk rebelled against around the same time.

Don Henley (b. 1947) and Glenn Frey (b. 1948) were the Eagles' core, the main songwriters, and the only continual members. They were serious about success and about their songwriting and made the decisions, held together by an adversarial comradeship that set the course for the general atmosphere of turbulent intensity within the band. Frey, born in Detroit, played guitar and had worked with Bob Seger before meeting Henley, born in Texas, who played drums. They worked together in Linda Ronstadt's band, and, for a brief period, so did the other founding members. Bernie Leadon (b. 1947), born in Minneapolis, who played lead guitar, pedal steel guitar, and banjo, had played in the Flying Burrito Brothers and other bands with musicians from the Byrds. Randy Meisner (b. 1947), born in Nebraska, played bass and had been in Poco and RICKY NELSON's Stone Canyon Band. Some of them backed Ronstadt on *Silk Purse* (1970), a straightforward, somewhat bland, country rock album that shows that neither she nor they had yet found their sound.

All members of the band sang, and the Eagles' signature harmonies, developed from country music traditions, remained part of their sound in all its phases. Their debut, *Eagles* (1972), is their most country-sounding album, with prominent banjo and pedal steel. Three songs hit the top 40: the jaunty "Take It Easy" (written by Frey with Jackson Browne), the mellow "Peaceful Easy Feeling," and the hard rocking "Witchy Woman." The recordings were done in England, as were those for their next album, with producer Glyn Johns, who had worked with the Beatles, the ROLLING STONES, and the WHO.

Desperado (1973) was a series of songs about an outlaw gang with a subtext that commented on rock stars as outlaws and people's deeds that catch up with them. "Tequila Sunrise" was a moderate hit, but "Desperado" was never issued as a single (though it received a lot of radio play and has been often covered by others, including Linda Ronstadt). When the album did not sell to expectations, there was a shift in sound for the next one, 1974's *On the Border.*

Guitarist Don Felder (b. 1947), from Florida, was added during the recording, which was started in London but finished in L.A., and his slide playing contributes to the more rock-oriented direction, though banjo and pedal steel are present on some

The Eagles (Michael Ochs Archives.com)

tracks. "The Best of My Love," an acoustic ballad, was their first number-one song.

With *One of These Nights* (1975), they had their first number-one album. The hits were the title song, a midtempo rocker with a disco beat, the countryish "Lyin' Eyes," and the orchestrated waltz "Take It to the Limit." Leadon quit the band a few months later, disagreeing with the musical direction. He was replaced by guitarist and vocalist Joe Walsh (b. 1947), from Cleveland, who had been in the James Gang and had hits as a solo artist. *Their Greatest Hits 1971–1975* was released next, the second of four Eagles albums in a row to reach number one.

Hotel California (1976) left country rock behind. The title song and "New Kid in Town" hit number one, and "Life in the Fast Lane" was also a hit. The band continued the international touring they had done almost from the beginning. In 1977 Randy Meisner quit, exhausted, and was replaced by Timothy B. Schmit (b. 1947), who had replaced him once before, in Poco in 1970, and had been in that band ever since.

The Long Run (1979) took two years to make, but from the black-and-white cover to the sterile production, it lacked vitality. It went to number one as usual, and although it generated more hits, the band was drained by infighting and drug abuse and drifted apart.

One more album was released, consisting of previously recorded material, *Eagles Live* (1980), a double. The band split up in 1982. All members pursued solo careers, and two of them made it big. Frey had hits with songs in movies and television. Henley had hits, too, the first a duo with a former lover, Stevie Nicks of FLEETWOOD MAC.

A best-selling tribute album by new country acts, called *Common Thread: Songs of the Eagles* (1993), publicized them anew while it reaffirmed their country origins. The Eagles re-formed in 1994 for memorable shows at exorbitant, and widely criticized, ticket prices. *Hell Freezes Over,* the live album from the tour of the same name, boasted four new songs and an acclaimed acoustic version of "Hotel California" amid other favorites. It topped the charts, just like in the 1970s. The Eagles were inducted to the Rock and Roll Hall of Fame in 1998, re-formed again for live shows, and did another tour in 2003–05. Whether in jest or in earnest, the tour was called "Farewell I."

Electric Light Orchestra

One of the most popular and successful of all rock bands, Electric Light Orchestra, from England, delivered creative compositions and brilliant arrangements that mixed rock and classical traditions into highly crafted commercial pop. During their peak, from 1974 to 1981, nine of their albums each sold either gold, platinum, or multiplatinum. Their elaborate stage shows made them one of the top headliners on the stadium circuit, and they broke attendance and box office records.

In about 1969 Roy Wood (b. 1946), guitarist and songwriter of an eclectic Birmingham band called the Move who were having big hits in the United Kingdom (but not the United States), conceived of a new band, to be called Electric Light Orchestra. It was to experimentally mix rock with jazz and classical music, and carry on in the vein of the BEATLES' "Strawberry Fields Forever" and "I Am the Walrus." Intrigued, Jeff Lynne (b. 1947), guitarist for the Idle Race, also from Birmingham, joined the Move. Both groups had, on occasion, employed classical ideas and instruments, as had other British groups such as the Beatles, the Moody Blues, Procol Harum, and Deep Purple, but none had string players as band members.

Lynne's father was a Chopin fan and Lynne had sung in a boys' choir. He had been turned on to rock and roll by seeing DEL SHANNON in 1960, and, as an adolescent, got intrigued by tape recorders and electronics, rigging up a primitive home studio. In 1968 he had visited the Beatles in the studio while they were recording the *White Album*. While in the Move, Lynne wrote "Do Ya," which turned out, in 1972, to be their only chart success in the United States. With the Move still in existence, though not for long, Wood, Lynne, and the band's drummer, Bev Bevan (b. 1946), plus others, recorded and started performing as the Electric Light Orchestra. Though their first album was moderately successful and the first single did well, Roy Wood left, with some of the players, to form Wizzard; that group was to have success in the United Kingdom but never in North America.

Bev Bevan and Jeff Lynne then rebuilt the band with new musicians, including what became their standard string section of two cellists and a violinist, plus Richard Tandy (b. 1948, another ex-Move member) on keyboards. Though the lineup would change with nearly every album, Bevan, Lynne, and Tandy stayed throughout the band's existence. The second album, *ELO II,* contained their version of CHUCK BERRY's "Roll Over Beethoven" (1973), which begins with the introduction from Beethoven's Fifth Symphony. It was their breakthrough single and would be the only one of their 26 American hits not written by Lynne, who produced them all. Though he generally shunned publicity, the few photographs of the band presented on album covers gave him a familiar image: a big head of frizzy hair and a beard, plus, usually, sunglasses.

Electric Light Orchestra toured every year from 1972 to 1979, extensively in the United States and Europe, with an awe-inspiring laser light show, a technique they helped pioneer. For the 1978 tour to promote *Out of the Blue,* the double album considered to be their best work, which sold 5 million copies worldwide, they used a massive stage prop that resembled the spaceship on the album's cover painting. When the top part opened, the band was playing within. It was made of fiberglass and aluminum, cost about $100,000, needed seven trailers to transport, and took 35 people a day and a half to erect.

The Beatles' influence was evident in much of their music and acknowledged occasionally in their lyrics, such as in "Evil Woman" where the line "there's a hole in my head where the rain comes in" refers to "Fixing a Hole" from *Sgt. Pepper's Lonely Hearts Club Band,* which Lynne has stated is his favorite album.

Not only did ELO encompass a wide range of styles, from tender ballads to classical overtures to disco-beat pop to heavy rock and roll, they had vast palette of sounds. The strings provided baroque figures, ethereal swirls of triplets, and powerful lines, while the KEYBOARDS included the stately grand piano and the funky Hohner Clavinet and capitalized on the vast tonal possibilities of the newly available synthesizers. The vocals were at times processed with effects such as echo, vocoder, phase shifter, and various treatments, such as the telephone timbre that opens "Telephone Line." ELO took background singing to a new level: it was used orchestrally, building on the influence of the Beatles and the BEACH BOYS, sometimes using the bass and falsetto sounds of DOO-WOP music, or the classical chorale. The chord progressions were always in motion, whether moving above pedal tones, in logical, stepwise sequences of upward- or downward-moving lines that employed diminished and augmented chords, or creating new variations based on 1950s clichés. The lyrics concerned the search for identity, the contrast between fantasy and reality, love and its loss and the hope for its return ("Sweet Talkin' Woman," "Turn to Stone"). Their rock and roll songs, using simple catchphrases like "Don't Bring Me Down," lent themselves to being covered by local bands, for the arrangements of their other songs were too elaborate.

The use of strings was one of the most notable features of ELO—*Eldorado* (1974) even used a 40-piece orchestra—but the role of the string section diminished by the late 1970s as the synthesizer was used even more. By the last album, *Balance of Power* (1986), ELO was down to its three stalwart musicians, with no string players in sight. They also had not performed live for three years, but returned to play a benefit show in Birmingham, England, and three more shows in Germany, where they had done much of their recording. Their last albums, while still producing hits, were less inspired and the band split up.

After producing George Harrison's acclaimed comeback album *Cloud Nine* (1987), Lynne and Harrison, with Tom Petty, BOB DYLAN, and ROY

ORBISON, worked together as the Traveling Wilburys. Lynne produced solo albums for each of them (except Dylan), as well as tracks or full albums for Randy Newman, Duane Eddy, DEL SHANNON, Brian Wilson of the Beach Boys, and Roy Wood. Lynne produced the two "new" songs for the Beatles' *Anthology* project, and then an album for Paul McCartney. For these and his own work, such as the solo album *Armchair Theater* (1990), Lynne returned to a more organic way of recording, using natural room echoes and avoiding synthesizers—getting back to the way music was made and recorded in the 1950s and 1960s.

Bev Bevan and other former ELO members, including bassist Kelly Groucutt and violin virtuoso Mik Kaminski, as well as Louis Clark, who had assisted with ELO's string arrangements from 1974 to 1980, reunited under the name Electric Light Orchestra, Part II. Through much of the 1990s, they toured to appreciative audiences, recording studio albums of new songs and live albums of greatest hits. Jeff Lynne was not involved and was reportedly not impressed.

In 2001 Lynne reclaimed the band name and put out *Zoom*. Released as by Electric Light Orchestra and true to the band's sound, it was basically a solo album, recorded during more than two years at his home studio with a handful of guests on certain tracks (including Ringo Starr and George Harrison, who each play on two). The album was a pleasure to ELO's fans but lacked a hit single and did not sell well. A full touring band was assembled, but after a few dates—filmed and later released on DVD—the tour was aborted due to poor ticket sales. In 2003 a resurgence of interest in ELO came when a Volkswagen commercial used "Mr. Blue Sky," originally a moderate hit from *Out of the Blue*, in a version recently rerecorded by Lynne.

Everly Brothers, The

The top duo in rock, their specialty was close harmony singing. Don (b. 1937), sang lead and Phil (b. 1939), sang the high harmony. From their debut hit, "Bye Bye Love," a song that went up the pop, country, and rhythm and blues charts in 1957 and is still popular today, they were a major influence on younger harmony singers, like their near contemporaries SIMON AND GARFUNKEL, the BEATLES, and the Hollies.

In their heyday, from 1957 to 1962, they had scads of hit records, some of them million sellers, from pop rock to harmonized rock and roll to orchestrated ballads such as "Let It Be Me." They are in both the Rock and Roll Hall of Fame (1986, among the 10 first inductees) and the Country Music Hall of Fame (2001). They were given a star on the Walk of Fame in Hollywood (1986), and given a Lifetime Achievement Award (1997), by the National Academy of Recording Arts and Sciences (the Grammy organization).

Their father, Ike Everly, was a renowned fingerpicking guitarist who worked for a time with his two brothers. The siblings were ex-coal miners who left Kentucky (where Don was born) and moved to Chicago (where Phil was born) and played in the honky-tonk bars there. Ike's family then moved to Iowa, where, at the ages of six and eight, the brothers, as "Baby Boy Phil," and "Little Donnie" started to sing on the radio with their father and their mother, Margaret. They sang country, folk, and gospel, and the duet singing was influenced by the Delmore Brothers and the York Brothers. Later the Everly Brothers acknowledged these foundations in the albums *Songs Our Daddy Taught Us* (1958) and *Roots* (1968). The family moved again to other locations, wherever radio contracts could be had.

Ike's connection with Chet Atkins led to a move to Nashville. Atkins was a key music industry figure who was also known as "Mr. Guitar," and he respected Ike—who had inspired him on the GUITAR—and found his boys to be talented, friendly, and intelligent. The Everly Brothers made their recording debut doing country music but soon found their stride with pop songs aimed at the teenage market. They also played at the Grand Ole Opry and received acclaim from the country audience.

The Everly Brothers (Michael Ochs Archives.com)

"Bye Bye Love" was written by the husband and wife team of Boudleaux and Felice Bryant, but labels had turned down the song all over Nashville. Once it was recorded and became a hit, the winning formula was kept for other songs: Don played an introduction on acoustic guitar using BO DIDDLEY–influenced rhythms, and Phil harmoned over Don's lead vocal (sometimes Don sang a few lines alone). They used lyrics that teenagers could identify with, and employed professional backup by some of Nashville's top session musicians (including Atkins). The Bryants went on to write many of their other hits, such as "Wake Up Little Susie," "All I Have to Do Is Dream," "Bird Dog," and "Problems." Other hits were composed by the brothers: Don wrote "('Til) I Kissed You," Phil wrote "When Will I Be Loved," and together they wrote "Cathy's Clown."

They performed on TV and did extensive touring, both strumming acoustic guitars, always well groomed and, thanks to all their previous experience, very professional. In the late 1950s, when many of rock and roll's top acts were down or out, the Everly Brothers kept on having hits. A stint in the U.S. Marines did take them away for a period in the early 1960s. When they returned they were two years into a 10-year contract for a new label. They had more freedom and were able to use the same studio and the same musicians as before, but with the shift in management, they no longer had access to the Bryants' compositions.

Singing together, touring together, being stuck in an image of themselves as teenagers, being thought of as a unit rather than as individuals, having hits sporadically and then not at all, and for a time being more popular in England than America created a lot of stress. After a fight on stage at a show in California in 1973, the brothers split up the act. Each made solo albums, but the public missed the Everly Brothers. Their father died and they sang together at his funeral, but afterward they did not speak to each other for several years.

Their eventual reconciliation was underlined by a magnificent concert in 1983 at London's Albert Hall. Dressed in tuxedos and backed by a top band that included guitarist Albert Lee, they sang to a rapturous audience. The show was an emotional event for all, and the resulting double album and video spread the happy news that the Everlys were back together. Buoyed by the response, they recorded again and had a comeback hit written by Paul McCartney: "On the Wings of a Nightingale" (1984). Though they made only three more studio albums, they returned to the concert circuit. This time they kept going for another 18 years, retiring from the road in 2001.

As special guests on Simon and Garfunkel's reunion tour of 2003, they performed again to the delight of attendees, who already connected the two acts not just by sound, but because Simon and Garfunkel had included "Bye Bye Love" on their last studio album, *Bridge over Troubled Water* (1970).

Besides all the awards mentioned above, there have been two biographies: *The Everly Brothers: Walk Right Back* (1984, updated 1998) by Roger White, and *Ike's Boys: The Story of The Everly Brothers* (1988) by Phyllis Karpp. Additionally, there have been television documentaries, including TNN's *The Life and Times of The Everly Brothers* (aired first in 1996) and A&E's *Biography* episode titled *Brothers in Harmony* (aired first in 1999). A musical version of their life story was performed throughout most of 1998 at Nashville's Ryman Auditorium (the historic home of the Grand Ole Opry). The brothers have made peace with their past, and now, though they live in separate cities and have different pursuits, they stay in touch, performing on occasion in Las Vegas or for homecoming concerts in Kentucky.

Fleetwood Mac

Fleetwood Mac's is one of the oddest and most fascinating of rock's success stories. They went from being a respected 1960s all-male British blues band to an adored mixed-gender Los Angeles–based pop band with three Britons and two Americans. In the 1970s they forged a creative, emotional, mystical, grown-up kind of rock. In the process they became the epitome of success and excess and sold unprecedented numbers of records. Despite mental and physical illness, drug abuse, alcoholism, religious fanaticism, affairs, divorce, bankruptcy, legal problems, power struggles, stressful world tours, and more than a dozen different lineups, Fleetwood Mac is still making music.

Two lineups of Fleetwood Mac, representing eight of the 16 players to be considered official members over the years, are in the Rock and Roll Hall of the Fame. What is consistent between these two lineups, and all the other ones, is the Fleetwood of the name, drummer Mick Fleetwood (b. 1942), and the Mac part: bassist John McVie (b. 1945). They are best friends, a loyalty based on mutual admiration, honesty, and humor.

Six of the inducted members are from the early chapters in the band's history. Originally the band was formed around the brilliant Peter Green (b. 1946), one of the most highly regarded blues guitarists to come out of Britain in the 1960s. Green had replaced ERIC CLAPTON in John Mayall's Bluesbreakers, and both McVie and Fleetwood had been with Mayall. McVie was with Mayall the longest, but kept getting fired for being drunk (and

then rehired). A second guitarist was added before their first performance at a festival in 1967, where the band was billed as "Peter Green's Fleetwood Mac featuring Jeremy Spencer." (McVie was briefly not available, so Bob Brunning filled in on BASS; he remained a friend and later wrote two books on the band.) Jeremy Spencer (b. 1948) was a musical chameleon with an uncanny ability to play slide GUITAR and sing like Chicago bluesman Elmore James. He also was a devotee of 1950s rock and roll, and could sing in the style of Elvis and BUDDY HOLLY. For amusement the band would do parodies of 1950s rock, using the moniker Earl Vince and the Valiants.

Spencer was less capable of playing second guitar behind Green, so a third guitarist was added in 1968: Danny Kirwan (b. 1950). He was still a teenager, and his talent was intuitive and soulful, but Kirwan was nervous and volatile. This formation had several hits in the United Kingdom, such as the number-one instrumental "Albatross." They had only one, however, in America: "Oh Well," whose lyrics give an indication of Green's beliefs: "God come to me and said . . . stick by me, I'll be your guiding hand." During a visit to Chicago, Fleetwood Mac recorded with some of their musical heroes, resulting in a double album, *Blues Jam at Chess* (1969).

One by one, all three guitarists left the band due to mental health problems. Acid trips caused a personality change in Peter Green. He was disturbed by material wealth and adulation—fans called him the Green God—and he developed a religious fixation, growing a beard and wearing a robe and crucifix on stage. He wrote about his disillusionment in "Man of the World"; about his anguish and demons in "Black Magic Woman" (1968; a hit for SANTANA in 1971); and about something that is trying to drive him mad in "The Green Manalishi (With the Two Prong Crown)." Green left in 1970 and, despite many rough periods, has sporadically returned to music with solo albums and guest appearances (sometimes uncredited on Fleetwood Mac albums). In the 1990s he released two well-received albums of Robert Johnson songs and was present and performed at Fleetwood Mac's 1998 induction into the Rock and Roll Hall of Fame.

Like the others, Spencer was inspired by old blues and rock and roll, but was bothered that he could not envision a way that the music could develop. Despite his sometimes crude stage antics, he, like Green, was religious, took too many drugs, and felt unworthy of adulation. In Los Angeles before a show, he went for a walk and disappeared. He was found five days later, a new recruit—head shaved and apparently brainwashed—in a religious cult called the Children of God. He did play music again, with others from this movement. In 1972 Kirwan was fired after smashing his guitar in frustration before a gig and refusing to perform. He managed to continue in music for a while, but has since been living in psychiatric hospitals and care centers.

In 1968 John McVie married Christine Perfect (b. 1943), a classically trained piano player in another blues band on the same circuit, Chicken Shack. She also made a solo album and had a big hit from it. On the departure of Peter Green in 1970, Christine McVie came in to fill out the sound. She knew the material well, having already participated, uncredited, on Fleetwood Mac recordings.

Before the 1975 arrival of the remaining two Hall of Famers, Americans Stevie Nicks (b. 1948) and Lindsey Buckingham (b. 1949), several transitional figures passed through Fleetwood Mac. Bob Welsh, a guitarist from Los Angeles, contributed much to the band, allowing it to evolve. He did five albums with Fleetwood Mac; *Future Games* (1971) and *Bare*

Trees (1972) are especially good. The latter has Welsh's "Sentimental Lady," which he redid after leaving the band, gaining a top-10 hit in 1978. On Kirwan's departure, vocalist Dave Walker came in, from another British blues band, Savoy Brown, for one album. Guitarist Bob Weston, from Long John Baldry's band, came in at the same time as Walker and did two albums, but was fired for having an affair with Mick Fleetwood's wife.

Before Welsh left, feeling artistically drained and having marital problems, he encouraged the band to move to L.A. There Mick Fleetwood, while checking out a new studio, heard a song from an album called *Buckingham Nicks* that had been recorded there. Impressed by the guitarist, Lindsey Buckingham, Fleetwood asked him to join the band, but Buckingham insisted that vocalist Stevie Nicks be included. The two were in their late 20s then, and though a glamorous and very talented couple, they were living through hard times; their album had been a flop. They had gone to the same high school, played in a band around San Francisco for three years (where Nicks was influenced by JANIS JOPLIN), and moved together to L.A. to try to make it as a duo.

All parties agreed, and the two new members, with Fleetwood and the McVies, made the quintessential lineup and the extraordinarily popular *Fleetwood Mac* (1975) and *Rumours* (1977) albums. Buckingham, like his hero Brian Wilson, was a gifted writer, musician, and vocalist, and a wizard in a recording studio. Nicks had a husky, sexy voice and a mystical presence inspired by fairy tales and fantasy. It ran through her compositions, such as "Rhiannon (Will You Ever Win)," which Nicks would introduce as being about a Welsh witch, and she played up the image by wearing shawls and wispy dresses. Her female fans took to wearing the same type of clothes at concerts. Christine McVie wrote and sang "Over My Head" and "Say You Love Me."

Those three songs, all from *Fleetwood Mac*, were all big hits and the band's first in America. The album took a long time, more than any other

Fleetwood Mac (Michael Ochs Archives.com)

album, to climb up the charts, finally hitting the top spot in 1976. By the time *Rumours* was recorded, all of the couples were breaking up: Fleetwood's marriage, the McVies' marriage, and the romance of Buckingham and Nicks. The record was made under intense emotional strain and the influence of cocaine, which band members had begun using. The members were proud, passionate, vulnerable, stubborn people who were, above all, a band, one that had magical chemistry in their music. The turmoil was channeled into work, and the work produced art that not only revealed the emotions behind it but that also resonated with the times: liberated, hedonistic, and confused. Four songs hit the top 10: "Go Your Own Way," "Dreams," "Don't Stop"

and "You Make Loving Fun." *Rumours* sold and continued to sell, staying at number one for more than six months, and remaining on the charts for more than two years. It is one of the half dozen biggest-selling albums ever. With their record successes and tours Fleetwood Mac was, at the time, the biggest band in the world.

Two years later the more experimental double album *Tusk* (1979), sold 4 million copies, a relative failure after the huge sales of the previous albums. It still had two big hits: the title track, featuring a university marching band, and "Sara" (written by Nicks). Before *Mirage* (1982), the fourth studio album with this lineup and the third to hit number one, Fleetwood Mac put out a live album and Nicks,

Buckingham, and Fleetwood all put out solo albums. Nicks' solo career was particularly successful, with hit singles, albums, and tours. In the mid-1980s she quit cocaine (but struggled for some years afterward with prescription sedatives), and John McVie, scared by a seizure brought on by alcohol, put an end to his drinking.

Tango in the Night (1987) was the final studio album from the classic incarnation. It hit the top 10 and contained four hit singles, but Buckingham then departed to work on his own. He was replaced by two guitarists, who were already friends, who brought new energy to the band. Rick Vito, from Pennsylvania, noted for his distinctive slide guitar style, had worked with John Mayall, Roger McGuinn, Jackson Browne, and Bob Seger. He toured with Fleetwood Mac and participated in *Behind the Mask* (1990), but then left for a solo career. Billy Burnette, son of Dorsey Burnette of the seminal ROCKABILLY band the Rock 'n Roll Trio, had already made several solo albums and had his compositions recorded by a list of artists when he joined Fleetwood Mac. He stayed until 1996, and can be heard on *Behind the Mask* and *Time* (1995).

The lineup for *Time* did not include Stevie Nicks—she dropped out in 1993—but did have Dave Mason, who had been in Traffic and had a solo career in the 1970s, and Bekka Bramlett, who joined Fleetwood Mac in 1992. Bramlett, like Billy Burnette, had not only been in Mick Fleetwood's solo projects but was also a second generation rock star. She is the daughter of Delaney and Bonnie Bramlett, whose 1970s band, Delaney and Bonnie and Friends, had a run of hits, including "Never Ending Song of Love" (1971), and had included at various times several rock greats, including Dave Mason as well as ERIC CLAPTON.

Mick Fleetwood's biography came out in 1990, and his book of photos plus commentary came out in 1992: *My Twenty-Five Years in Fleetwood Mac*. The classic formation reunited in 1997, 30 years after the band began and 20 years after *Rumours*. They looked healthy and unified. After all they had been through, a feeling of family seemed to override

any bitterness. *The Dance* was a live-in-the-studio album (also a video) of new and old songs. After the world tour that followed, Christine McVie, tired of traveling, left the band. In 2003 came *Say You Will*, Fleetwood Mac's first studio album in more than a decade.

folk rock

Folk rock emerged in the mid-1960s as a mix of the ideologies and sounds of the folk revival with those of the BRITISH INVASION. Years before, rock players had made arrangements of folk songs, and several had been hits. In 1956 BILL HALEY AND HIS COMETS did "Rockin' through the Rye," an arrangement of "Comin' through the Rye," a Scottish song from the 1700s. In 1958 RITCHIE VALENS rocked up "La Bamba," a traditional Mexican wedding song, and in 1964 the ANIMALS, from England, did "House of the Rising Sun," a traditional American song. Folk rock was not created, however, until the BYRDS, who were grounded in the folk revival, experienced in acoustic presentation, and familiar with folk repertoires, adopted rock's instrumentation and rhythmic approach.

Folk rock's arrival in 1965 was announced by the Byrds' two number-one hits: "Mr. Tambourine Man," a BOB DYLAN composition, and "Turn! Turn! Turn! (To Everything There Is a Season)," a biblical text adapted by Pete Seeger. Dylan himself contributed to the momentum by "going electric" at the Newport Folk Festival that summer, though he had already released tracks on which he was backed by a rock band. His folk rock had more blues and rock and roll elements and ultimately proved to be more durable, if less commercial, than most of the folk rock discussed here. Dylan's electric style marks the beginnings of ROOTS ROCK.

The Byrds' recipe of doing Dylan songs or others written in a similar poetic folk style (often containing a critique of society or a statement of proud individuality) with BEATLES-type rock accompaniment was emulated by many bands, giving folk rock a brief but successful heyday (1965 to 1967). For most acts, folk rock was only a phase or an aspect of their repertoire.

Other hallmarks of the style are clear harmony singing and some instrument that provides a "jingle-jangle"—a pleasing, high-pitched metallic sound. Dylan had used that expression in "Mr. Tambourine Man" and the Byrds had done the obvious by including tambourine on their recording of the song. The chiming sound of Jim McGuinn's electric 12-string GUITAR, processed with compression, provided another jingling element. A Dylan song, a tambourine, a 12-string guitar, and harmony singing made a dynamite combination, but this narrow set of characteristics was too restrictive to last.

Folk rock soon diffused into a broader spectrum of sounds involving more orchestration and other influences. The jingle-jangle was provided sometimes by harpsichord, as in "The 59th Street Bridge Song (Feelin' Groovy)" (a Paul Simon composition) by Harpers Bizarre, or glockenspiel, as in the BEACH BOYS' "Sloop John B," a Trinidadian folk song from the 1920s popularized by the Kingston Trio. The Lovin' Spoonful's "Do You Believe in Magic" used the Autoharp for its jingle-jangle.

The Lovin' Spoonful were from New York, as were SIMON AND GARFUNKEL ("The Sounds of Silence") and the Youngbloods ("Get Together"), but most folk rock came from Los Angeles. Besides the Byrds, Beach Boys, and Harpers Bizarre, other L.A. acts that did folk rock were the Association ("Windy"), the MAMAS AND THE PAPAS ("California Dreamin'"), the Grass Roots ("Where Were You When I Needed You"), Sonny and Cher ("Baby Don't Go"), Barry McGuire ("Eve of Destruction"), the Turtles ("It Ain't Me Babe"), the MONKEES ("Last Train to Clarksville"), BUFFALO SPRINGFIELD ("For What It's Worth"), and Love (the *Forever Changes* album).

Further up the coast, the style found a home in San Francisco, with the We Five ("You Were on My Mind"), and the JEFFERSON AIRPLANE, whose debut album was folk rock. They soon shifted to psychedelic music, but like most of the other PSYCHEDELIC ROCK bands there, their roots in the folk revival remained evident. A version of folk rock developed in the United Kingdom, as can be seen in particular songs by the BEATLES, the ROLLING STONES, DONOVAN, and later with Fairport Convention, Steeleye Span, and others.

From the late 1960s on, the SINGER-SONGWRITER movement continued the mix of folk and rock elements, but the British invasion flavor was dropped, leaving a more purely American product.

Four Seasons, The

They are the most successful and longest lasting of the white vocal groups to come out of DOO-WOP. The Four Seasons emerged in the early 1960s with interesting compositions and catchy arrangements that featured the spectacular falsetto lead singing of Frankie Valli (b. 1937). They were one of the few American groups that predated the arrival of the BEATLES and managed to keep their popularity during the BRITISH INVASION. They are sometimes considered an East Coast counterpart to the BEACH BOYS. Their songs were not just about romance; they also reflected the tough, Italian working-class reality of urban poverty and survival of their native New Jersey in contrast to the Beach Boys' suburban ease and idealized endless summer of blondes and surfing in California. Both acts were influenced by jazz vocal groups as well as R&B vocal groups. They once recorded a single together, "East Meets West" (1984).

By 1970 the Four Seasons had placed 40 songs in the top 100, 13 of them in the top 10, including four number-one hits between 1962 and 1964: "Sherry," "Big Girls Don't Cry," "Walk Like a Man," and "Rag Doll." As Frankie Valli and the Four Seasons, they had five more hits between 1975 and 1980, including the number-one "December, 1963 (Oh, What a Night)," their biggest hit ever. Frankie Valli had a parallel career as a solo artist, with hits from 1966 to 1980. The biggest were "Can't Take My Eyes Off You" (1967), "My Eyes Adored You" (1974), and "Grease" (1978), from the film of the same title.

The staple elements in the Four Seasons' story are not the record labels (there have been more than a dozen), nor group members (they have come and gone), but the lead vocalist, Frankie Valli, whose falsetto singing defined their sound, and the writers who penned most of the groups' hits and produced their recordings: Bob Gaudio and Bob Crewe.

Born Francis Castelluccio, Frankie Valli took his stage name from a hillbilly singer named Texas Jean Valley who not only encouraged him, but tried to pass him off as her younger brother. She got him into her (real) brother's country and western band,

Four Seasons (Michael Ochs Archives.com)

and in 1953, she helped him make his first record, under the name of Frankie Valley. It was "My Mother's Eyes," a standard played by pop, blues, and jazz artists that was introduced in a 1928 movie. With his mother, Frankie had gone to concerts of jazz bands, and once, when he was seven, he was impressed by seeing Frank Sinatra; they later became friends. The first time his mother ever heard him sing, however, was when she heard the record. Frankie, the oldest of three boys, had not done his singing around the family home in the projects; he had been skipping school to hang out with the bad boys and perfect his skills as a pool-playing hustler, singing doo-wop on street corners. He also had to learn how to defend himself against bullies and gangs because he was short (five feet, seven inches) and skinny.

In a group called the Four Lovers, Valli had his first chart record in 1956 with a song written by Otis Blackwell. This led to an album, an appearance on *The Ed Sullivan Show,* and lots of nightclub engagements. Teaming up with Bob Crewe, an independent New York producer who had coauthored the hit "Silhouettes," got the Four Lovers work as studio backup singers. In 1959 Bob Gaudio (b. 1942), the classically trained keyboard player in the Royal Teens (whose hit was "Short Shorts") joined Valli, then singing with Tommy Devito (b. 1936) and Nick Massi (b. 1935), and the hit-making lineup was set. They soon changed the group's name to the Four Seasons, after a New Jersey bowling alley where they had tried to get an engagement.

Bob Gaudio wrote "Sherry" in 15 minutes. The day after the Four Seasons sang it on TV on Dick Clark's *American Bandstand,* their record label got orders for 180,000 copies and the song was soon at number one. Their follow-up hits proved it was not just a fluke. On tour in England, they heard the BEATLES, and their label, Vee Jay (primarily an R&B label), followed their suggestion and picked up the American distribution rights for the Beatles. Those records are now highly collectible, for it was not until the Beatles were on Capitol that they had North American success.

The Four Seasons signed to the Philips label and kept having hits, even under the pseudonym The Wonder Who, but by 1967, they found the shift in music to more relevant sounds harder to weather. They tried to do a concept album in 1968 but when it flopped, confusion set in. Crewe dropped out around this time, and Gaudio took on production duties. Another difficulty was that Valli was having hearing problems—so bad that he had to read lips to understand a conversation—caused by a rare disease that made a calcium-like buildup in the inner ear. He passed through a period of suicidal depression, and, through risky but ultimately successful operations, regained his hearing.

By 1970, with the group's fortune at a low ebb, Valli and Gaudio bought out the last original member. From this point onward they owned all rights to the name; future members were actually employees. The two also had kept the rights to the publishing and master recordings of their early hits, thus they were able to control reissues. From the group's beginnings, Valli and Gaudio had a deal between them, sealed by a handshake and honorably maintained over the years, that they would evenly split whatever money the other made from their creative endeavors together, whether from performing or from songwriting royalties.

A move to Motown looked promising but bore little fruit and the group broke up, having sold 85 million records and had more songs hit the charts than any other American act. Valli put his energies into his solo career. The phenomenal success of *Grease* (1978), set in the 1950s and starring John Travolta and Olivia Newton-John, with Valli in a cameo playing himself and singing the theme song (written by Barry Gibb), gave him his biggest ever solo hit, plus new young fans. Valli and Gaudio reactivated the group in 1980. Billy Joel's "Uptown Girl" (1983) paid them tribute by mimicking their sound. The Four Seasons were inducted into the Rock and Roll Hall of Fame in 1990.

garage rock

Influenced by the harder side of the BRITISH INVASION, namely the music of the YARDBIRDS, the ANIMALS, the ROLLING STONES, and the KINKS, garage was the do-it-yourself music of disenchanted middle-class suburban high school boys. Its heyday was 1965 and 1966, between the first wave of the British invasion and the wave of studio expertise heralded by the BEATLES' *Sgt. Pepper's Lonely Hearts Club Band* (1967). Also in that time period came folk rock and the beginnings of PSYCHEDELIC ROCK, and garage has elements of both.

Born of a snarly attitude, garage band lyrics often spoke in cynical tones of failed young love and teenage pressures and frustrations. Garage music is sometimes called '60s punk, and it is the spiritual and musical forerunner of the PUNK ROCK that emerged in the mid-'70s with the RAMONES, Sex Pistols, and others.

Of the thousands of garage bands across the world, few achieved hits, and most that did were one-hit wonders. In the 1980s extensive reissuing of rare 45s stretched to a great many volumes in numbered series of vinyl (and later CD) albums called *Nuggets, Pebbles, Boulders, Back to the Grave,* and *Highs in the Mid-Sixties,* among others.

Wearing mod fashions like striped pants with wide belts, paisley shirts or turtlenecks, leather vests, medallions, and Beatle boots, garage musicians played intense, driven, trashy, simplistic music getting tremendous variety out of shifting major chords and blues guitar riffs played through fuzz tone pedals. Following the model of the Dave Clark Five and the Animals, many bands used organs, specifically the Vox Continental organ with a red top and steel tubular legs, as did the top groups like Paul Revere and the Raiders, Sam the Sham and the Pharaohs, the Sir Douglas Quintet, the Blues Magoos, and the Seeds. Other top garage bands were the Electric Prunes, Standells, Chocolate Watch Band, and the Music Machine. The last five named were all from California, but other bands came from all over: Paul Revere and the Raiders, for instance, began in Idaho, relocated to Portland, Oregon, and then again to Los Angeles. Sam the Sham and the Pharaohs recorded in Memphis, Tennessee, but were from Texas, the home of the Sir Douglas Quintet. The Blues Magoos were from New York.

Perhaps the best description of a garage rock band is this one: "The typical punkadelic band came from suburban Anywheresville and consisted of one kid who'd grown up copying Chet Atkins licks on his uncle's hollow-body [guitar], another who'd had 10 years of classical piano lessons, a hyperactive woodshop dropout on drums, a lead singer with a range of three-and-a-half notes and a bass player brought in for his ability to attract girls. They borrowed the down payment on their instruments from their parents and rehearsed in the drummer's garage."[9]

The sound of teenage energy was what sold the records. Certainly it was not the richness of the harmonic language, at least in the cases of "Psychotic Reaction" by the Count Five or "Pushin' Too Hard" by the Seeds (both hits from 1966), as each are entirely made up of a one-bar pattern containing two chords a tone apart, except for periods in the former where the tonic chord stays static. In the majority of garage songs, however, the possibilities of tonalities made from only major chords were thoroughly explored. The perfect example, and probably the song that set off this mid-1960s fad, was "Hey Joe."

In the 1980s garage music was revived by many groups, and in the 1990s a series of rock festivals in New York City under the name Cavestomp reunited several of the 1960s bands and featured an international cast of contemporary supporting bands. One of the ongoing festival's organizers was Little Steven Van Zandt (of BRUCE SPRINGSTEEN's band), whose syndicated radio show *Underground Garage* currently has a vast listening audience. Garage music is alive and well.

girl groups

Girl groups consisted of young women—teenagers, most of them—singing fervently, yet fatalistically, about the insecurities of adolescent life. Its incomprehensibility could only be alleviated by uniting with (or at least fantasizing about) the object of desire, an idealized, irresistible boy, who was rebellious, misunderstood, or sensitive (or maybe all three). If captured, the boyfriend would be a protector, and if married, the union would be permanently banish loneliness.

The heyday of the girl groups was from the late 1950s to the mid-1960s. The first girl group hit is generally thought to be "Maybe" (1958) by the Chantels, high school friends from the Bronx in New York City. Stylistically, "Maybe" is DOO-WOP, but since women up to that point were scarce in doo-wop, their success inspired many others to follow, including the SHIRELLES. The doo-wop influence can be heard in the nonsense syllables sung in the background on girl group records, with "doo-lang" being a favorite. Once the Shirelles began having big hits in 1961, the girl group era really got underway. More than 500 groups recorded. There

were a few one-hit wonders, and fewer who had sustained careers. For something that was supposed to be ephemeral and teenage and very much a part of its time, girl group music has had an astonishing impact and longevity.

Unsurprisingly, since the roots of the girl group style are in R&B, most of the girl groups and the solo vocalists whose records had that sound (accompanied by uncredited backup singers), were black. There were some white girl groups, such as the Angels ("My Boyfriend's Back") and the Shangri-Las ("Leader of the Pack"). There were even some groups of mixed gender, such as the Essex ("Easier Said Than Done") and Ruby and the Romantics ("Our Day Will Come"), who had female lead singers and whose music is accepted in the girl group category. The producers and songwriters, for the most part, were white, although there were black producers too, such as Richard Barrett with the Chantels, and the teams at MOTOWN, who were behind the Marvelettes ("Please Mr. Postman"), Martha Reeves and the Vandellas ("Heat Wave" and "Dancing in the Street"), and the Supremes. The Supremes were the most successful act to come out of the style, though their music, especially after their early period, often transcended the category, and whose evening-gowned image was more glamorous than most girl groups, who played up their girlishness by wearing pink, frilly outfits and the like, and beehive hairdos, or who presented a bad-girl image.

Because their music was marketed on 45rpm singles (which rarely came with pictures) and few of the groups toured, most of the listening audience was unaware of the singers' race. The performers were essentially anonymous. That made it easy for personnel to be replaced, overlapped with another group, or completely substituted by another group if need be. In any case, what was important was the ability to connect. What the girl groups sang about was universal: the search for love. In itself, that did not set their music apart, for love is the standard topic for pop songs. What distinguished the girl group records was the emotional punch in the lyrics and the singers' conviction in delivering them, plus the high caliber, in the best songs anyway, of the songwriting.

Girl group songs were usually crafted by professionals, many of them working out of the Brill Building in New York City, though girl group music came from other centers, including Detroit, Philadelphia, and Los Angeles. The Brill Building team of Jeff Barry and Ellie Greenwich, along with PHIL SPECTOR, who was the most famous producer in the style, wrote "Be My Baby," (1963) by the Ronettes, perhaps the quintessential girl group song; "Da Doo Ron Ron," by the Crystals; and "Chapel of Love," by the Dixie Cups. Barry and Greenwich also wrote (with Shadow Morton) "Leader of the Pack" by the Shangri-Las. Another famous male-female writing team based in the Brill Building was Gerry Goffin and Carole King, who wrote the first girl group song to hit number one: "Will You Love Me Tomorrow" (1960) by the Shirelles. They also wrote "One Fine Day" (1963) by the Chiffons and "The Loco-Motion" (1962) by Little Eva.

The BEATLES were influenced by girl groups, and their early albums featured some of their songs, such as "Chains" (another Goffin-King composition) originally by the Cookies, "Please Mr. Postman" by the Marvelettes, and two songs by the Shirelles: "Baby It's You" and "Boys." The girl groups coexisted on the charts with the BRITISH INVASION groups, but not for long. The turmoil of the 1960s resulted in great changes in society and in music styles, which eclipsed the innocent earnestness of the girl groups.

The public has retained a fondness for the girl group style and its memorable hits. Several of them have been remade. Van Halen, Linda Ronstadt, and Phil Collins have all reprised girl group songs from Motown. In 1980 AEROSMITH redid "Remember (Walkin' in the Sand)," originally recorded by the Shangri-Las in 1964. The Manhattan Transfer had a top-10 hit in 1981 with "The Boy from New York City," originally recorded by the Ad Libs in 1965. "The Loco-Motion," recorded in 1962 by Little Eva, was a hit for Grand Funk Railroad 12 years later. The Crystals' "Da Doo Ron Ron" was a number-one

hit in 1977 for TV idol Shaun Cassidy. Betty Everett's "Shoop Shoop Song (It's in His Kiss)" (1964) was a 1991 hit for Cher (whose career began with girl group singing).

The Go-Go's and others revived the sound in 1980s, and its influence can be heard in the music of artists as diverse as Bette Midler, the B-52s, the BEACH BOYS, the RAMONES, Patti Smith, BLONDIE, and BRUCE SPRINGSTEEN. In recent decades, feminist academics have probed the girl group phenomenon as a mirror of American culture, finding much to say about songs like Lesley Gore's "You Don't Own Me" and "It's My Party," and "He Hit Me (And It Felt Like a Kiss)" by the Crystals.

glam rock

Also known as glitter, glam (short for "glamour") began in the early 1970s. Musically it was fairly straightforward HARD ROCK, but its image was unconventional. Glam brought drama and spectacle to stage shows and highlighted sexuality with male musicians who wore outrageous costumes that blurred gender expectations. The KINKS' "Lola" (1970) and Lou Reed's "Walk on the Wild Side" (1973) addressed the issue with their lyrics about transvestites. DAVID BOWIE, ALICE COOPER, Marc Bolan of T. Rex, the New York Dolls, and other male artists dressed as women, wearing fishnet stockings, jewelry, makeup, lipstick, dresses, platform-heeled boots, and so on. When Bowie dropped his Ziggy Stardust character, he continued to play with gender stereotypes, returning as the Thin White Duke, an almost robotic version of an elegant gentleman in a suit.

An early predecessor of glam was the VELVET UNDERGROUND, whose lyrics (written by Lou Reed) often concerned sexuality. Few American acts were involved with glam rock aside from the New York Dolls, who were not commercially successful, and Alice Cooper, who were. KISS picked up on the wild outfits and makeup but avoided the gender-bending overtones by looking like characters from science fiction or comic books.

Glam was more popular in England, where it was first known as "heavy metal bubblegum." It was created to be blatantly marketable, and it resulted in numerous hits by Slade, Gary Glitter, and the Sweet, whose hits such as "Ballroom Blitz" (1975) are stellar examples of the brash, propulsive energy for which glam was famous. Glam also looked back to the 1950s in records like David Essex's "Rock On" (1973), which mentions song titles and the late actor James Dean, and the Rubettes' "Sugar Baby Love" (1974), which featured DOO-WOP style background vocals. Roxy Music, Roy Wood's Wizzard, Elton John, QUEEN, and Mott the Hoople ("All the Young Dudes," 1972), all took part in glam.

Though most of its energy had dissipated by the time disco and PUNK ROCK arrived, both picked up on glam's love of outrageous costumes, and punk picked up on its rhythms. In NEW WAVE music Annie Lennox of Eurythmics played with the norms of gendered wardrobes by dressing, for example, as a tart in a blonde wig or in a man's suit with close-cropped orange hair. Glam was revived in the 21st century by new bands, most notably the Darkness (from England), and Robin Black and the Intergalactic Rock Stars (from Canada). A host of glam tribute acts currently operate in many different countries.

Grateful Dead, The

From their first show in 1965 to their last in 1995, the Grateful Dead epitomized the San Francisco sound and were ambassadors of the hippie philosophy they had helped create in the Haight-Ashbury district of that city. Though the members came from diverse musical backgrounds, they passionately incorporated elements of all of them into a unique sound. It garnered for them millions of fans, called "deadheads," who turned their devotion into a lifestyle. By the 1990s this beloved unit, often just called the Dead, was not only the top-grossing act on the live circuit, but the most successful touring band ever. Their desire to play better and to hear themselves and have the audience hear them clearly

led their sound team to invent and develop the most sophisticated PA (public address) systems in the music business. The Grateful Dead were also a paragon of how a communal organization can follow its own experimental impulses while making music and doing business on its own terms, still managing to be popular and successful as well as uplift and unite people. As promoter Bill Graham, a friend of the band, said: "The Dead are not the best at what they do, they are the only ones who do what they do."

The deadheads saw themselves as one huge family. In the early days, the fans were, like the band, hippies. In later years the deadhead ranks were swelled by the children of the baby boomer generation who carried on the spirit of the 1960s. Hordes of deadheads lived a nomadic life, taking long breaks from work or school to follow the band as it toured across the country. Like modern gypsies, they traveled in cars or vans, showing up at every concert. Some attended the concert, others just hung out, camping in the parking lot. To the sound of tapes of live shows and with the smell of incense and marijuana smoke in the air, vendors sold crafts, tie-dyed clothes, homemade food cooked on portable gas stoves, and beer. The Grateful Dead sometimes played a run of shows—consecutive days at the same venue—and for that time, the parking lot scene would function as a temporary town. People who wanted to attend the show but had no ticket would hold up a hand-printed cardboard sign or put up one finger, a gesture that meant "I want one ticket." It was called "miracling," and referred to a line in the song "I Need a Miracle" (1978). Sometimes it worked, if someone donated an extra ticket. Being "kind" was highly valued, and the phrase "Are you kind?" from "Uncle John's Band" (1970) was put on bumper stickers.

Being a dedicated deadhead was called being "on the bus," after a line in "The Other One" (1968), composed by Bob Weir. He sang: "The bus came by and I got on, that's when it all began, with Cowboy Neal at the wheel of a bus to Never Ever Land." He was referring to a 1939 school bus transformed by author Ken Kesey and his "Merry Pranksters," a gang of creative psychedelic eccentrics, who in 1964 drove across the United States from San Francisco to New York. They named the bus "Furthur." The driver, "Cowboy Neal" of the song, was Neal Cassady, who had (under a pseudonym) been the protagonist in Jack Kerouac's *On the Road* (1957), the classic book of Beat literature. In late 1965 and early 1966 (when LSD was still legal), Kesey had hosted parties, known as "acid tests," that became the prototype for the Grateful Dead's scene and their musical approach, as they were the house band.

Though the Grateful Dead had no official leader, Jerry Garcia (1942–95) was their central figure, a musical guru and one of rock's iconic personalities. From a musical family, he was inquisitive and talkative and had a philosophy of letting things take their own course, which became the band's modus operandi. He sang in a reedy, sincere, and expressive voice and played lyrical lead GUITAR with pristine tone and great skill. He had also been a bluegrass banjoist. Phil Lesh (b. 1940) was an intellectual with perfect pitch. He took up the BASS to join the group but had previously played trumpet in a big band, composed avant-garde pieces, and been involved with electronic music. The gentle but imposing-looking Ron "Pigpen" McKernan (1945–73) played organ, guitar, and harmonica and was steeped in blues and R&B. In their early years he was the showman of the band, rousing the audience with his forceful delivery. Bob Weir (b. 1947), the youngest, played rhythm guitar and had previously sung folk songs. Bill Kreutzmann (b. 1946) played DRUMS and had been in R&B bands. Joining them in 1967 was a second drummer, Mickey Hart (b. 1943), whose parents were both drummers.

Aside from vocalist Donna Godchaux (b. 1945) who was in the band through most of the 1970s, the other members of the Grateful Dead were all keyboard players. Tom Constanten (b. 1944), known as T. C., joined the band at the end of 1968, playing on some of their essential recordings and adding timbral colors with organ, harpsichord, and prepared piano (an avant-garde technique that involved attaching or dropping odd objects onto the strings of an acoustic piano). He left the band in early 1970. As Pigpen's health diminished from alcohol abuse, so did his role in the band. Keith Godchaux (1948–80) joined in 1971, two years before Pigpen died, and stayed until 1979. Godchaux was replaced by Brent Mydland (1952–90). After Mydland's death from a drug overdose, the KEYBOARDS chair was filled by Vince Welnick (b. 1951), formerly of the Tubes, who was in the band from 1990 until its demise in 1995. During the first year and a half of his tenure, he was joined by another keyboardist: Bruce Hornsby (b. 1954), who had his own solo career before and after his time in the band.

Before they were called the Grateful Dead, they were the Warlocks, playing mostly covers of R&B tunes. Previously, Garcia, Weir, and McKernan had been in the all-acoustic Mother McCree's Uptown Jug Stompers, doing songs from the 1920s and 1930s. Rhythm and blues and jug band songs carried into the Grateful Dead's repertoire, and later they would often return to acoustic music for a portion of their show. They also wrote some of their own songs. However, unlike their rootsy cover songs, few of these stuck in the repertoire until they started working with the lyricist Robert Hunter (b. 1941), who had played folk music with Jerry Garcia in the early 1960s. Hunter's lyrics were full of evocative images. They were set to music by members of the band, usually Garcia. Like BOB DYLAN, Hunter had a poetic gift, and he was fond of writing songs that were generated by intuitive creativity. Other songs of his were more novelistic and described a mythical earlier America populated by unpretentious characters such as cowboys and miners and other underdogs trying to survive or gamble with the cards that fate has dealt them.

During their 30 years together, the Grateful Dead played 2,318 documented shows. They had such a loyal and devoted following that every aspect of their career has been studied. The statistic for the number of shows played comes from *Dead Base X: The Complete Guide to Grateful Dead Song Lists*

(1997) by John W. Scott, Mike Dolgushkin, and Stu Nixon. In its foreword, written by Steve Silberman, a coauthor of *Skeleton Key: A Dictionary for Deadheads* (1994), which explains the jargon developed by the deadhead subculture, *Dead Base X* is described as "a detailed account of the creative odyssey of the most-recorded human beings who ever lived." The Grateful Dead were recorded at every turn by their own organization, and a great many live recordings have and are still being issued from "the vaults," and they were recorded by their fans, who were encouraged to do so by the band. The "taper's section" was a forest of microphone stands, and tape trading, as well as live radio broadcasts, spread the Dead's fame better than any form of advertising could have. The ethics of taping prescribe that no money should change hands, and so it was an activity based not on capitalism but on sharing, and many friendships developed through it. Collectors of cassette tapes (the preferred medium is now digital) were often so enraptured by the Grateful Dead that they collected and listened to little else. A common piece of humor known as "You Know You're a Deadhead When . . ." included these as characteristics: "None of your tapes have names on them, just dates" and, because the trading was done through the mails, "You have the postal rates memorized." Listening to the Dead, however, introduced their fans to the heritage of American music, for the band covered songs from rock and roll, blues, R&B, folk, and country traditions.

On their earliest recordings—1965 demos for the Autumn label when they were still called the Warlocks—they played garage, FOLK ROCK, BRITISH INVASION–style blues, and early psychedelia. They were a young band but their sound had been tightened by a recent gig that had them playing five nights a week for six weeks. One of the songs, "I Know You Rider," a traditional song that was a favorite of West Coast bands, remained in their repertoire until the end. They performed it 549 times, and of the 500 or so songs they are known to have done on stage, only five other songs were played more often.

Typical Grateful Dead shows consisted of one and a half or two dozen songs that might be ancient folk songs, old jug band tunes, 1940s bluegrass, 1950s rock and roll or Chicago blues, 1960s soul or honky-tonk, and their own compositions. Some of the songs would launch the band into several minutes of fearless jamming. They would hypnotically develop intertwining musical lines while riding a rhythmic feel, following their intuition and bouncing ideas off each other. The dynamics and intensity would rise and fall in the flow of ideas and inspiration within the band, fed by the energy of the crowd. These unguarded moments of reaching for something profound and intangible through a process that was almost telepathic and definitely spiritual was a conscious goal for the band and a major attraction for their fans. They often arrived at a state of collective awareness, in which the music seemed to be playing the players and the audience was an integral participant and contributor to the experience. Their concerts have been likened to primal rituals, and the deadheads to a tribe, their devotion like a religion.

Their first album, *Grateful Dead* (1967), was recorded and mixed in less than a week, and showed their roots in folk, blues, and R&B. The week before, they had played, along with other local bands, at the Human Be-In, an outdoor "happening" in San Francisco. That event showed the hippie community that it was larger than anyone realized, and, through the media coverage, soon enticed thousands of people to come to California to be part of the so-called summer of love. The album, aside from the vocal overdubs, was essentially live in the studio, recorded on a four-track tape recorder.

The Dead's second and third albums involved a lot of studio experimentation, which other groups, such as the BEATLES, the BEACH BOYS, and the JEFFERSON AIRPLANE, were also doing at the time. *Anthem of the Sun* (1968) was done on an eight-track recorder, and through tape splicing, sections of live performances were joined with studio recordings into an unprecedented and densely layered collage of sound. Assembling the album took a lot of time and energy and record company money. They were under contract to Warner Brothers, and label chief Joe Smith's faith in the band was eventually rewarded; the general public was not convinced until the 1970 albums. With *Aoxomoxoa* (1969) the newly invented 16-track recorder inspired much creativity. The album took more than six months to complete, and it marked the integration of Robert Hunter into the Dead's creative inner circle as chief lyricist. He cowrote, with Garcia and Lesh, all eight of the album's songs, which were more complex than the cover songs. Like its predecessor, *Aoxomoxoa* was adventurous but not particularly commercial.

Live/Dead (1969) was a double album, the first 16-track live recordings ever made. It is considered one of rock's quintessential live albums. The band was at a creative peak, with adventurous jamming and musical explorations. The mind-expanding "Dark Star," one of the Grateful Dead's most celebrated pieces, goes on for more than 23 minutes. The title of "The Eleven" refers to its unusual time signature of 11 beats per measure. Their space travels are balanced by the earthiness of the R&B of "Turn On Your Love Light," a Bobby "Blue" Bland song sung by Pigpen that the band uses as a vehicle for improvisation, and a 10-minute version of "Death Don't Have No Mercy," a song by Reverend Gary Davis, the blind black guitar evangelist whose complex finger-picking was an inspiration to acoustic guitarists.

By the end of the 1960s the psychedelic music scene in general had nearly exhausted itself, and the next two albums returned the Dead to their roots. This time they brought a more profound understanding and new inspiration from the Americana approach of the BAND and the vocal harmonies of Crosby, Stills and Nash. Traces of country and western are part of the blend, highlighted by Garcia's involvement with the pedal steel guitar. *Workingman's Dead* and *American Beauty* (both 1970), recorded live in the studio, contained well-crafted songs that were beautifully performed. These were their most accessible albums to date and gave them entry into the top 30 charts for the

first time. "Uncle John's Band," from *Workingman's Dead,* and "Truckin'," from *American Beauty,* were their first hits on the pop singles charts, and FM radio made "Casey Jones" and "Friend of the Devil" into standards. A line from "Truckin' " has been repeatedly used to describe the Dead experience: "What a long, strange trip it's been."

Grateful Dead (1971), also known as "Skull and Roses" for the cover image (taken from a 19th-century print, which became one of their logos), was an accessible live album. It introduced a leaner, harder rock sound that incorporated ROCKABILLY and honky-tonk into their repertoire. It also included an address where fans could write to get on a mailing list, one of their first moves, expanded upon in later years, in maintaining a line of communication with the deadheads. *Europe '72* (1972), a triple live album, showed the Dead instrumentally and vocally stronger, having added keyboardist Keith Godchaux and vocalist Donna Godchaux. It was their most popular album to date.

Through the series of studio albums that followed, the Dead continued to grow musically, bringing in funk and MOTOWN to their mix: *Wake of the Flood* (1973), *From the Mars Hotel* (1974), *Blues for Allah* (1975), *Terrapin Station* (1977), *Shakedown Street* (1978), and *Go to Heaven* (1980). During that time there was one live album, *Steal Your Face* (1976), and after it there were two: the acoustic *Reckoning* and the electric *Dead Set* (both 1981). Though the band kept touring, there was a long gap before the next release.

Onstage in summer 1986, Jerry Garcia lapsed into a near-fatal diabetic coma that lasted for five days. When he came out of it, he had lost much of his ability to play guitar and had to relearn how. After a period of convalescence and months of practice, he returned to a standing ovation. This energized him, and 1987 was a strong year for both the Dead and the Jerry Garcia Band, which sold out 13 nights on Broadway. The Grateful Dead went back into the recording studio for the first time in years, and their hard work resulted in their only top-10 album, *In the Dark* (1987). It contained their only top-10 single, "Touch of Grey," with Garcia's poignant chorus proclaiming "I will survive." A new generation of fans arrived, but the increased numbers brought problems. The family of deadheads sometimes felt like a mob, and undercover police arrested people engaged in illegal or irresponsible acts at or near Dead concerts. The group wore out its welcome in certain regions, and the band and community groups among the fans urged more responsible behavior. The band continued to tour, and backed up Bob Dylan for some shows, documented in *Dylan and the Dead* (1989). Their final studio album was *Built to Last* (1989). In 1990 Garcia began using a MIDI setup with his guitar, and its sonic possibilities were a great inspiration. It allowed him to trigger synthesized sounds, including saxophone, violin, and other instruments.

During this period Garcia's health worsened. He had heart and lung problems, and he ate too much, drank too much, and smoked too much. Once known as Captain Trips for his use of LSD, he had by now reportedly shifted his drug intake to cocaine and heroin. Garcia's exhaustion led to 22 canceled concerts in 1992. His attempts to improve his condition were inconsistent; he succeeded in regaining his health temporarily, and then slipped back into his addictions. After a difficult 1995 tour, marred by violence and mishaps, Garcia checked into a drug rehabilitation center. At age 53 he died of a heart attack in his sleep while at a drug and alcohol treatment facility.

By the end of his life, he was a gentle gray-bearded father figure whose smiling face and optimism represented the survival of hippie idealism. As had happened in 1980 with the murder of John Lennon, his death was mourned by millions and seen as the end of an era. Garcia's death brought forth a flood of eulogies from fans, musicians, and even politicians. The reminiscences of thousands of "netheads" (participants in the extensive online deadhead community) were posted on the Internet. The surviving members declared that the Grateful Dead was no more.

The members of the Grateful Dead had regularly made solo albums and taken part in side projects. Besides the Jerry Garcia Band, Garcia had formed Old and in the Way, a short-lived bluegrass band, and collaborated with many musical colleagues, including keyboardist Merle Saunders, mandolinist David Grisman, and the New Riders of the Purple Sage, a COUNTRY ROCK band that he joined temporarily as the pedal steel guitarist. The surviving members the Grateful Dead continued to play in various formations of their own. They later regrouped with new players as the Other Ones, and then as The Dead.

Dozens of archival recordings, from single CDs to elaborate box sets of studio and live material, have been produced for the insatiable appetites of those touched by and still discovering the legacy of the Grateful Dead. Alongside the recordings, there is an industry of books on the band. Mickey Hart's fascination with drumming has included authoring *Drumming at the Edge of Magic: A Journey into the Spirit of Percussion* (1990) and *Planet Drum: A Celebration of Percussion and Rhythm* (1991).

"The Grateful Dead" is the name of a folktale about a traveler who spends his last penny to pay the debts of a corpse so it can be buried. He is later befriended by one who is revealed to be the ghost of the deceased. Garcia picked the name, feeling it held power. The motif of goodness and its repayment was an underlying theme in the history of the Grateful Dead. They promoted a faith in freedom, a joyous spirit, and a belief in basic human kindness. They treated their fans with respect and donated millions of dollars to environmental causes and social and cultural concerns through their own charitable foundation. They played community-building free concerts and benefit shows.

The Grateful Dead played a unique role in the history of American music. They brought the improvisational aspect of jazz to rock and roll, using it to recast the roots of rock. To these foundations, they added a body of original compositions. Their freewheeling approach to repertoire sources and their exploratory musicianship was picked up on by the JAM BANDS of the 1980s and 1990s, whose fans carried on the type of dedication exhibited by the deadheads.

grunge

Grunge is a form of ALTERNATIVE ROCK that got underway in the late 1980s in the Pacific Northwest, especially Seattle, Washington, and was popular in the 1990s. The rise and fall of grunge is an example, as was San Francisco in the 1960s, of an isolated, local scene that developed away from the scrutiny of major record labels and mass media, and that was discovered, popularized, and exploited in short order. The participants, who never really courted commercialization in the first place, had to deal with its effects.

Grunge, sometimes called the "Seattle sound," came to worldwide attention in the early 1990s with the success of NIRVANA's *Nevermind* (1991), its featured song "Smells Like Teen Spirit," and the song's video. Nirvana and PEARL JAM are the best-known and most successful grunge bands, but other top bands in the style include Soundgarden and Alice in Chains, also based in Seattle; plus Everclear, from Portland, Oregon; Stone Temple Pilots, from San Diego; and the Smashing Pumpkins, from Chicago. Other important Seattle bands were Green River (pioneers whose members went into Mudhoney, Mother Love Bone, and eventually Pearl Jam), the Melvins, Screaming Trees, and some side projects that made only one CD each: Temple of the Dog and Mad Season. Los Angeles had Tool, Hole (led by Courtney Love, who married Kurt Cobain of Nirvana), and Blind Melon, which had three members from Mississippi and which was aligned more with classic rock than grunge. Once grunge became popular, grunge bands were to be found in Australia, in England, and all across North America.

Grunge is a cross between PUNK ROCK and HEAVY METAL, with influences ranging from 1960s rock (the WHO, the BEATLES) to 1980s indie rock (the Pixies), and it can be seen as the antithesis of glam-influenced pop metal (known as "hair metal" for the coiffures of the musicians). The early roots of grunge were in the "Northwest sound" of the 1960s, a style that featured powerful drumming, R&B songs, and screamed vocals. The Wailers were the founders of the Northwest sound, but the Sonics were closest to what became grunge. Grunge used punk's intense singing style but took a more pop-oriented approach to melody and sometimes included harmony singing. It used prominent drumming and slowed-down heavy-metal-type riffs played by guitarists who favored a loud, distorted sound (via effects pedals such as fuzz and wah-wah), and who liked feedback. Though the term *sludge* is often used to describe the sound of grunge, actually it explored a wider range of timbres, at times including other instruments such as acoustic guitar, mandolin, or cello. Nirvana and Alice in Chains released "unplugged" (acoustic) albums, and Stone Temple Pilots performed on the MTV *Unplugged* show.

Depression and low self-esteem were undercurrents in the lyrics, but the anguish was artistically and intelligently channeled into musical form. Organized noise can be pleasing and cathartic at the same time. Teenagers recognized themselves in the lyrics of the grunge bands and identified with them, taking Kurt Cobain of Nirvana and Eddie Vedder of Pearl Jam as spokesmen for a generation (though Cobain was extremely uncomfortable with the role). Grunge appealed to many who were unimpressed by pop idols like Madonna and Michael Jackson. In grunge they found something less manufactured and more unpredictable.

Grunge was supported by local independent record labels and fanzines—photocopied magazines produced by fans whose chief resource was their enthusiasm. Once the scene was discovered by the outside world, it received coverage in the established music press, on television, and on radio (especially college radio). Major labels bought the bands' contracts from the independent labels where they got their start: for example, Nirvana went from Sub Pop to Geffen Records and Soundgarden from Sub Pop to A&M. By then major labels had been alerted to the buzz around the Seattle bands, and Alice in Chains signed directly to Columbia and Pearl Jam to Epic.

The basic grunge outfit was plaid flannel shirts, baseball hats worn backward over long hair, faded and ripped jeans, and bulky shoes or boots. The day-to-day, seemingly careless clothing not only made no concession to glamour (and thus distanced itself from the conventions associated with other rock styles), but it also connected to the Northwest's logging heritage. This antifashion became commercialized in glossy magazines and on fashion runways and was sold in chain stores when grunge became a fad.

The Seattle grunge scene was the backdrop of the film *Singles* (1991), a romantic comedy directed by Cameron Crowe and starring Matt Dillon. The soundtrack is an excellent survey of the style. While it omits Nirvana, it includes Screaming Trees, Alice In Chains, Mudhoney, Chris Cornell (solo and with Soundgarden), Pearl Jam, and Mother Love Bone. The soundtrack also features Jimi Hendrix (a native of Seattle), and the Lovemongers (a side project of Heart, the Seattle rock band led by the Wilson sisters, Ann and Nancy), as well as Paul Westerberg (of the Minnesota band the Replacements). Another notable film is *Hype! Surviving the Northwest Rock Explosion* (1996), a documentary that presents the origins and later developments of the Seattle scene, including early footage of Nirvana, plus other bands, known and obscure.

Soundgarden formed in 1984, making it one of the first bands in what became the grunge scene. The fledgling Sub Pop label put out the band's first records in 1987, and two years later they were the first underground Seattle band to get signed to a major label. Soundgarden featured the wailing voice of Chris Cornell and the imaginative guitar playing of Kim Thayil. They had three million-selling albums. *Badmotorfinger* (1991) included "Rusty Cage" (covered in 1996 by country legend Johnny Cash on *Unchained*). The emotionally raw *Superunknown* (1994) hit number one, sold 5 million copies, and contained their best-known song,

"Black Hole Sun," which has a psychedelic edge. *Superunknown* is an excellent and cohesive set that is full of complex arrangements delivered with a punch. It is not only considered their best, but is one of the best albums of the decade. *Down on the Upside* (1996) is a mature, underrated disc. As the last studio album from the band (which broke up, amicably, the following year), it is seen as the end of the grunge era (though before Kurt Cobain died in 1994, he had been often photographed wearing a "Grunge is Dead" T-shirt). Cornell later joined former Rage Against the Machine members in Audioslave.

Alice in Chains came to grunge from heavy metal. Their sound incorporated odd time signatures and discordant harmonies. Featured members were Jerry Cantrell and Layne Staley. Both sang, played guitar, and wrote songs, though Cantrell was the lead guitarist (and a very fine one), and Staley's tortured voice handled most of the lead vocals. Staley's drug use caused the band to fragment temporarily in the mid-1990s. He took a successful detour with a side project called Mad Season that included one member each from Pearl Jam and Screaming Trees. Five Alice in Chains albums sold a million copies each, including *Dirt* (1992), *Jar of Flies* (1994, a mini-album, the first and only one to reach number one) with "No Excuses," *Alice in Chains* (1995) with "Heaven Beside You," and *MTV Unplugged* (1996). The compilation *Live* (2000) is the last of their charting records. Staley died of a heroin overdose in 2002 at the age of 34.

Stone Temple Pilots, featuring vocalist Scott Weiland, had great success with *Core* (1993), *Purple* (1994), *Tiny Music . . . Songs from the Vatican Gift Shop* (1996), and *No. 4* (1999), all million-selling albums. Accused of being derivative at the start of their career, they developed into a creative force that mixed grunge, alternative, 1960s rock, and even jazz. Weiland later was in Velvet Revolver with three former members of Guns n' Roses.

The Smashing Pumpkins were together from 1988 to 2000. They were led by guitarist and songwriter Billy Corgan, whose breathy, ethereal, and impassioned vocals were supported by the band's fierce barrage of sound. They had a number-one album, the ambitious and diverse *Mellon Collie and the Infinite Sadness* (1995), which spawned several hits, including "1979." The album had many moods and covered many styles. It is, along with the guitar-dominated *Siamese Dream* (1993), among their five albums that made the top 10. In 2000, after releasing their last album and touring in North America, Europe, and the Far East, they played their final shows at the small club where they did their first gig. Fans came from far and near, and tickets sold for about $1,000 each.

Everclear, a trio, formed in Portland, Oregon, in 1992. Their breakthrough album was *Sparkle and Fade* (1996). This, plus the follow up *So Much for the Afterglow* (1997) showed that grunge had room to grow. Art Alexakis plays guitar and sings, in a grainy voice, somewhat autobiographical songs drawn from difficult experiences. Alexakis grew up in a broken home, had an older brother and a first girlfriend who died of heroin overdoses, and survived a lot of moving around, a suicide attempt, and his own drug addiction. Everclear's bassist was Craig Montoya, and its drummer was Greg Eklund. Their best-selling album is *Songs from an American Movie Vol. One: Learning How to Smile* (2000), boosted by its hit single "Wonderful." The song's lyrics portray a child's feelings on watching his parents fighting, fearing their separation and dreading the future. Volume two's subtitle is *Good Time for a Bad Attitude*. Since then they have continued recording and touring, though in 2004, Montoya and Eklund left the band. Alexakis, retaining the Everclear name, brought in other musicians.

Though Alexakis managed to quit drugs before Everclear formed, drugs, especially heroin, were rampant in the grunge scene. Several bands had members who were addicts, like Nirvana and Stone Temple Pilots. Many lost members through lethal overdoses, including Smashing Pumpkins, Mother Love Bone, Mad Season, Hole, Blind Melon, and Alice in Chains. While drugs were decimating the

ranks, the critical backlash against the commercialization and subsequent trivializing of grunge made it less credible.

Musically, by expanding the parameters of the style, bands broke away from the grunge tag (which many hated, musician and fan alike) by fusing it with elements of folk, country, psychedelia, southern rock, progressive rock, jazz, blues, funk, hiphop, soul, and gospel. While the result blurred the concept of grunge as a style, it seems to have been replaced by the idea of grunge as an era: the period from the early 1990s to the mid-1990s. However it is perceived, the influence of it reverberates in the music of later acts, including Alanis Morissette, Creed, Puddle of Mudd, and Nickelback. Of the grunge acts, a few still survive, having developed their individual sound beyond the early sound of grunge. Pearl Jam is thriving, and others, such as Everclear, are still in the running.

guitar

The guitar is the most important instrument in rock and roll. Acoustic guitar is found in ROCKABILLY, with players strumming the way ELVIS PRESLEY did. It is found in FOLK ROCK songs and featured guitar instrumentals like "Embryonic Journey" by Jorma Kaukonen of the JEFFERSON AIRPLANE. There is acoustic guitar in the style of the SINGER-SONGWRITERS and other folk and country influenced rock. Still, the electric guitar is rock's iconic instrument.

Rock guitar has several foundations. Blues, hillbilly, gospel, and folk had all produced original and popular acoustic guitarists. The first electric guitars on the market arrived in 1936. During the next 15 years, notable players such as Charlie Christian in jazz, T-Bone Walker in rhythm and blues, Sister Rosetta Tharpe in gospel, and Lightnin' Hopkins, John Lee Hooker, Muddy Waters, and B. B. King in blues broke a lot of ground. Country music had its innovative players also, including Merle Travis in honky-tonk, Eldon Shamblin (one of Bob Wills' Texas Playboys) in western swing, and Arthur

"Guitar Boogie" Smith. Rock's early electric guitarists were close to their roots.

The first electric guitar solo that is considered rock and roll, according to Jim Dawson and Steve Propes' 1992 book *What Was the First Rock 'n' Roll Record?*, was by Les Paul, who had a country music background but played jazz. It occurs on a 1951 pop version of a jazz standard, "How High the Moon," sung by Paul's wife Mary Ford; the recording is famous for its technological advances using the tape recorder as well. The lead guitarists who played with BILL HALEY also showed a jazz influence. Out of the blues tradition came CHUCK BERRY, rock's prototypical guitar-playing frontman, and BO DIDDLEY, who had ideas from Afro-Cuban and Spanish-American rhythms. Scotty Moore, who played with Elvis Presley, drew from the blues and his country roots, as did the other great guitarists of rockabilly. In the late 1950s Duane Eddy and Link Wray popularized the guitar in the INSTRUMENTAL ROCK field, which was further developed in the early 1960s by the SURF guitarists, starting with Dick Dale. Dale's "Miserlou" was a standout track 30 years later on the soundtrack to the 1994 film *Pulp Fiction*.

With the arrival of the BRITISH INVASION, new guitar players came to prominence. The BEATLES' lead guitarist was George Harrison, whose principal inspirations were CARL PERKINS and Chuck Berry. Harrison's use of the electric 12-string guitar in the Beatles film *A Hard Day's Night* (1964) was influential. In the hands of Jim (later, Roger) McGuinn of the BYRDS, it became a signature sound of folk rock. He popularized the electric 12-string guitar and influenced the sound of Tom Petty and the Heartbreakers and R.E.M., among others. Keith Richards of the ROLLING STONES based his style on those of Chuck Berry, Bo Diddley, and early blues guitarists.

The role of "guitar hero"—a flashy soloist with an impressive command of blues-based licks—was established in the mid-1960s in England. The British blues bands around London were the breeding grounds of a group of great guitarists. Some of the most famous passed through the YARDBIRDS: ERIC CLAPTON, who went to John Mayall's blues band before forming CREAM and having further adventures; Jeff Beck, who led his own band with Rod Stewart as vocalist before making important jazz rock fusion albums in the early 1970s; and Jimmy Page, who started LED ZEPPELIN. Peter Green took Clapton's place in Mayall's band before forming FLEETWOOD MAC, which, in their first incarnation, was perhaps Britain's best blues rock unit.

Upon JIMI HENDRIX's arrival in Britain, his outrageous stage antics and mastery of blues rock guitar both intimidated and inspired other players. His recordings and tours created an indelible impression, and many guitarists, including Robin Trower and Stevie Ray Vaughn, followed his lead; many still do.

In America, Mike Bloomfield, first with Paul Butterfield and then the Electric Flag, was an early guitar hero who started playing with blues veterans around Chicago. Bloomfield was so influential in his playing that his choice of Gibson Les Paul guitars drove up the price of the particular models. From Texas, Johnny Winter, who could not have looked more white (he is an albino), nor sounded more black, was influenced by the Texas blues guitarists. Winter exploded onto the rock scene in 1969. By then many American guitarists had taken the British blues influence into their own music. AEROSMITH started out playing songs by Cream and Fleetwood Mac. SANTANA had a huge hit with Green's composition "Black Magic Woman." Duane Allman of the ALLMAN BROTHERS BAND was strongly influenced by Eric Clapton as well, and they played together on Derek and the Dominos' *Layla* album.

Psychedelic players, who were usually grounded in more than one earlier genre, added a penchant for lengthy improvisations. Among them were Jerry Garcia, with the GRATEFUL DEAD; John Cipollina and Gary Duncan, with Quicksilver Messenger Service; Robbie Kreiger, with the DOORS; and David Gilmour, with PINK FLOYD. Further developments in the history of the guitar in rock are described in the entries on PROGRESSIVE ROCK, HEAVY METAL, PUNK ROCK, GRUNGE, JAM BANDS, and ALTERNATIVE.

Haley, Bill, and His Comets

Bill Haley (1925–1981) was the first rock and roll star. He set the blueprint for the new genre by mixing country with R&B and emphasizing a solid dance beat, hot solos, and lyrics with teen themes and slang. He was the first to put a rock and roll song on the pop charts: "Crazy, Man, Crazy" in 1953. His "Rock Around the Clock" (1954) is the biggest-selling and perhaps best-known rock song of all. In later years his happy, carefree music came to epitomize the good times of early rock and roll and the 1950s.

Haley's career had several phases: the country years (1940s to early 1950s), the early hits on independent labels (1951–53), the move to the Decca label and the hit-making years (to 1960), the relocation to Mexico (in 1961) where he became a star, the lean years (the mid-1960s), and the rock revival (from 1968 onward).

Haley grew up near the town of Chester, Pennsylvania, in a musical home. His father played the banjo, and his mother, who was born in England, played classical piano and gave lessons. A doctor's botched operation when Bill was an infant left him blind in his left eye, and as a result he was shy and self-conscious. This disability precluded military service in World War II. His trademark "kiss curl" (a lock of hair that hung over his forehead), served to distract people from noticing his blind eye. As an adolescent, he was inspired by Gene Autry, the famous singing cowboy movie star. Haley taught himself to sing and yodel and play guitar by imitating songs on the radio. In his teens he enter-tained at local amusement parks and got a spot on a popular radio show.

The first professional group he worked with was the Down Homers (1946–47). In early 1946 they recorded two picture discs for the Vogue label. It was thought until recently that Haley was then part of the group, making this his earliest record and a valuable collector's item. Actually, according to the group's leader, he joined afterward. A recording of a 1946 radio show with this group has recently come to light, and on it Haley plays rhythm guitar, sings backing vocals, and takes the lead on "She Taught Me to Yodel." On returning to Chester after being on the road, Haley hosted a radio show. Years later, in an interview he said that his biggest influence came from rhythm and blues, Dixieland jazz, and country and western records.

Haley formed his own band, the Four Aces of Western Swing (1948–49). They recorded (thus making Haley the first of the rock and roll icons to do so), and their repertoire included cowboy songs, honky-tonk, novelty songs, pop tunes, and comedy numbers. To this repertoire his next band, Bill Haley and the Saddlemen (1950–52), added rhythm and blues. One of their records was "Rocket 88" (1951), a cover of the celebrated R&B song by Jackie Brenston and His Delta Cats, and it was a hit in Philadelphia.

Another R&B cover in 1952 gave them a regional hit: "Rock the Joint," done previously by Jimmy Preston and His Prestonians, a Philadelphia jump blues band. Haley kept "Rock the Joint" in his repertoire for the rest of his life, often performing it as an encore. In 1953 the band, still on the local Essex label but no longer wearing cowboy outfits and now called Bill Haley and Haley's Comets (referring to Halley's comet), had their previously mentioned hit, "Crazy, Man, Crazy."

On the strength of that, Decca, a major label, contracted the group—henceforth known as Bill Haley and His Comets—for two songs, which were recorded in April 1954. One was "Rock Around the Clock." The studio was in a converted ballroom in New York City, whose high ceilings provided a resonant acoustic space. The producer was Milt Gabler, who had worked with jazz stars such as Billie Holiday, Louis Armstrong, and Ella Fitzgerald. Gabler had also produced the top R&B star Louis Jordan and His Tympany Five, who had been a huge success in the 1940s and had left Decca just the year before. Gabler would produce Haley's classic Decca recordings from 1954 to 1959, plus two more songs in an attempted comeback in 1964.

"Rock Around the Clock" was a brilliant-sounding record, and the performance has never been bettered despite a multitude of cover versions. The crack of the snare, the slapping of the bass, the urgency of Haley's vocal, the immediacy of the lyrics, and the astonishing guitar solo all portrayed the enthusiasm that was summed up in the word *rock*. It was unique, and it was a modest hit, selling 75,000 copies. That was enough for Decca to sign them for more recordings.

For their follow-up, Haley and his group reworked BIG JOE TURNER's "Shake, Rattle and Roll." They cleaned up the lyrics and changed the R&B feel to rock and roll. It made the top 10 in July 1954, and was the first rock and roll song to sell a million copies.

Then "Rock Around the Clock" had another turn. The songwriting credit for it is shared by two men. Max Freedman was a Tin Pan Alley songwriter who had cowritten the hit "Sioux City Sue" in 1945. "Jimmy DeKnight" was a pseudonym for James E. Myers, a self-promoting bandleader and drummer from Philadelphia. After serving in World War II, Myers entered the record and publishing business.

His role in the writing of "Rock Around the Clock" may have been as little as suggesting that "rock" would sound better than "dance" in the title. What Myers did with it after it was written is more important: he got it placed in the 1955 film *Blackboard Jungle*. One year after it was recorded, "Rock Around the Clock" was on the market again, as the movie's theme song.

The film is about a teacher who tries to communicate with his students who are juvenile delinquents. In one scene they smash his jazz records, which he brought to school to play for them. In *Blackboard Jungle*, rock and roll, in the form of "Rock Around the Clock," was presented as the background music of youth rebelling against authority. Movie audiences made the connection and rallied to the call. Newspapers reported incidents of attendees dancing in theater aisles and, in some places, tearing up the seats. *Blackboard Jungle* popularized "Rock Around The Clock" and it became rock and roll's international anthem. In 1955 it topped the charts in both the United States and the United Kingdom. Over the years, 25 million records of "Rock Around the Clock" have been sold, an unmatched achievement.

Hollywood got on the rock and roll bandwagon. The first of the so-called rock exploitation pictures was *Rock Around the Clock* (1956), in which Bill Haley and His Comets perform six songs. In *Don't Knock the Rock* (1956) they do four.

In February 1957 Haley became the first American rocker to tour England. On his arrival in London, he and his band were mobbed by fans. He made many return visits, and is still remembered there as an icon. He had an impact on a whole generation, among them the BEATLES and Graham Nash (later in the Hollies and in Crosby, Stills and Nash), who fondly remembers Haley's 1957 show in Manchester. During Haley's difficult tour of Europe in 1958, a riot at a show in Berlin nearly halted all momentum. That year, "Skinny Minnie," using a BO DIDDLEY beat, was his last big hit in the States.

The German label Bear Family has released two box sets documenting phases of his career. *The

Decca Years and More (five CDs) includes all the hits and dozens of lesser-known 1950s tracks, some excellent and some dire. Haley applied his rock and roll style to old pop tunes and standards, folk tunes from many countries, and numerous instrumentals, such as his last two hits. *The Warner Brothers Years and More* (six CDs) covers the recordings made in the United States in the 1960s. Despite financial and marital problems and some difficulty in keeping musicians, he continued to perform internationally. His tenure at Warner Brothers was brief; after leaving that label, he then recorded for various small labels. The recordings show his versatility, and include country standards, covers of rock and roll classics, some unusual instrumentals, and different backup bands, from contemporary rock to mariachi. The box set also includes some live recordings. At Haley's show at Madison Square Garden in 1969, he received a standing ovation of nearly 10 minutes.

Not included in these box sets are the recordings done outside of the United States. Haley moved to Mexico (far from tax collectors and divorce lawyers), and recorded there from 1961 to 1966. He sang in Spanish, had many hit records, and was the country's most popular purveyor of the twist. In 1968 he started recording for the Swedish label Sonet.

In 1974 "Rock Around the Clock" charted again in the United States, boosted by Bill Haley and His Comets' performance in *Let the Good Times Roll* (1973), a rock revival concert film, and by its presence on the soundtracks of *American Graffiti* (1973) and as the theme song to the new hit TV series *Happy Days*. The song also charted again that year in the United Kingdom, having already recharted there in 1956 and 1968.

Bill Haley and His Comets (Michael Ochs Archives.com)

The band's stage act was a fast-paced variety show leavened with comedy, as Haley shared the spotlight with his talented musicians, all dressed in plaid dinner jackets. The best-known was Rudy Pompilli, who played sax (and sometimes clarinet or flute) on almost all the studio recordings and live shows from 1955 to 1975. His wild sax playing was featured regularly, and "Rudy's Rock" was a hit for Bill Haley and His Comets in 1956. Pompilli also acted as the band's manager, dealing with the pay and the hiring and firing of musicians. Another attraction was the acrobatic acoustic bass playing, as done by Marshall Lytle or Al Rex, with the player riding the instrument or holding it over his head or above him while lying down. Guitarists were also featured, such as Danny Cedrone, who created the fabulous guitar solo on "Rock Around the Clock" but who died a few months after it was recorded. Frank "Franny" Beecher, who had played guitar with Benny Goodman, took his place and was often showcased with instrumentals like "Guitar Boogie" and "Steel Guitar Rag."

In 1976 Rudy Pompilli died of cancer. Haley was disconsolate to lose his right-hand man, his sax player of 20 years. Haley kept playing for a while, but his heart was not in it. He then stopped for more than two years, living quietly and not thinking much about fame or music. When he returned, Haley found it hard to work with other sax players. Alcoholism and the effects of a brain tumor led to erratic behavior onstage and off, though he rose to the occasion for some good final recordings and a 1979 comeback tour of Europe, which included a command performance before Queen Elizabeth II.

Near the end of his life, in Mexico or at a residence in Texas when not on the road, he became paranoid and deluded. He made bizarre and unnerving phone calls, ranting for hours in the middle of the night, to former associates in Pennsylvania. In 1981, he died in his Texas home, of natural causes attributed to a heart attack. Despite his poor health, he had been working on an autobiographical project, and there were plans for a new record and a tour of Germany.

Since Haley's death, several groups have carried on his sound. Some were short-lived reunions, others had tenuous links to Haley. Three acts, all with official pedigrees, were performing in the 2000s. Drummer John Lane was a Comet (from 1965 to 1968), as was bassist Al Rappa (from 1959 to 1969). They worked together touring North America in the early 1980s as Bill Haley's Comets. A few years later they parted, each to head his own touring Comets group.

Because Rappa holds the rights to use the Comets name and that of Bill Haley, another group, formed for a reunion show in 1987, has had to skirt around the issue. This band includes five 1950s Comets. Four were in the band back in 1951: bassist Marshall Lytle, pianist Johnny Grande, saxophonist Joey D'Ambrosio, and drummer Dick Richards. All but Richards were on "Rock Around the Clock." Franny Beecher joined Haley in 1955, and now, in his 80s, still amazes audiences with his guitar playing. They have worked under various names, such as the Original Comets, the 1954–55 Comets, Tribute to Bill Haley Featuring his Original Comets, or just the Original Band. Whatever they are called, this group, truly the oldest rock and roll band in the world, has received much attention and been given rave reviews by the rockabilly revivalists and nostalgia fans. They have revived many old songs and added new ones. One of those, from their fifth CD, called *Aged To Perfection* (2002), is "Viagra Rock," which received a lot of radio play.

Bill Haley was first. His music was made to be danced to and teenagers loved it. He carried the torch for rock and roll, and his former band members have done the same into the 21st century.

Though international fans still regard Haley as rock royalty, in the United States his stature is smaller. Many rock critics assert that he just happened to be at the right place at the right time. When younger, more dynamic and unorthodox stars like LITTLE RICHARD, ELVIS PRESLEY, and CHUCK BERRY arrived, so their logic goes, Haley was shown to be what he was, a chubby, unsexy, middle-aged man who got lucky and was pushed aside by the more authentic rock and roll artists. True, Haley was less glamorous, and he was almost 10 years older than Elvis, for example, but pioneers have no rules to follow or expectations to live up to. Bill Haley and His Comets came out of the earliest sources of rock and roll and maintained traditions of precise, crowd-pleasing professional concerts. If rock and roll can have an establishment, they were it. But teenagers and even their parents bought their records, and those records proved to have timeless appeal.

Bill Haley and His Comets are getting reevaluated as impressive live concert recordings show up, such as a 1955 show in Cleveland, some songs from the Olympia Theatre in Paris in 1958, and Armed Forces Radio broadcasts from 1962. Bill Haley is in the Rock and Roll Hall of Fame, but the Comets are not, an omission that current fans are hoping can be rectified.

heavy metal

One of the most durable of rock styles, it emerged as a less blues-influenced branch of hard rock in the early 1970s and developed into something more brutal. The term was first used in print in the early 1960s novels of William Burroughs, though its use in connection with a music style stems from a line in STEPPENWOLF's "Born to Be Wild" (1968). From its beginnings in England, it has spread and permutated into many substyles, such as hair metal and thrash metal (also known as speed metal), both strong in Los Angeles, and black metal, death metal, and nü metal. Metal also influenced hardcore PUNK ROCK and ALTERNATIVE ROCK and contributed to the formation of GRUNGE. The JIMI HENDRIX Experience, Deep Purple, and LED ZEPPELIN—all bands that formed in the 1960s—were essential influences on heavy metal and are themselves sometimes considered as part of the style. They can, however, as readily be considered hard rock.

Metal is loud rock that features fiery instrumental technique, guitar riffs, powerful vocals, a warrior-like energy (its participants and audience are almost exclusively male), and commonly has morbid, even disturbing, lyrics. Its underlying dread derives from a sense of diminished hope for humanity, and its rise in the early 1970s coincided with the fading of the hippie dream of utopia. Metal lyrics are imbued with forebodings of doom expressed in apocalyptic metaphors and sinister ideas of power often expressed in satanic images. Difficult and contentious aspects of society—war, politics, religion, drugs, morality, and environmental deterioration—are addressed with intelligence and cynicism.

These concerns are underscored in band names and album titles. Associations with death are seen, for example, in Slayer (*Reign in Blood*), Megadeth (*Rust in Peace, Countdown to Extinction*), and Metallica's *Kill 'Em All;* with religion in Black Sabbath (*Heaven and Hell*), Judas Priest, Helloween, and *Shout at the Devil* by Mötley Crüe; with madness in *Diary of a Madman* and *Bark at the Moon* by Ozzy Osborne, and *Operation Mindcrime* by Queensrÿche; with violence in *Appetite for Destruction* by Guns n' Roses and *Tooth and Nail* by Dokken; with toxins in Poison and Anthrax and with stings in Scorpions, Venom, and W.A.S.P.; with vermin in Ratt (*Out of the Cellar*); and with hardship in Skid Row.

Fans of heavy metal are known as metalheads or headbangers (for the common practice of nodding the head in time to the music). Fans declare their allegiances and express their fierce loyalty to particular bands by wearing T-shirts and patches emblazoned with their logos and album cover artwork. They draw versions of the same on notebooks, desks, and jean jackets. Album covers often feature a painting of archetypal figures or scenes. A band's image is expressed in these visual arenas, as well as by their looks and costumes, their stage props and production, and, of course, their lyrics and musical style. Image is an essential part of how they position themselves within the genre and differentiate themselves from their competitors in the marketplace.

Metal's instrumentation is typical for many other types of rock: DRUMS, BASS, and a GUITAR or two, plus perhaps keyboards. Guitarists have fast and intricate playing styles, and, building on the innovations of JIMI HENDRIX and Jimmy Page, explore various sonic effects and tricks. Some of these involve dexterous use of the hand, such as palm-muting, or fingers, such as harmonics and tapping (the hammering-on of notes high on the guitar neck with the picking hand, which allows for fast arpegiating and leaps); some come from the exploitation of guitar design such as tremolo ("whammy") bars that raise and lower the pitch; and others from effects devices such as wah-wah pedals and amplifier manipulations. Some of these approaches are adopted by bassists as well. Drummers play muscularly on expansive kits that sometimes include two bass drums. Singers have stylized, forceful voices, and sing with dramatic emphasis, from a growl to a high-pitched wail.

The line of pure metal runs from Black Sabbath to Iron Maiden, which is to say, from the start of metal in the early 1970s to what is known as the New Wave of British Heavy Metal (abbreviated as NWOBHM) in the late 1970s and early 1980s. Black Sabbath, whose name refers to witchcraft, wrote on many themes, including the occult, but unlike some later bands they were not Satanists. Their second album, *Paranoid* (1971), with its screamed vocals, ponderous tempos, and lyrics about madness and society's ills, is cited as one of the records that laid out the blueprint for heavy metal. The members at the time were vocalist Ozzy Osborne, guitarist Tony Iommi, drummer Bill Ward, and bassist Geezer Butler. *Paranoid* sold millions (as did several other of their records), and it contained their only two radio hits: "Paranoid" and "Iron Man." Despite many changes in lineup over the years, Black Sabbath (and Ozzy Osborne in his solo career) has influenced hundreds of bands.

The New Wave of British Heavy Metal, a phrase created by a magazine in the 1970s, referred to younger bands that were less commercially slick and more threatening and primal than the likes of Led Zeppelin and Black Sabbath. Iron Maiden made a series of classic metal albums such as *Number of the Beast* (1982), *Piece of Mind* (1983), and *Powerslave* (1984). Def Leppard had many million-selling albums, including *Hysteria* (1987) which spawned the number-one pop ballad "Love Bites" and six other chart hits. AC/DC was from Australia but moved to the United Kingdom in 1976. With *Back in Black* (1980), created while mourning the death of their original vocalist Bon Scott, they made one of heavy metal's most celebrated records, and one of the biggest-selling albums ever. Motörhead's loud and fast style was more influential than record sales indicate: it pointed the way to both thrash metal, and, by attracting punk fans, hardcore. Judas Priest had a string of gold and platinum albums, including *Screaming for Vengeance* (1982), and they popularized the concept of two guitarists in a heavy metal band as well as what became typical metal attire: leather, studs, and spikes. Also involved were regionally famous or lesser-known bands, such as Angel Witch and Diamond Head and, later on, Venom. In this phase metal was influenced by punk's energy, and metal songs were shorter, faster, and less self-indulgent, with lots of power chords and speedy guitar solos.

"Hair metal" is a somewhat derogatory term for macho, heterosexual 1980s bands whose elaborate coiffures were a major part of their image. To metal they added elements of GLAM ROCK (androgyny expressed in hair, makeup, and costumes) and pop (love songs, the slow ones known as power ballads). Los Angeles was the center of hair metal, and many of the city's bands had great success. Van Halen, a hard rock band whose image was partly hair metal, was innovative, especially the guitar style of Eddie Van Halen. His guitar solo feature "Eruption" (1978) inspired guitarists to greater heights and helped usher in a classical influence (also seen in the playing of Ritchie Blackmore, formerly of Deep Purple, Randy Rhoads with Ozzy Osborne, and Yngwie Malmsteen). Every album Van Halen made from 1978 to 1998 made the top 10, except their debut, which made the top 20. While they and Mötley Crüe, Ratt, Poison, and Guns n' Roses hit the mainstream with their pop metal, purists disapproved.

More to the taste of metal purists were the bands that played thrash or speed metal, a style influenced by the NWOBHM as well as by punk, with METALLICA, Megadeth, Anthrax, and Slayer among the top bands. Metallica's *Master of Puppets* (1986) established the style as commercially viable. Slayer's obsession with death and satanic imagery inspired a new substyle called death metal, which featured down-tuned guitars, fast drumming that favored double-pedaled bass drums, and vocalists who screamed or growled almost unintelligible lyrics. Death metal expanded after the mid-1980s with such bands as Possessed, Celtic Frost, Sepultura, Morbid Angel, Obituary, Massacra, Death, Entombed, Sodom, Master, Deicide, and Cannibal Corpse.

In the late 1980s a bleak variation of death metal called grindcore was epitomized by Napalm Death. Around the same time, a mechanical type of metal called industrial metal incorporated electronic instruments (drum machines and synthesizers). Industrial metal bands include the Swans, Killing Joke, Skinny Puppy, Ministry, Nine Inch Nails (led by Trent Reznor, whose lyrics expressed hate and anger), and Fear Factory.

The next wave, a more extreme and savage style called black metal, came in the early 1990s, especially with bands from northern Europe, such as Samael, from Switzerland; Bathory, from Sweden; and Mayhem, from Norway. Venom's fast, distorted sound and occult fascination was a forerunner; their *Black Metal* (1982) album gave the style its name. Black metal's uncompromising stance and fundamental nihilism was expressed in dissonance and distortion and a kind of drumming called blast beat. Vocalists affected hoarse, snarling guttural singing and lyrics obsessed with death, suffering, and disease. Image was vital for many bands, with a type of makeup called corpse paint, and costumes included armor and weapons that recalled the Dark Ages. By the end of the 1990s, black metal was flirting with melody and diverse influences from folk to electronic while remaining distant from mainstream tastes. Another gloomy style was called doom metal. It was eerie with a gothic atmosphere, using slow tempos, orchestral song structure, and operatic female vocalists alongside growling death metal-style male singers.

Alternative metal, also called funk metal, took influence from African-American rhythms (bands include Primus, Ugly Kid Joe, and Red Hot Chili Peppers), but it was nü metal that found the most commercial success in the 1990s with a mix of metal and rap. Precedents were the collaborations done by Run-D.M.C., whose 1986 remake of AEROSMITH's "Walk This Way" included Aerosmith's vocalist and guitarist, and Anthrax's cover of Public Enemy's "Bring the Noise" with Public Enemy's Chuck D. Nü metal features jerky drumming, heavily distorted guitars tuned lower than concert pitch, and rap-influenced vocals. Rage Against the Machine was a bridge from the 1980s to nü metal bands of the 1990s, such as Korn, Deftones, and Limp Bizkit.

In fulfilling its mandate as hard-driving, antisocial rock, heavy metal has changed with the times, incorporating influences from all over. It has vacillated from the conventionally attractive to the repulsive, yet has always found, from Europe to Japan, a seemingly insatiable audience for its intensity. Despite or perhaps because of its bombastic presentations and its fixations on the morbid side of life—which make it a target for parody, as in the 1984 movie *This Is Spinal Tap*—it has proved to be vital as a social and musical force. Its malleability and resilience indicate that it will likely continue to thrive, even if other styles may wither.

Hendrix, Jimi (1942–1970) *innovative guitarist*

Though he died in 1970, Jimi Hendrix is still universally acclaimed as rock's greatest and most inventive guitarist. When he burst onto the scene in London in fall 1966, it seemed like he came out of nowhere (actually, he had been backing up R&B musicians across America for years). In England his explosive GUITAR playing and dynamic stage antics thrilled audiences and intimidated the established players, including ERIC CLAPTON and Pete Townshend (of the WHO).

Hendrix made hit singles and recorded three acclaimed studio albums. From his first public performance with the Jimi Hendrix Experience in October 1966 to his last, shortly before he died, he played constantly, with barely a month off: more than 500 documented shows, including the two most legendary ROCK FESTIVALS, Monterey and WOODSTOCK. His tours took him all over the United Kingdom, to almost a dozen European countries, to 34 U.S. states, and into Canada. Hendrix revolutionized electric guitar playing and influenced almost everyone who heard him, from a whole generation of rock contemporaries to Miles Davis, George Clinton, and Stevie Ray Vaughn.

Four years almost to the day that he first arrived in London, he died there at age 27. The cause, as noted on the death certificate, was inhalation of vomit due to barbiturate intoxication. Although the conflicting details surrounding his death have led to much speculation, it is considered accidental, not suicide. His career can be divided into five phases: the formative period, the R&B years, the time with the Jimi Hendrix Experience, the final year of his life, and the posthumous legacy.

He was born in Seattle, Washington. His name at birth was John Allen Hendrix, but at the age of three it was changed to James Marshall Hendrix when his father, who had not been consulted about the choice of name, returned from serving in the U.S. Army. Jimmy, as he was known, was nine when his parents divorced, and he was raised by his father, although he still saw his mother occasionally. He became enamored of his dad's blues and R&B records, and went to see ELVIS PRESLEY when he came to Seattle in 1957. In 1958 when Hendrix was 15, his mother died of a ruptured spleen, the result of long-term alcoholism. That summer he took up the guitar, playing left-handed on a right-handed instrument held upside down. Soon he was practicing with friends, learning songs from 45s, such as Ray Charles' "What'd I Say." When they started to play teenage dances at recreation centers, Hendrix got an electric

guitar. He joined and gigged with the Rocking Kings and other local bands. Friends remembered him as shy, kind, and crazy about the guitar.

He dropped out of high school, and then got picked up by the police for riding in a car that a buddy had stolen. In 1961 he joined the army, later training in the 101st Airborne as a paratrooper. He did about 25 parachute jumps. While in the service he met and played in a band with bassist Billy Cox. In 1962, after Hendrix broke his ankle during a jump, he was honorably discharged. With Cox, he then began playing around the South.

This began the second phase, which lasted until mid-1966. Under the name Jimmy James, he served his musical apprenticeship on the so-called chitlin circuit as a sideman for top R&B acts, including LITTLE RICHARD, the Isley Brothers, Ike and Tina Turner, and Don Covay, as well as Joey Dee and the Starliters, best known for "Peppermint Twist." He also played guitar in a touring package show headed by Sam Cooke that included Jackie Wilson, the Valentinos (with Bobby Womack), Chuck Jackson, and B. B. King. Hendrix recorded with some of them, as well as others such as Curtis Knight, King Curtis, and Lonnie Youngblood. Youngblood remembered him as a carefree person and exceptional musician who liked to practice and could energize the band but was too shy to enjoy being out front. Hendrix signed contracts rather indiscriminately during this period that would haunt him later. After he became famous, these early sessions (along with some bogus recordings) were marketed in a multitude of guises. Few of them provide much insight into what Hendrix would soon become. One of the most notable, and certainly the most successful of these recordings with Hendrix as a sideman, is Don Covay's "Mercy Mercy," a top-40 hit in 1964.[10]

This phase ended in summer 1966 when Hendrix met his future manager Chas Chandler. Hendrix, then in New York City, had decided to sing and front his own band, called Jimmy James and the Blue Flames, a quartet that included 15-year-old Randy California (who would later form Spirit in Los

Angeles). They played in Greenwich Village for little money, doing blues and R&B injected with feedback, and quickly developed a following. Sometimes they worked with blues singer John Hammond. Linda Keith, girlfriend of Keith Richards, was very impressed by Hendrix and brought several music business people to see him. None shared her enthusiasm until she brought Chas Chandler, the bassist from the ANIMALS, who were about to break up. Chandler wanted to get into management, and persuaded Hendrix to move to London—it was at this time that they agreed to change the spelling of his name to Jimi. In London they auditioned players for the Jimi Hendrix Experience, choosing two younger musicians: Noel Redding, a guitarist who switched to bass, and Mitch Mitchell, a jazzy drummer who had played R&B with Georgie Fame's Blue Flames. Chandler took on a comanager, helped organize the repertoire, and produced the recordings, engineered by Eddie Kramer, who worked with Hendrix from this point on.

During this third period, from fall 1966 to mid-1969, with the Jimi Hendrix Experience, he did most of his best work. They blended the American and British approaches to blues, R&B, and soul with the power trio energy of the Who and CREAM (who had formed just before the Experience), and the emerging psychedelic style, creating an exciting form of pop. The British rock audience, so deeply influenced by black American music, was bowled over to hear a black American player who had mastered those styles and pushed them further using rock's vocabulary.

The first gig they played was in Paris. It came at the invitation of Johnny Halliday, a big star in France who had seen Hendrix play in a London club and asked him to open his show at the Olympia Theatre. After much touring, the Experience made their American debut at the MONTEREY POP FESTIVAL in June 1967. As seen in the film *Monterey Pop*, Hendrix and the band give a powerful performance, including his showman tricks of playing guitar with his teeth and behind his back. For the set's climax, in an ritual with erotic overtones, he laid his guitar (still noisily

Jimi Hendrix Experience (Michael Ochs Archives.com)

feeding back) on the stage, kneeled it front of it, squirted lighter fluid on it, and set it on fire. It is one of rock's indelible images and legendary moments. The festival appearance created a sensation, and with his recordings selling well and incessant touring, Hendrix was soon a star in America.

The breakup of the Experience in 1969—Chandler had already withdrawn—marks the start of the fourth phase, which lasted until the death of Hendrix a little more than a year later. He experimented with different kinds of music and recorded prolifically, but was unable to focus on making a new album. His personal life was confused and his professional affairs were in disarray: there were problems with finances and contracts and frustrations with management. Increased drug use did not help. At the end of the year, Hendrix formed Band of Gypsys to try a funkier direction. It was an all-black trio, with his old friend Billy Cox on bass and

Buddy Miles, from the Electric Flag, on drums and vocals. The group was unsatisfying and played only a few gigs, though the antiwar "Machine Gun" from the live *Band of Gypsys* (1970) is one of his top recordings, even if the album was released to fulfill an obligation from an old contract.

Hendrix retained Cox and brought Mitch Mitchell back, and began working on a new record to be called *First Rays of the New Rising Sun.* It was never finished, though a reconstructed version came out in 1997. The band was augmented with additional players at Woodstock. Their last big show—performing again as a trio—was in August 1970 at England's Isle of Wight festival. Hendrix's exhaustion was apparent, as was the gap between his desire to continue to experiment musically and the audience's expectations for outrageous stage behavior.

Jimi Hendrix has many well-known songs. "Hey Joe," "Purple Haze," and "The Wind Cries Mary," his first three singles, all made the top 10 in the United Kingdom. "Hey Joe" was a song he had done in Greenwich Village. Previously it was a hit for the Leaves (the first to record it), and most of the other Los Angeles bands also did it, including the BYRDS, but Hendrix's slowed-down, definitive version, was based on the one by folksinger Tim Rose. "Purple Haze," with its strident opening and intense solo, was his first American hit. Its title allegedly refers to a type of LSD, and it contains one of his most famous lines, "'Scuse me while I kiss the sky." "The Wind Cries Mary," like "Purple Haze" and most of his studio output, was an original composition and showed another side of his writing: gentle and lyrical. All three songs were included on the American release of his debut album, *Are You Experienced* (1967).

The delicate "Little Wing" (an often-covered song) and "If Six Was Nine" (used in the film *Easy Rider*) come from *Axis: Bold As Love* (1967). On this album his writing showed more depth, and there was greater variety of musical styles, along with some impressive studio manipulations.

"All Along the Watchtower" and "Voodoo Chile" come from *Electric Ladyland* (1968), a more eclectic

work augmented by other musicians, including members of Traffic and JEFFERSON AIRPLANE. The playing, songwriting, arrangements, and production are all splendid on this celebrated double album. The Hendrix recording of BOB DYLAN's "All Along the Watchtower" (1968) is the definitive version; even Dylan later adopted Hendrix's arrangement. Hendrix was very inspired by Dylan, whom he met briefly in the Village, from the poetry and symbolism in his lyrics to his frizzy hairstyle. Hendrix covered three other Dylan songs: "Like a Rolling Stone," "Drifters Escape," and "Can You Please Crawl Out Your Window?"

To hear the Hendrix version of "The Star Spangled Banner" that he performed at Woodstock is to hear a nightmarish interpretation that seemed to symbolize, in its violent screeches and thunderous dive bomb effects, the nation's anguish over the war in Vietnam, the race riots, and the generational struggles of the 1960s. It was something he had been working on for almost two years. He had incorporated the theme into performances of "Purple Haze," and then into a suite that he introduced as "This Is America," which also included a bit of the theme song of *Bonanza,* a TV western. The Woodstock performance came at the close of the festival. Most of the audience had already left, but "Star Spangled Banner" was widely heard, as it was included in the film and on its soundtrack album.

After Hendrix died, Eddie Kramer organized much of the unreleased material in a series of albums. The live ones and the first with studio tracks were the most impressive, but after a while the barrel was fairly well scraped. In the mid-1970s Alan Douglas, who had been a friend of Jimi's, was brought in, and during the next two decades he had new parts overdubbed onto some unfinished material, a controversial effort. An album he compiled of Hendrix's blues recordings was better received. In July 1995 Al Hendrix gained control of his son's estate, with Jimi's sister Janie Hendrix-Wright acting as executor. This move was made with the financial and legal help of Microsoft cofounder Paul Allen, who was behind the Experience Music

Project, a lavish museum in Seattle dedicated to Hendrix's memory and the history of rock and roll. Kramer was brought back into the fold, and a major reissuing program began in 1997. It included remastering, reorganizing posthumous releases, and a box set of live and previously unreleased tracks and rarities.

From his foundation in the blues, Hendrix took the electric guitar into new territory. Not only was he a virtuoso technically, but with his Fender Stratocaster tuned slightly low and strung with light-gauge strings that facilitated bending, and a bank of amplifiers, typically Marshalls, he created new sounds. He exploited feedback, distortion, and effects pedals (like the newly invented wah-wah). He infused these sounds with the kind of inspiration, sophistication, and emotional range that was occasionally found in jazz or blues but previously unknown in rock. In addition, he was an excellent songwriter who could arouse passion or use science fiction, fantasy, and spirituality to reflect philosophically on the nature of life. Despite his insecurity as a vocalist, he became an engaging and effective one.

Besides the massive amounts of Hendrix recordings on the market, there is a seemingly endless number of other forms of tribute to his influence: books, magazines, Web sites, documentaries, exhibits, conferences, tribute bands, and, as always, young musicians who want to play like him.

Holly, Buddy (1936–1959) *influential singer and songwriter*

The basic description is that Buddy Holly was a bandleading, guitar-playing singer from a conservative town in Texas called Lubbock. His originality and innovations were presented in cleverly simple love songs of beguiling honesty. He changed the course of rock and roll and he died at age 22 in a plane crash while on tour. Who he was, what he did, and what happened to him have been covered in great detail. What he meant and still means to people is harder to describe. Buddy Holly is one of the great musical icons of the 20th century. His legacy has been celebrated in print, recordings, concerts, plays, films, and festivals.

The Buddy Holly Story (1978) was a popular Hollywood film that helped to create Holly's reputation and build the legend. Gary Busey did an excellent job in the title role and actually performed the music, rather than lip-synching. The film's celebratory mood was appreciated, but it played with the facts of Holly's life, even substituting fictional characters for his producer and fellow musicians. So Paul McCartney, whose band the BEATLES was named in reference to Holly's Crickets, and who later acquired the publishing rights to Holly's compositions, financed the making of the documentary *The Real Buddy Holly Story* (1987). In it, Holly's kin, members of the Crickets, the EVERLY BROTHERS, and other people who had known him, were interviewed and the historical record was set straight. It also presented most of the known film footage of Holly in performance.

In his youth he and his two brothers played music and took lessons. Buddy tried out violin, piano, mandolin, and banjo, but settled on the guitar. He and Bob Montgomery, his first musical partner, did country songs by honky-tonk and bluegrass artists and some of their own. Calling themselves Buddy and Bob, both playing acoustic guitar and singing in the brother duet tradition, they performed on the radio and recorded some demos as early as 1952. The act was sometimes augmented by friends, including future Crickets Sonny Curtis on fiddle and guitar, and, by 1955, Jerry Allison on drums. (Curtis would not be in the Crickets until after Holly's death.) When ELVIS PRESLEY's records came out, and he then came to Lubbock to perform, Holly, like other musicians, were mightily impressed and shifted from country to ROCKABILLY. Allison, Curtis, and bassist Don Guess accompanied Holly on 1956 recordings made under contract for Decca in Nashville, including an early version of "That'll Be the Day," but the label did not yet comprehend the emerging rock and roll market, instead seeing them as a country act. Decca released two singles that went nowhere and did not pick up the option

Buddy Holly and the Crickets (Michael Ochs Archives.com)

to renew the contract. Holly was devastated but determined to try again.

He had already met Norman Petty, almost 10 years his senior, with whom he would make his classic records. Petty was a bandleader who had set up a home studio with modern equipment in his hometown of Clovis, New Mexico, after making some money in 1954 with a pop version of the Duke Ellington composition "Mood Indigo." Petty had intended it for his own use, that is, to record his trio, which included his wife Vi, but studios were rare in the region, and he had began making demos and vanity recordings for younger musicians, which

is how Holly met him. ROY ORBISON had cut "Ooby Dooby" there and it was a local hit, leading him to a contract with the Sun label of Memphis, where he redid the song and had a national hit with it. Another song, also recorded in 1956, became a number-one hit the next year when picked up by the Roulette label of New York City: "Party Doll" by Buddy Knox and the Rhythm Orchids. With few options, Holly returned in 1957 to Clovis, 100 miles northeast of Lubbock, to do more demos.

He redid "That'll Be the Day," backed by Allison on drums and his old friend Larry Welborn on bass. In exchange for Petty's studio time and to entice him to shop for an established label to release the song, Holly cut Petty in on the songwriting and publishing credits. He had little to lose and the possibility of something to gain. Petty tried his contacts in New York, and, after several rejections, managed to place it with Brunswick, a low-profile but artistically independent subsidiary of, ironically, Decca. The demo version was released and eventually climbed to number one in the United States and the United Kingdom. Because a clause in the old Decca contract forbid an artist to record for another company material already recorded for Decca, the band—which had solidified as Holly, Allison, bassist Joe B. Mauldin, and second guitarist Nikki Sullivan—chose the name Crickets. The clause was intended to protect the songs already recorded but did not restrict the artist from finding a new home, so Petty negotiated a separate contract under Buddy Holly's own name, since he was obviously the star of the band, for the Coral label, another subsidiary of Decca. By releasing records under the name the Crickets (which generally had background vocals) on one label, and as by Buddy Holly (which generally did not) on another, the act could gain double the exposure. In the recording process, the musicians did not differentiate between the two entities: what was released under which moniker was decided later.

The ploy worked. "Peggy Sue" and "Oh, Boy!" soon followed "That'll Be the Day" into the top 10. While Holly was alive, a total of 10 songs charted: five by the Crickets, four by Buddy Holly, and one with Jerry Allison singing, issued under his middle name, Ivan. Among them were "Maybe Baby," "Rave On," and "Heartbeat." Besides the prolific recording of his own songs, Holly also recorded songs written by Chuck Berry, Fats Domino, Roy Orbison, Bobby Darin, Little Richard, Paul Anka, and Felice and Boudleaux Bryant, composers of many hits for the Everly Brothers.

In fall 1957 Buddy Holly and the Crickets raised their profile by touring almost nonstop for three months across the United States and in Canada. At the end of the year, Sullivan quit the band, tired of the road. The others continued as a trio, touring through most of 1958, in the United States, in Australia, and in the United Kingdom. They also appeared several times on television shows hosted by Dick Clark, Ed Sullivan, and Arthur Murray, and on shows in London.

In late 1958 Holly parted with the Crickets, moved to New York, and married Maria Santiago. He also broke off his business dealings with Norman Petty, unsatisfied with his financial accounting. In his last months Holly's musical evolution had completely passed through rockabilly into pop, especially ballads. He veered toward the smoother, lighter (and whiter) vocal sounds of the Everlys, Bobby Darin, and Paul Anka. Holly's last recordings—solo demos of a dozen new songs and favorites recorded in his New York apartment—are reflective and mostly slow in tempo.

With a new backup group that included future country star Waylon Jennings, at the end of January 1959 Holly joined a touring package called Winter Dance Party. Also on the bill were Dion and the Belmonts, Ritchie Valens, the Big Bopper, and the now-forgotten Frankie Sardo. They did 11 dates in a row through the Midwest. After the February 2 show at the Surf Ballroom in Clear Lake, Iowa, Holly, Valens, and the Big Bopper, fed up with the breakdowns and heating problems in the tour bus, boarded a chartered plane to fly to the next stop. They never made it. In snowy weather, the plane crashed minutes after takeoff, and they and the pilot were all killed. This event was immortalized as "the day the music died" in Don McLean's number one song "American Pie" (1971). Amid international mourning, Holly's "It Doesn't Matter Anymore," recorded the month before in New York with a string orchestra, was released and became a huge hit.

Holly's records had been even more popular in the United Kingdom than in the States, and they kept selling there longer, throughout the 1960s. Holly and the Crickets had toured there in 1958, and the British have retained a special fondness for his music. The idea of a self-contained group of guitar, bass, and drums who wrote their own songs and sang their own backup (a misconception, as most of the singing behind Holly was done by others), in other words, the standard approach of most rock and roll bands, can be traced at least in part to Buddy Holly and the Crickets. The Beatles, when still known as the Quarrymen (which contained John Lennon, Paul McCartney, and George Harrison), chose "That'll Be the Day" for their premiere recording, a vanity record made in Liverpool in 1958. Harrison sang Holly's "Crying, Waiting, Hoping" at the Beatles' 1962 audition for Decca, and his vocal on "Reminiscing" was recorded at the Star Club in Hamburg later that year. McCartney and Lennon harmonized on "Words of Love," issued on *Beatles VI* (1965), and the Beatles played Holly songs on other occasions, such as during the rehearsals for *Let It Be* (1970). Lennon sang "Peggy Sue" on his solo album *Rock 'n' Roll* (1975). Holly's influence was also huge on other artists of the BRITISH INVASION, such as the Searchers and the Hollies (named in his honor). Several of them had hits in America in 1964 and 1965 with Holly songs, including the ROLLING STONES ("Not Fade Away"), the Hullabaloos ("I'm Gonna Love You Too"), and Peter and Gordon ("True Love Ways").

In his lifetime, Holly's influence was evident in songs like Robin Luke's "Susie Darlin' " (1958). After his death, other Americans kept the Holly sound alive. Bobby Vee, whose career was launched when he was asked to fill in for the very next show of the ongoing Winter Dance Party, retained elements of his style and recorded an album of Holly songs. He also recorded with the Crickets, who had their own ongoing career with a nucleus of Sonny Curtis, Joe Mauldin, Jerry Allison, and a succession of different vocalists. Tommy Roe's "Sheila" (1962) was in the Holly style, and the Bobby Fuller Four reprised his "Love's Made a Fool of You" (1966). Songs from Holly's catalog continued to be covered by all manner of artists. ERIC CLAPTON's short-lived band Blind Faith covered "Well All Right" in 1969 and Santana had a hit with it in 1978, the year that *The Buddy Holly Story* renewed interest in Holly. During the same period, Holly's music provided several artists with hits: Linda Ronstadt ("It's So Easy"), Leo Sayer ("Raining in My Heart"), and the BEACH BOYS ("Peggy Sue"). In the mid-1980s James Taylor had a hit with "Everyday," already once successful for John Denver in 1972. Thousands of other artists covered Holly's songs and still do.

Holly was one of the initial inductees into the Rock and Roll Hall of Fame in 1986. Interest in him remains high, as older fans still delight in his songs and younger ones discover him. For example, between 1989 and 2002 the stage musical *Buddy* ran for more than 5,000 performances in London's West End, grossing £46 million (around $84 million). It earned an additional $365 million on Broadway in New York and in road productions.

instrumental rock

Some people can't sing. Some people can't write lyrics and some people can't seem to hear them. Not everything needs to be said. The best approach to music is through feeling, and some feelings can't be put into words. New and unique sounds are more captivating than common ones. All these reasons seem to apply to instrumental rock, but whatever the reason, the instrumental has always been popular in rock, especially from the mid-1950s to the mid-1960s.

When voices are heard and nothing else, it's called a cappella. When instruments are heard and little else, it's called an instrumental. Instrumentals are everywhere in music: classical has its symphonies and concertos, jazz its hot improvisations and big band tunes, blues its solo pieces, country its pickin' and grinnin', and R&B its honking and squealing saxophone solos. An instrumental is a record or a performance in which an instrumentalist or group of them is featured throughout a piece. Lead singing is incompatible with the concept, but some background singing can be accepted, even the occasional spoken or shouted phase.

Instrumental blues, whether by ensembles or solo pianists and guitarists, had long been popular. One of the most durable pieces, "Guitar Boogie" (1948) by Arthur Smith and his Crackerjacks, was picked up by budding guitarists and remained as a source for variations for decades. Instrumental rock started with Bill Doggett's "Honky Tonk (Parts 1 and 2)," a blues shuffle in R&B style that hit number two in 1956. Doggett recorded for the King label of Cincinnati, which would soon sign James Brown. "Honky Tonk," with its memorable solos by electric guitar and tenor sax, supported by Doggett's organ, was so lengthy that the single split it into two parts. It became a standard repertoire item in the live sets of thousands of artists, from Clarence "Gatemouth" Brown to Moby Grape.

In 1958 instrumental rock became a fad in the wake of "Tequila," a number-one hit for the Champs from Los Angeles. Early stars were the guitarists Link Wray and Duane Eddy, and the Ventures, a quartet. Link Wray's distorted sound is still influential and he still performs. He has been called the father of the power chord, first heard in "Rumble" (1958). Duane Eddy had his first hit that year, too, and his low twangy sound was so popular that he is still rock's top-selling instrumentalist. One of his nearly 30 hits was "Peter Gunn," which he redid in 1986 in collaboration with the techno-pop group Art of Noise, gaining a top-10 hit in the United Kingdom. The Ventures, from the Seattle-Tacoma area, are rock's top-selling instrumental combo. Their biggest hits are two different versions of "Walk Don't Run" (1960 and 1964), and the theme for the TV series "Hawaii Five-O" (1969). The band was extremely influential for beginning guitarists, some of whom learned from Ventures play-along records.

Drummer Sandy Nelson also sold a lot of records with "Teen Beat" (1959) and "Let There Be Drums" (1961). In Britain the Shadows, Cliff Richard's backup band, reigned as the top instrumental group. Jorgen Ingmann redid one of their songs called "Apache" (1961)—named after the American

Indian tribe but sounding like it came from outer space. Using spacey sounds to evoke space itself was what gave the Tornadoes, another English group, a number-one hit in 1962 with "Telstar," named for one of the world's first communications satellites.

More earthy, from the same year, was the rocking R&B of "Green Onions" by Booker T and the MG's, featuring the organ of Booker T. Jones and the guitar of Steve Cropper. Their name stood for "Memphis Group," and they were the house band for many of the great soul singers who recorded in Memphis. They had more than a dozen additional instrumental hits of their own. Cropper and bassist Duck Dunn were in the *Blues Brothers* movie and band, and they, along with Jones, are often seen at televised award and tribute shows backing up the featured artists.

Lonnie Mack interpreted CHUCK BERRY's "Memphis" as a guitar instrumental in 1963 and put three more songs on the charts, the last one an updated oldie: "Honky Tonk 65." By then surf instrumentals were popular, though before long they were supplanted by the BRITISH INVASION. Surf instrumentals are discussed under SURF ROCK, a style that had vocals as well.

There was barely any room for instrumentals in the vocally rich British invasion, though there were a few. The BEATLES did one at their very first recording session when they backed Tony Sheridan in Germany. It was George Harrison's "Cry for a Shadow," a tribute in sound and name to Cliff Richard's band. The Beatles did one other instrumental late in their career, "Flying," on *Magical Mystery Tour* (1967).

After their remake of "Apache," called "Apache '65," Davie Allan and the Arrows had further hits with instrumental soundtrack music for biker films, such as "Blue's Theme" (1967) from *The Wild Angels.* Allan was a session guitarist from Los Angeles. His career was revitalized in the 1990s by new CDs and tours. In performance he was as rocking as ever,

playing mostly his own beautifully constructed compositions, which are inspired by the music of film and television composer Henry Mancini.

The heyday of the rock instrumentals lasted until 1966, though they continued to be made and enjoyed. In the 1970s two innovative electric guitarists, both shy of the spotlight, emerged out of the shadows to become venerated musicians. Neither Roy Buchanan nor Danny Gatton had hit records but both sustained careers through album sales and performances, inspiring many players along the way with their tone, technique, and ideas. One of Buchanan's skills was his mastery of controlled harmonics. Gatton was known as the Master of the Telecaster, and his blend of rock and roll and jazz was dubbed "redneck jazz." At different times, Buchanan and Gatton were each called the world's greatest unknown guitarist. Both suffered from depression and, tragically, each committed suicide.

PROGRESSIVE ROCK gave new impetus to the instrumental, as on the albums by keyboardist Rick Wakeman and the flashy acoustic guitar showpieces like "Mood for a Day" (1972) by Steve Howe, both from the group Yes. The albums of jazz rock instrumentals that Jeff Beck, formerly of the YARDBIRDS, made in the mid-1970s found an audience. Many others pursued instrumentals and soundtrack work, such as guitarist Robbie Kreiger of the DOORS. Hard rock took some impetus from progressive rock, as in "Frankenstein" (1973) by the Edgar Winter Group, which put the emphasis again on sax and keyboards, and in the soaring instrumentals of the ALLMAN BROTHERS BAND, with their harmonized guitar leads.

Since the 1970s few rock instrumentals have been hits, though musicians have never lost interest in creating them. Much of their energy went to make soundtracks. The revival of interest in surf music encouraged much important research into the history of instrumentals and stimulated the creation of new music.

jam bands

The jam band style began in the 1980s and was widespread in the 1990s. The term *jam* comes from jazz sessions in which musicians, often from different ensembles, would get together after hours to improvise over standards. As the name of a style, *jam bands* refers to units with rock instrumentation (or that play to rock audiences) that include improvisation and experimentation in their music along with a willingness to incorporate elements from other genres. As in PROGRESSIVE ROCK, a 1970s British style, the technical ability of jam band musicians is extraordinary, but jam bands put less emphasis on spectacle, are more eclectic in their approach, and have far less inspiration from European classical music, drawing instead from American blues, folk, and jazz sources. They also place more emphasis on groove rather than segmented song forms, preferring to create intricate improvised segues that provide transitions from one tune to the next.

The roots of the jam band style go back to the 1960s, particularly the music of the GRATEFUL DEAD and the ALLMAN BROTHERS BAND, who had a penchant for long improvisations and took inspiration from blues and jazz. FRANK ZAPPA was another pioneer. Like these artists, the jam bands incorporated elements of other styles and genres, and in jam bands one may hear rock, jazz, blues, bluegrass, funk, soul, reggae, metal, rap, and worldbeat.

The essential setting to hear jam bands is in live concerts, where the players can stretch out and interact with their large and loyal followings. Unlike a typical rock concert, audiences do not come expecting to hear bands play their greatest hits (though they may hope to hear favorite songs). Jam bands are famous for their sound, for their abilities, for a catalog of albums (which most fans are quite familiar with), and for the atmosphere created during their concerts, but not so much for hits. Most do not have any hits to speak of, not in the typical pop sense: songs get airplay but are rarely released as singles. Two common phrases describe what happens at concerts, one for the bands—"they never play the same show twice"—and one for the audience—"you never know what to expect."

The audience for the style is primarily middle-class college students who are part of a neo-hippie subculture. Many fans travel, like the Deadheads who followed the Grateful Dead, to see their preferred bands over many nights as they tour. Many take advantage of the bands' encouragement of tapers (people who make recordings—on tape or in digital media—of live shows) and traders (tapers and others who collect and exchange live recordings). There are policies for taping; it is, for example, confined to a special section of each venue. Likewise, there is an etiquette for trading: the chief rule is that no money be exchanged. With all the taping and trading, again as with the Grateful Dead, the jam bands have engendered a word of mouth network. In publications and on Web sites, fans track their repertoires statistically and rate and debate the shows and renditions. These activities bring attention to the bands and are beneficial in enlarging their audience and maintaining its interest in their development.

Phish, from Vermont, which began in 1983, and the DAVE MATTHEWS BAND, from Virginia, which began in 1991, are the most popular jam bands. Other prominent acts in the style are Widespread Panic; Ben Harper; Blues Traveler; String Cheese Incident; Bela Fleck and the Flecktones; Rusted Root; the Derek Trucks Band; moe.; Medeski, Martin, and Wood; the Spin Doctors; Col. Bruce Hampton and the Aquarium Rescue Unit; Strangefolk; Gov't Mule; Big Head Todd and the Monsters; God Street Wine; Leftover Salmon; Galactic; and Donna the Buffalo. The Allman Brothers Band and the Grateful Dead (until its demise in 1995 and various offshoots since) remain important in the jam band scene.

Phish formed at the University of Vermont and played clubs around Burlington, building a fan base. Their lineup settled to be guitarist Trey Anastasio, bassist Mike Gordon, keyboardist Page McConnell, and drummer Jonathan Fishman. Once their first recording was released in 1988, they began touring extensively. They have since released many other studio recordings and a series of live CDs. By the mid-1990s they were one of most successful touring bands in the United States.

They were wildly eclectic and amazingly proficient. After playing some of their intricate compositions they would go into a Duke Ellington swing piece, an old-fashioned a cappella barbershop quartet number, or a cover of BOB DYLAN, the JIMI HENDRIX EXPERIENCE, the Beastie Boys, LED ZEPPELIN, Stevie Wonder, or who knows what. For special events like Halloween and New Year's Eve shows, they have been known to perform entire albums from start to finish, in order. The WHO's *Quadrophenia*, PINK FLOYD's *Dark Side of the Moon,* the BEATLES' *White Album,* and the TALKING HEADS' *Remain in Light* have all been done live on stage by Phish. Their approach is playful, even silly at times, and they readily accommodate guests, such as Bela Fleck, onstage and in the studio. For their fans, a big part of the adventure is the unpredictability, and

hearing a few musical fumbles is a small price to pay for seeing a great band go out on a creative limb. Phish disbanded in 2004.

Those who love jam bands can follow them around and see them night after night; those who do not have difficulty understanding why anyone would. In a period where much music being made for the masses is being fabricated in sonic laboratories full of technical wizardry, to watch music being played live the way jam bands do, a way that defies expectations, is an appealing alternative. It speaks highly of human creativity and it can provide a welcome and shared experience of vitality.

Jefferson Airplane (also Jefferson Starship)

Jefferson Airplane were one of the principal San Francisco PSYCHEDELIC bands (along with the GRATEFUL DEAD, Big Brother and the Holding Company, Country Joe and the Fish, and Quicksilver Messenger Service), and the first to record. They were also the only one to have top-10 hits in the 1960s. They had two, the indelible "White Rabbit" and "Somebody to Love." They were an extremely inventive, eccentric, and prolific band, and their music intelligently and poetically articulated the concerns of the hippie generation with its antiestablishment stance, leftist idealism, and use of psychedelic drugs. Jefferson Airplane played some of the most important ROCK FESTIVALS, including the MONTEREY POP FESTIVAL, WOODSTOCK, and Altamont.

The band has one of the most convoluted histories in rock, with changes of personnel and solo albums and side projects aplenty. In the 1960s they were called Jefferson Airplane (from a joke name for an imaginary bluesman, Blind Thomas Jefferson Airplane, a derivation of the name of a real bluesman from the 1920s called Blind Lemon Jefferson). In the 1970s they were Jefferson Starship, and in the 1980s simply Starship. The personnel overlapped during each change, and musically one can hear how the later incarnations developed from the previous as the band played FOLK ROCK, acid rock, hard rock, and NEW WAVE–influenced synthesizer pop, with some ballads included in each period. That the early Jefferson Airplane bore virtually no sonic resemblance to the later Starship is unsurprising, for by the end of the 1980s, no one in Starship had ever been in Jefferson Airplane. Nonetheless, each unit had a different musical identity that suited its era, and each managed to find its audience: all three bands had top-10 hits.

They were called Jefferson Airplane from 1965 to 1973. During this time, they made seven albums, and all but the first, the folk rock *Takes Off* (1966) and the last, the live *Thirty Seconds over Winterland* (1973), made the top 20. In their peak years, 1967 to 1969, they consisted of vocalists Marty Balin (b. 1942) and Grace Slick (b. 1939), guitarists Paul Kantner (b. 1941) and Jorma Kaukonen (b. 1940), bassist Jack Casady (b. 1944), and drummer Spencer Dryden (1943–2005). Slick had a regal beauty and was witty and sarcastic, and she and JANIS JOPLIN (with Big Brother and the Holding Company and then in her solo career) were very charismatic, the most prominent female rock artists in the 1960s. They altered perceptions of what roles women could have in the music world and in the culture at large.

The richness of the talents within the Jefferson Airplane was a blessing, but also led to rivalries and differences over direction. The band was run as a democracy, and each member was given a chance to shine. Grace Slick, whose clear voice and imaginative phrasing was unmatched in rock, and Paul Kantner, who previously played banjo and whose chiming, folky 12-string rhythm guitar provided rhythmic support, were aligned (they had a child together in 1970). Both are outspoken, assertive, and sometimes contentious. Their songs covered counterculture and fantasy themes that related to contemporary concerns. They were also users and sometimes abusers of alcohol and drugs. Marty Balin took a more moderate position, but he could be temperamental and tended to withdraw during conflict. He could sing soulfully and be convincing on rocking numbers, but his specialty was romantic

serenades. Their voices soared and intertwined, each taking the lead at times. Another faction was Jorma Kaukonen, whose lead guitar style evolved from its folk origins into something more electric and passionately intense, and Jack Casady, whose thundering, agile bass lines made him one of the chief exponents of that instrument. They had been friends before the band started, and musically they pushed towards a harder sound. Spencer Dryden, aligned to Slick romantically for a period and aligned as well with Kaukonen and Casady as part of one of rock's mightiest rhythm sections, added powerful drumming that propelled the groove while adding timbral variation.

Balin, Kantner, Kaukonen, and Casady were present on the first album, and Slick and Dryden came in for the second, the seminal *Surrealistic Pillow* (1967), one of the finest examples of San Francisco psychedelic music in its first bloom, still showing its folk roots alongside the harder acid rock. It contained "White Rabbit" and "Somebody to Love." Slick brought the songs with her when she left another San Francisco band, the Great Society (formed after seeing one of the Jefferson Airplane's first gigs), to replace Signe Toly Anderson, who wanted to spend more time with her husband and their baby. Anderson would occasionally sing again with her old bandmates in later decades. Dryden came in to replace Skip Spence who, as a guitarist, would soon be a founding member of Moby Grape.

Slick's composing of "White Rabbit" was influenced by jazz trumpeter Miles Davis's album *Sketches of Spain* (1960) and the rhythm used in French composer Maurice Ravel's "Bolero" (1928). Because its enigmatic imagery was clearly from Lewis Carroll's book *Alice's Adventures in Wonderland* (1865), "White Rabbit" escaped the censorship usually accorded to songs that had (or were suspected of having) drug references. It was an unusual and effective song, an anthem that has retained its power to evoke the spirit of the times. The same is true of the hard-driving "Somebody to Love," which became a theme song for 1967's so-called Summer of Love. It was written by Darby

Slick, Grace's brother-in-law, and had been recorded by the Great Society in a gentler version.

Because of the great success of their second album, RCA gave the band unlimited studio time for their next. They took full advantage of it to try drug-influenced artistic experiments, as the Grateful Dead did with *Anthem of the Sun* around the same time, with the newly expanded (to eight tracks) multi-track tape recorder. What they created on *After Bathing at Baxter's* (1967) included freeform collages of sound effects, spoken bits, and percussion, and each side of the album was mixed into one long flow. Though Balin's songwriting credits are minimal here, Kantner emerged as a songwriter, and his compositions, "Ballad of You and Me and Pooneil" and "Watch Her Ride," made the singles charts. As with other San Francisco hippie bands, they avoided making a formula out of their past successes, continuing, as ever, to pursue their own muse. With *Crown of Creation* (1968), they kept the effects but relied more on song structures and, despite the dark themes, it earned them their second gold record.

Bless Its Pointed Little Head (1969) and *Live at the Fillmore East* (recorded in 1968 but not released until 1998) are exciting live sets showing the band in top psychedelic jamming form. *Volunteers* (1969) included the politicized title track, and "Wooden Ships," a postapocalyptic vision written by Kantner with David Crosby and Stephen Stills (who also recorded it in Crosby, Stills and Nash). It is the first of Kantner's science fiction songs. "Good Shepherd," sung by Jorma Kaukonen, is an old folk hymn they learned from a Library of Congress recording made in Virginia in 1936 (under the title "Blood Stained Banders" by Jimmie Strothers). It foreshadowed Kaukonen's future career in Hot Tuna and his solo recordings. Again, Balin was barely present in the songwriting credits, and left not long afterward, disillusioned with the band and disgusted by the selfish hedonism of the rock and roll scene.

Bark (1971), the first release on the Grunt label, a group-owned subsidiary of RCA, and *Long John Silver* (1972) show Kaukonen's growth as a guitarist.

He contributes some of the best material on these albums. The band was still very popular, and both albums made the top 20, but despite being full of interesting ideas, they have an aimlessness about them that reveals the band's decline. *Thirty Seconds over Winterland* (1973), containing mostly live versions of songs from their last two albums, was their final album.

Kaukonen and Casady had already formed a blues-based duo called Hot Tuna that developed a loyal following and has recorded prolifically since 1970. It continued, on and off, whether or not either or both was involved in the larger band. There was so much energy and creativity among the Jefferson Airplane's members that solo albums and side projects were numerous; this contributed to the lack of focus on their last albums. There were some new members as well. In 1970 Dryden left to join New Riders of the Purple Sage, and he was replaced by Joey Covington. Covington in turn was replaced in 1972 by John Barbata, formerly of the Turtles. "Papa" John Creach, an elderly black violinist whose energetic playing and bright tone acted like a second lead guitar and whose presence pleased the audience, was in the band from 1970 to 1972, and that year David Freiberg, formerly of Quicksilver Messenger Service, came in as a vocalist.

From 1974 to 1984 the band was called Jefferson Starship. The first use of the name was in 1970, for an album project of Kantner's: *Blows against the Empire,* credited to Paul Kantner/Jefferson Starship, which included Slick, Casady, and Freiberg, as well as David Crosby, Graham Nash, and three members of the Grateful Dead: Jerry Garcia and their two drummers. (All of them plus others were also on Crosby's first solo album, *If Only I Could Remember My Name.*) It earned a gold record for sales and for its theme of three friends who hijack a starship to create a new, free society away from a repressive government, it was the first record nominated for science fiction's Hugo Award. The Jefferson Starship band had 17 charting songs. The melodic lead guitar style of young Craig Chaquico contributed to their more contemporary sound. Their biggest hit was "Miracles," sung by Marty Balin, who had rejoined his mates, from their number-one album *Red Octopus* (1975). The seven-year relationship of Kantner and Slick broke down soon afterward. Slick's behavior was quite erratic, and she quit the band in 1978 while on tour overseas. Balin, tired of ego clashes, also quit, leaving Kantner as the only Airplane veteran. Later Slick rejoined and then, in 1984, unhappy with the band's hard rock direction, Kantner quit. A struggle for the name led them to drop the "Jefferson" part.

From 1984 to 1990 they were known as Starship. Taking a commercial direction and using songs by outside writers, they put 11 pop tunes and ballads on the charts, including three number ones: "We Built This City" and "Sara," both from *Knee Deep in the Hoopla* (1985), the first album under this name, and "Nothing's Gonna Stop Us Now" (1987), the theme for the movie *Mannequin*. Not long afterward, Slick, the last vestige of the Airplane in the band, departed, tired of its bland corporate approach. They continued to have hits until 1991.

In 1989 the Jefferson Airplane briefly reunited— all the core members except Dryden—for a tour and an eponymous album (which was not well received). Fans were delighted to see the band again, but while the inclusion of several side musicians beefed up their sound, it seemed to dilute their purpose. Afterward, Slick declared her retirement, though she has returned as a guest vocalist from time to time.

In the 1990s Starship continued as "Starship featuring Mickey Thomas" (the lead singer who joined in 1979). In the early 1990s Kantner used the name Paul Kantner's Wooden Ships (thus making a reference to the Jefferson Airplane) for an acoustic trio, but despite legal wrangling over the use of the "Jefferson" name, since 1992 he has led a unit known as Jefferson Starship—The Next Generation. Joining him, at least some of the time, are Marty Balin and Jack Casady (who continues with Kaukonen in Hot Tuna). The female vocalist role was handled very capably by Darby Gould and then by Diana Mangano.

The band's metamorphosis into a lightweight, albeit very successful, pop band has tended to obscure the Jefferson Airplane's status as a musical and cultural force of great magnitude. Similarly, the sustained popularity of "White Rabbit" and "Somebody to Love," while keeping the band's name in public awareness, has overshadowed their other recordings, which are not just vital to an understanding of the idealistic and tumultuous 1960s and its aftermath, but are spectacular music in their own right.

Several books have been written on the band. The earliest book, *Jefferson Airplane and the San Francisco Sound* (1969), was by Ralph J. Gleason, who championed them from the beginning even before he cofounded *Rolling Stone* magazine in 1967. Grace Slick has written an autobiography, *Somebody to Love? A Rock-and-Roll Memoir* (1998), and Paul Kantner has done a double CD called *A Guide through the Chaos (A Road to the Passion): The Spoken Word History of the Jefferson Airplane and Beyond* (1996). In 2003 Jeff Tamarkin wrote *Got a Revolution! The Turbulent Flight of Jefferson Airplane,* an affectionate and carefully documented tome that covers the music and the conflicts and puts everything in cultural perspective.

Joplin, Janis (1943–1970) *influential rock-blues singer*

Though her professional career lasted less than five years, Janis Joplin is a cultural icon. She emerged from the San Francisco dance hall circuit, part of the Haight-Ashbury hippie culture, as an unconventional, remarkable singer who conveyed tremendous emotional power. She was also a flamboyant, charismatic woman with an electrifying presence who was not afraid to express herself. Janis Joplin took center stage when there were few women in rock. For her individuality, her accomplishments, her liberated bisexuality, and songs from a female perspective like "Women Is Losers," she is a feminist symbol.

Her infamous hedonism, less desirable in a role model, was used to soothe a wounded psyche and was acted out through promiscuity and alcohol and drug use. Her public image went from a stylish and free-spirited hippie chick wearing feathers and bangles to a more outrageous persona nicknamed Pearl, a brash, Southern Comfort–drinking floozy that was a caricature of some of her idols. It was an image she felt she had to live up to. *Pearl* is the title of her final album. While making it, she died of an accidental heroin overdose.

In performance she was totally involved with singing, "all hoarse and insistent and footstamping . . . shrieking for delivery from some terrible, urgent, but not entirely unpleasant, physical pain."[11] She is considered the best white blues singer, and her chief inspiration was Bessie Smith, the great classic blues singer who died in 1937. Less than two months before her own death, Joplin financed a headstone for Smith's grave. Besides the blues, Joplin also sang folk, country, and gospel in her early period. She got famous singing BLUES ROCK and acid rock with Big Brother and the Holding Company. In her final period she shifted into soul music.

The eldest of three children, she was born and raised in Port Arthur, Texas, a small oil refinery town where she had a stable family life. Janis was a loner and a thinker, and she turned to art for solace. She became a reader of literature, history, and philosophy, a passion she got from her father that she continued all her life. A social outcast who was insecure about her looks, she was deeply hurt when once named "Ugliest Man on Campus."

Though she recorded only four studio albums, many live recordings have since been made available commercially and on bootlegs. The earliest Joplin recordings were done in 1963 and 1964 in Austin, where she felt more freedom in the arts community around the University of Texas (and also got into booze and drugs). The recordings are in the folk revival spirit. They capture the kind of music she played in coffeehouses around Texas and on visits to the bohemian meccas of San Francisco's North Beach and New York City's Greenwich Village. To the sound of acoustic guitar and occasional harmonica, Joplin sang songs by the female blues singers and the jug bands of the 1920s and 1930s, as well as a few original blues. In 1965 she recorded four songs of the same type in San Francisco, accompanied by a Dixieland jazz band. Soon she went back to Texas to get off drugs and find her direction. She enrolled in college but was not satisfied.

Joplin returned to San Francisco, and in June 1966 she joined Big Brother and the Holding Company, who were already playing as a quartet. They had gotten together the summer before through regular jam sessions held in the basement ballroom of the old Victorian mansion, now a boardinghouse, where some of them lived. The band was guitarist Sam Andrew (who had a rock and roll background and a knowledge of classical music), guitarist James Gurley (an intuitive musician with an intense way of playing lead solos, not with a guitar pick, but with his fingers), bassist Peter Albin (who had been a folkie), and drummer David Getz (who was also a visual artist). They shared the vocals, but included instrumentals in the repertoire. When they decided to look for a female vocalist (like JEFFERSON AIRPLANE had, who formed around the same time), their manager, Chet Helms, who knew Joplin from Austin, sent for her to come to San Francisco and audition. Joplin and the band clicked. She started working with them right away, developing from a folk singer to a rock singer.

From June to August Big Brother and the Holding Company played around San Francisco, mostly at the Avalon Ballroom and the Fillmore Auditorium, the city's two most important rock venues. They also played at the Red Dog Saloon in Virginia City, Nevada, whose hippie community energized and then populated San Francisco's psychedelic scene. The band also played a couple of gigs down the coast, including one in Monterey. Their breakthrough into the big leagues would take place there one year later.

In August 1966 Big Brother went to Chicago to play a month's residency at a nightclub called Mother Blues. Over many sets and many nights the band tightened up immensely, but few people

Janis Joplin (Michael Ochs Archives.com)

the Holding Company's set was so riveting that they were asked to repeat it so it could be filmed.[12] One song appears in the film *Monterey Pop:* Janis tears into "Ball and Chain," and very little of the rest of the band is shown. Some of them had heard Big Mama Thornton singing the song in a nightclub in San Francisco, and Janis had asked and received her permission to sing it. The band changed the song to a minor key and recast it into something new.

In the festival audience were record industry personnel, who expressed keen interest in the singer and the band. Albert Grossman, who also managed BOB DYLAN, became their new manager and got them signed that fall to Columbia, which bought off their contract with Mainstream. In February 1968 Big Brother and the Holding Company began touring on the East Coast, playing New York and other places for the first time.

In the spring the band started recording their next album. Progress was slow in the studio, so the band was also recorded live. *Cheap Thrills* (the title edited by Columbia from the proposed *Dope, Sex, and Cheap Thrills*) captured not only the depth and intensity of Joplin's singing, but also the band's brilliant and raw instrumental interplay and power. Released in August, the album went to number one, and is one of the most significant albums of the decade. "Piece of My Heart" became a hit, and "Summertime," the old standard in a new arrangement with intertwining lead guitars, became a signature song. Mainstream put out two singles from their archives, and both went into the charts. The band, Janis mostly, got a lot of publicity. They did big shows and commanded high fees, but some people in the business and press suggested that the gentlemen were not up to her level. In the fall Grossman announced that she would leave the others. For six months after the album's release, the band toured until Joplin did her farewell shows with Big Brother at the end of 1968.

Weeks later she did her first gig with a new outfit (Sam Andrew stayed with her), the Kozmic Blues Band, which favored keyboards and horns. It was a more conventional, soul-influenced sound. They

came—the hippie scene had yet to develop in Chicago—and the contract was cut short. The band signed to the small local Mainstream label, partly out of pride and partly out of desperation. They began an album in Chicago and finished it in Los Angeles. A couple of singles were released to little reaction. The band continued to play extensively in California.

The album did not come out until two months after they caused a sensation at the MONTEREY POP FESTIVAL in June 1967. They, along with the rest of the psychedelic bands from San Francisco, were lesser known and underrecorded compared to the acts from Los Angeles and New York, as well as the international acts on the bill. Big Brother and lasted one year, until December 1969. In that period they toured all over the United States and did a stint in Europe. They made one album, *I Got Dem Ol' Kozmic Blues Again Mama!*, which went to number five. It included "Try" and other favorites, and "Kozmic Blues" was a moderate hit on the charts. It was, like all her subsequent singles, released under Joplin's name only. The band had good players, but the lineup kept shifting and seemed to lack chemistry no matter who was in it.

In April 1970 she reunited for a show with Big Brother, and the next month did her first with her new lineup, the Full-Tilt Boogie Band. She felt more comfortable with this band, and they hit the road, taking part in the Festival Express as it traveled by train through Canada, documented in the film *Festival Express*. Her use of drugs and alcohol had not diminished and it made her behavior sometimes erratic. In August, days after their last concert, Janis attended, despite mixed feelings, her 10-year high school reunion in Port Arthur. Recordings for *Pearl* began the next month, and were nearly completed when she died in her Hollywood hotel room.

The album was released in early 1971 and went to number one. "Mercedes Benz" was an instant classic, and "Me and Bobby McGee" was the hit, her only number-one single.

Big Brother and the Holding Company did two more albums for Columbia. In the late 1980s they reunited with all the original male members, and to the present have toured and recorded again, featuring a younger female vocalist. Rather than try to imitate Joplin, the singers that have worked with the band add their own significant talents.

Over the years much Joplin product has been released: live albums, greatest hits, film and television documentaries, a box set, and several plays and biographies. For years, there have been rumors of a forthcoming movie biography, but as of this writing, none has materialized. A Porsche that Joplin bought in 1968 and had a band roadie friend custom paint with fanciful nature scenes, symbols, and bright colors is now a museum piece, having been shown at the Rock and Roll Hall of Fame and at 1960s-themed exhibits. These things are reminders of what a bright and brief flame Joplin was.

keyboards

The piano and the other keyboard instruments such as organ and synthesizer have a sequence of keys that sound notes when fingered. In each octave of 12 notes is a pattern of seven white and five black keys, and most instruments have several octaves. The piano has the most, with 88 notes: seven full octaves plus a portion of another. The concept of dividing the octave into 12 equal parts—which nature does not do—is a system called equal temperament. It was conceived in Europe and universally adopted there by 1800, spreading to everywhere that had a cultural link to that continent. Asia and Africa and other locales do not base their music on the same system and so have a different basic sound.

The piano, the instrument of great classical composers and showy virtuosos, was invented in Europe. The piano was used in all of the root genres of rock and roll. Although it is most readily perceived as guitar music, rock and roll has incorporated keyboards since the beginning. Several early stars claimed the piano as their instrument, such as FATS DOMINO, LITTLE RICHARD, and JERRY LEE LEWIS. More recently, the piano is associated with players whose music is as much pop as rock, such as Carole King, Elton John, and Billy Joel.

Numerous rock bands include a keyboard player. Some had two, for example the BAND (with Garth Hudson and Richard Manuel) and Procol Harum (with Gary Brooker and Matthew Fisher). Some have a member who doubles on the instrument. One does not immediately think of keyboards in connection with, say, the BEATLES, LED ZEPPELIN, or Van Halen, but each had a bassist or guitarist or two who occasionally played keyboards on their records. Respectively, their names are Paul McCartney and John Lennon, John Paul Jones, and Eddie Van Halen. QUEEN's vocalist Freddie Mercury was, like Eddie Van Halen, a classically trained pianist who played keyboards sometimes. Even groups with no keyboard in their lineup employ one from time to time. BUDDY HOLLY had organ on some of his records, and on "Everyday," his producer's wife, Vi Petty, played the bell-like celesta, an orchestral keyboard whose name means "heavenly." Billy Preston played the organ on some later Beatles recordings.

Preston played a Hammond organ. Invented in the 1930s, it has, despite its bulk, been the most popular organ for gospel, jazz, R&B, and rock. The Hammond, especially the beloved B-3 model, is often used in conjunction with a Leslie speaker, a large cabinet that has within it a rotating horn with a variable speed that sweeps sound past listeners' ears in a pleasing manner. A partial list of American Hammond players includes Booker T. Jones of Booker T and the MGs, whose instrumental music bordered R&B and rock and whose first and biggest hit was the influential "Green Onions" (1962); Goldy McJohn of STEPPENWOLF; Doug Ingle of Iron Butterfly; and Lee Michaels, who was usually accompanied only by a drummer and had a hit with "Do You Know What I Mean" (1971). In England, Stevie Winwood brought his Hammond sound to the Spencer Davis Group, Traffic, Blind Faith, and then his solo career. Jon Lord of Deep Purple was an impressive soloist on tracks like "Hush" and "Woman from Tokyo." PROGRESSIVE ROCK players used the Hammond extensively as part of their keyboard arsenal, including Rick Wright of PINK FLOYD, Keith Emerson of Emerson, Lake and Palmer, and Rick Wakeman of Yes. More recently it has been used by Page McConnell of Phish, one of the JAM BANDS.

New Orleans is home to a long line of great piano players stretching back before Jelly Roll Morton (1890–1942), who claimed to have invented jazz. In the 1940s Professor Longhair and Fats Domino were among the first New Orleans R&B pianists to record. Others soon followed. Little Richard was from Georgia, but he recorded in New Orleans and based much of his style on local wildman Esquerita. There was also Larry Williams, whose songs the Beatles liked to cover; the clowning Huey "Piano" Smith, whose "Rockin' Pneumonia and the Boogie Woogie Flu" (1957) was reprised in 1973 by Johnny Rivers; Allen Toussaint, a performer, songwriter, and arranger; and Dr. John, who became the ambassador for the New Orleans piano tradition.

Blues pianists contributed much to early rock and roll. CHUCK BERRY's records featured Johnny Johnson, and BO DIDDLEY's usually had either Lafayette Leake or Otis Spann (of Muddy Waters' band). Harry Vann "Piano Man" Walls, a staff pianist at Atlantic Records, had a distinctive and exciting style that enlivened records by the likes of the Drifters, Ruth Brown, the Clovers ("One Mint Julep"), and BIG JOE TURNER ("Shake Rattle and Roll"). Boogie-woogie pianists, with their thundering left-hand patterns, were very influential on the R&B players as well as on country musicians. Jerry Lee Lewis, whose influences included boogie-woogie and honky-tonk, made piano an accepted instrument in ROCKABILLY. Ray Manzarek of the DOORS made use of his boogie-woogie roots by playing with his left hand the bass parts of songs such as "Light My Fire" and "Riders on the Storm."

Gospel was another source of inspiration for rock players. Aretha Franklin came out of gospel, but her pop career never took off until she signed with Atlantic Records. Her first for them, "I Never Loved a Man (The Way I Love You)" (1967), featured her own spectacular piano playing.

Ray Charles, an iconic figure, popularized the electric piano with "What'd I Say" (1959), his first top-10 hit on the pop charts. The instrument was manufactured by Wurlitzer, and in the 1970s this type of electric piano became part of the signature sound of Rick Davies of Supertramp ("Dreamer," "The Logical Song," and "Goodbye Stranger") and Donald Fagen of STEELY DAN ("Do It Again"). Another famous brand of electric piano was the Fender Rhodes, invented in the 1940s by Harold Rhodes. Its action resembles that of an acoustic piano. Instead of the acoustic piano's felt-covered hammers striking strings, the Rhodes has rubber-tipped hammers striking metallic tines (similar to tuning forks). This normally gives a chiming sound, but when notes are played with more force the sound is somewhat distorted, thus giving the instrument a wide expressive range. The Rhodes was very popular in the 1960s and 1970s, but its use is more common in jazz fusion (as in Herbie Hancock's "Chameleon"), and pop ballads (Billy Joel's "Just the Way You Are" and Stevie Wonder's "You Are the Sunshine of My Life") than it is in rock. It is found in PAUL SIMON's wry "Still Crazy after All These Years."

In the 1960s many BRITISH INVASION acts had keyboards. Manfred Mann, Alan Price of the ANIMALS, Mike Smith of the Dave Clark Five, and Stevie Winwood, as mentioned, played the organ. They influenced American GARAGE ROCK bands that typically included a portable organ. The lightweight Pianet, invented by the German company Hohner in 1962, had no sustain pedal and sounded a little like a jazz guitar but more aggressive in the low register and more like a music box in the upper. It was used by the Beatles ("The Night Before," "I Am the Walrus"), Herman's Hermits ("I'm into Something Good"), and the Zombies ("She's Not There"). Others who used it were the Guess Who from Canada ("These Eyes") and Three Dog Night from California ("Joy to the World"), as well as Led Zeppelin ("Misty Mountain Hop") and Queen

("You're My Best Friend"). The YARDBIRDS' "For Your Love" featured studio musician Brian Auger on the harpsichord, a baroque keyboard instrument with a silvery sound whose keys cause strings to be plucked, unlike the piano, whose keys cause strings to be struck. As a solo artist Auger, on various keyboards, was a pioneer of jazz rock fusion. Some British blues musicians played the piano, like Ian Stewart with the ROLLING STONES; John Mayall, who played several instruments; and Christine McVie, who joined FLEETWOOD MAC. The versatile Nicky Hopkins played piano with Jeff Beck, Quicksilver Messenger Service, and the Rolling Stones.

Another keyboard instrument used by British bands was the mellotron, popularized by the Beatles ("Strawberry Fields Forever"), the ROLLING STONES ("2000 Light Years from Home"), and Mike Pinder of the Moody Blues. Pinder had helped develop the instrument during the 18 months that he worked in the factory where they were made. The keys of the mellotron trigger the playback of short loops of tape on which instruments have been recorded. Its most characteristic sound is one called "3-Violins," but the brass and breathy flute sounds were also popular. The instrument's notoriously finicky mechanism ceased to be an issue once the original sounds were available as samples that could be loaded into synthesizers. In this form, mellotron sounds have returned to rock, used by such bands as the Smashing Pumpkins, Crowded House, RADIOHEAD, the Wallflowers, and, again, the Rolling Stones.

The Hohner Clavinet was a favorite instrument with funk bands. It was basically an electric version of the clavichord, the earliest type of stringed keyboard instrument, which dates from the 12th or 13th century and was common until the time of J. S. Bach. The Clavinet came to prominence in 1972 with Stevie Wonder's "Superstition" and Keith Emerson's playing on Emerson, Lake and Palmer's "Nutrocker" (a rock adaptation of Tchaikovsky's *The Nutcracker Suite*). Emerson, like Tony Banks of Genesis, was among the many classically trained progressive rock players who elevated the status of keyboards in rock. Rick Wakeman of Yes also played

on albums by DAVID BOWIE and had a solo career with keyboard-dominated concept albums. Richard Tandy of ELECTRIC LIGHT ORCHESTRA had a similar classical background, but his band was closer to the pop rock tradition of the Beatles.

Blues and R&B were fundamental influences on many American rock bands. Gregg Allman's Hammond organ playing is a vital component of the ALLMAN BROTHERS BAND. SANTANA began as the Santana Blues Band, and organist Gregg Rolie carried on when the band's name was shortened. The GRATEFUL DEAD's long line of keyboard players began with Ron "Pigpen" McKernan, a blues and R&B specialist, and continued with Keith Godchaux, Brent Mydland, Bruce Hornsby (who also led his own band), and Vince Welnick. Al Kooper came out of the Blues Project, added organ to BOB DYLAN's "Like a Rolling Stone," helped found Blood Sweat and Tears and participated in the *Super Session* (1968) album with Mike Bloomfield and Stephen Stills before maintaining a solo career. Oklahoma-born Leon Russell had played sessions for PHIL SPECTOR and came to notice as the keyboardist in Joe Cocker's band, playing on hits like "The Letter" (1970), which boosted his solo career.

Synthesizers became popular in progressive rock bands, and were picked up by other players as well. Edgar Winter, a Texan and the keyboard-playing brother of blues guitarist Johnny Winter, had a number-one hit with the instrumental "Frankenstein" (1973). Gary Wright, a New Jersey–born vocalist and keyboard player formerly of the British band Spooky Tooth, was the first to have an all-keyboard band. On *The Dream Weaver* (1975), all the parts, except for drums and vocals, are played by various keyboards: electric piano, Clavinet, organ, and synthesizer, which provided the sounds of woodwinds, violins, and bass. The public approved: the album, the title song, and "Love Is Alive" all made the top 10.

Synthesizers would become more sophisticated and widespread in the years to come. One style that used them extensively was NEW WAVE. In that era, players such as Greg Hawkes of the Cars, Jools Holland of Squeeze, Benmont Tench of Tom Petty and the Heartbreakers, Jerry Harrison of Talking Heads, and Jimmy Destri of Blondie kept keyboardists in the public eye. Though some styles of rock have little place for keyboards, such as Punk Rock, Heavy Metal, and Grunge, the classic sounds will remain and new types of keyboards will be invented. There will be styles that include them, great musicians to come up with new ideas, and fans to appreciate them.

Kinks, The

One of the first generation of London-based British Invasion bands, they had top-10 songs in the 1960s, 1970s, and 1980s. Their strength came from the talent, interplay, and sometimes tension between brothers Dave Davies (b. 1947, lead guitar) and Ray Davies (b. 1944, vocals, rhythm guitar), who were joined by Peter Quaife (b. 1943, bass) and Mick Avory (b. 1944, drums). Ray Davies blossomed into one of the best and most prolific songwriters of his generation. His songs have clear and intriguing musical ideas, and his lyrics range from poetic depictions of emotional moments in relationships to tragicomic vignettes of modern life, often with particular insight into the suburban British experience, painted through keen observations or empathetic (even when satirical) portraits.

In their first phase, 1964 to 1967, with nearly a dozen hits, all produced by Shel Talmy, the Kinks established themselves with three top 10's in a row: "You Really Got Me," "All Day and All of the Night," and "Tired of Waiting for You." The first two (and "Till the End of the Day" from 1965) were powerful rockers based on chord riffs that locked the Guitar (playing shifting major chords) to the Bass (playing the chords' roots). This style, a Kinks trademark, made them not only highly influential to American Garage Rock but to all later heavy rock. A garage band example is the Chocolate Watchband; they covered the Kinks' version of the blues song "Milk Cow Blues" as well as "I'm Not Like Everybody Else."

With "A Well Respected Man" and "Dedicated Follower of Fashion," the social commentary side of Ray Davies' writing emerged, continuing with "Sunny Afternoon" and "Dead End Street" and expanding into concept albums, which he produced, starting with *The Kinks Are the Village Green Preservation Society* (1968) and *Arthur (Or the Decline and Fall of the British Empire)* (1969). After three years off the singles charts, the Kinks, unlike many of their British invasion peers, returned to commercial success, principally with "Lola" (1970), a tale of mistaken sexual identity. The corrupt music industry was also a theme in their songs, as the band endured many hassles. There were some personnel shifts in the bass role and additions of keyboards and horns. They formed their own record company, Konk, in 1974. Always a touring band, their approach became more theatrical, with roots in British music hall traditions.

Beginning in the late 1970s, the Kinks experienced a resurgence of popularity. In 1978 Van Halen reprised "You Really Got Me" and gained their first hit. In 1980 the Pretenders had a hit with a Ray Davies song, "Stop Your Sobbing." (Chrissie Hynde, the leader of the Pretenders, and Davies were married.) The Kinks themselves had a string of top 40 albums between 1977 and 1983, the year they again had a huge hit single with "Come Dancing." Subsequent recordings did not meet such success, though to the delight of fans the band continued to tour into the 1990s.

To date, the last Kinks album of new recordings is the double CD *To the Bone* (1996), a marvelous, mostly acoustic retrospective set of the band playing great new versions of hits and obscure songs from their career. In 1995 Ray Davies published his autobiography, *X-Ray: the Unauthorized Autobiography*, and then toured as a solo performer, documented on the CD *Storyteller* (1998). In 1997 Dave Davies published, *Kink: An Autobiography*, and then toured with his own band in a show called Kink Kronikles. Several Dave Davies albums, live and studio, have been released. Both brothers have continued to tour individually, though Dave postponed much of his 2004 schedule to recover from a stroke.

KISS

This hard rock band from New York can be seen as part of the glam movement, which featured costumes and outlandish stage shows. Unlike most glam acts, however, they were not androgynous cross-dressers playing with gender stereotypes but were inspired by fantastic characters, the kind seen on Halloween night or in comic books. In the 1970s, along with those of ALICE COOPER, KISS's live shows revolutionized the art of rock performance by bringing theatrical elements to its stages. Their painted faces and flashy, grotesque costumes and platform boots were only the frontline of KISS's elaborate, macabre presentations. There

was also fire breathing, "blood" spitting, smoke bombs and other pyrotechnics, a giant illuminated logo of the band's name, and assorted props such as hell hounds with glowing eyes. In the 1990s laser and 3-D effects were added.

Besides being showmen, KISS were entrepreneurs. The gimmickry of their act was translated into merchandising spin-offs. They inspired a pinball machine, were in a film (*Kiss Meets the Phantom of the Park*), and their own series of comic books. Their fans, known as the KISS Army, loved the fantasy, loved the music, and loved the band. The film *Detroit Rock City* (1999), named for an early song, depicts four teenagers in 1978 who will

KISS (Michael Ochs Archives.com)

stop at nothing to get to a KISS concert. Many of the band's fans were captivated as children or adolescents and remained loyal to the band into adulthood. They went to the shows, bought the records, and at KISS conventions and expos, where band members would appear, they purchased the collectibles. After ELVIS PRESLEY and the BEATLES, KISS is the most collectable rock act. On the market are licensed (and bootleg) products such as: die-cast cars, Halloween costumes, dolls, posters, photos, magazines, books, shirts, belt buckles, videos, press kits, backstage passes, lunch boxes, school supplies, games, makeup kits, radios, toy guitars, bubble gum cards, and unused concert tickets. To know the value, one could consult one of the price guides to KISS collectibles. As of 2001 there is a Kiss Kasket (for sale at $5,000). Gene Simmons, the band leader and marketing mastermind, suggests that the coffin, decorated with images of the members and the words "Kiss forever," could be used to celebrate life too and that it would make a good beer cooler. Any of these purchases can be made on a KISS Visa credit card.

Their first two albums were not big sellers when first released, but the band was building their fan base from their live shows. Their third, *Dressed to Kill* (1975), made the top 40, but fittingly, a live recording, the double album *Alive!* (also 1975), gave them their first top 10 placement. Their other best-selling albums include *Alive II* and *Love Gun* (both 1977), *Revenge* (1992), and *Psycho-Circus* (1998), their last record of new material. One of their top singles was the anthemic "Rock and Roll All Nite" (1975), which charted twice in the same year, first in a studio version and then in a live version. Their biggest hit singles were "Beth" (1976), an untypical ballad, "I Was Made for Lovin' You" (1979), in disco style, and "Forever" (1990), cowritten by Michael Bolton.

Bassist Gene Simmons (b. 1949) and guitarist Paul Stanley (b. 1951) met in 1968. After crossing paths numerous times as part of separate bands, they decided to work together in 1971 in one called Wicked Lester. That group recorded an unreleased album, but Simmons and Stanley split from the other members in 1972 with the intent to form a band with a more visual approach. Simmons and Stanley found drummer Peter Criss (b. 1947) through an ad Criss had placed in *Rolling Stone* magazine that said "Drummer available . . . willing to do anything to make it." To round out the band with a lead guitarist, they advertised in New York's *Village Voice* newspaper. They auditioned at least 50 guitarists, and picked Ace Frehley (b. 1950). All four of the band's musicians were also singers.

They chose the name KISS, in all capital letters, which made it seem like it was an acronym. Detractors said it stood for "keep it simple, stupid," while religious fundamentalists believed the rumor that it stood for "knights in Satan's service" (the band never denied this, as it was good publicity to let people wonder). The reality was that they just liked the name, and later realized that it fit with glam rock. More importantly, it was a simple word that was understood even by non-English speakers.

They developed their characters and makeup based on aspects of their own personalities. Simmons' character is "The Demon," Stanley's "The Starchild," Frehley's "The Spaceman," and Criss' "The Cat." They wore makeup for their first gig in 1973, and, until they decided to "unmask" in 1983, always appeared in full regalia for public appearances. Going without makeup then gave them headlines in the press, and the publicity and the image change boosted record sales and concert attendance. Putting it back on more than a decade later achieved the same result.

Gene Simmons and Paul Stanley are the mainstays in the band's lineup. Criss had a near-fatal car accident in 1979. He recovered but left the band the next year. From the 30 or more drummers that auditioned, Eric Carr won the position, adopting the persona of "The Fox." After he was stricken with cancer and died of a brain hemorrhage in 1991, he was replaced by Eric Singer. Frehley left in 1982, and the lead guitar spot was filled by Vinnie Vincent, whose persona was "The Wizard." He departed in 1984, replaced by Mark St. John. KISS at that time was no longer wearing makeup. St. John played on only one album before getting sidelined by arthritis; he was replaced by Bruce Kulick. In 1996 the original lineup reunited and returned to wearing makeup. Their reunion tour was the highest-grossing tour that year.

They announced their farewell tour in 2000 but were still touring as of 2004. Peter Criss departed in early 2001 over a contract dispute, and Simmons and Stanley, who own the rights to the band name, rehired Eric Singer, who performed in Criss' cat makeup. When the farewell tour ended but the others decided to not retire after all, Frehley, disapproving, dropped out. Tommy Thayer, formerly of the band Black and Blue, was hired in his place and wears Frehley's "Spaceman" makeup. These events have been hotly debated by fans. Some, who attended their concerts, tended to approve, because the band remained musically strong and was willing to play songs from their entire catalog, not just the material that was done by the original lineup. Others derided the actions as based on greed, feeling that KISS had turned into a tribute band. These arguments are brought up for every legendary band that has had shifts in personnel, from the ROLLING STONES to the BEACH BOYS. There are, in fact, more than 100 KISS tribute bands, in North America, South America, Europe, Australia and New Zealand, and Japan: all places where the real band has performed.

Gene Simmons has written two autobiographies, *Kiss and Make-Up* (2001), which describes his upbringing in Haifa, Israel, and the history of the band, and *Sex Money Kiss* (2003), which contains more on his philosophy of life, particularly on the topics named in the book's title.

Led Zeppelin

Critics detested them for being pompous and exhibitionist. Music purists reviled them for reworking blues classics and folk themes into hard rock bombast and the arrogance of claiming songwriting credits for others' ideas and compositions. Christian organizations accused them of spreading satanic messages that could supposedly be heard by playing their records backward. Punks thought they were boring. But fans loved them. Their concerts broke box office records, their albums sold in gigantic quantities, rappers would later sample them, authors would write books, and Web sites by the dozens would detail their uncredited influences, discuss trivia, offer to sell memorabilia or trade bootlegs, analyze their lyrics, and transcribe their guitar and bass lines into tablature (a way of writing music by indicating the hand positions with numbers).

With GUITAR, BASS, DRUMS, and voice, Led Zeppelin emerged from England in the 1960s to capture the loyalty of millions around the world in the 1970s with their heavy rock chemistry. Into an electric blues rock foundation, Led Zeppelin incorporated elements of acoustic British folk, down-home blues, early rock and roll, and California psychedelia. Later they added funk and ethnic influences. Their album covers were enigmatic and their lyrics sometimes obtuse, with references to pagan rituals, *The Lord of the Rings,* and drugs. They paved the way for HEAVY METAL and underlined the shift in importance from singles to albums. Despite never being released as a single, "Stairway to Heaven" is one of the world's most played songs. Classic rock stations continue to program other Led Zeppelin favorites, such as "Whole Lotta Love" (their biggest chart hit), "Communication Breakdown," "Dazed and Confused," "Immigrant Song," "Black Dog," and "Kashmir."

When the YARDBIRDS broke up in 1968, their lead guitarist Jimmy Page, who had followed ERIC CLAPTON and Jeff Beck in that role, fulfilled the band's last contracted dates with a new lineup. Vocalist Robert Plant and drummer John Bonham had played in Band of Joy, a Birmingham group, and bassist and keyboard player John Paul Jones was a session musician and arranger in recording studios. All were in their early 20s. Page was the only well-known member at that point, but all were remarkable talents.

Peter Grant, the Yardbirds' last manager, stayed on with Page's new band. He negotiated a big deal: a lucrative, long-term, exclusive contract with Atlantic, the New York independent label that was branching out from R&B into rock (they had recently signed CREAM and the Bee Gees, among others). The group's debut album, just called *Led Zeppelin,* was recorded within two weeks in little more than 30 hours of studio time, but before it was released, in January 1969, the band toured the United States opening for Vanilla Fudge, a heavy rock band who recorded for a subsidiary of Atlantic. Audiences immediately took to Zeppelin.

Led Zeppelin's name was inspired by a remark made by Keith Moon, the drummer for the WHO, at an impromptu recording session in 1966 that included Jeff Beck, Jimmy Page, and John Paul Jones. Someone said that if the players were to form a band, it would go over like a lead balloon (a common expression for failure), and Moon reputedly added, "like a lead zeppelin." Their manager changed the spelling so it would be properly pronounced.

In reference to the name, the first album cover used a famous photo of the tragic 1937 crash of the *Hindenburg,* a German zeppelin (a dirigible, or steerable balloon-like airship named for the count who developed it) at the moment it burst into flame. For Led Zeppelin, the photo not only underscored the band's name, but the image of the cigar-shaped dirigible was extremely suggestive. Their music and the strutting, bare-chested, long-haired stage presence of Plant and the low-slung guitar and leaned-back poses of Page were a forerunner of heavy music that expressed, often aggressively or boastfully, male sexuality.

Led Zeppelin (Michael Ochs Archives.com)

The first album was produced (as were all subsequent Zeppelin albums) by Jimmy Page to have a huge sound. It sold very well, and was favorably compared to the music of Cream and JIMI HENDRIX. One critic said that Page "had somehow made two very important discoveries: spaced-out heavy rock drove barely pubescent kids crazy; the Sixties were over. And so, with virtually no critical support, Led Zeppelin was soon the biggest new band on earth."[13]

The record seems to have been modeled after Jeff Beck's 1968 album *Truth* (on which John Paul Jones played organ on one song). Both discs have a heavy blues orientation, a powerful singer backed by a guitar-bass-drums lineup (on most cuts), plus a reworked Yardbirds song, a traditional folk instrumental on acoustic guitar, and a cover of Willie Dixon's "You Shook Me."

In 1969 the band toured constantly, as headliners now, and quickly released their follow-up, simply called *Led Zeppelin II,* recorded in various studios on the road. Three appropriations of blues songs led to lawsuits. "Whole Lotta Love" was done first by Muddy Waters, as "You Need Love," but Led Zeppelin's rendition was inspired by seeing the Small Faces do it. The song's author, Willie Dixon, was not credited (the songwriting credits on the album named the four members of Led Zeppelin). Nor was Dixon credited for "Bring It On Home" (Page and Plant were), a song he had written for Sonny Boy Williamson. Both suits was settled out of court in favor of Dixon. The third one was "The Lemon Song," again credited to the band members but taken from Howlin' Wolf's "Killing Floor," with the lemon-squeezing lines lifted from Robert Johnson's "Traveling Riverside Blues." In another out-of-court settlement, Howlin' Wolf's publisher sued and won for copyright infringement.

Led Zeppelin III (1970) was a departure: the cover was psychedelic and, though it contained some typically heavy numbers, such as "Immigrant Song," the emphasis on acoustic material alienated some fans. "Gallows Pole" was a treatment of a traditional folk song known on both sides of the Atlantic. By the end of 1970, with the BEATLES having just split up,

Led Zeppelin's concert grosses, attendance figures, album sales, and popularity poll winnings indicated that they were the world's top rock band.

Their untitled fourth album (1971) is Led Zeppelin's best known and, some say, their best work. Their selling power was such that the gatefold cover had no words on it—no title, no band name—just a photo of a ruined wall (representing the old) near row housing and tall apartment towers (representing the new). On the wall is a framed print of a man doubled under a load of branches he carries on his back. The inside cover, also devoid of words, is a drawing of a robed and bearded man who signifies wisdom—the Hermit from the tarot cards—standing on a mountain and holding up a lighted lantern that contains a six-pointed star. He is looking below to a village and a small figure who is climbing toward him. The album is referred to variously as *IV, Untitled,* or, because of the four runes printed on the record label, *Four Symbols, Runes,* or *Zoso* (an alphabetical approximation of the runes). The album contains the masterful "When the Levee Breaks" (credited to all members, plus Memphis Minnie, the blues legend), classics like "Black Dog" and "Rock and Roll," and "The Battle of Evermore," which featured vocals by Sandy Denny of the British folk rock band Fairport Convention.

It also contains what some consider the greatest rock song of all, "Stairway to Heaven." The introduction (borrowed from "Taurus" by Spirit), is especially appealing to guitarists because, with its contrary motion, it sounds complex and therefore impressive, yet is not hard to play. So many budding guitarists learned it that some guitar stores instigated a "No Stairway to Heaven" policy because their employees were sick of hearing customers play it: this was dramatized in a scene from the film *Wayne's World* (1992). The song's arrangement is a minihistory of music in just under eight minutes. The first two verses, accompanied by acoustic guitar and recorders, have a medieval sound highlighted by the minor key. The accompaniment for the next pair of verses, with acoustic guitar, electric guitar, and bass, take listeners into the 20th century. Drums are added for verses five and six, moving listeners stylistically into rock. A new progression—a repeating two-bar pattern—is the backdrop for the guitar solo. In the final (seventh) verse, Robert Plant sings an octave higher against this pattern, slightly modified, moving listeners to 1971 and the newly emerging heavy metal style. The lyrics are open to interpretation, but they evoke the universal concern of materialism versus spirituality. In this song, some claim, the words "my sweet Satan" (or similar) can be heard if the song is played backward; others claim this is a hoax perpetuated by preachers. The song ends with Plant's lowered, unaccompanied voice, bringing listeners back to the human, the simple, and the title.

Houses of the Holy (1973), Zeppelin's fifth album, also had a gatefold cover with no indications inside or out. The enigmatic cover photo, taken in Ireland, depicts young, naked blond children climbing a rock formation. According to Page, it is meant to convey a feeling of expectancy for the music on the record. The inside photo shows an adult facing a castle while holding aloft one of the children in a gesture that seems like he is making an offering to the sun as it rises. The diverse music confounded critics, but contrasted folk ballads with hard rock, with touches of REGGAE thrown in. The tour broke attendance records previously set by the Beatles.

In a 1974 arrangement with Atlantic, the band created their own imprint, a label called Swan Song, to which they signed a few other acts, such as Bad Company and the Pretty Things. The first release on Swan Song was *Physical Graffiti* (1975), a double album. On the cover is the facade of an old building in New York City. Cutouts allow the viewer to see various figures inside the windows, such as the band members, anonymous characters, and identifiable personalities, including Charles Atlas, Elizabeth Taylor (as Cleopatra), Marlene Dietrich, JERRY LEE LEWIS, the queen of England, King Kong, Lee Harvey Oswald, and Neil Armstrong. Again the music was diverse, spanning hard rock, blues, and the vaguely Middle Eastern sounds of "Kashmir." At this time, Led Zeppelin was the world's most commercially successful band. All six of their albums were on the charts in 1975, an unprecedented and unduplicated feat.

Led Zeppelin did a sold-out tour of the United Kingdom, but when Plant and his family were injured in a car crash in Greece, plans for further touring were dropped. After a delay for convalescing, *Presence* (1976) was released. It had a sparser sound that lacked the band's usual sense of grandeur. It was recorded in Germany, and achieved platinum sales through advance orders, but sales dropped off once it was released. "Achilles' Last Stand" was a standout performance, but much of the rest of the record was a disappointment. The cover artwork, again enigmatic but with the theme of old and new, features a small black object whose presence has been introduced into photos from the 1930s and 1940s.

The Song Remains the Same (1976) was the name of a concert film and the accompanying double album soundtrack. The footage was shot at New York's Madison Square Garden in 1973, and the film was augmented by numerous surreal and bizarre fantasy sequences that featured the band members, including a gangster-style shootout, knights sword fighting, motorcycle riding, and so on.

The aborted tour was rescheduled in 1977 and started in the United States. Their audiences totaled more than a million people. An infamous incident in which Bonham, manager Peter Grant, and a bodyguard were arrested for beating up one of promoter Bill Graham's security staff tarnished the band's reputation. Days later, when Plant learned of the death of his six-year-old son from a viral infection, the tour was canceled. During the months of inactivity that followed, speculations were that the band would break up.

In 1979 they made what turned out to be their last album. *In Through the Out Door,* recorded in Sweden, had a somber feeling, and Jones contributed more than usual to the record. It mixes some new sounds, such as the ROCKABILLY of "Hot Dog," a Caribbean influence, and synthesizers. There were six versions of the cover, all with the same photo of

a man sitting in a funky barroom, but taken from different perspectives.

That year they did two shows in England, and next year did a short tour of Europe, presenting a more austere sound that may have been inspired by the rise of PUNK ROCK. In fall 1980 John Bonham died from asphyxiation (he inhaled his own vomit following a drinking binge). Not long after, the surviving members of Led Zeppelin announced they would not continue without him.

In 1982 one last album was released. *Coda* (the term for a concluding passage in a piece of music) gathered together some unreleased live and studio tracks. The stark cover seemed appropriate.

Jones went back to session work and production, keeping a low profile that was raised by some solo albums around the turn of the 21st century. Plant had a successful solo career, making many hit records and albums and touring. Page did a movie soundtrack and then in 1984 reunited with Plant in the Honeydrippers, a back-to-the-roots project that included Jeff Beck and Nile Rodgers (of Chic). Their sole record had only five songs but two were hits: "Sea of Love," a remake of Phil Phillips' 1959 hit, and "Rockin' at Midnight," Roy Brown's 1949 sequel to his own "Good Rockin' Tonight" (a song popularized by Wynonie Harris in 1948 and ELVIS PRESLEY in 1954). Then Page, with vocalist Paul Rodgers of Bad Company, fronted a new band called the Firm, which managed some moderate hits. Page also did a solo album, one with vocalist David Coverdale of Whitesnake, and worked with the Black Crowes.

Led Zeppelin reunited publicly for two special events: Live Aid in 1985 (with Phil Collins on drums) and the Atlantic Records 25th Anniversary Concert in 1988 (with Jason Bonham, John's son, on drums). In 1994 Page and Plant reunited for an acoustic concert featuring some Zeppelin tunes and some new compositions. It was presented on an MTV special called *Unledded,* on the *No Quarter* album, and on a world tour. A second reunion came in 1998, for an album of all-new material, *Walking into Clarksdale,* and further live dates.

Led Zeppelin's influence is pervasive. Though they were lax in crediting their sources, fans have traced them back, discovering artists in downhome blues (Bukka White, Sleepy John Estes, Robert Johnson, Blind Willie Johnson), urban blues (Howlin' Wolf, Muddy Waters, Albert King, Otis Rush), British folk (Bert Jansch, Davey Graham, Annie Briggs), and developing an appreciation for styles that influenced Zeppelin's sound, namely Celtic, Indian, Arabic, Moroccan, and Caribbean music.

The sonority of later music changed with the influence of Zeppelin's huge sound (via studio effects) of Bonham's drums, the mix of acoustic and electric sounds, and even the instruments (Page's use of the Les Paul guitar gave it additional status). Their influence can be seen in the basic approach of bands such as Heart, while guitarists from AEROSMITH to Guns n' Roses to METALLICA like to throw in riffs and quotes from Led Zeppelin songs. Pop bands like Frankie Goes to Hollywood and rappers like the Beastie Boys and Ice-T sampled their beats and riffs. Tribute bands from around the world play their repertoire and copy their sound.

"Stairway to Heaven" in particular has been parodied. One version, called "Stairway to Gilligan's Island," by Little Roger and the Goosebumps, was released in 1978 as a joke: it copied the arrangement but used the melody and words to the theme song of the TV sitcom *Gilligan's Island*. It was suppressed by Led Zeppelin's manager, but later, when Robert Plant heard it, he thought it was funny and gave permission to rerelease it. A band called Dread Zeppelin made a career out of doing songs the way Elvis Presley would have if he liked Led Zeppelin songs and wanted to do them reggae style.

Since the 1990s Page has overseen Led Zeppelin's back catalog. Various CD box sets and collections, with remastered sound and artistic sequencing, have sold very well. The first box set sold more than a million copies. A double CD of live performances recorded in the BBC studios came out in 1997. *How the West Was Won* (2003) was the name given to both a three-CD set of a 1972 concert and a two-

DVD set of early 1970s concerts. Both hit number one on their respective charts.

They are the only band to have all of their original albums reach the Billboard Top 10. Most of them went to number one. Only the Beatles have sold more records. Perhaps the reason Led Zeppelin's music has lasted is that it was so solidly founded on traditional music yet, through creatively integrating diverse genres, managed to transcend its sources.

Lee, Brenda (b. 1944) *female rock singer*

She was one of the first female vocalists in rock and roll, and certainly one of the youngest. She first recorded in 1956 at age 11, and her big voice made a stark contrast to her diminutive frame. Her name at birth was Brenda Mae Tarpley, and she was billed as Little Brenda Lee on her records and as Little Miss Dynamite in promotional material. Lee's clear voice, effortlessly flexible and instantly recognizable, conveyed innocence and confidence. She grew up near Atlanta, Georgia, her singing influenced by the R&B of Ray Charles and FATS DOMINO, the gospel of Mahalia Jackson, and local, unrecorded blues singers. Her recordings, mostly made in Nashville, have the sheen of pop production, and her repertoire encompassed country, ROCKABILLY (which brought her attention in the rockabilly revival), novelty songs, ballads, and standards. A consummate interpreter of songs, she never composed her own.

Brenda Lee had been winning talent contests since she was five, had her own radio show not long after, and appeared on a country music variety show on network TV when she was 11. By the time of her 12th birthday, before she had a hit record, she had started recording for Decca, been on three more top TV shows, and done a three-week engagement in Las Vegas. She recorded for Decca from 1956 to 1970; 51 of those songs made the pop charts, a dozen of them in the top 10.

In 1959 Lee toured to great acclaim in England and France (where a publicity stunt hinted that she

Brenda Lee with Elvis Presley (Michael Ochs Archives.com)

the international tour circuit she would mix in rock and roll songs.

Though her last charting single in the pop field was in 1973, between 1969 and 1985 she consistently scored country hits. From 1988 to 1990 she starred in a Nashville musical. She has sung frequently for charitable causes and served for eight years on the board of directors of the Country Music Association. Lee has received numerous awards, including induction into the Country Music Hall of Fame in 1997 and the Rock and Roll Hall of Fame in 2002. Also in 2002, her autobiography, written with noted country music historian Robert Oermann, was published: *Little Miss Dynamite: The Life and Times of Brenda Lee*. It describes her rise from poverty, the story of her career, and the blessings of a long, happy marriage and loving extended family. To the delight of her loyal fans, this effervescent, legendary lady continues to record and tour.

Leiber, Jerry (b. 1933) and Mike Stoller (b. 1933) *songwriting team*

Leiber and Stoller were a songwriting team from Los Angeles. "Hound Dog" was one of their early compositions. It was first a hit for Big Mama Thornton, a blues singer from Texas. The backgrounds of the participants at her recording session in 1952 in Los Angeles show how rock and roll was a hybrid kind of music. There were the Jewish songwriters, a black singer, and a band comprised of Louisiana blues guitarist Pete Lewis, Puerto Rican bassist Mario Delgarde, and Greek R&B drummer and bandleader Johnny Otis, who considered himself "black by persuasion" (and who later had a rock and roll hit of his own in "Willie and the Hand Jive" in 1958).

Another of Leiber and Stoller's early blues songs was "Kansas City" (recorded often, but not successful until done by Wilbert Harrison in 1959). The two writers went on to compose, and produce in most cases, a host of black acts, including Ruth Brown ("Lucky Lips"), Ben E. King ("Spanish

was really a 32-year-old midget). "I'm Sorry" and "Sweet Nuthin's" were her first major hits, in 1960, the same year "Rockin' around the Christmas Tree" hit (it charted again the next two years at Christmastime). After the mid-1960s she concentrated on the country market, but for live shows on

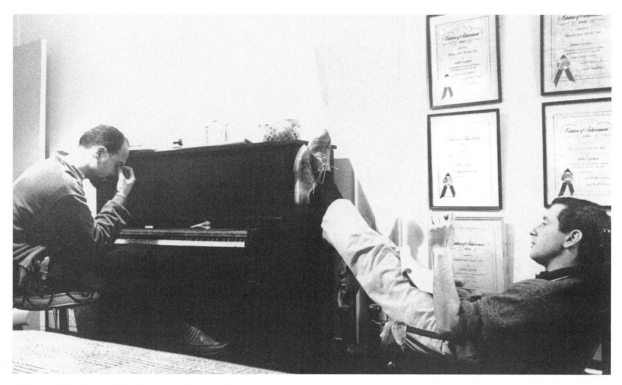

Leiber and Stoller (Michael Ochs Archives.com)

Harlem," "Stand by Me"), La Vern Baker ("Saved"), the Robins ("Riot in Cell Block #9," "Smokey Joe's Café"), the Clovers ("Love Potion #9"), the Drifters ("Drip Drop," "Fools Fall in Love"), and particularly the Coasters ("Yakety Yak," "Poison Ivy," and "Charlie Brown"). They were active in the 1970s, producing an album for Procol Harum.

Their music was honored in the 1990s in the Broadway musical *Smokey Joe's Café*.

Lewis, Jerry Lee (b. 1935) *rock and roll pioneer*
Legendary Jerry Lee Lewis, nicknamed "the Killer," was born in Ferriday, Louisiana. On the Sun label of Memphis, he established himself as a major star with "Whole Lotta Shakin' Goin' On," "Great Balls of Fire," and "Breathless," all top-10 hits in 1957 and 1958. His rhythmically assured and versatile "pumping" piano style was influenced by church music and country players such as Moon Mullican, who played western swing and honky-tonk. Lewis' other early inspirations include Al Jolson, Jimmie Rodgers, Hank Williams, Holiness preachers, and the black rhythm-and-blues musicians he observed as a youth.

Born in poverty, Lewis began at age nine to play piano at the home of an aunt. His father, a carpenter and a bootlegger, seeing his son's passion and talent, mortgaged their house to buy him a piano. By emulating the playing styles of a local preacher and black musicians whom he spied on during nightclub appearances, Lewis was soon performing at school assemblies, talent shows, tent revivals, and on the radio. Previous to landing at the Sun label in Memphis, drawn by the success of ELVIS PRESLEY, Lewis had attempted to break into the

Jerry Lee Lewis (Michael Ochs Archives.com)

music business in New Orleans, Shreveport's *Louisiana Hayride* stage show, and Nashville.

A highly skilled instrumentalist and vocalist, Lewis wrote few songs. His is the art of the stylist, able to put a personal stamp on a vast and diverse repertoire. He is also a man of contradictions, tormented by conflicts between rock and roll hedonism and his religious upbringing.

Lewis captivated legions of fans with his flamboyant attitude and unpredictable, charismatic showmanship in stage, television, and film appearances. His blond hair falling in his face, he exhibited seemingly boundless energy and a menacing sexuality while carrying out various stage antics: standing on the piano, playing it with arms and feet, kicking over the stool, even lighting the instrument on fire.

In 1958 scandal nearly killed his career. While he was on tour in England, the press scorned him for marrying his 13-year-old cousin (her father was Lewis' bassist) while his previous marriage was still valid. Despite the ensuing boycott, Lewis continued recording and performing wherever he could. In 1961 he hit with a version of Ray Charles' "What'd I Say." He soon returned to England, this time greeted as a star. Lewis' full comeback came only in the late 1960s through a series of hits on the country charts.

His position in music is that of royalty, for his talent, persistence, longevity, international touring, and a huge legacy of recordings. Several biographies and films describe his vital music and fascinating persona while detailing his erratic behavior, alcohol and drug problems, bouts of ill health, tax debts, wild escapades, and six marriages.

Little Richard (b. 1932) *rock singer and pianist*
Little Richard is one of rock and roll's most outrageous characters, and perhaps its wildest and most exciting performer, willing to do just about anything to rile up an audience. He is unpredictable on stage but has been known to stand on the piano, pretend to be struck dead during a show and then come to life singing, and tear off his clothes. His music mixes fervent gospel feeling with rhythm and blues, all set to a rock and roll beat.

Little Richard's fame was secured with the hits recorded, mostly in New Orleans, for the Specialty label from 1955 to 1957. On the road his thrilling, pounding piano and magnificent, powerful voice was backed by a tight band called the Upsetters. Not only did he drive audiences to a frenzy, he inspired artists such as ELVIS PRESLEY, BUDDY HOLLY, and the BEATLES, who sang his songs, James Brown and Otis Redding, who imitated him, Mick Jagger and Paul Simon, who idolized him, and JIMI HENDRIX and Billy Preston, who played in his band.

He was born Richard Penniman and raised in Macon, Georgia, under the oppressive racial segregation then prevalent in the South. He grew up poor, a mischievous boy in a large, religious family. The god-versus-devil conflict that tormented many early rock and roll musicians—the view that one should dedicate oneself to God and not play hedonistic, sinful music like rock and roll—was especially real for Little Richard. As a youth he recognized that he was gay, and that, too, was a source of conflict.

He left home to do music and got his first professional experiences singing with traveling bands and variety shows in which he would sometimes perform in drag. In Atlanta, Richard was influenced by R&B star Billy Wright, "The Prince of the Blues," and he copied his gospel-style blues singing, entertaining abilities, stage clothes, tall pompadour hairdo (also known as a conk), and use of makeup. Through Wright's contacts, Little Richard made, for RCA in 1951 and 1952, his first records. He was backed by Wright's band, and musically he was still in Wright's shadow, but he did gain a local hit.

A month after his last RCA session, Richard's father was murdered. Richard returned to Macon, and, as the principal breadwinner for the family, got a job washing dishes at the Greyhound bus station. There, as a way of talking back to his employers without actually saying anything offensive, he came up with the nonsense syllables that open "Tutti Frutti": "womp-bomp-a-loo-momp-a-lomp-bomp-bomp."

Richard's piano playing changed to something wilder under the tutelage of S. Q. Reeder, a gay gospel and R&B pianist from South Carolina whose stage name was Esquerita. Esquerita's late 1950s recordings are some of the most untamed in rock's history, but by then he was marketed as a Little Richard imitator.

Richard formed a band called the Tempo Toppers that toured the South. In 1953 they recorded without success in Houston, Texas, for the Peacock label. A second session, with Little Richard backed by the Johnny Otis Orchestra, was not issued at the time. The Upsetters were formed next, with two saxophone players, and they, too, went on the road, drawing crowds and building up a reputation.

Lloyd Price, who had a big hit on Specialty in 1952 with "Lawdy Miss Clawdy," saw them play in Macon. He was impressed by the music, and Richard was impressed by Price's Cadillac. In 1955, at Price's suggestion, Richard recorded a demo and sent it to Specialty. Label owner Art Rupe eventually bought out their contract from Peacock. He set up a recording session in New Orleans with producer Robert "Bumps" Blackwell. The backup band was composed of the same studio musicians who recorded with FATS DOMINO. The initial songs they cut were unremarkable, but then, during a lunch break at a local club, Richard started showing off at the piano, singing a lewd song. Blackwell saw potential in it, and had Richard sing it to a lyricist who wrote a cleaned-up version. At the end of the session, they managed to get it recorded. "Tutti Frutti" was unlike anything on the market, and was a big hit. Like most R&B or country songs that were released on independent labels and that showed commercial promise, it got redone as pop music by a more established artist. Pat Boone, who already had six hits, covered "Tutti Frutti" and it was an even bigger hit for him, though his recording is now merely a curio, while Richard's original is world famous.

Richard's next hit was his biggest: "Long Tall Sally." There were many more. Soon he was Specialty's top artist, with such hits as "Jenny, Jenny" and "Keep A Knockin' " and some that were redone by others, like "Rip It Up" (also a hit for BILL HALEY AND HIS COMETS), and "Lucille" (also a hit for the EVERLY BROTHERS). In the 1960s, besides the BEATLES' versions of his songs, including "Long Tall Sally," additional Little Richard songs were covered, such as "Good Golly Miss Molly" (by CREEDENCE CLEARWATER REVIVAL, also Mitch Ryder and the Detroit Wheels), and "Miss Ann" (by Johnny Winter).

Little Richard starred in three rock and roll movies: *The Girl Can't Help It* (1956), one of the best of its kind, and two with disc jockey and promoter Alan Freed: *Don't Knock the Rock* and *Mr. Rock and Roll* (both 1957). He toured in the United

States and Europe, but during a tour of Australia he had a change of heart. He cut the tour short, and gave up rock and roll for religion. Richard entered theological college, married a religious woman who knew little of his past, and cut gospel songs for various labels. Specialty kept releasing singles from its archives, and some of them were hits. Though he kept reading his Bible, the marriage did not last, nor could he stay away from rock and roll.

His return came during a 1962 tour of England with Sam Cooke. He tried singing gospel, but concert-goers were bewildered. One night, when Cooke did a powerful set, Richard could not stand to see him (or anyone) steal the show. His narcissism won out, and he pulled out all the stops, singing rock and roll and using all his antics. It was during this tour that he met the Beatles and they shared stages in England and in Germany.

In 1964 he returned briefly to Specialty, with Bumps Blackwell again producing. "Bama Lama Bama Loo" gained moderate sales. That year he shifted to the Vee Jay label, where he had one more charting single, and JIMI HENDRIX, then working as a sideman on the R&B circuit, played on a few

Little Richard (Michael Ochs Archives.com)

recordings. For Vee Jay and other labels Richard remade his classic songs and tried soul or contemporary music. Over the next years, as the ROCK REVIVAL gained momentum, he toured often.

In 1969 he signed to the Reprise label. With them he made three albums, one with his New Orleans cronies, and had two songs chart. Canned Heat's "Rockin' with the King," featuring Little Richard on vocals and keyboards, was a moderate hit in 1972. He was his usual outrageous self in the rock revival concert film *Let the Good Times Roll* (1973). In 1976, following the death of one of his brothers, he again left rock and roll for religion, and rejected his homosexuality.

In 1984 the excellent and popular biography *The Life and Times of Little Richard, The Quasar of Rock,* by Charles White, which included much interview material by Little Richard and people who were close to him, brought him back in the limelight and seemed to help him integrate the disparate aspects of his life. In 1986 he sang the theme song for the movie *Down and Out in Beverly Hills:* "Great Gosh A' Mighty" was his biggest U.S. hit since 1958. Also in 1986, he was inducted into the Rock and Roll Hall of Fame.

In the 1990s he was given further awards, and his version of "Itsy Bitsy Spider" on a children's disc was so popular that he did a whole children's album for Walt Disney Records: *Shake It All About.* Over the years he has collaborated with many artists, including the BEACH BOYS, New Edition, Living Colour, the Bangles, Philip Bailey, Elton John, and Tanya Tucker. As a celebrity rock and roll star and media evangelist, Little Richard has often been on television for interviews and performances. He has also been hired as a spokesperson in commercials. His songs have graced several soundtracks.

Dick Clark called him the greatest rock and roll legend of our time. He is not alone in that estimation.

Mamas and the Papas, The

This vocal group of two men and two women met in New York's Greenwich Village folk scene. They polished their smooth blend of harmonies in the Virgin Islands before moving to Los Angeles in 1964. Success came with their first single, "California Dreamin'," one of the songs that, to this day, symbolizes the 1960s.

The first nine of their 15 hits made the top 20. "Monday, Monday," their other million-seller, won a Grammy in 1966. Most of their hits were originals, such as "Creeque Alley," which described their early history. They also covered songs by other artists. "I Call Your Name," for example, was a BEATLES song, and "Dedicated to the One I Love" had been done by the SHIRELLES, who got it from the "5" Royales.

John Phillips (1935–2001) was the leader and main songwriter. His teenage bride Michelle Phillips (b. 1945), a former model, was the only one without previous experience in folk revival singing groups. The large and endearing Cass Elliot (1941–74) had a charismatic presence. All had fine voices that intertwined beautifully, but Denny Doherty (b. 1941), from Canada, had a particularly glorious tenor. In sound and look they typified the groovy happiness of the emerging hippie movement, but within the group a lot of anguish came from a love triangle when Denny had an affair with Michelle, and the unrequited love that Cass had for Denny.

John's abilities as a songwriter brought him success outside of the group as well. "Me and My Uncle" was recorded first by Judy Collins but popularized by the GRATEFUL DEAD. They performed it more than any other song in their repertoire, more than 600 times between 1966 and 1995. In 1967 John wrote and produced Scott McKenzie's "San Francisco (Be Sure to Wear Some Flowers in Your Hair)," which served as something of an advertisement for the Summer of Love and the MONTEREY

The Mamas and the Papas (Michael Ochs Archives.com)

POP FESTIVAL. Phillips coauthored "Kokomo," a number-one hit in 1988 for the BEACH BOYS.

That legendary festival had been masterminded largely by Phillips and the group's producer Lou Adler, who had written "Wonderful World" for Sam Cooke before getting into record production and label management. The Mamas and the Papas closed the Monterey Pop Festival, though they did not consider it to be one of their best performances. The next year, John and Michelle divorced and the group broke up. Mama Cass had some solo hits from 1968 to 1970, notably "Dream a Little Dream of Me," a standard from 1930. John Phillips put out a solo album in 1970. The group reunited briefly in 1971 for an unsuccessful album.

Cass Elliot died in London in 1974 of a heart attack (not from choking as first reported). In the 1980s the old Papas with new Mamas (John's daughter Mackenzie, and Spanky McFarlane, of the group Spanky and Our Gang), revived the Mamas and the Papas for the oldies circuit. When Doherty dropped out, Scott McKenzie took his place, and then, despite other shifts in personnel, John carried on.

John and Michelle each put out an autobiography in 1986. Michelle's was *California Dreamin': The True Story of the Mamas and the Papas,* and John's, describing how he eventually won a lengthy battle with alcohol and drug addiction, was *Papa John: A Music Legend's Shattering Journey through Sex, Drugs, and Rock 'n' Roll.* The years of abuse took their toll, however, and in the 1990s Phillips had a liver transplant.

When the group was inducted into the Rock and Roll Hall of Fame in 1998, Denny and John and Michelle sang "California Dreamin' " at the ceremony. In 2001, at 65, John Phillips died in Los Angeles, of heart failure. An album called *Pay, Pack and Follow,* containing 1970s recordings by John accompanied by members of the ROLLING STONES, was released posthumously. Denny's stage show, called Dream a Little Dream: The Nearly True Story of the Mamas and the Papas, presented his captivating storytelling and singing with a backup band.

Metallica

The most popular of all HEAVY METAL bands was formed in 1981. Worldwide they have sold 90 million albums, 57 million in the United States alone, where seven of their recordings have each sold 5 million or more copies. *Metallica* (1991), also known as *The Black Album,* stayed on *Billboard's* top-100 album charts for more than five years. Of American groups, only the EAGLES and AEROSMITH have higher sales.

Metallica injected speed and energy into heavy metal, helping to establish a sound called thrash metal or speed metal that featured growled vocals, fast tempi, and lightning guitar riffs. It drew some of its impulse from PUNK ROCK and was also influenced by what was known as the New Wave of British Heavy Metal. By diversifying their sound to include, at times, influences from earlier roots music such as blues, country, and R&B, plus ballads, tuneful vocals, acoustic guitars, and symphonic backing, Metallica were accused of selling out by some of their fans. In the process, however, the band not only expanded the parameters of heavy metal, but also increased its audience.

Metallica's name was borrowed from a possible name for a fanzine that a friend was planning to launch. The band began in Los Angeles when drummer Lars Ulrich (b. 1963), who had the chance to put a song on a compilation of metal bands, met vocalist and rhythm guitarist James Hetfield (b. 1963). Each had independently placed an ad in the same paper looking for musicians to play with. They are Metallica's main writing team and its only consistent members. At first they were joined by Dave Mustaine on lead guitar and Ron McGovney on bass. McGovney recorded on their demos (which were never released but did circulate widely) but was replaced before their first album by Cliff Burton, formerly of the San Francisco band Trauma. Ulrich and Hetfield were very impressed upon seeing Trauma perform in Los Angeles and invited Burton to join Metallica. He refused, but later agreed if the band would relocate to San Francisco. They did, to get him to join, but also because they were better received there than in Los Angeles, where glam metal was in vogue. At their first headlining show in San Francisco, a local band named Exodus, with guitarist Kirk Hammett, opened the show. When Dave Mustaine's erratic behavior caused him to be fired, Kirk Hammett (b. 1962) came in as his replacement, and his manic, speedy lead runs became a Metallica trademark. (Mustaine later founded Megadeth, who have sold 15 million albums, including *Countdown to Extinction* [1992].)

In Scandinavia in 1986, during the tour to promote their third album, *Master of Puppets,* Metallica's tour bus hit a patch of ice and the driver lost control. The bus overturned and Burton was killed. The band returned to America and, after auditions, chose Jason Newsted (b. 1963) from the hardcore band Flotsam and Jetsam as his replacement. Newsted stayed with the band for 15 years, but left in 2001 and worked with his own, called Echobrain, as well as the Canadian band Voivod and Ozzy Osbourne, of Black Sabbath, one of the foundational influences on metal.

With each album Metallica broadened their approach. Their first, *Kill 'Em All* (1983), was a dramatic debut that presented their command of rhythm, with its relentless drive, intense riffs, and tempo shifts. *Ride the Lightning* (1984), recorded in Copenhagen, showed musical growth in instrumental technique and more mature lyrics. The title track is about someone who is a condemned prisoner, or dreams that he is, imagining his execution by the electric chair. One piece is an extended instrumental that featured Burton's bass playing. Another distinctive song is "Fade to Black," a slower song whose lyrics portray the thoughts of someone on the verge of suicide. The album's breadth set Metallica apart from Anthrax, Slayer, Megadeth, and other speed metal bands.

Master of Puppets (1986) marked their signing to Elektra, an established label that had been the home of the DOORS. This album, among their best work, made the top 30 and showed the acceptance of the band and speed metal in general. They toured with Ozzy Osbourne and increased their fan base immensely.

Following Burton's death, the first sessions recorded with Newsted were a selection of relatively obscure cover songs by British metal and hardcore bands that had inspired Metallica. They were released as *The $5.98 EP: Garage Days Re-Revisited* (1987). It was reissued in 1998 as part of a double CD called *Garage Inc.* that also included other covers. Some were newly recorded, others were rare early tracks.

. . . and Justice for All (1988), was their first top-10 album and "One" their first charting single; it made the top 40. Metallica got a lot of media coverage and performed their hit at the 1989 Grammy Awards (but lost, controversially, to Jethro Tull). *Justice* is their most ambitious work: the songs are long, the structures complex, and the guitar parts layered multiple times (which tended to obscure the bass line). Lyrically it dealt with themes of personal independence, and stylistically it showed how metal did not have to rely on the blues. They toured extensively to support the album.

Their fifth album, *Metallica* (1991), also known as *The Black Album* or *The Snake* for its simple cover, featuring only a snake and the band's logo, was their first number one. It brought them into the mainstream. For this album they used producer Bob Rock, who had worked with Bon Jovi, in order to be more commercial. The arrangements were leaner and smoother, the singing more tuneful, the songs simpler, and the themes more personal than ever. Five songs from it made the singles charts, with "Enter Sandman," still one of their best-known songs, making the top 20. The tour lasted about three years and took them to 37 countries. A lavish product, called *Live Shit: Binge and Purge* (1993) consisted of a double CD recorded in Mexico and three concert videos. It was packaged in a cardboard replica of a touring trunk and, despite its size and price, went into the top 30.

In the early 1990s, groups like NIRVANA and PEARL JAM popularized GRUNGE, and Metallica reacted by introducing lighter guitar textures and more groove-oriented rhythms on *Load* (1996). Older fans were dismayed at the changes in music, band members' short haircuts, and even a new logo, but *Load* and *ReLoad* (1997), the second volume from the same recording sessions, both went to number one. "Until It Sleeps," from *Load,* is Metallica's only top-10 single to date.

After the previously mentioned *Garage Inc.,* with its rock, punk, and metal cover songs, the next album was *S&M* (which stood for "symphony plus Metallica") in 1999. It was a double set of live performances that Metallica had done with the San Francisco Symphony Orchestra, directed by Michael Kamen, who had worked with the band on "Nothing Else Matters" from *The Black Album.* The concerts covered old songs plus two new ones composed for the event, and was released on CD and on video and DVD. Both *Garage Inc.* and *S&M* made the number-two spot on *Billboard.*

In 2000, when Metallica—along with rap artist Dr. Dre—decided to sue Napster (the peer-to-peer file-sharing Web site) for distributing their music without monetary compensation, public opinion was divided. The band originally requested that Napster remove their songs from its directory of available files. When it refused but offered to close the accounts of users who traded Metallica songs, Lars Ulrich delivered, in person, a list of more than 300,000 users who had downloaded or uploaded Metallica files in a single weekend. The next year, Metallica and Napster agreed to an out-of-court settlement. Though the band never actually sued any fans for copyright infringement, the whole affair was very controversial. Ulrich, who stated that the band had no problem with the trading of concert recordings but was concerned only with studio recordings being given away, was portrayed as a greedy and pompous rock star out of touch with his fans. Those in favor of Metallica's stance agreed that all artists merit compensation for their work, that the band had paid their dues and deserved their rewards, and that they were taking a position that would benefit many other bands who did not have the resources to fight a practice that was thought to

be deeply hurting the record industry in general. Those opposed to Metallica's stance felt that the band did not need the money, that file sharing benefited bands (especially lower-level ones) by exposing their music more widely (and that Metallica's own career had been boosted by people copying and sharing their early demos), that downloading their music for free was justifiable because the band had lost the respect of fans, and that file-sharing was a revenge for the public's frustration over the high cost of purchasing music. Internet discussions and articles in publications made efforts to explain the complexities of finances in the record business.

In 2001, at the suggestion of their management, the band brought in Phil Towle, a 64-year-old former psychotherapist and performance coach, in hopes of repairing relationships among the members and preventing Newsted's split. He left the band anyway, but the other members and their producer continued to work with Towle to process unfinished business. This included grieving over the death of Cliff Burton, working out their animosities toward each other, and arranging a meeting between Lars Ulrich and Dave Mustaine, fired from the band in 1983, to voice their differences. During much of this time, Hetfield was in rehabilitation for alcohol and other addictions. A 2004 documentary, *Metallica: Some Kind of Monster,* shows the band in therapy. They are not the first band to take this route, but their willingness to embark on it and allow it to be filmed reveals how psychotherapy may be useful in helping rock musicians survive the pitfalls of fame.

The bass position vacated by Jason Newsted was filled temporarily by Bob Rock, their producer, who played on *St. Anger* (2003). The album was loud, fast, raw, and angry, and it was presented as a return to form. It debuted at number one on the album charts in 30 countries and won a Grammy Award. For its minimalist approach and noisy production values, some found it another bold and interesting development. Others found it disappointing, citing the unappealing sound of the snare drum, the use of repetitive riffs, the lack of guitar solos, the overlong songs, and for seeming to emulate the music of bands that Metallica once inspired.

Perhaps no other band has had such deeply loyal and devoted fans from early in their career turn so strongly against them. From *The Black Album* onward, each change has caused consternation. Some have declared the band past the point of no return, that they have betrayed their genre by being once revolutionary and then just trendy, and that they are a mockery of their former selves. Depending on which disgruntled fan is talking, the band started to go downhill at almost every turn: after the first album; when Cliff Burton died; when they started working with Bob Rock; when James Hetfield cut his hair, or started taking singing lessons, or stopped drinking; or when Jason Newsted quit the band. Despite the bitching, Metallica remains one of the industry's top-grossing bands on the concert circuit, where they were in the top ten in 2000 and 2003. Rob Trujillo (b. 1964), formerly of Suicidal Tendencies and Ozzy Osbourne's band, is the latest bassist. The band toured with him to great acclaim, and the story continues.

Monkees, The

The BEATLES were known as the Fab Four, and they wore their fabulousness well. The Monkees were called, even by their fans, the "prefab four," meaning not that they predated the Beatles but that they were prefabricated, like a house that has been designed and manufactured and just needs assembly. It was a humorous but accurate description of their origin. Two television producers decided to create a fictional band to emulate the Beatles as they were presented in their films *A Hard Day's Night* (1964) and *Help* (1965)—funny and zany and apt to burst into song. The talented young men that made up the Monkees were all that. However, they chafed against the manufacturing process of their music—written by professionals and, aside from the vocals which the members provided, recorded by top studio musicians—until they gained artistic control and actually, remarkably, became a real band with their own sound and style. Despite their lightweight image, their musical output was diverse and sometimes sophisticated. Some of their music is classic pop rock and has held up over the years.

Like *Beatles, Monkees* was a two-syllable plural word with one purposefully misspelled letter indicating a life-form. Monkeys are animals, beetles are insects, but there was another model: the BYRDS, a FOLK ROCK group based, like the Monkees' TV show, in Los Angeles. Musically, the Monkees incorporated the sounds of both the BRITISH INVASION and of folk rock, especially on "Last Train to Clarksville," their first hit, a number one. On some songs they showed a COUNTRY ROCK influence, a style the Byrds helped pioneer.

The TV producers, Bert Schneider and Bob Rafelson, advertised in *Daily Variety* for four folk and rock musicians who could act and do comedy. More than 400 people answered the ad, including Stephen Stills (later of BUFFALO SPRINGFIELD and Crosby, Stills and Nash), Danny Hutton (later of Three Dog Night), and Paul Williams (who became a successful solo artist and songwriter). The field was narrowed down after a round of auditions that determined the candidates' singing and acting ability, charisma, sense of humor, and ability to improvise. Four were chosen to star in the situation comedy series about a struggling band.

Though all took turns singing lead, Davy Jones (b. 1945) was cast as the lead singer and was the heartthrob of the group. He was born in Manchester, and his British accent was an asset in the time of Beatlemania. He had experience in musical theater. Micky Dolenz (b. 1945) had been a child actor; he played the drummer and would write a few of their songs, including one that was a hit only in England. Mike Nesmith (b. 1942) was already a guitarist, and he developed into a fine songwriter. "Mary Mary," for example, was covered by the Paul Butterfield Blues Band, and "Different Drum" was a hit for Linda Rondstadt. Peter Tork (b. 1944), in the role of bassist, had been a folk singer. The slapstick comedy, fast editing, and appealing camaraderie of the actors gave the quirky but

The Monkees (Michael Ochs Archives.com)

wholesome show an upbeat quality, and response to it was sensational. It ran for two seasons, from September 1966 to March 1968. In each of the 58 episodes, the group would do a song or two. Monkee merchandise was very popular as well.

Of the professional writers who contributed songs, the first were Tommy Boyce and Bobby Hart. They wrote the show's theme song (with the catchy line "Hey, hey, we're the Monkees"), "Last Train to Clarksville," "(I'm Not Your) Steppin' Stone," recorded earlier by Paul Revere and the Raiders, and a popular song for garage and later punk bands to cover, "Words," and "Valleri," the Monkees' last top-10 hit. Neil Diamond wrote "I'm a Believer," their second hit and second number one, and "A Little Bit Me, a Little Bit You," also a million-seller. "I'm a Believer" is their most popular song, and was a number-one hit also in the United Kingdom, which embraced the TV show. Carole King and Gerry Goffin, the husband-and-wife team who had written several GIRL GROUP hits, wrote "Pleasant Valley Sunday," a critique of suburban life. "Daydream

Believer," another million-selling number-one song, was written by John Stewart of the Kingston Trio. Boyce and Hart had hits of their own, and Diamond, King, and Stewart all had successful careers as solo artists.

The Monkees' albums were also very popular: the first four all went to number one, each selling between 2 million and 5 million copies. The fifth, released just after the show's second season ended, sold a million. Though *The Monkees* was a comedy show about a band, it gave the impression that they played their own instruments on their records, so when it was revealed that their recordings were made by studio musicians, the audience felt betrayed. To counteract the controversy, the third album, *Headquarters,* was, aside from the French horn and cello parts (and some of the bass parts), completely their own playing. As well, they went on tour, mismatched with the JIMI HENDRIX Experience (new to American audiences) as their opening act.

After the TV show ceased, the Monkees made their own feature film. *Head,* cowritten and coproduced by Jack Nicholson, was innovative but too surreal and psychedelic for their teenybopper audience. It did give them some credibility with the hippies. Commercially it was a flop, but artistically it worked, and it is highly regarded today. It contained "Porpoise Song," a superb psychedelic song written by Goffin and King. The group then appeared in a mediocre TV special called *33 1/3 Revolutions Per Monkee.* Dispirited, Peter Tork left the group, and the others continued for two more albums as a trio. Nesmith left the group in 1970 for a solo career, and had some success as Michael Nesmith and the First National Band, scoring a hit with his composition "Joanne." He also ran a successful film and video production business. Dolenz and Jones soldiered on a duet, still called the Monkees, for one album before breaking up.

Changes (1970) did not chart until reissued in 1986, when the band reunited (without Nesmith) for a lengthy and highly successful 20th-anniversary tour and a new album. They gained a top-20 hit with "That Was Then, This Is Now." Their popular-ity had continued because their show was kept on television in syndicated reruns, and later was revived again on MTV, garnering them new and younger fans. The Rhino label reissued all of their recordings: original albums with bonus tracks, greatest hits discs, and box sets, plus videos of their shows, later reissued as DVD box sets of the complete first and second seasons. Nesmith took part in another reunion in 1996 and another new album and tour.

In the 1990s reruns of the shows were being aired in more than 40 countries. *Daydream Believers: The Monkees Story* (2000), a made-for-TV movie, cast actors who looked like the Monkees, and the DVD release includes commentary and interviews with three of the original members (all but Nesmith). The trio version of the group toured again in 2001, and one concert has been released, to fans' acclaim, on DVD. Two of the members, Jones and Dolenz, have written autobiographies. Teen idols had been prefab stars in the 1950s, but the Monkees were a model for numerous later acts created by producers, from the boy bands to the Spice Girls.

Monterey Pop Festival (1967) *landmark music festival*

Considered the first-ever rock festival, the Monterey Pop Festival (June 16–18, 1967) marked the handing of the torch from Los Angeles to San Francisco as the next vital regional cultural hearth. Essentially, this meant the passing of FOLK ROCK and the rise of PSYCHEDELIC ROCK. All five of San Francisco's top psychedelic bands were there: the JEFFERSON AIRPLANE, Country Joe and the Fish, Quicksilver Messenger Service, the GRATEFUL DEAD, and Big Brother and the Holding Company. The latter benefited most, getting signed to Columbia on the impression made by JANIS JOPLIN.

Certain performers and their stage antics—Otis Redding mesmerizing the audience, the WHO smashing their instruments, and JIMI HENDRIX burning his guitar—are now canonized in rock history. After WOODSTOCK, Monterey is the best remembered of the hundreds of rock festivals; the two are also the most documented. Discussions of Monterey are *de rigueur* in rock history books, and its sounds can be heard on a box set of four compact discs, the *Monterey Pop* film (1968; later expanded on DVD), plus the tapes and videos of additional performances that circulate among collectors.

Organizers John Phillips of the MAMAS AND THE PAPAS and their producer Lou Adler were regarded with suspicion by the San Francisco musicians who questioned their motives and disliked their Los Angeles show-business image but eventually agreed to perform. Not only were the Mamas and the Papas considered rich and phony hippies, but Phillips had written and produced Scott McKenzie's single "San Francisco (Be Sure to Wear Flowers in Your Hair)," which was already on the charts. Another paean to the Haight-Ashbury scene, sung first at the festival, was Eric Burdon and the ANIMALS' "San Franciscan Nights," which became a hit later that summer. ("Monterey," their tribute to the weekend, was a hit at the end of the year.)

Besides the Mamas and the Papas, who announced the festival on *The Ed Sullivan Show*, and Scott McKenzie, Los Angeles was represented by Johnny Rivers, a dynamic nightclub entertainer whose hits were mainly POP ROCK versions of black R&B songs, and folk rock acts the Association, BUFFALO SPRINGFIELD, and the versatile BYRDS. The BEACH BOYS, though advertised, were in crisis after several extremely successful and creative years and did not perform.

Other styles that were represented at Monterey were: East Coast SINGER-SONGWRITER pop folk (SIMON AND GARFUNKEL, Laura Nyro), soul (Lou Rawls, Booker T and the MGs, Otis Redding), BRITISH INVASION (the Who, Eric Burdon and the Animals), plus Ravi Shankar's Indian ragas, and a world-jazz mix from South African–born trumpeter Hugh Masekela. Aside from L.A. folk rock and San Francisco psychedelia, the strongest contingent came from blues and BLUES ROCK, including the Paul Butterfield Blues Band, the Steve Miller Band, the Electric Flag, the Blues Project, Al Kooper, Canned

Heat, and the Jimi Hendrix Experience, who were making their debut in America. The Jimi Hendrix Experience introduced a new format, the power trio: a singing guitarist backed only by (very proficient) bass and drums. Blues rock proved to be the most durable of all the styles present at the Monterey Pop Festival, and it is played to this day everywhere electric guitars are to be found.

For the players, the audience, the police, and the townspeople, Monterey managed to live up to its advertised motto of "Music, Love, and Flowers." For the record industry, Monterey was something like a trade fair—a place where labels could shop for new acts and observe new trends.

Motown

Motown is the name of a record label that developed its own style of rhythm and blues. Its incredible popularity began in the early 1960s. Motown stood for "motor town," and was thus a reference to the label's location, in Detroit, Michigan, the center of automobile manufacturing in North America. Motown launched the careers of dozens of important acts, including Smokey Robinson and the Miracles, the Supremes, the Four Tops, the Temptations, Marvin Gaye, Stevie Wonder, and the Jackson Five (with a young Michael Jackson).

From its start Motown was a source of inspiration and repertoire for rock acts. For example, the BEATLES covered Barrett Strong's "Money," the first hit on Motown, the Marvelettes' "Please Mr. Postman," and the Miracles' "You Really Got a Hold on Me." The ROLLING STONES did Marvin Gaye's "Hitch Hike" and "Can I Get a Witness," the Miracles' "Going to a Go-Go," and the Temptations' "Ain't Too Proud to Beg." CREEDENCE CLEARWATER REVIVAL made "I Heard It through the Grapevine" famous again after it had already been a hit for two different Motown acts, Gladys Knight and the Pips and Marvin Gaye. Vanilla Fudge rearranged the Supremes' "You Keep Me Hangin' On," and Phil Collins redid their "You Can't Hurry Love." Martha and the Vandellas' "Dancing in the Streets" was a hit for the MAMAS AND THE PAPAS, Van Halen, and a duet of Mick Jagger and DAVID BOWIE.

The label was founded by Berry Gordy. His ambition and hard work made the operation such a success that it became the most profitable black-owned music business in the United States. Prior to starting the label, Berry's efforts at being a boxer and a record store owner had been failures. He went to work on the Ford assembly line, but he quit to become a professional songwriter and prospered when his songs were hits for Jackie Wilson, including "Reet Petite" (1957) and "Lonely Teardrops" (1958). After observing a vocal group called the Matadors (later known as the Miracles) in an audition, Gordy was taken by their youthful talent and charm. Before long he went into the record production business to promote them.

Berry Gordy and the group's lead singer, Smokey Robinson, were mutually encouraging and they became close friends. Together they wrote the Miracles' "Shop Around" (1960), Motown's first million-seller. In the lyrics, a mother gives advice to her son to not be hasty in love, to find a girl whose love is true. Her words are set to a gospel chord progression, giving them a sermonlike quality. That this landmark recording should deal with family values was appropriate, for not only did the people who worked at Motown feel like a family, but the business was supported by the Gordy clan. They had lent him money to start it, and several of his family members were to work for the company. Robinson was prominent as an artist, a writer, and a producer, and he became Motown's vice president. One of his songs was the beloved "My Girl," a 1965 hit for the Temptations, the most successful and long-lived R&B act in the field.

Using the idea of the assembly line, Gordy built up several divisions of labor. The company's headquarters was a house nicknamed Hitsville USA, with Gordy's residence on the second floor, a reception area on the main floor, and a studio in the basement. Operations soon expanded to a series of other houses in the neighborhood. Several individuals and teams each had a specialty. There were songwriters, producers, engineers, publicists, graphic artists, and promoters. A choreographer created dance steps and rehearsed the acts. A woman ran the charm school, grooming the young artists, mostly from ghetto environments, to exude pride, confidence, and accomplishment by teaching them how to be polite and act professionally in social settings. The house band was known as the Funk Brothers. They belatedly came to be recognized because of a film called *Standing in the Shadows of Motown* (2002) that grew out of a project to honor bassist James Jamerson, a little-known electric BASS player of immense influence.

Motown's motto was "The Sound of Young America." The music was fresh and wholesome, rooted in gospel and blues but aimed not at black youth or white youth or any other race, but at everyone. The songs were emotional and genuine, with yearning, romantic lyrics set to infectious rhythms ideal for dancing. The arrangements were imaginative but not difficult to grasp, and Motown never succumbed to a formula sound. Of the songwriters, who worked in friendly competition with each other, the most successful were the team of Eddie Holland, Lamont Dozier, and Brian Holland known as Holland-Dozier-Holland. In 1966 they won eight Broadcast Music International (BMI) awards for the year's most performed songs; the Beatles were second with five awards. Over a three-year period in the mid-1960s, they wrote 28 hits that made the top 20. When they left Motown in 1967 over a royalty dispute, neither they nor the company would have such success again.

Many Holland-Dozier-Holland songs were sung by the Supremes, including "Where Did Our Love Go," "Baby Love," "Come See About Me," "Stop! In the Name of Love," and "Back in My Arms Again." In gowns and wigs, the Supremes were elegant, and before lead singer Diana Ross left for a solo career in 1969, they had placed 33 songs on the pop charts, a dozen of them number-one hits. Gordy then focused his energies on Ross's thriving solo career and her chances as a Hollywood actress—she did act in a few films—but in doing so withdrew from the general running of Motown. Its last great act was the Jackson Five. Gordy cowrote their first hit, "I Want You Back" (1969), the first of four consecutive number-one hits. Michael Jackson, only 11 at the time, was the star of the show and went on to massive fame in the 1980s.

Motown's move to Los Angeles in 1971 dismantled most of the structure that had run so well in Detroit. By then was less needed anyway. That year two Motown artists, Stevie Wonder and Marvin Gaye, fought for and won the right to have complete artistic control over their recordings. Wonder produced a remarkable series of albums in the 1970s. Gaye released the landmark LP *What's Goin' On* (1971) and continued having hits until he was fatally shot by his father in 1984. By the early 1970s, the Temptations had weathered changing styles, but most of the other acts had folded or were in decline. The Supremes, without Diana Ross, continued to have hits on a more moderate scale until 1976.

From the mid-1970s into the 1980s, several Motown stars defected to other labels, though Motown retained enough of its established acts and developed new ones, such as the Commodores and Rick James, to maintain its position of importance. In 1983 the company celebrated its 25th anniversary with a successful TV special. The Motown Historical Museum, in the restored Hitsville building, opened in 1985 and remains an important Detroit tourist attraction.

In 1988, the year he was inducted into the Rock and Roll Hall of Fame, Berry Gordy sold Motown Records to MCA and Boston Ventures for $61 million. He retained ownership of Jobete, his publishing company. Boston Ventures later bought out MCA's interest and in 1993 sold Motown Records to Polygram, based in Holland, for $325 million. Motown, now a subsidiary of Universal Music, is still active as a record label. Some of the legendary artists are still on the roster and others have been brought back, while several new artists have had success. Gordy sold off Jobete, which controlled the rights to virtually all of the 15,000 songs composed at Motown, to EMI in increments. In 1997 they acquired 50 percent for $132 million. In 2003 EMI bought another 30 percent for $110 million, and in 2004 they bought Gordy's remaining 20 percent for about $80 million. The songs continue to generate royalty income from radio airplay and soundtrack use, and from commercial licensing for new recordings and such growing markets as cell phone ring tones and karaoke.

n

Nelson, Ricky (Rick Nelson) (1940–1985)
rockabilly singer

Ricky Nelson was the first TV star to become a rock and roll star. He truly grew up in public, for he and his whole family—dad, mom, and older brother David—played themselves on *The Adventures of Ozzie and Harriet.* It was one of the most popular and longest-running early sitcoms, first on the radio from 1944, and then on TV from 1952 to 1966. With hit records, more than 50 of them, from 1957 to 1973, Ricky Nelson himself was one of the most popular and longest-lasting of the rock and roll artists. Many of his hits, including "Poor Little Fool," "Travelin' Man," "Hello Mary Lou," and "Garden Party," are regularly heard on oldies radio programs.

His parents were show business veterans. His father, Oswald (known as Ozzie), had led a dance band in the 1930s, and his mother, Harriet, had been the band's vocalist. When Ricky wanted to sing and make records too, Ozzie had the connections, and he became his son's manager. In 1957, at age 16, Ricky made his first record. Both sides were big hits: "A Teenager's Romance" was a slow song of the kind that used to be called a "rockaballad," and "I'm Walking" was a ROCKABILLY cover of a FATS DOMINO hit. Ozzie then negotiated a deal with Imperial Records that gave him and Ricky complete control over song selection. The first record for Imperial earned a gold record, and both sides were hits: one an oldie and the other a ROCKABILLY song.

Rockabilly, the kind recorded on the Sun label of Memphis by CARL PERKINS and ELVIS PRESLEY (who personally encouraged Nelson), was one of Ricky's chief inspirations. He surrounded himself with great rockabilly talent. His guitarist was from Louisiana: James Burton was just one year older, but already a veteran rocker, having played on the original "Suzy-Q" with Dale Hawkins. Burton was a very exciting and influential player who went on to be one of the most recorded guitarists in history,

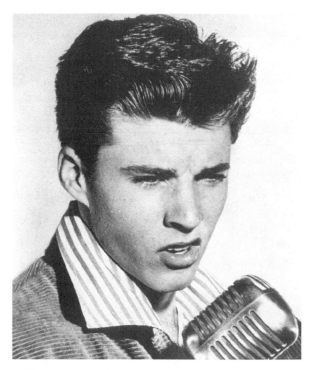

Rick Nelson (Michael Ochs Archives.com)

working with a who's who of music stars. Nelson, like Elvis Presley, used the Jordanaires for background vocals. Several of his early hits were written by Johnny and Dorsey Burnette, brothers from Memphis who had been part of the Rock 'n Roll Trio, later recognized as one of the finest of all of the 1950s rockabilly bands.

Nelson's other big influence was the music of his parents. Not only were some of his hits new versions of songs from the 1920s to the 1940s, popularized by the likes of Glenn Miller, Billie Holiday, and Bing Crosby with the Andrews Sisters, but his singing style was cool and smooth like a swing-era crooner. Applying this to rockabilly, while keeping the style's rhythmic drive, gave him more commercial success than any other rockabilly artist, aside from Elvis.

With his good looks and light voice, he was a prototype for the teen idols who came after him, and his youthfulness was played up in his first hit and others like "Young Emotions" and "Waitin' in School." When he turned 21 he indicated that he had grown up by dropping the "y" from his first name. As Rick Nelson he reflected on all that in "Teen Age Idol" (1962).

Later in the 1960s, he was one of the pioneers of COUNTRY ROCK. In the early 1970s, he got into the reflective SINGER-SONGWRITER style and did FOLK ROCK versions of BOB DYLAN songs. His last big hit was "Garden Party" (1972), about an oldies show at Madison Square Garden where he was booed for his hippie image and new repertoire, which included the ROLLING STONES' "Honky Tonk Women." The lyrics of "Garden Party" state "If memories were all I sang, I'd rather drive a truck . . . you can't please everyone so you've got to please yourself."

In the 1980s he returned to rockabilly and was an important and beloved figure during that music's revival. He died in 1985 on the way to New Year's Eve gig in a plane crash that also took the lives of his fiancée and four members of his band. The next year he was voted into the Rock and Roll Hall of Fame.

new wave

New wave is a term that was coined by the record industry and applied in the late 1970s to emerging American and British bands. The idea was to distinguish them as something more palatable than PUNK ROCK, which had arrived a little earlier. There were many similarities: lyrics that criticized society, few instrumental solos, pumping bass lines that repeated the root note of a chord, performers using jerky, quirky body movements on stage, and an obsession with fashion and unconventional clothes. New wave and punk reacted against both disco and the established traditions in POP ROCK. Bands like FLEETWOOD MAC and PINK FLOYD, huge at the time, were considered irrelevant, corporate, and formulaic, and they were derisively called dinosaurs (in other words, big, lumbering creatures whose days of domination were numbered).

The differences between punk and new wave were in their intent and their constituency. Punk was rebellious and confrontational. It took a minimalist approach to sound, usually reducing the sonic palette to the basics: GUITAR, BASS, DRUMS. Its participants and audience, at least in the United Kingdom, were primarily disaffected lower-class youth who felt there was no future. Their music was distorted and their clothes were meant to shock. New wave was more experimental and artistic. It took an expansive approach to sound, broadening the sonic palette to embrace portable keyboard synthesizers—readily available by the 1980s and relatively inexpensive—and diverse influences from electronics to DOO-WOP to REGGAE. New wave's participants and audience tended to be more affluent and better educated. Their attitude was more positive—they did not promote anarchy like punk did. Their music was sonically clear and their clothes were garish and outlandish, but in a glamorous way that was meant to entice. In simpler terms, punk had a street sensibility and new wave had an art school sensibility. Because of that, new wave was more accepting of musical difference as well as less rigid in gender stereotypes. New wave had room for many female performers, and also for homosexual males.

The term *new wave* united a variety of acts that all tried to do something new, but there were two main sources. The first was punk. It had made an unforeseen opening in rock and roll that allowed for a new direction, and some people favor the use of the term *post-punk* to describe the arty and challenging bands that were connected to it. The second was what has been called synthpop. PROGRESSIVE ROCK had expanded the role of synthesizers in rock, and some people try to reserve the term *new wave* to describe bands that made prominent use of them. Those bands were pop-based and oriented towards dancing, borrowing some of the big beat sound of disco. However, because some of the so-called post-punk bands, like TALKING HEADS, were there at the start of punk but followed their own course, it does not seem appropriate to refer to them by that term. Because there are many other strands included in new wave, such as various new versions of older forms from ROCKABILLY to ska, the simplest thing is to stick with *new wave* as the term for all.

One way to sort out the multitude of new wave acts is by country. Though most of them came from England or the United States, there were acts from Canada (Men Without Hats, the Spoons, Martha and the Muffins), Australia (Men at Work, Icehouse), New Zealand (Split Enz), Scotland (Big Country), Ireland (the Boomtown Rats), Norway (a-ha), Germany (Nina Hagen, Nena), Austria (Falco), and elsewhere.

English new wave's best-known acts included Elvis Costello, the Police, Culture Club, the Pretenders, Duran Duran, and Wham! Culture Club's Boy George created a sensation with his charismatic charm and androgynous glamour; their biggest hits were "Do You Really Want to Hurt Me" (1982) and "Karma Chameleon" (1984). The Pretenders were lead by Chrissie Hynde, from Ohio. They proved quite durable, with hits from 1980 to 1994 (their biggest was "Back on the Chain Gang" in 1983), and resilient: two of their members died of drug overdoses within a year. Duran Duran was the most commercially successful of all the new wave acts, British or American, in the United States. Their

first hit entered the charts in 1982, their last in 1997. Among their many triumphs were "Hungry Like the Wolf" (1982), "The Reflex" (1984), and "A View to a Kill" (1985, the theme to a James Bond movie), the latter two both number-one songs. Dozens of acts were important, such as the Jam, Joe Jackson, XTC, the Psychedelic Furs, Talk Talk, and Nick Lowe. New wave had a darker, introverted side that came to be known as goth. It was exemplified by Bauhaus, the Cure, Siouxsie and the Banshees, and Joy Division (which became New Order after the suicide of front man Ian Curtis).

The biggest names in American new wave were the Cars, Talking Heads, and BLONDIE. Also important were the B-52's, Cyndi Lauper, the Go-Go's, the Bangles, Devo, Tom Tom Club (an offshoot of Talking Heads), Oingo Boingo, Wall of Voodoo, 'til Tuesday, and a host of others. The Cars, Blondie, the Go-Go's, and the Bangles are also considered POWER POP, and the terms *new wave* and *power pop* (as well as just *rock*) have also been applied to Tom Petty and the Heartbreakers, Cheap Trick, Marshall Crenshaw, and the Romantics, among others.

New wave's heyday was from the late 1970s to the mid-1980s. Its biggest boost came when MTV went on the air in summer 1981. A television station completely devoted to music videos was a new idea, and new wave provided much of its content. Videos made image as important as sound and gave an introduction to many acts, such as Adam Ant, Spandau Ballet, Haircut 100, the Thompson Twins, and a Flock of Seagulls, that perhaps would not otherwise have had much impact, and made stars of Culture Club, Duran Duran, and others. British acts, like the above named, seemed to be able to take advantage of the situation to make clever, mysterious, and fashionable videos. A constant stream of music videos on television changed buying habits. For example, Men at Work had two number-one singles—"Who Can It Be Now" (1982) and "Down Under" (1983)—more because of TV than radio.

The excitement of the times was documented in *Urgh! A Music War* (1981), a concert movie (and soundtrack album) filmed in 1980. It was filmed in New York, Los Angeles, London, and France. Several of the featured acts made names for themselves in new wave: the Police, Orchestral Manoeuvres in the Dark (also known as OMD), XTC, Echo and the Bunnymen, the Go-Go's, UB-40, Klaus Nomi, Gary Numan, and Gang of Four. Most of the acts in the film were connected to I.R.S. Records or its related booking agency, F.B.I. The I.R.S. label was founded by Miles Copeland (the older brother of Stewart Copeland, the drummer in the Police) in the late 1970s, and was one of the first successful independent punk rock and new wave labels.

In the new wave era, synthesizers were available in cheap, toylike consumer versions, like the ones made by Casio, and more musician-oriented versions, like the Yamaha DX-7. With a flick of a digit, one could make dozens of different sounds, and by playing with one or two fingers, a person could sound interesting without possessing proper piano technique. People who had never played before were happy to get onstage and experiment with sound. Synthesizers gave new wave acts a futuristic side, and the tensions of a society absorbing evermore technological advances were played out in humorous ways, from robotic stage movements to science-fiction inspired fashions. Devo, from Akron, Ohio, made it an essential part of their act: they looked and sounded like mutants, or at least like people in industrial uniforms pretending to be robots. Their name came from the word *devolution,* the idea being that humans were not evolving but doing the opposite. Their first album is called *Q: Are We Not Men? A: We Are Devo!* (1978).

Another early band with a new wave sound was the Cars, from Boston. "Just What I Needed" and "My Best Friend's Girl," their first of more than a dozen hits (all written by guitarist Ric Ocasek), both made the top 40 in 1978. Their use of punk's pulsing eighth-note rhythms gave them a driving underpinning for their clever and catchy midtempo songs. The idea of the car as something sleek and manufactured for the use and pleasure of the masses is apt, for the Cars' music had the crafts-

manship and polished sheen of pop music. Their music mixed the old and the new: the basic structures of 1950s rock and roll and the vocal harmonies of the 1960s with the relentlessness of punk, the new sound of the synthesizer, and some use of electronic percussion. Ocasek's melancholy, somewhat weary-sounding voice seemed detached while singing his emotional and poetic, at times surrealistic, lyrics.

An awareness of earlier music styles was a common thread for many of the acts, not just the power pop bands, under the banner of new wave. The "two-tone" bands of England (Madness, the Specials, the Selector, the English Beat), so named for their black-and-white checkerboard logos and the racial integration within the bands, revamped ska, a style predating reggae that originated in Jamaica. Reggae itself found its way into punk bands (especially the Clash) and new wave bands such as UB-40 and the Police. The Stray Cats and a host of others revamped 1950s rockabilly into something more powerful and more fashion-conscious.

The synthesizer bands were inspired by Kraftwerk, from Germany, whose album *Autobahn* made the top 10 in the United States in 1975. British new wave artists particularly took to the synthesizer; they were inspired also by Roxy Music, whose string of hit singles in the United Kingdom began in 1972, but who had only sporadic hits in the United States. Gary Numan's "Cars" hit the U.S. top 10 in 1980, as did Soft Cell's "Tainted Love" in 1982. The Human League had several hits, including two number ones: "Don't You Want Me" (1982) and "Human" (1986). Depeche Mode had great success, and former Depeche Mode member Vince Clarke's Yaz and Erasure were also popular. The Pet Shop Boys, a duo, had a number one in their first hit: "West End Girls" (1986).

A fine example of a new wave hit featuring the synthesizer is the first and biggest hit for Eurythmics (the duo of Annie Lennox and Dave Stewart). "Sweet Dreams (Are Made of This)" was a number-one single in 1983. It featured sequenced keyboards, a drum machine, and Lennox's soulful vocals. The worldly lyrics of the verses ("Who am I to disagree . . . everybody's looking for something") contrast with the uplifting lines in the bridge: "Hold your head up . . . keep your head up . . . movin' on." The solo is the synthesized sound of a string section of violins. Lennox's orange hair and playful but subversive fooling around with gender stereotypes in a series of smart videos gave them a strong image.

In its heyday, some established stars, such as DAVID BOWIE and Hall and Oates, adopted elements of new wave in certain songs, as did some up-and-coming artists, such as Madonna, who incorporated it into her pop disco style. Once new wave had run its course, its component strands separated again. The so-called post-punk side was carried on in ALTERNATIVE ROCK. The revivalist impulse continued to be identified with each respective style. The exploration of the synthesizer and electronic instruments was carried, through the influence of New Order and others, into house and electronica. Power pop kept going as it had before new wave started. The goth bands were forerunners of a much wider movement. The pop side of new wave continued as pop rock.

New wave has proved durable in many ways. Several of its stars have had lengthy careers, for example Annie Lennox (of Eurythmics), George Michael (of Wham!), Sting (of the Police), Cyndi Lauper, and David Byrne (of Talking Heads). The records have retained a nostalgic value and an undeniable ability to get people dancing, and its catchy bass lines and hooks have been sampled for current dance records.

Nirvana

They formed in Aberdeen, Washington, in 1987, and in their short career, until the death of Kurt Cobain, Nirvana emerged as the iconic representative of a new style called GRUNGE. Grunge music and the surrounding subculture emerged from Seattle, where it had developed from a strong local scene supported by independent labels such as Sub Pop.

Similar things were going on in other cities at the same time.

Nirvana was a trio. Kurt Cobain (1967–94) was a bright, melancholic, and charismatic performer and a gifted lyric writer and singer. His versatile voice had an endearing raspy quality, with a broad dynamic range from a whisper to a raging scream, sometimes in the same song. His guitar playing was engaging and powerful, not for his soloing but for his unusual chordal riffs. Bassist Krist Novoselic (b. 1965) and drummer Dave Grohl (b. 1969) both occasionally sang backup. For the original compositions, Cobain would come up with the basic concept on acoustic guitar, and Novoselic and Grohl would help determine the song's structure and feel. The lyrics were often based on something Cobain had seen on television or read in a newspaper. The songs were made more striking by his penchant for taking on someone else's character and singing the lyrics in the first person.

Nirvana was influenced by underground bands such as Sonic Youth, the Vaselines, the Pixies, the Melvins, and Mudhoney. Their sound drew from hard rock and PUNK ROCK and mixed Cobain's melodic singing and raw guitar with Novoselic's rhythmic bass underpinning the riffs and Grohl's intense and agile drumming driving the ensemble. They also played acoustically sometimes, and a handful of their recordings feature cello. Cobain said: "People have opened up to an appreciation of hard rock in punk, and it's great that they've fused together. Now it's time to appreciate the pop side. Attitude is one thing. But a good song is the most important thing. It's the only way to really touch someone."[14]

Cobain and Novoselic met in 1985 and played in various bands, forming Nirvana at the end of 1987. In its early days several drummers passed through the band. Chad Channing was there for the first album, *Bleach* (1989), Sub Pop's first album release. *Bleach* was done in three days and cost $600 to record. The album shows the group in a formative stage, with "About a Girl" more pop-sounding than what other grunge bands were doing at the time. Melody floating above noisy, heavy riffs was an appealing mix, and the band attracted a cult following.

Grohl, formerly of a Washington, D.C., band called Scream, joined in the fall of 1990, just before Nirvana did a brief tour of England. His arrival strengthened their sound immediately and elated the others, inspiring a burst of group songwriting. For months they rehearsed daily. After members of Sonic Youth urged one of Geffen Records' representatives to see Nirvana in concert, the band was signed to that label. For the producer, the band chose Butch Vig, an associate of Sonic Youth and the Smashing Pumpkins.

With the new label's resources, they were able to take more time for their second album. The band was in good spirits, happy with their new lineup, their new contract, and being in sunny Los Angeles with some spare money to do some partying after recording sessions. They were not yet famous, and the sessions were done casually, without pressure. By the time recording was finished, the band had spent $130,000, twice their initial budget and a far cry from the $600 it cost to record *Bleach*.

Nevermind (1991), with a cover image of a naked baby underwater, a fishhook with a dollar bill on it dangling in front of him, brought Nirvana an unexpected and spectacular rise to fame. "Smells Like Teen Spirit" was hailed as an anthem for its generation. It is a catchy song whose lyrics were smart but largely indecipherable, except for the odd phrase like "Here we are now, entertain us" and "Oh well, whatever, never mind." Less than three weeks after *Nevermind* was released, it was certified as a gold record. It has sold 18 million copies worldwide, 10 million in the United States. Over the next few months the band toured Europe, Australia, Japan, and Hawaii. The video for "Smells Like Teen Spirit" was in heavy rotation on MTV, the album hit number one on the *Billboard* charts, and Nirvana was on the cover of *Rolling Stone*. The grunge scene exploded, as other bands and grunge clothing styles became fashionable. Since that time, *Nevermind* has regularly been named as one of rock's top albums, and

many consider it the best grunge album, and even the best album of the 1990s.

Cobain, who exuded despair and angst, was seen as the spokesman or a John Lennon–type figure for the so-called Generation X.[15] He rejected that role, and the band, taken off guard by the whirlwind of their huge success, approached their fame as anti–rock stars, with humor, ambivalence, cynicism, and sarcasm. For example, as seen on Nirvana's *Live! Tonight! Sold Out!* (1994) video, in England on the *Top of the Pops* television show, where the instrumental track was prerecorded, they subvert the fantasy that the band is actually performing "Smells Like Teen Spirit" by letting on that they are miming. Cobain strums while his other hand slides up and down the guitar neck, but the fingers are kept straight, rather than forming chords. Novoselic jumps around and swings the bass in a way that would be impossible if he were actually playing. At one point Grohl stands up and waves his arms in the air while the drum beat continues. The vocal track, however, is live, but even on that Cobain plays with expectations by singing it in an odd voice, pitched one octave lower than on the hit record, while almost swallowing the mike.

Cobain was a troubled soul and suffered from bipolar disorder, which is sometimes seen in people with artistic temperaments who are sensitive and highly creative. He was also afflicted with a painful and mysterious stomach ailment. In pain and wearied by the commercialism of the music industry, he became reclusive and addicted to heroin. In early 1992 Cobain married Courtney Love of the band Hole, and they had a daughter. Even as parents, they reportedly continued to use heroin.

The gap before the next Nirvana studio album was filled with *Incesticide* (1992), a collection of outtakes, demos, B-sides, and live sessions recorded for the BBC. Cobain felt guilty about how polished *Nevermind* sounded, and was uncomfortable with the fame it brought, so for the band's third (and last, as it turned out) studio album, *In Utero* (1993), they aimed for a uncompromising and unpolished sound. The album is harsh and dark, full of extremes and expressions of inner turmoil, with inspired songwriting. It also went to number one. Some songs comment on fame and its cost, and another example of the sarcastic antistar attitude is "Radio Friendly Unit Shifter." The title suggests that it will be suitable for airplay and will sell a lot, but radio shunned it: it is full of feedback and Cobain screaming "what is wrong with me?"

During the three-month tour to support *In Utero*, Nirvana performed an acoustic show for MTV's *Unplugged* series, a remarkable contrast to their grunge style. They brilliantly reinterpreted some of their songs in the acoustic setting, adding cover songs by Leadbelly, Devo, the Vaselines, DAVID BOWIE, and three by the Meat Puppets (on which they are joined by two members of that band, Cris and Curt Kirkwood). The band gave an emotional and subtle performance. Cobain was relaxed and soulful, Grohl subtly played his drums with brushes, Novoselic played acoustic bass and accordion, and a second guitarist, Pat Smear, formerly of the Germs, was added to lineup. The show was aired on television before Cobain's death but not released on CD until afterward. Both *MTV Unplugged in New York* (1994) and another concert album made number one on the *Billboard* chart. *From the Muddy Banks of the Wishkah* (1996) was another reminder of what a great live act Nirvana was: loud, frenzied, and somewhat sloppy, but full of vitality.

Though the coroner's report indicated that Cobain died of self-inflicted gunshot wounds on April 8, 1994, there is speculation that he was murdered. Apparently he was contemplating a divorce and retiring from music. In print, on Web sites, and in film, various theories, possible motives, and inconsistencies in the case have been presented and suspicions cast.

A legal struggle pitted Dave Grohl (now in a successful band called Foo Fighters) and Krist Novoselic against Cobain's widow, Courtney Love, over the ownership of Nirvana's music. It was finally resolved, resulting in the release of *Nirvana* (2002), a greatest-hits album with one previously unreleased studio track, "You Know You're Right," the last song Nirvana recorded together. *With the Lights Out* (2004), a box set of three CDs and one DVD, collects B-sides, tracks from compilations and live shows, and home demos.

Cobain kept a journal from around the time that Nirvana began until just before his death, filling 22 notebooks with his thoughts, song lyrics, and drawings. His writing is by turns morbid and humorous. It gives insight into his depression and his thoughts on fame, and reveals his knowledge of rock music's history and his desire to be part of it. A sampling was published as *Journals* (2002), which reproduced actual handwritten notebook pages.

In their brief career Nirvana took risks and achieved their goal of making music that mattered. In the process they became one of the most influential rock acts since the BEATLES.

Oasis

This British band is famous for more than its dense, GUITAR-dominated Britpop style and the high quality of music during their rapid rise. Alongside the hit singles, top albums, and sold-out stadium shows, is the bad behavior of the outrageous, volatile Gallagher brothers. Liam Gallagher (b. 1972) sings lead, and Noel Gallagher (b. 1967) plays guitar, writes almost all of the songs, and shares the lead vocals. They are the core and only consistent members of Oasis. The music press, the mainstream gossip columns, and more than a dozen books about the band have noted the bickering, the booze, the drugs, the marriages, the marital infidelity, the fistfights, the insulting remarks about other musicians, the canceled gigs and aborted tours, the rumors of the band's imminent breakup, and the comings and goings of the other members. The publicity has done wonders for Oasis. Their unpredictability has created an air of danger and uncertainty around them.

They came to notice with music that had a 1990s sound and sensibility but drew from earlier artists, particularly the BEATLES. Three years after their formation in 1992, Oasis seemed as big as their heroes. The initial rehearsals, demo recordings, and getting signed to a recording contract were all done in short order. Then a series of hit singles made Oasis so popular that their first album, *Definitely Maybe* (1994), entered the U.K. charts at number one. Their second, *(What's the Story) Morning Glory?* (1995), did the same. These musically rich and assured efforts are considered to be their best. Oasis then did a sold-out tour of the United States. This is the period when the fans called them "The Best Band in the World." The concert film called *There and Then* (1996) shows them at their peak. As it begins Noel Gallagher comes onstage and faces the audience—tens of thousands of cheering fans—with arms outstretched, repeatedly lifting his hands to command more applause, then, arms over his head, bows a few times in reverence to the crowd. The first gesture seems consistent with the band's reputation for egotism and arrogance, the second appears as worshipful, another trait they exhibit, at least with reference to the Beatles.

The Beatles influence was never hidden: there is a Beatlesque quality to much of their music. One song is reminiscent of the Beatles' "Hey Jude," others of the Beatles album *Abbey Road.* An early Oasis single, called "Live Forever," had a picture sleeve that depicted John Lennon's childhood home. Oasis did a version of the Beatles' "I Am the Walrus" in concert and released it as the B-side of another single. Liam Gallagher and his wife named their child Lennon.

There was so much anticipation for Oasis' third album, *Be Here Now* (1997), supposedly named after a remark John Lennon made, that customers lined up in front of retail shops. Within a day (or a week—sources differ), 800,000 copies were sold in the United Kingdom. However, despite a couple of hit singles and hot sales, some listeners started to lose interest in the band, finding the songs lacking in substance and overly long. Those who found the music stale and bloated attributed it to the band's party lifestyle. A compilation of B-sides called *The Masterplan* (1998) was welcomed, but *Standing on the Shoulders of Giants* (2000), was seen as a decline. Two founding members were gone, and the well of inspiration appeared to be running dry: some lyrics and songwriting were weak, and the band's influences were too transparent. *Familiar to Millions* (2000) was a live double CD (also released on video and DVD) of performances at Wembley Stadium. *Heathen Chemistry* (2002), a more democratic effort, was spotty, but in its best moments seemed to indicate a return to form. *Don't Believe the Truth* (2005) shows that the band's attitude is still one of its best assets, even as the references to 1960s British pop rock are clearly in the foreground.

Orbison, Roy (1936–1988) *singer and songwriter*

Orbison was a gentle man with a fabulous voice and a talent for writing excellent songs that touched people deeply. ELVIS PRESLEY called him "the greatest singer in the world." Roy Orbison was plain looking, an unlikely star whose black hair, dark glasses, and almost motionless stance on stage gave him a distant, enigmatic image. It seemed appropriate though, for his emotional songs did not need a showy presentation. He began in his native Texas, recorded his best-known music in Tennessee, toured extensively, and was enormously popular in the United Kingdom, Europe, and Australia even when his recording career was in decline in the United States. He died suddenly after making a spectacular comeback that was supported by several of the other biggest stars in rock.

With his soaring, distinctive, almost operatic voice, accompanied by swirling orchestration, rhythmic punctuations, and tender, even celestial background singing, Roy Orbison made some of the most loved music in the rock and pop field. He expressed desolation in "Crying," melancholy in "Only the Lonely (Know How I Feel)" and "It's Over," and yearning in "In Dreams" and "Dream Baby (How Long Must I Dream)." The songs of heartbreak and desire were tempered by other feel-

ings: promise and reassurance in "Blue Angel," happy surprise when the lady walks back toward him in "Oh, Pretty Woman," and triumph, when she chooses him over his rival in "Running Scared." All those songs were top-10 hits between 1960 and 1964. The universality of the emotions, the sophistication of the compositions (most written by Orbison, usually with a co-author), the quality of the presentation, and, of course, his glorious singing have made them timeless.

Born in Vernon, Texas, near the Oklahoma border, he was raised nearly 400 miles to the southeast in Wink, Texas, near the New Mexico border. His father supervised oil crews and his mother was a nurse. Roy was ridiculed as a child for his beady eyes and glasses, and the emotional scars stayed with him. He received his first guitar at age five as a birthday present from his father, who taught him how to play. By eight years old he was singing in public and on the radio, and at 13 he formed his first band, the Wink Westerners. After high school he went to North Texas State University, where he planned to be a geologist and then a schoolteacher.

Around this time he had a band called the Teen Kings. Some of the music they performed in 1956 for a television broadcast was preserved and issued on CD in 2001. It shows them to be a competent working ROCKABILLY band influenced by Elvis Presley and doing some of the hits of the day, such as "Blue Suede Shoes." Also in 1956, the band went to the Clovis, New Mexico studio of Norman Petty (who would become famous as BUDDY HOLLY's producer) to cut a record. "Ooby Dooby" was written by fellow students and "Trying to Get to You" was inspired by Presley's version. "Ooby Dooby" became a regional hit and led to Orbison getting signed by Sun. The Teen Kings moved to Memphis and rerecorded the two songs. The band backed him on some of the two dozen additional songs he did at Sun, but when they broke up in 1957 and went home, Orbison stayed in Memphis. Some of his Sun songs are rockabilly, others point to his later style. The Sun version of "Ooby Dooby" became his first national hit in 1956, reaching number 59 and leading to live and television appearances. From mid-1956 into 1958 Orbison toured regularly from Canada to Florida with CARL PERKINS, Johnny Cash, and many others.

The flip side of the Sun version of "Ooby Dooby" was "Go Go Go," his first recorded original, retitled "Down the Line" when done by JERRY LEE LEWIS and RICKY NELSON. In 1957 another Sun rockabilly artist named Warren Smith had his only pop hit with an Orbison composition, "So Long I'm Gone." Orbison never recorded it, but it gave him his first composer royalties. In 1958 his song "Claudette," named for his wife, was a hit for the EVERLY BROTHERS, the B-side of "All I Have to Do Is Dream." Buddy Holly recorded two of his songs. At this point Orbison was more successful as a songwriter than as a performer. Through the Everlys' contacts Orbison obtained a songwriting contract with a Nashville publisher, and he moved there in 1958. He recorded briefly for RCA, but the two singles went nowhere.

Roy Orbison (Michael Ochs Archives.com)

He signed to the Monument label and finally made the charts for the second time with "Uptown" (1960). The next hit was his commercial break-through: "Only the Lonely (Know How I Feel)." The ensuing string of hits also occasionally included up-tempo songs that recalled his rockabilly roots, such as "Mean Woman Blues," which Presley had done in 1957. In 1963 Orbison headlined a U.K. tour which included the BEATLES, becoming lifelong friends with the band, particularly George Harrison. It was on this trip that Orbison adopted sunglasses as part of his image; it began out of necessity because he had left his regular glasses on the plane. In 1965 he toured Australia with the ROLLING STONES.

That year he signed with MGM, then a record company as well as a film studio, because they had more clout with promotion. Orbison starred in only one film, a muddled comic western called *The Fastest Guitar Alive* (1967), playing a Confederate spy with a gun hidden inside his guitar. Orbison looked uncomfortable except when singing. He did have eight hits while at MGM. None were really big. Generally the songs were forgettable and the production was bland. In 1966 his wife Claudette died in a motorcycle accident while they were both out riding. He endured another tragedy two years later when, while he was on tour in the United Kingdom, two of his three sons died in a fire at his home in Nashville. He remarried in 1969, to a German-born teenager named Barbara Wellhonen, whom he had met at a club in the United Kingdom. They had two children together.

Even when Orbison was no longer having hits in America, others had hits with his songs. "Blue Bayou," a top-30 hit for him in 1963, was a bigger hit for Linda Ronstadt years later. "Crying" was redone by Don McLean in 1981, "Oh, Pretty Woman" by Van Halen in 1982. His songs were also used in film soundtracks: for example, "In Dreams" was featured prominently in David Lynch's film *Blue Velvet* (1986) and "Oh, Pretty Woman" in *Pretty Woman* (1990), starring Julia Roberts.

The album *Class of '55* (1986) reunited Orbison with his mates from the Sun label: Carl Perkins,

Jerry Lee Lewis, and Johnny Cash. In 1987 Orbison reprised "Crying" in a duet with k. d. lang, and he was inducted into the Rock and Roll Hall of Fame. BRUCE SPRINGSTEEN made the introductory speech and sang with his idol. *Roy Orbison and Friends: A Black and White Night* was a television special filmed in 1987 at Los Angeles's Coconut Grove. It was produced by his wife Barbara, who had become his manager. The musical director was T-Bone Burnett, and the well-rehearsed supporting cast included Bruce Springsteen, Jackson Browne, Elvis Costello, k. d. lang, Bonnie Raitt, Jennifer Warnes, Tom Waits, and a rhythm section of guitarist James Burton and other veterans of Elvis Presley's early 1970s touring band. They played with obvious respect and restraint, and Orbison, despite being a heavy smoker, sounded as powerful as ever and gave a triumphant performance, casting a spell on the audience and countless watchers who have seen its frequent broadcasts on public television or purchased the video or DVD.

Shortly afterward, while working with producer Jeff Lynne (of ELECTRIC LIGHT ORCHESTRA) on tracks for a new album, Orbison and Lynne, together with BOB DYLAN, Tom Petty, and George Harrison, formed the Traveling Wilburys. Their *Volume One* (1988) was a big hit, and they took turns singing on "Handle with Care," the album's hit single. One of the lines Orbison sang, written specifically for him by Harrison and Lynne, was "I'm so tired of being lonely, I still have some love to give." It caused listeners to recall his great songs and remind them that he still had something to offer. The following year, amid the renewed interest in him and his music, with a new album just recorded, Orbison died of a heart attack while visiting his mother.

That album, *Mystery Girl,* came out posthumously in 1989. It was his only album to make the top 10. It contained "You Got It," written by Orbison, Lynne, and Petty, the first Orbison single to make the top 10 since 1964, and the haunting "She's a Mystery to Me," written for him by Bono and the Edge of U2. Unfinished tracks were completed under Lynne's supervision for the acclaimed *King of Hearts* (1992).

Pearl Jam

Along with NIRVANA, Pearl Jam is one of the top bands to come out of Seattle in the GRUNGE style of the 1990s, and the only one of stature to remain active into the 21st century. Their music is diverse and intelligent, and though they love and acknowledge their hard rock and punk influences, they have pursued their own muse. At full force they are loud and melodic; they can also play brooding acoustic ballads with understated intensity. Their fan base is huge and, though they lost some of their following after their first three albums and self-imposed distance from what Joni Mitchell called (in "Free Man in Paris") "the star-making machinery behind the popular song," they have garnered new fans and regained old ones with their new material and admirable actions.

Pearl Jam came to attention with the accessible debut *Ten* (1991), one of their finest efforts and, with 12 million copies sold in the United States to date, their most popular album. Two other of their albums have sold in great quantities: *Vs.* (1993), one of the fastest-selling records in history, has sold 7 million copies, and *Vitalogy* (1994), 5 million. Unlike nearly every other successful album of the 1990s, those two had no supporting videos. Their first six studio albums made it either to number one or two on the charts.

Like other grunge bands, they took a dim view of the music marketing industry and found ways to subvert it. Some bands were uncomfortable with their fame and seemed to make purposefully uncommercial records. Pearl Jam made the records it wanted to make, but did things on their own

terms in other areas as well. The video for "Jeremy" (from *Ten*), is a disturbing look—based on a true story of a student who shot himself in front of his classmates—at the subject of disturbed children. When MTV asked Pearl Jam to change the ending, they did, but they abstained from making videos for years (a move that boosted what is called "street credibility" but hindered their career). "Jeremy" won numerous awards and is considered one of the best rock videos. When they tried to keep the ticket prices down for their concerts, Pearl Jam instigated a valiant legal battle against Ticketmaster (the band lost). To counteract bootleg recordings, they released their own "official bootlegs," multiple-CD sets of every date of their 2000–01 tour, more than 70 altogether, each of a complete show.

Before Pearl Jam formed, two of its founding members had played together for years. From 1984 to 1988 guitarist Stone Gossard (b. 1966) and bassist Jeff Ament (b. 1963) were in Green River, a band inspired by early PUNK ROCK and GLAM ROCK. Their 1987 recordings mark the start of the grunge movement. In 1988 Green River fragmented into two bands: Mudhoney, whose music was basic riff-driven hard rock, and Mother Love Bone, whose hard rock was more slick. Gossard and Ament went to Mother Love Bone, which released *Stardog Champion* (1990). When that band's vocalist, Andy Wood, died of a heroin overdose, Temple of the Dog was formed as a tribute to him to make one album. Temple of the Dog were Gossard, Ament, and Chris Cornell and Matt Cameron of Soundgarden, plus lead guitarist Mike McCready (b. 1966), and vocal-

Pearl Jam (Alison Braun/Michael Ochs Archives.com)

ist Eddie Vedder (b. 1964), from San Diego. How Vedder joined is an interesting story. Via a mutual friend, Jack Irons (the drummer of Red Hot Chili Peppers), Vedder heard a demo tape made by Ament, Gossard, and McCready. He dubbed his own vocals onto it and mailed it back to Seattle. They approved, and Vedder soon moved there.

Pearl Jam then formed and played their first show in fall 1990. All the members of Temple of the Dog except Chris Cornell would be in Pearl Jam, though Matt Cameron (b. 1962) did not join until a series of other drummers had passed through the band. Dave Krusen was on the first album, Dave Abbruzzese was on the second, Jack Irons (b. 1962) joined in 1994, and Cameron replaced him in 1999.

Eddie Vedder's voice is tremulous and impassioned, a magnificent primal roar, and he is a possessed and riveting performer. Stone Gossard's and Mike McCready's guitar parts are textured, inter-

locking, imaginative, and soulful, and the power-house rhythm section creates formidable grooves. Their albums, while drawing on the band's many strengths, are all different as they rejected any impulse to formula and continued to evolve. The band's lyrics are often anguished and depressing, expressing the personal and commenting on social issues: child abuse, greed, drug use, corruption, politics, guns, racism, war, and tragedy. They are, however, quite touching, set to uplifting, life-affirming music that comes from an underlying belief in self-reliance, love, and hope. Their peaks are many and their output is very strong, if somewhat rambling and inconsistent. Following a collaboration with NEIL YOUNG (*Mirrorball*, 1995, issued only under his name) and some experimental albums, in 1999 they scored their biggest hit with a cover of a 35-year old classic, J. Frank Wilson's "Last Kiss." Pearl Jam's version had originally been issued as a single available only through their fan club until radio listeners clamored for its commercial release.

Pearl Jam has stayed true to their roots, and their love of music and respect for their fans shows. They have sincerely tried to live up to their ideals by creating original music in a restrictive commercial context and by contributing to charitable causes. In concert they make music at a high level, giving energy and getting it back from the crowd. Their marathon sets include lengthy jams, guest artists, songs from all their albums, and covers of old punk and rock nuggets, such as songs by John Lennon, the WHO, CREEDENCE CLEARWATER REVIVAL, Neil Young, the English Beat, and the Buzzcocks (who have been their opening act). As true believers, in music, in their group, and their audience, they are a stellar example of a band that carries the torch for rock and roll.

Perkins, Carl (1932–1998) *guitarist and rockabilly pioneer*

One of the pioneers and chief ambassadors of ROCKABILLY, Perkins was an excellent lead guitarist, singer, and songwriter. Raised on a farm, he was grounded in gospel and country music, and taught guitar by a black neighbor. From age 14, with his older brother Jay on rhythm GUITAR, Carl developed his style in the rough honky-tonk bars around Jackson, Tennessee, their hometown. Their youngest brother, Clayton, joined them when he got big enough to play the upright BASS.

One night in 1955 the Perkins Brothers Band played at the local university. A young couple was dancing near the stage, and at home after the show, Carl could not stop thinking about how the young man had admonished his date not to scuff his new shoes. Rising from his bed at 3 A.M., Carl went to the kitchen and wrote "Blue Suede Shoes" on the only paper he could find: a brown paper potato sack. He soon recorded it in Memphis for SAM PHILLIPS, who had already put out two of Carl's records. Neither of those had made a splash, but "Blue Suede Shoes" got him out of the cotton fields for good. ELVIS PRESLEY soon had a hit with it, but before that, Perkins' version did what no other record had done before: it made the top five on three different charts—country, R&B, and pop. This shows not only how appealing the song was to different markets, but also how early rock and roll was a hybrid music, a mix of white and black elements that found favor with a mass audience.

En route to New York to perform on television, Carl and Jay were injured in a car accident, temporarily halting the band's momentum. As a recording artist, Perkins managed, despite leaving the independent Sun label for the major label Columbia in 1958, to place only four other songs on the charts. Jay died that year of complications from the accident. Dispirited by these events, Carl went through a period of low morale and alcoholism. Nonetheless, he was a big influence on other rockabillies, especially RICKY NELSON.

In 1964 and 1965, at the height of Beatlemania, Perkins toured in England. George Harrison had been particularly influenced by his guitar playing, and the BEATLES recorded several of his songs, including "Matchbox" (with Perkins present at the session), and "Honey Don't," which raised his profile and his royalty earnings.

From 1965 to 1976 he toured as part of the Johnny Cash Show. In their first year together, as described in Perkins' autobiography, *Disciple in Blue Suede Shoes* (1978), they became born-again Christians and renounced their addictions. Cash had a big hit with Perkins' "Daddy Sang Bass," about family gospel singing. Several other country acts also had hits with his compositions.

The rockabilly revival in the 1980s was another boost, and Perkins again played with a family band, this time with sons Greg (bass) and Stan (drums). Among his accolades was a Grammy Award for the 1986 album *Class of '55* (recorded with his old friends and Sun label mates Johnny Cash, JERRY LEE LEWIS, and ROY ORBISON), and his induction into the Rock and Roll Hall of Fame in 1987.

A second book on his life, *Go, Cat, Go! The Life and Times of Carl Perkins, the King of Rockabilly* (1996), coauthored with David McGee, was coupled with his last album, *Go Cat Go* (1996), on which he sings again with Cash, as well as with Willie Nelson, and John Fogerty (of CREEDENCE CLEARWATER REVIVAL), Tom Petty, Paul Simon, and each of the surviving Beatles. John Lennon, like JIMI HENDRIX, was represented by an archival recording of "Blue Suede Shoes."

Having survived bouts with cancer, Perkins died of a stroke in 1998. That year a video of Perkins with Paul McCartney called *My Old Friend,* was released. In 2003 McCartney bought the publishing rights to nearly two dozen Perkins songs, including "Blue Suede Shoes," "Honey Don't," and "Matchbox."

Phillips, Sam (1923–2003) *record producer and owner of Sun Records*

Sam Phillips not only was the owner of Sun Records, he produced and engineered the early recordings made for this legendary label of Memphis, Tennessee. In the history of rock and roll, Sun is the most important of the multitude of independent record labels (indies) that sprang up in the late 1940s and 1950s. Few of the artists he recorded had recorded before, including Elvis Presley. Before him, Phillips had recorded blues by such notables as Howlin' Wolf, B. B. King, Junior Parker, Roscoe Gordon, Rufus Thomas, Little Milton, and James Cotton. Presley and many of his label mates, including Carl Perkins, Jerry Lee Lewis, and Roy Orbison did rockabilly, while others, including the great Johnny Cash, did country music. Sun records have a special sound, partly because Phillips had a remarkable ability to get the most out of his artists and partly because of the warm, enveloping tape echo, called slap-back echo, that he invented and applied to the records.

Phillips and his label are held in the utmost esteem by rock fans. A television documentary of his life was titled *The Man Who Invented Rock and Roll* (2000), and a set of interviews with Phillips, published in 1990 in *Now Dig This,* a British magazine devoted to 1950s rock and roll, was called "The Most Important Man in the World." These descriptions are obviously hyperbole but indicate the level of respect for Phillips' achievements. The claim that Phillips invented rock and roll is based on two notions. One is that Elvis Presley's 1954 Sun records, which Phillips produced, mark the beginning of rock and roll. They do not, despite the celebrations in 2004 purporting to mark the 50th anniversary of its birth. Bill Haley had been playing rock and roll since 1952 and had four hits on the charts, including "Rock Around the Clock," before Elvis recorded for Sun. Rather, Presley's records mark the birth of rockabilly, just one of the styles that made up the rock and roll genre in that period. The second notion is also common: that "Rocket 88" (1951) by Jackie Brenston and His Delta Cats, which Phillips produced, is the first rock and roll record. As strong a case could be made for Wynonie Harris' "Good Rockin' Tonight" (1947).

First rock and roll record or not, "Rocket 88," a number-one hit on the R&B charts, is one of the most important specimens of early rock and roll and possibly the first use of one of its characteristic sounds: a distorted guitar tone. The band's guitar amplifier had been damaged when it fell off the roof of their car as they traveled from Clarksdale, Mississippi, to Memphis, but the idea to make the resulting distortion a feature of the record was Phillips'. The band was really Ike Turner's Kings of Rhythm, to which Brenston belonged. Since he wrote the song, sang and played sax on it, it came out under his name. At the time of this recording, Phillips had not yet launched his own label, so he leased it to Chess in Chicago.

Born in Florence, Alabama, Phillips worked throughout most of the 1940s in the radio industry, mostly as an announcer. His studies in audio engineering gave him the background to open his own business, called Memphis Recording Service, in a small storefront in downtown Memphis in 1949. He installed recording equipment at the studio and had some relatively portable gear he could carry in the trunk of his car to social gatherings. His business card read "We Record Anything-Anywhere-Anytime." He began to record musicians at the studio and to sell or lease the masters to different labels. Some of his recordings did well, but when relationships with the labels became strained, Phillips launched his own in spring 1952.

Sun was a small operation, and promotion and distribution all took time and energy. Phillips himself would load up his car and drive to visit disc jockeys and distributors in various cities. Once Elvis Presley started having success, other artists with similar styles came knocking. With rockabilly becoming popular, Phillips abandoned the blues market. When RCA bought Presley's contract in the fall of 1955 for $35,000—a huge sum at the time for an artist whose popularity was still only regional—Phillips was able to stop worrying about going bankrupt. Sun then had hits with Carl Perkins ("Blue Suede Shoes"), Jerry Lee Lewis ("Great Balls of Fire") and Johnny Cash ("Folsom Prison Blues," "I Walk the Line"). Other now-legendary rockabillies such as Sonny Burgess, Billy Lee Riley, Warren Smith, and Ray Smith had regional fame. To diversify, Phillips launched subsidiary labels, and one of them scored with "Raunchy," a saxophone instrumental by Bill Justis.

Scandal caused Lewis' star to fade, though Sun kept recording him. Perkins and Cash both signed to the major label Columbia in 1958, the year Phillips bought a bigger studio not far from the original. More hits were recorded there, such as "Mona Lisa," an old standard rocked up by Carl Mann, and "Lonely Weekends," a rock song with a gospel feel by Charlie Rich, later a country star. However, by the late 1950s Phillips was less directly involved in the business, and other producers tried diversifying in order to remain current. Most of these records were unsuccessful then and are less satisfying now. It is the earlier recordings that have lasting appeal, whether they were hits or not or even issued at the time.

In the 1960s other Memphis labels came to prominence. Stax and Hi had great success with soul music. Though Sun was in decline, Phillips had wisely invested in businesses: radio stations, the Holiday Inn hotel chain, and property. In 1969 he sold the entire Sun catalog to entrepreneur Shelby Singleton. Often asked to speak about his involvement in the history of rock and roll, Phillips had the eloquence and zeal of a southern preacher. He was

Sam Phillips (Colin Escott/Michael Ochs Archives.com)

justifiably proud of his ability to spot and nurture talent, but of his accomplishments he was particularly pleased that his work in music had helped break down barriers between the races. He was inducted into the Rock & Roll Hall of Fame in 1986.

The original Sun location is open daily as a tourist attraction, but at night it also is a functioning modern studio. Def Leppard, Bonnie Raitt, Billy Swan, and U2 have recorded there, as well as various artists paying tribute to Sun's early days.

Pink Floyd

Though Pink Floyd, from England, is now inactive, it remains a legendary act with legions of fans. Each of their three incarnations was fueled by the creativity of a different member. In the mid-1960s Syd Barrett (b. 1946), an eccentric but fragile character who sang lead, wrote the songs, and played lead GUITAR, was their guiding force. They were the top band on London's PSYCHEDELIC ROCK scene. Barrett's erratic behavior, attributed to psychic damage caused by LSD, led to his departure following their debut album. The quartet that carried on was creatively led by bassist and vocalist Roger Waters (b. 1944). In the 1970s they became famous as one of the most innovative exponents of PROGRESSIVE ROCK, with *Dark Side of the Moon* (1973) as their finest achievement on record. After making *The Wall* (1979), they fragmented. Waters developed a solo career, and the others continued, under the direction of guitarist David Gilmour (b. 1944), to use the Pink Floyd name for stylistically cohesive but less groundbreaking recordings. The contributions of keyboardist Richard Wright and drummer Nick Mason (both born in 1945), were essential in all phases (though both were out of the band for short periods).

In 1965, having come out of various short-lived units, Pink Floyd (with Barrett, Waters, Wright, and Mason) quickly became popular in London's emerging hippie milieu. Like the British beat groups that preceded them, they took inspiration from American music. To invent the band's moniker, Barrett put together the names of two down-home blues guitarists whose records were in his collection, Pink Anderson and Floyd Council. At Pink Floyd's early gigs, alongside versions of American rock and roll and blues songs, they experimented with feedback, had slides projected over them while performing, and explored lengthy instrumental passages. The title of their debut album, *The Piper at the Gates of Dawn* (1967), comes from the children's book *The Wind in the Willows*. Barrett's songs have lyrics that recall the enchanted storybook realm of childhood as part dream and part nightmare.

To counterbalance Barrett's nerve-wracking instability, David Gilmour, a friend who had earlier coached him on guitar, came into the band. They were a quintet only briefly, as Barrett's declining condition forced the others to ask him to leave. Pink Floyd's second album, *A Saucerful of Secrets* (1968) contained only two tracks with Barrett: "Jug Band Blues," which he wrote and sang, and "Remember the Day." Otherwise, it was recorded as the quartet of Waters, Wright, Mason, and Gilmour. This lineup would endure for more than a decade and make Pink Floyd's finest albums. *A Saucerful of Secrets* showed that the band was capable of carrying on without Syd Barrett. All participated in the songwriting, but Roger Waters was responsible for most of the lyrics. Where Barrett's lyrics tended towards whimsical fantasy, Waters' outlook was more world-weary.

Barrett made two solo albums in 1970, helped by Waters and Gilmour: *The Madcap Laughs* and *Barrett*. Pink Floyd's "Shine On, You Crazy Diamond" and the title of the album on which it appears, *Wish You Were Here* (1975), were dedicated to Syd Barrett. His collected recordings, including rare tracks, were issued on a box set called *Crazy Diamond* in 1993.

Pink Floyd took sound and lights to new levels in their live shows, using special effects and surround sound. This gave a cinematic quality to their work, making them naturals for movie soundtracks, which is what their next album was. *More* (1969)

Pink Floyd (Michael Ochs Archives.com)

was made for a film with an antidrug message: the title refers to an addict's insatiable craving. Other films would use their music, such as *Obscured by Clouds* (1972), an original score.

Ummagumma (1969) is a double album with one disc from a live concert and the other a studio disc on which each member took a turn as composer and featured musician. Though indulgent, it served as a sketchbook for future explorations. *Atom Heart Mother* (1970) explored the fusion of classical music and rock. It made number one on the British charts.

Meddle (1971) also went high on the British charts, and spent a year on the U.S. charts. The standout track, which took one whole side of the vinyl album, is "Echoes," a 23-minute opus that is a pinnacle in Floyd's repertoire and contains one of Gilmour's famous guitar solos. It became a concert favorite.

Pink Floyd at Pompeii (1972), a film of the band playing in the ancient amphitheater in Italy, is interspersed with interviews and some studio shots taken during the recording of their next album, *Dark Side of the Moon* (1973). This album is a landmark in music. It is one of the most popular albums ever made, spending a record-breaking time, more than 14 years, on the charts. It has continued to sell to the present day. It also marks the rise and continued popularity of what can be called headphone culture: listening as an intimate act, to which one brings concentration and invests the art with a personal interpretation. The technology that enabled Pink Floyd to create, with the help of sound engineer Alan Parsons (who later had fame as an recording artist under his own name), an album of unprecedented clarity and rich sonority, also enabled the rise of a connoisseurship in the act of listening to rock. High-quality home stereos were becoming big business and, with good speakers or headphones, intent listeners could appreciate the craft that went into the record at every level, and hear the details, including the sound effects and the spoken-word excerpts. Once the Sony Walkman was invented, years later, individuals could listen not just in the comfort of their homes, but anywhere. *Dark Side of the Moon* has the reputation as a superb audio experience.

The music is well conceived. "Money," from *Dark Side of the Moon* and their first hit single in the United States, uses tape loop techniques: the sound of coins and a cash register repeat in a rhythmic way. The song, like much of their material, is in a medium-slow tempo and a minor key, but is distinguished by an odd meter: the bluesy riff behind the verses takes seven beats to complete before it repeats. In a song about money, Pink Floyd came up with a time signature that one has to count (like money).

Another reason for the album's phenomenal popularity is found in the themes. Rather than pop music's typical invocation to dance or romance, which are social occurrences, the album expresses gloomy and pessimistic themes—stress, death, madness. The bright production and remarkable clarity of the sound offsets the lyrics about greed, insanity, the inexorable passage of time and the inevitability of death, the struggle to survive, the futility of war, and the indifference of the sun and the moon. The album hit a deep collective nerve. The band's contributions were augmented by the sax of Dick Parry and some spectacular backing vocals of tremendous vitality.

Pink Floyd would then make fewer but more ambitious LPs. Their next album came after touring and a period of rest. *Wish You Were Here* (1975) was seen as anticlimactic by the press, but the fans made it number one on both sides of the Atlantic. *Animals* (1977), a reference to George Orwell's chilling futuristic novel *Animal Farm*, was an embittered view of the human species but was nonetheless a commercial success. By this time, Pink Floyd's live shows had developed into monumental productions. The band used props, such as a giant inflatable pink pig, and huge screens showing visual effects and film clips. Before the next album, Gilmour and Wright released solo albums, and there were rumors that the band was splitting up.

The Wall (1979), a double album, was Waters' epic. Its main theme is alienation. The band presented it in a massive stage production in selected cities, and a film version was made. "Another Brick in the Wall (Part II)," with the lines "We don't need no education . . . no thought control . . . teacher, leave those kids alone," was their biggest hit: a number-one single in the United States and the United Kingdom.

The band fractured when Wright left, due to conflict with Waters. Pink Floyd made *The Final Cut* (1983) as a trio. Waters' antiwar theme and bleak visions of the present day were meant as a requiem for the dreams of postwar society. Following a period of inactivity for the band with some outside projects, Waters departed for a solo career, assuming Pink Floyd was over. David Gilmour and Nick Mason fought Waters for the rights to use the band's name. They won, and resurrected it for *A Momentary Lapse of Reason* (1987), on which Gilmour's artistic vision was at the forefront. Though the band was officially just he and Nick Mason, Richard Wright played on it as a hired hand. He rejoined as a full member partway through the tour supporting the album. This trio lineup made the live *Delicate Sound of Thunder* (1988) and *The Division Bell* (1994). They toured, with additional musicians, for two record-breaking years, performing their new material and their greatest hits in 15 different countries before more than 10 million fans. The albums sold very well, but critics found them self-consciously full of references to, but not as good as, their older music. Some fans claimed to find more substance in Roger Waters' solo records.

A milestone in Waters' solo career was his staging of *The Wall* at the site of the former Berlin Wall for an audience of some 250,000 people. A host of guests participated, including Cyndi Lauper, Van Morrison, Sinéad O'Connor, the BAND, Bryan Adams, and Marianne Faithfull. The recording charted, and all proceeds went to a disaster relief charity.

Pink Floyd's mark on popular music is indelible. Their influence can be heard in the likes of Coldplay and RADIOHEAD. The music that they made is loved by a vast and loyal constituency. Because Pink Floyd was far more concerned with the conceptual content of their music than with fame—most of their album covers do not even have a photo of the band—the members have remained individually inconspicuous. Their relative anonymity has made it easier for the numerous tribute bands, some touring internationally in prestigious theaters and even stadiums, to concentrate on the music and the visuals and be little concerned about wearing any particular costuming.

pop rock

From pop music came concepts of orchestration, clichéd chord progressions such as the "Blue Moon" progression, professional songwriters and their lyrics about romantic longing, and the mechanisms of distribution, publicity, hype, and exploitation.

Brill Building pop is one of most obvious places to see the how pop interconnected with rock. The Brill Building is in New York City, a few blocks north of the area known as Tin Pan Alley, the traditional home of the music publishing industry. In the rock era, particularly in the years between ELVIS PRESLEY's arrival and Beatlemania, the Brill Building was the workplace of professional songwriters who created pop rock for adolescents. It was a hive of activity where more than 150 music businesses were located.

One of the most prominent songwriters was Neil Sedaka, a classically trained pianist from Brooklyn, whose career provides a view of the role of Brill Building pop in the larger story of rock. Sedaka was one of the few who also became a recording star. (Carole King, for whom Sedaka wrote "Oh! Carol," is another.) Sedaka had 20 hits, including "Oh! Carol," on RCA under his own name between 1958 and 1966. He began a songwriting partnership with neighbor Howard Greenfield, who wrote lyrics, when they were high school students. Their first hit as writers was "Stupid Cupid" for Connie Francis (1958); one of their last was "Love Will Keep Us Together" by Captain and Tennille (1975).

Sedaka's hits articulated the euphoria of young love ("Calendar Girl"), its concerns ("The Diary"), and the transformation that growing up brings ("Happy Birthday, Sweet 16"). Several of their songs use terms derived from religion: "Little Devil," "Next Door to an Angel," "The Answer to My Prayer," and "Stairway to Heaven" (not the LED ZEPPELIN song); biblical characters appear in "Run Samson Run" ("there's a little of Delilah in each and every gal").

With a signature sound of his own bright voice, often singing overdubbed harmony to his lead vocal or featured prominently among the background singers, Sedaka used in his songs the conventions of the pop music of the day—the "Blue Moon" progression and DOO-WOP-type vocals—while adding creative touches. For example, in "Breaking Up Is Hard to Do," a number-one hit in 1962 and still his best-known song, the bridge modulates effortlessly through two new keys before resolving back to the original one.

In the mid-1970s after signing with Elton John's Rocket label, Sedaka enjoyed a second period of hit making. He scored two number ones: "Laughter in the Rain" (also the title of his 1987 autobiography) and "Bad Blood" (on which John sang background vocals), and placed six more songs on the charts, including a slower remake of "Breaking Up Is Hard to Do." A shift to the Elektra label brought two final hits, the last one in 1980, a duet with his daughter

Dara. With a large fan base in North America as well as England, Sedaka continues to be a popular concert act into the 21st century.

An example of a pop rock group is the Association, who were an extraordinarily successful six-piece Los Angeles soft rock band formed in 1965. Versatile and adept, they presented an amiable grooviness set to earnest and harmonized vocals. Months of intense rehearsal led to extensive live work, which earned them a large following before the hits came. The first one was the atypical "Along Comes Mary" (1966), whose Dylanesque lyrics and veiled reference to marijuana along with its rhythmic drive and shifting chords put it close to GARAGE ROCK style. The FOLK ROCK "Windy," with its flute and prominent backing vocals, was reminiscent of the MAMAS AND THE PAPAS. It was a million-seller, as were the romantic "Cherish" and "Never My Love." As perfect pop ballads and as declarations of love, appreciation, and commitment, both songs have retained their popularity over the years. The Association did much of their live work away from the typical 1960s venues of ballrooms and rock festivals, and although they were the opening band at the MONTEREY POP FESTIVAL (1967), they and their audience (more mainstream than for most rock acts) were more at home in cabarets and concert halls. Rock critics have dismissed them for their middle-of-the-road blandness expressed as wholesome professionalism, but radio played their music and the public loved it. Their *Greatest Hits* is one of the longest-selling albums. The band split up in 1972, not long after the death by drug overdose of their bassist. The Association re-formed in 1979 and resumed touring internationally.

POWER POP is one way pop and rock continued as a combination, though the pop side of rock has generally become so pop that much of it does not really qualify as rock. Such is the case for the music of Madonna, the Spice Girls, the boy bands, Britney Spears, Christina Aguilera, and the like. Avril Lavigne, for one, has put the rock back in pop rock by adding the crunch of rock guitar and some of the energy from PUNK ROCK.

power pop

Power pop has attracted musicians and produced hit records in every decade since the 1970s. Though it can incorporate elements from earlier and later styles, power pop is founded on the mid-1960s music of the BEACH BOYS, the BYRDS, the BEATLES, and all the BRITISH INVASION bands that mixed hard and soft elements. The style features short, smart, energetic songs with strong melodies, clear lead vocals and enthusiastic harmony singing, irresistible hooks, good production, lyrics about romantic love, and economical solos delivered by punchy electric GUITAR. The result can be deceptively simple: catchy music with intricate details.

The term was coined by Pete Townshend of the WHO during a 1966 interview when asked to describe his band's music. Other acts that were influential on later power pop bands were the Small Faces, the KINKS, the Hollies, the Searchers, and the Move—all from the United Kingdom—plus the Beau Brummels, from San Francisco. Because of the strong influence of the Byrds, with their trademark chiming electric 12-string guitar sound, power pop is sometimes called jangle pop.

Power pop is a well-known term, and although it lacks universal acceptance, it is a useful one to describe such a long tradition. That tradition is somewhat obscured by more general terms like POP ROCK or *melodic rock,* or more specific terms related to particular periods. In the late 1970s and early 1980s, when NEW WAVE was prominent, acts that made music that fits under the definition of power pop—such as the Cars, Tom Petty and the Heartbreakers, the Romantics, the Bangles, the Go-Go's, and, at least in some of their work, Blondie—were considered part of new wave. British counterparts Squeeze, XTC, and Nick Lowe are highly respected artists that are well-known in America, while others are known for having a moderate hit or two, such as the Records and the Jags. When ALTERNATIVE came along later in the 1980s, bands such as Let's Active and R.E.M. (who were based in Byrdsian jangle pop) were thought of as part of that.

Power pop as a style in itself, that is to say after the 1960s, got underway in the early 1970s with Badfinger, Big Star, and the Raspberries. Badfinger were from Wales, and recorded for the Beatles' label, Apple. In their first incarnation, as the Iveys, they made the charts with "Maybe Tomorrow" (1969). As Badfinger, between 1970 and 1972 they had three top-10 hits in a row, including "Come and Get It" (written and produced by Paul McCartney) and "Day after Day" (produced by George Harrison). After vocalist and guitarist Pete Ham committed suicide in 1975, Badfinger disbanded. Two members reformed the group in 1978 with additional players, and they had two more hits. Bassist Tom Evans, present from the band's beginnings, also committed suicide, in 1983. *Without You: The Tragic Story of Badfinger* (2000), a book by Dan Mantovina that includes a CD, provides the full picture.

Big Star, from Memphis, ignored the ROCKABILLY, blues, gospel, and soul traditions of their hometown (though guitarist Alex Chilton drew from them on his later solo records), and made three albums of brilliant power pop. Their name proved to be wishful thinking rather than a prophecy, for Big Star's albums barely sold at all (the third was not even released at the time). They have since become widely revered, especially after Paul Westerberg wrote a song called "Alex Chilton" on the Replacements' *Pleased to Meet Me* (1987), which includes the lines "I'm in love with that song . . . I never travel far, without a little Big Star." Big Star has been tremendously influential—for example, the Bangles revived their "September Gurls"—and are now canonized as essential listening.

The Raspberries, from the Cleveland area, did have commercial success, placing seven songs on the charts from 1972 to 1974, including "Go All the Way" and the autobiographical "Overnight Sensation (Hit Record)." Vocalist Eric Carmen had a vibrant solo career, charting another dozen songs into the late 1980s. Other power pop hits from the 1970s include "Brother Louie" (1973) by Stories, from Boston; "I'm on Fire" (1975) by the Dwight Twilley Band, from Tulsa, Oklahoma; and "My

Sharona" and "Good Girls Don't" (both 1979) by the Knack, from Los Angeles. Cheap Trick, based in Chicago, had more than a dozen hit singles, including "I Want You to Want Me" from the multi-platinum *At Budokan* (1979), recorded live in Japan. Two more big hits, both in 1988, were "The Flame" and "Don't Be Cruel" (a new version of the ELVIS PRESLEY song). In 2004 Cheap Trick toured as the opening act for AEROSMITH. The Flamin' Groovies began in the mid-1960s in San Francisco and chose to ignore that city's PSYCHEDELIC ROCK movement, remaining true to their 1950s and early 1960s inspirations. Best known for their "Shake Some Action" (and the album of the same name) from 1976, they developed an international cult following.

Tom Petty and the Heartbreakers emerged in the 1970s with a power pop sound. Petty grew up in Gainesville, Florida, where he was born in 1953. As a teenager he played in bands, and, as bassist with Mudcrutch, a top local group, he played for two years on the Florida bar circuit. They moved to Los Angeles in 1974 to try to make it, but split up when their single didn't take off. In 1976 Petty, now on guitar, regrouped with two of the players, guitarist Mike Campbell and keyboardist Benmont Tench. Adding two others from Gainesville, drummer Stan Lynch and bassist Ron Blair, they adopted the name Tom Petty and the Heartbreakers.

With their first album, they seemed to bridge rock and new wave. Petty and his band hit their stride by their second album, but then their record company went bankrupt, leaving a mess of legal problems to sort out. They were back on track with *Damn the Torpedoes* (1979), which contained their first big hit, "Don't Do Me Like That." In the 1980s Petty consolidated his position as a radio hit maker with a strong touring band. His sound was built on 1960s rock, and he has paid homage to it. Along the way, he was accepted as a colleague by stars of his own and the previous generation. He wrote songs with Roger McGuinn of the Byrds, and Petty had a hit with a version of the Byrds' "So You Want to Be a Rock and Roll Star." He also had a hit with the Searchers' "Needles and Pins" with Stevie Nicks of FLEETWOOD MAC on background vocals. Petty and the Heartbreakers backed her on her solo album and did the same for DEL SHANNON. Petty also worked with Dave Stewart of the Eurythmics. He toured with BOB DYLAN in the mid-1980s and then was one of the Traveling Wilburys, a collaborative band of Dylan, ROY ORBISON, George Harrison, and Jeff Lynne (of ELECTRIC LIGHT ORCHESTRA). By the 1990s Petty was a top artist whose material consistently sold well.

The majority of power pop bands since the 1980s have produced some superb music and developed a fan base while gaining only moderate sales. Important artists include the Plimsouls and Jules Shear (both based in Los Angeles), the dB's (originally from North Carolina), the Shoes (Illinois), and 20/20 (Oklahoma). Marshall Crenshaw, from Detroit, had a hit with "Someday, Someway" (1982). The Smithereens, from New Jersey, had a few hits, including "A Girl Like You" from *11* (1989), their most popular album. Since their debut album in 1989, which gave them two hits, Enuff Z'Nuff, from Chicago, have made 10 acclaimed albums and toured in Europe and Japan. Matthew Sweet, who was born in Nebraska and worked out of Los Angeles after spending time in Athens, Georgia, and New York City, came to attention with "Girlfriend" and had his biggest hit with "Sick of Myself" from *100% Fun* (1995). Into his power pop sound he added a more distorted guitar sound. The Posies, from Seattle, carried the torch for power pop during the GRUNGE phase. The Gin Blossoms, from Arizona, had a big hit with "Follow You Down" and six more charting songs in the mid-1990s. Fastball, from Austin, Texas, made the top 10 with "The Way" (1998). The Canadian band Sloan, from Halifax but based in Toronto, has earned an international fan base and, since 1992, created an impressive catalog of recordings. Each member writes and sings lead.

Aimee Mann was schooled at the Berklee College of Music in Boston and she sings, plays guitar and BASS, and writes emotionally direct and compelling songs in the tradition of rock SINGER-SONGWRITERS, tracing the tradition back to the Beatles and Ray Davies of the KINKS. Mann's music is brilliant pop rock with a plaintive quality. Some of her songs are like short stories, many of them vignettes of failed relationships either romantic (she went out with Jules Shear, and after they broke up they wrote an album of songs about it) or referring to problems within the music business. As part of the band 'Til Tuesday, she had a major label contract and a hit with "Voices Carry" (1985). She made two acclaimed solo albums in the 1990s, gaining additional notice for songs contributed to soundtrack albums and as an opening act for Bob Dylan. The *Magnolia* movie soundtrack (2000), issued under her name since she was the featured artist, introduced her to a new audience. Her music has continued to mature and she is now on her own label where she has complete artistic freedom. She is one of legions of independent artists directing their own career with the help of a manager or small team. Respected for her integrity and perseverance, Aimee Mann is one of the most talented of these artists to find that a Web site can be an effective route for communicating tour dates and information about recordings.

Power pop will no doubt remain a vital stream of popular music. Even if it never reaches the heights of popularity of the bands that inspired it, it will continue to engage musicians and find listeners who appreciate the creativity and individuality that can be generated from such classic sources.

Presley, Elvis (1935–1977) *the King of Rock and Roll*

Though he died in the 1970s, Elvis Presley is still the King of Rock and Roll and no one has come to dethrone him. He is the most successful of all recording artists, in terms of both hit songs and hit albums. He was the top artist of the 1950s, was second only to the BEATLES in the 1960s, and was still one of the top 10 artists in the 1970s.[16] Presley's public seemed insatiable in their desire to buy his records: more than 150 of his songs made *Billboard* magazine's pop singles chart, and there were 85 songs on the country chart, 52 on the adult contemporary chart, and 35 on the R&B chart. More than 100 Elvis Presley albums also charted. His likeness is still instantly recognized around the world and he is in the halls of fame for rock and roll, country, and gospel.

There are many Elvises. The early one created a new form of rock and roll called ROCKABILLY and, with his television debut in 1956, became the biggest phenomenon ever in the world of entertainment. He contributed mightily to putting rock and roll on the map and excited fans like no one before.

Then there is the 1960s Elvis, who made many movies, most of them inconsequential. He still managed to sell massive amounts of records even while his style seemed to become outmoded with the arrival of the Beatles and the entire BRITISH INVASION and all that came after. In 1968 Presley made a dramatic comeback via a television special. It was his first TV appearance in eight years and it showed that he had lost none of his onstage power and charisma. Wearing black leather, in good humor and excellent voice and accompanied by his old bandmates, he returned to his rock and roll roots. To the audience it was a revelation; for Presley himself it was a revitalization. He never made another film and returned invigorated to the studio and to the concert stage.

The 1970s Elvis is yet another one. The live performing continued, in Las Vegas and on the road across America. Wearing flashy outfits and fronting large bands, Elvis played to sold-out venues, setting attendance records. This Elvis became bored and bloated, an increasingly pathetic figure whose performances mixed brilliance with moments of banality. He died in his opulent and garishly decorated mansion, Graceland. There is one more Elvis, for the millions of devoted fans who loved him then and now: the personal Elvis, an entity that transcends all of these images, a force that uplifts and inspires.

Elvis Presley was born in the middle of the Great Depression into poor circumstances in Tupelo, Mississippi. He was raised as an only child; his twin brother had been stillborn. When Elvis was 13, he and his parents, Vernon and Gladys Presley, moved to Memphis. He enjoyed and absorbed many kinds of music: gospel, country, blues, and pop. After graduating from high school, Presley worked various jobs, including as a truck driver, adopting the sideburns and slicked-back hair common to many truck drivers at that time. He also shopped for colorful clothes on Beale Street in Memphis, the cultural and commercial center for blacks throughout the whole mid-South area. Though his looks made him stand out, it was an expression of individuality rather than rebellion. He had good manners and was very close to his mother.

Having noticed the sign for the Memphis Recording Service in the window of the small building that was also the home of the Sun label, Presley went on two occasions, in 1953 and early 1954, to make one-copy vanity records. On these he sang pop ballads to hear what his voice sounded like and in the hope that the proprietor, SAM PHILLIPS, would discover him and want to make a record with him. The secretary took note of his name. Months later, Phillips decided to give him a try.

At that exploratory session in July 1954, Elvis, as before, sang and played his acoustic GUITAR. This time he was backed by Scotty Moore and Bill Black, who played electric guitar and upright BASS respectively, and who had recently made a record at Sun as members of a hillbilly band. The recording session did not seem to be fruitful, but in an unguarded moment during a break Elvis started playing "That's All Right," a tune he had heard by Mississippi bluesman Arthur "Big Boy" Crudup. Phillips was impressed, they worked up an arrangement, and it was captured on tape. To find another song suitable for a flip side, after some experimentation they radically reworked "Blue Moon of Kentucky," a song by Bill Monroe and the Bluegrass Boys that had been a hit in the 1940s. These two Presley recordings are considered the birth of rockabilly.

Following strong positive reaction to the songs on a local radio show hosted by Dewey Phillips (no relation to Sam Phillips), one of the most popular and powerful disc jockeys of his time, Presley and his band were added to a package show of country stars that played in Memphis at the end of the month. Since Presley had almost no previous performing experience, the leg shaking he did that caused such a commotion of excitement in the young girls in the audience could be attributed to nerves.

Over the next year and a half, Presley made four more singles at Sun and toured relentlessly throughout the South. On record and onstage he was accompanied by Scotty Moore and Bill Black. They were sometimes billed as the Blue Moon Boys, in reference to "Blue Moon of Kentucky"; it also helped align them with country music when audiences and disc jockeys were not sure in which category to place them. The Sun recordings were made with a process invented by Sam Phillips called slapback echo, which gave a full sound to the trio in the studio, but on live dates the band seemed thin-sounding and so added drummer D. J. Fontana.

Another blues song done as rockabilly by Presley was "Good Rockin' Tonight." Recorded in 1947 by its composer, Roy Brown, it was immediately covered by Wynonie "Mr. Blues" Harris. Though Harris boasts "Tonight she'll know I'm a mighty man," the stronger power is the music itself: "Everybody's going to rock tonight." Church men Elder Brown and Deacon Jones leave their happy homes to go "jumpin' and a stompin' at the jubilee." "Sweet Lorraine, Sioux City Sue, Sweet Georgia Brown, Caldonia too" (all famous ladies whose names are song titles), will "be there jumpin' like mad" and rockin' their blues away. After Presley did "Good Rockin' Tonight," Pat Boone did it as pop (1959), and James Brown as soul (1967). A 1984 version, actually a cover of a sequel to the original song, called "Good Rockin' at Midnight," was a hit for the Honeydrippers, with vocals by Robert Plant of LED ZEPPELIN.

None of Presley's Sun records made the pop charts, but some did well in the country charts and in the jukebox trade. As if to underline the cultural and musical blending of Presley's style and rockabilly itself, each of the five Sun singles had one song that came from a white source and one from a black source. These records and the touring, which included an appearance at the Grand Ole Opry in Nashville (which was not a total success), and multiple appearances at the Louisiana Hayride in Shreveport, Louisiana (which were), showed that Presley was having a big impact. Musicians were impressed and copied his style. Audiences, especially the females, were ecstatic, for Presley was a charismatic and very physical performer with erotically charged stage moves: swaying, swiveling his hips, dropping to his knees, and always causing a pandemonium in the crowd.

Colonel Tom Parker, who had gone from a carnival huckster to the manager of country music acts, including Hank Snow and Eddy Arnold, saw Presley's potential and became his manager. Their relationship was not without problems, but their arrangement continued until Presley's death. Parker set up a deal whereby RCA Records bought Presley's contract from Sun—for $35,000, the largest sum ever paid for a country artist—at the end of 1955, and got him onto national television in January 1956. Television played a vital role in Presley's rise to fame. In a one-year period Elvis would appear on TV a dozen times: six times on *Jackie Gleason's Stage Show* (hosted by big band stars Tommy and Jimmy Dorsey), twice on *The Milton Berle Show,* once on *The Steve Allen Show,* and three times on *Toast of the Town* (hosted by Ed Sullivan). The second Berle broadcast, in which Presley's gyrations during "Hound Dog" were criticized for being vulgar, led to Steve Allen's attempt to defuse the controversy with humor: Presley wore formal clothes and sang the song to a basset hound. For Presley's final Sullivan appearance (January 1957), in which Sullivan sincerely compliments Presley for being "a real decent, fine boy," the instructions to the cameramen were to film Presley "from the waist up." (Some sources suggest that Colonel Tom Parker may have orchestrated this as a publicity stunt.)

Presley's first recording session for RCA occurred in January 1956, two days after his 21st birthday. It was held in Nashville, and Moore, Black, and Fontana were present (they would continue to be part of his recordings for another two years). The backing group was augmented by the addition of two Nashville session musicians (who both had careers as recording artists): Chet Atkins on electric guitar and Floyd Cramer on piano. Also present were the Jordanaires, a gospel vocal group who would do many pop and gospel recordings and live appearances with Elvis. The expansion of the ensemble—to be expected in the setting of a Nashville session for a major label, but also due to the RCA engineers' inability to duplicate the expansive sound of Sam Phillips' slap-back echo—was part of the evolution of rockabilly. The first session produced one of the most important rock and roll records ever made: "Heartbreak Hotel," a bleak but poetic vision of despair.

As he had with Sun, Presley recorded more than rockabilly. His RCA recordings included pop, country, and gospel. Some rock and roll purists, while naming certain songs as exceptions, see the whole of his subsequent recorded output as an artistic decline. In truth, when Presley was engaged with his material, he made some great music in every phase of his career. Just as true, after his first years, especially with the unadventurous songs that were commissioned for his movies, he was often disinterested.

Elvis Presley made 31 motion pictures. They served primarily as vehicles for his performances, and they shifted his image from dangerous rock and roll star to innocuous family entertainer. The four films made in the 1950s are rated higher than the often pointless 1960s movies, though even some of his final movies have merit. The 1950s films are *Love Me Tender* (1956, set in the time of the Civil War), *Loving You* (1957, about a truck driver who became a pop star), *Jailhouse Rock* (1957, with memorable choreographed dance sequences), and *King Creole* (1958, set in New Orleans and considered his finest film). These films, particularly the last two, show that Elvis had great potential as a serious actor. By the time *King Creole* was released, Presley was in the army. It has been speculated that, since the United States was not at war then, the fact that Presley was drafted had something to do with

Colonel Tom Parker's plan to clean up his image. During his tour of duty RCA continued to release songs and have hits with them. Presley served in Germany, where he met his future wife, Priscilla Beaulieu, when she was 14 years old; they married in 1967 and the next year had their only child, Lisa Marie Presley. On Presley's return, he was as popular as ever. He capitalized on the army look in the film *G.I. Blues* (1960). That year he also made *Flaming Star,* and every year from then on until 1969, he made two or three movies, except 1968. That year he was in four: *Live a Little, Love a Little, Speedway, Stay Away Joe,* and *Double Trouble.*

Elvis was a consummate interpreter of songs written by others. Although he was listed as a coauthor on some songs, these indicate financial dealings, not creativity. For example, the credits for "All Shook Up," "Don't Be Cruel," and "Return to Sender" read Blackwell/Presley. Otis Blackwell, whose other credits include "Great Balls of Fire" and "Breathless" for JERRY LEE LEWIS and other songs for Elvis that do not have Presley's name listed, never met him. After Elvis had a hit with their composition "Hound Dog," Jerry Leiber and Mike Stoller were asked to contribute others. Presley recorded more than 20 of them, including "Jailhouse Rock," "Treat Me Nice," "Trouble," and "Love Me." Presley also recorded about 20 songs by the great R&B songwriter Doc Pomus (many coauthored by Mort Shuman), including "Little Sister," "Surrender," "A Mess of Blues," and "Viva Las Vegas."

Presley had hits with all kinds of songs: rock and roll, ballads, and religious songs, such as "Crying in the Chapel." He redid a lot of old country and R&B songs, as well as old folk songs ("Love Me Tender" is based on "Aura Lee" from 1861, and "Frankie and Johnny" dates from the late 1800s), pop songs ("Are You Lonesome Tonight?" was a hit in 1927), and songs from Europe ("It's Now or Never" and "Surrender" were adapted from Italian songs, and "Can't Help Falling in Love" was inspired by a French song). Some of his repertoire dealt with difficult subjects, including "In the Ghetto," with its social commentary, and "Suspicious Minds," about jealousy.

The 1968 TV revitalization that sent him back on the concert trail seemed to drift away as he appeared to have exchanged one dulling treadmill (the movies) for another (live performances). Again his potential was underrealized. He was pampered, surrounded by sycophants, and isolated in a state of decadent unreality in his mansion. The breakup of his marriage in 1973 contributed to the decline of his spirits, and he gained weight and became more dependent on prescription drugs, though he performed up to two months before his death.

Elvis died at Graceland in 1977 at the age of 42. The cause of death was abuse of prescription drugs resulting in heart failure. The outpouring of public grief was astonishing. Elvis was buried on the grounds of Graceland, and a few years after his death, Graceland was opened as a tourist attraction. For the fans who come to Memphis from around the world to see it, it is a shrine. It is the most visited residence in the United States.

Hundreds of books have been written about Elvis. There are dozens of biographies, most notably the two volumes by Peter Guralnick: *Last Train to Memphis: The Rise of Elvis Presley* (1994), and *Careless Love: The Unmaking of Elvis Presley* (1999), which are accurate, objective and well written. There are books about performances, recording sessions, discographies, album covers, and bootlegs. There are books of musical analysis. There are reminiscences that aim to reveal his personality, secrets and love affairs, written by people who knew him: friends and family, his nurse, his cook, and the so-called Memphis Mafia (a group of men who were Presley's bodyguards, assistants, and confidants). Other books document specific aspects of his life: his beginnings, his movies, the army years, life at Graceland (including his favorite recipes), his meeting with the BEATLES, his kindness and charity, his relationship with his manager, his comeback, the files the FBI kept on him. Some books deal with his death (one asks: was he murdered by the mob?). There are books of

photographs, memorabilia, collectables, plus encyclopedias of all things Elvis, day-by-day chronologies, guides for beginners, and trivia quizzes. Some books contain writing inspired by Elvis, from love letters and poetry to short stories and novels. Then there are books about Elvis impersonators and Presley's status as an icon, such as *Dead Elvis: A Chronicle of a Cultural Obsession* by Greil Marcus. Presley was a deeply religious man who in death has become a saintlike figure; there is a book on a religious cult that worships him: John Strausbaugh's *E: Reflections on the Birth of the Elvis Faith*.

In 2002 "A Little Less Conversation," a 1968 single by Elvis remixed by JXL (a disc jockey from Holland) was used by Nike in television commercials during the World Cup soccer games. The new version went to number one in the United States and more than 20 other countries, and was included as a bonus track on the *ELVIS 30 #1 HITS* compilation. It was another international number-one album. In 2003 a remix of Elvis's 1969 "Rubberneckin'" by Paul Oakenfold, a renowned DJ from England, topped the U.S. singles chart.

Elvis Presley was a natural communicator who touched millions of people. He mirrored and contributed to profound changes in society, and his effect on world culture will continue to be felt for a long, long time.

progressive rock

Also known as art rock, symphonic rock, or just prog rock, this style developed out of PSYCHEDELIC ROCK in the 1960s, flourished in the 1970s, and has continued to the present. By incorporating diverse influences, especially classical music, into rock, its practitioners found new avenues of expression. The role of the KEYBOARD player, for example, was elevated to one of prominence, making stars out of Rick Wakeman, of the band Yes, and Keith Emerson, of Emerson, Lake and Palmer. Keyboard players, from having taken piano lessons, were familiar with and able to draw from the history of art music: baroque, classical, romantic, and 20th century.

Emerson, Lake and Palmer and Yes, plus King Crimson, Pink Floyd, Genesis, and Jethro Tull were all top bands in progressive rock. All were from England, and all were immensely popular in the United States. Additional British acts important in the style, such as Gentle Giant, Soft Machine, Caravan, the Strawbs, Camel, Renaissance, and Van Der Graaf Generator found American devotees. Progressive rock was popular throughout much of Europe, particularly in Italy, France, and Scandinavia, though acts from Europe tended to be less known in the United States. One exception was the Dutch band Focus, who had a U.S. top-10 hit in 1973 with "Hocus Pocus." Classical traditions were strong and deep in the United Kingdom and Europe, but were less part of the fabric of cultural life in the New World. While acts such as Frank Zappa, Chicago, Vanilla Fudge, and It's a Beautiful Day had elements of progressive rock in their music, few North Americans took up the style, preferring to draw more from native forms like blues, country, and jazz. Two notable exceptions are the band Kansas, and, from Canada, Rush.

Hallmarks of prog rock are lengthy, segmented compositions, intricate unison passages, odd time signatures and abrupt tempo changes, clear solo singing and fugue-style harmony vocals, and virtuoso instrumental technique. The keyboard instruments that progressive rock emphasized include the traditional grand piano of the classical concert stage and the organ from the church, as well as the modern electric piano, the recently introduced synthesizer, and the mellotron. The mellotron's keys triggered tape-recorded notes of violins or other acoustic instruments, giving a modernistic version of traditional orchestral sounds. The lyrics, usually well crafted but sometimes inscrutable, concern spirituality and mythology, history and war, fantasy and science fiction, and madness and the breakdown of society. Prog dealt with love abstractly, unlike pop music's "I love you" approach. Prog album covers are often paintings that depict fantastic or archetypal characters and imaginary realms with science fiction overtones. Progressive rock was the domain of male musicians, with few exceptions like vocalist Annie Halsam and lyricist Betty Thatcher of Renaissance. Its audience was primarily male as well.

By 1967, via blues and psychedelic jams, rock bands had already begun to experiment with longer forms, and classical orchestration and ideas had started to show up on album tracks. With the release of and nearly unanimous praise for the Beatles' *Sgt. Pepper's Lonely Hearts Club Band* (1967), rock's possibilities seemed endless. It was an album full of studio experimentation and unusual orchestration, and the creativity and depth of the music called for listening, not dancing. Also released that year was Procol Harum's debut album, containing the hit single "Whiter Shade of Pale," whose keyboard work owed much to classical precedents, and the Moody Blues' *Days of Future Passed*, the first rock album to feature a symphony orchestra. Other bands who mixed classical influences into rock were Electric Light Orchestra, Deep Purple, and the Nice. As rock found an alternative to short pop singles designed to get the body moving, the FM frequency on the radio came into vogue and provided a forum for extended, experimental music.

King Crimson's debut, *In the Court of the Crimson King* (1969), set the parameters for progressive rock: mystical and surreal lyrics, longish compositions with contrasting sections and tempo shifts, influences from classical, jazz, and rock, precise playing, dramatic mood changes, and a striking image on the album cover. "21st Century Schizoid Man" was ferocious, sinister, and chaotic, while "I Talk to the Wind" was pastoral and enchantingly beautiful. In presenting a range of moods from gloomy to uplifting, the band used a variety of instrumental timbres: gentle flute, jazzy saxophone and vibraphone, arpeggiating acoustic guitar, slashing electric guitar, and extensive use of the mellotron. Textures and dynamics ranged from soft, flowing melodies in subtle, atmospheric settings to distorted, frenetic riffs that verged on the cacophonic. The album cover painting is arresting. The outside of the gatefold cover is an extreme close-up of a terrified, screaming man; his crimson-and-blue face dissolves at the eye into blue space and crimson planets. The inside cover has a toothy, smiling moonlike head that exudes wisdom and serenity.

As in other spheres of popular music at this time, such as MOTOWN, where Stevie Wonder and Marvin Gaye had both lobbied for and won complete artistic control of their music, the progressive rock bands wrote their own songs, performed their music with no outside help, and acted as their own producers. They were able to express themselves creatively without hindrance. This freedom spurred them to push back boundaries, make grandiose statements, and present elaborate stage shows that combined epic music with costumes, props, and lights. Many progressive rock albums had a conceptual theme. Often there were tracks that featured individual band members, sometimes in adventurous solo performances.

Behind progressive rock's fascination with technology, from signal processors to multitracking to synthesizers, was an excitement in new possibilities. This was a period of space missions—humans first walked on the Moon in 1969—and early computers. Alongside a belief that technology could provide salvation for humanity was the awareness of technology's capability to enslave it. The future was regarded with a mix of optimism and dread, which was played out in romantic science-fiction fantasies or nightmarish visions of alienation and paranoia. There was also the sense that progressive rock was a bridge from the past to the future, thus the medieval settings and classical instrumental counterpoint.

Because progressive rock was an expression of the hippie counterculture, its musicians, to some extent at least, had antiestablishment ideals and were familiar with hallucinogens and Eastern spirituality. They had a sense of helping to create or pioneer a new world through blending traditional acoustic instruments with futuristic electronic ones, drawing from the classical music of Europe and the jazz and blues of America, and being familiar with the Christianity of the Western Hemisphere but also intrigued by the Eastern religions. The heyday of progressive rock was from 1969 to 1975, and its rise and fall parallels the spread and decline of the hippie movement.

"Roundabout" by Yes, a top-20 hit in 1972, helped make *Fragile* one of the best-known progressive rock albums. Listeners got to know the band members through their featured tracks. Rick Wakeman's "Cans and Brahms" used extracts from the third movement of Brahms' 4th Symphony, in which Wakeman transposed orchestral parts to different keyboards: he played the string parts on electric piano, woodwinds on grand piano, brass on organ, reeds on harpsichord, and contrabassoon on synthesizer. Jon Anderson overdubbed multiples of his voice for "We Have Heaven." Bill Bruford's drum beats formed the basis of a group piece called "Five Percent for Nothing." Chris Squire's bass produced all the sounds in "The Fish." Steve Howe's acoustic guitar composition "Mood for a Day" was widely copied by solo guitar players. *Fragile* and the albums that preceded and followed it (*The Yes Album* and *Close to the Edge*) made the group famous and influenced progressive rock's evolution.

Also influential were Emerson, Lake and Palmer. The band was named for each member, because they were already known from other groups: Keith Emerson had been in the Nice, bassist and vocalist Greg Lake came from King Crimson, and drummer Carl Palmer had been in Atomic Rooster. They made a specialty of adapting pieces from the classical repertoire, such as "Pictures at an Exhibition" (by Modest Mussorgsky, a Russian composer who lived in the 1800s), with lyrics added by Lake. Their "Lucky Man" (1971) was atypically delicate, and was one of their biggest hits.

Pink Floyd came out of the psychedelic scene in London to make the most successful of all progressive rock albums, *Dark Side of the Moon* (1973). Before Peter Gabriel left Genesis in 1975, they made several progressive rock records, including the ambitious double album *The Lamb Lies Down on Broadway* (1974). Jethro Tull, led by Ian Anderson, whose flute playing gave them a signature sound, evolved from their jazz, blues, and folk beginnings to make progressive rock records, including the popular *Aqualung* (1971) and the overblown *Thick as a Brick* (1972).

In spite of, or perhaps because of, progressive rock's daring arrangements and the awesome musicianship of its players, and its immense popularity live and on record, the style's detractors saw it as elitist and self-indulgent. It was perceived as emotionally cold music full of pointless virtuosic displays done by privileged white European males. Contrasted with the ROCK REVIVAL of the mid-1970s and the arrival of PUNK ROCK just afterward—both back-to-basics movements—the pomposity of progressive rock seemed a betrayal of the working-class roots and blues-based origins of rock and roll. Prog rock was easily ridiculed, and even the concept of the "muso" (a musician who through training or personal dedication tries to master an instrument) came into question. Part of this was a rejection of keyboards, of institutions, of historical ways of music making, and even of rational thought. Raw expression, according to this way of thinking, is preferable to crafted productions, and not only does it not need to be supported by musicianship, it is likely to be hampered by it. A rise in do-it-yourself music making and idiosyncratic approaches to singing and playing inevitably led to shorter and simpler songs and more intuitive and aggressive styles that favored the guitar. The mocking of progressive rock is not uncommon even now, among rock critics and musicians alike.

King Crimson disbanded in 1974; they re-formed between 1981 and 1984, and re-formed again in 1994. Only guitarist Robert Fripp has been in all incarnations of the band. Emerson, Lake and Palmer broke up in 1979, tired of the intensity of their work. They reunited in the 1990s for more recording and some live shows. Peter Gabriel left Genesis in 1975 for a solo career. The band continued, to great success, under Phil Collins' leadership, more pop than progressive. After changes in personnel and time off, Yes re-formed in 1983, gaining a number-one pop hit with "Owner of a Lonely Heart." Like the music of their progressive rock peers, their later output was somewhat simpler and more electronic, as analog synthesizers were replaced by digital ones and drum machines.

Progressive rock had a resurgence in the mid-1980s in England, as seen in the popularity of Marillion's *Misplaced Childhood* (1985). In the 1990s another resurgence of progressive rock occurred, with younger bands taking up the style internationally. A hybrid of progressive rock and HEAVY METAL, called progressive metal, gained popularity, with technical playing, concept albums, and extended pieces.

The progressive rock era of the early 1970s was a phenomenal period of experimentation, and while the style had pretentious and exaggerated moments, it also left a legacy of music that was truly original, effective, and touching.

psychedelic rock

Also called acid rock or psychedelia, psychedelic rock began in 1965 and was very popular until around 1970. Though it could be found almost anywhere, its most important centers were San Francisco, the city of its origin, Los Angeles, and London. San Francisco psychedelic music took its impetus from the folk music revival of the 1950s, in which many of its most important practitioners had participated. The catalyst for the folk revival musicians to adopt the rock band format was the BRITISH INVASION. Psychedelic music in Los Angeles was more aligned with pop traditions. In the United Kingdom it generally had a more intellectual character, was based more on rhythm & blues than folk, and was closer in sound to pop music.

Virtually none of the acts that made psychedelic music did so exclusively. The main exponents from the San Francisco area were the GRATEFUL DEAD, the JEFFERSON AIRPLANE, Big Brother and the Holding Company (with JANIS JOPLIN), Country Joe and the Fish, and Quicksilver Messenger Service. In the Los Angeles area, artists that played psychedelic music included the BYRDS, the DOORS, the BEACH BOYS, the Strawberry Alarm Clock, Love, Captain Beefheart,

Spirit, Iron Butterfly, the Electric Prunes, and the Peanut Butter Conspiracy. In England psychedelic music was an important phase for the BEATLES, CREAM, DONOVAN, PINK FLOYD, the YARDBIRDS, Traffic, Procol Harum, Eric Burdon and the ANIMALS, the Crazy World of Arthur Brown, the Move, the Hollies, the Small Faces, and, briefly, the ROLLING STONES. The Jimi Hendrix Experience was based there for a time, though JIMI HENDRIX was an American. Psychedelia was part of the music of acts in other cities too: New York had the VELVET UNDERGROUND, Vanilla Fudge, and the Blues Magoos, while Austin, Texas, had the pioneering 13th Floor Elevators.

As Michael Hicks points out in *Sixties Rock* (1999), one of the chief features of the style was the attempt to translate into musical terms the effects of hallucinogenic drugs, especially LSD, which had become available in artistic circles in the early 1960s and was legal until 1966. Glossy mainstream magazines like *Life, Newsweek,* and *Saturday Evening Post,* discussed LSD extensively in 1966 and 1967. Talk of mind expansion and sensual distortion affected people's perceptions even if they never tried drugs. An altered sense of time was expressed musically with slow tempi, lengthy renditions, meandering solos, and hypnotic repetition. A sense of unity was expressed in group improvisation and bands that had no official leader, as well as benefit concerts in aid of the local community. A sense of fluidity was expressed in idiosyncratic song forms, giving an organic, handmade quality or an air of innocence and freedom from convention. It was also expressed in odd harmonies and segues that joined contrasting sections together into a song or different songs into a whole album side. The vocabulary of psychedelic music highlighted animated bass lines, drones and scales inspired by the music of India, and soloing and modal chords from jazz. Lyrics made reference to mind expansion, drug trips, hippie philosophy, childhood images, archetypal characters, and fantasy realms, some derived from children's and science fiction literature.

Psychedelic rock was an expression of the hippie subculture, and in no previous style had social alternatives affected music making to the same extent. Psychedelia reflected the hippie credo of freedom and rejection of authority. Some musicians were attracted to psychedelic music because it is by nature an eclectic, less restrictive or formulaic style than others, such as bluegrass or Chicago blues. For certain bands that meant the freedom to play only their own compositions. For others it showed a way to take previous styles, particularly FOLK ROCK and GARAGE ROCK, into a new dimension. Communal living, a characteristic of the hippie lifestyle, led to elaborate collective compositions and arrangements and fostered near-telepathic interactions during improvisations on the bandstand. Psychedelic music was innovative, not only in its use of improvisation and attempts to tap into the subconsciousness, but in its rejection of the music industry's modus operandi. Psychedelic rock also catalyzed the development of light shows and concert sound systems and pioneered ways to use multitracking and such experimental electronic sound manipulations as feedback, phase shifting, backward taping, and timbre-changing devices, such as the wah-wah pedal for guitar. Affected by its own disdain for the music industry and its nonetheless successful growth, psychedelic music had a short and spectacular heyday.

In its early development in 1966 and 1967, psychedelic music tended to show its roots more directly, with garage and folk rock characteristics, and solos inspired by jazz and Indian music, as in "Eight Miles High" by the Byrds, "Psychotic Reaction" by the Count Five, "White Rabbit" by the Jefferson Airplane, and "Get Me to the World on Time" by the Electric Prunes. Songs then tended to become more orchestrated and more mannered, with an increasing use of studio-created effects, as in "Paper Sun" by Traffic, "San Franciscan Nights" by Eric Burdon and the Animals, and "Itchycoo Park" by the Small Faces (all 1967). Then it turned toward the theatrical and the "heavy," both in its lyric themes, such as the demonic "Fire" by the Crazy World of Arthur Brown, and the use of unison blues riffs as a chief motif, as in "In-A-Gadda-Da-Vida" by Iron Butterfly (both 1968).

Around 1970, most American psychedelic bands, that had not done so already headed for the grounding effects of COUNTRY ROCK and ROOTS ROCK. The Grateful Dead did that but also kept on with their psychedelia. British groups such as Pink Floyd pursued their own creative course, retaining elements of psychedelia and adding new influences, such as PROGRESSIVE ROCK. In the late 1980s a renewal of interest in 1960s music was spurred by nostalgic anniversary celebrations. It contributed to a revival of psychedelic music. In 1987 the media heralded the 20th anniversary of the "Summer of Love," that rapid growth of the hippie movement that occurred in San Francisco and spread internationally, and reported on the commemorative events. That year the Grateful Dead had their only top-10 hit, "Touch of Grey," and their increasing popularity helped also fuel the JAM BAND style. The media coverage of the 20th anniversary of the WOODSTOCK festival, in 1989, generated further interest in bands and music of the psychedelic era.

In the 1980s psychedelic rock was revived by many younger bands, a few of them producing outstanding albums. They rarely redid older songs, but their new compositions were presented in ways that showed the influence of the sounds of the 1960s. Among the prominent acts in this movement were Plasticland, from Milwaukee, and bands in Los Angeles who were part of an eclectic scene, held together by camaraderie if not musical cohesiveness, that became known as the Paisley Underground. It included bands who were connected to traditions of roots rock (the Long Ryders, Green on Red), jangly pop (the Bangles, who had the most commercial success), ALTERNATIVE ROCK (the Dream Syndicate), and psychedelia, notably the Three O'Clock (*Sixteen Tambourines*, 1982) and the Rain Parade (*Emergency Third Rail Power Trip*, 1983). Psychedelic music has expanded to be a global style, and has its festivals, publications, and bands who find new ways to explore the connections between mind and music.

punk rock

Punk began as a backlash against disco and pop and PROGRESSIVE ROCK. In 1976 and 1977, when the punk movement came into view, primarily in the United States and Britain, it caused consternation and confusion. It was a new and abrasive type of music, and seemed to come with a previously unknown subculture, one that looked angry and threatening and, at least in the United Kingdom, promoted anarchy. The general public was disgusted by the sight of unhealthy-looking kids with weird and strangely colored hair: it was cut jaggedly, stuck up in spikes, or shaved except for a central strip (a cut known as a mohawk).[17] Punks put safety pins through their skin and used them to hold together their torn clothing, which bore stated and implied confrontational messages.

Punk, as was its intention, disturbed the complacency of society. In its divisiveness and seeming impenetrability to outsiders, it declared its otherness. Musicians already involved in other styles found punk off-putting, decrying what they felt was its crude relentless, simplistic beat, and tuneless vocals. Of course, there was more musicality in it than they gave it credit for. Though most people rejected it, some found it liberating. One reason was that it offered a place for female musicians.

Punk's philosophy was born of anger, disillusionment, and boredom. In Britain and the United States there was a failing economy, mass unemployment, a malfunctioning government, and racial strife. New possibilities—for individuals, for society, for humanity—seemed unavailable. Things were not "getting better all the time," as the BEATLES had sung. What Johnny Rotten sang in the Sex Pistols' "God Save the Queen" (1977), was "There is no future in England's dreaming." "No future" became a punk slogan. In that song Rotten also sings: "They made you a moron . . . don't be told what you want . . . we are the poison in your human machine . . . we're the future, your future . . . no future for me, no future for you." If the future was closed, the past, in the form of musical traditions, or any kind of history for that matter, was largely dismissed out of hand. Only the present was left, and since it was bleak, life was a search for pleasure and stimulation. The names of bands suggested deviance, violence, and hopelessness: the Sex Pistols, the Buzzcocks, the Clash, the Stranglers, the Exploited, and the Damned, from England; the Dead Boys, Fear, and the Germs, from the United States.

In aiming to express themselves without hindrance, punk players and singers rejected musical ostentation and artifice. Punk was trying to offend, to shake things up, not to please (like pop music), or impress (like progressive rock). Out went KEYBOARDS, orchestration, solos, embellishments. For the most part, all that was left was slashing GUITARS, pumping BASS, thumping DRUMS, and snarling vocals singing frankly realistic lyrics. With few exceptions, it was aggressive, fast, and loud. Even within these limitations, there was much variety, and as musicians gained proficiency and widened their ambitions, punk developed further, drawing from other kinds of music. For example, by the time the Clash disbanded in 1985, they had incorporated REGGAE, ROCKABILLY, and rap into punk. The Jam built on the mod sound of the WHO and then drifted toward soul and R&B.

The roots of punk are in the GARAGE ROCK of the mid-1960s. Both had the same do-it-yourself ethic (abbreviated as DIY). This approach meant, in the punk era, a rise in local scenes, homemade fan magazines (fanzines), and independent record labels. It was like the early days of rock and roll in the late 1940s and early 1950s, when independent labels flourished for the first time. Punk did hearken back to early rock and roll, not just in its instrumentation, but in its directness and populist attitude. In that sense it shunned most of the music that had happened since the early 1960s. In "London Calling" (1979), a song of impending doom, the Clash sing that "phony Beatlemania has bitten the dust."

However, some music made since then was still valid to the punks, such as two audacious hard-rocking and highly energetic bands from Detroit that both made debut albums in 1969: the MC5,

and the Stooges, led by Iggy Pop. Several New York bands also were precursors of punk, starting with the VELVET UNDERGROUND, with their dark, gritty lyrics and noisy delivery. Their "I'm Waiting for the Man" (1967) is perhaps the first employment (aside from sparing use for effect by earlier bands), of a bass player constantly and rapidly repeating the root note of a chord, instead of making a moving or melodic bass line. This became a common device in punk, much simpler than previous styles of bass playing and much more viscerally powerful. It also went along with the DIY concept: one did not need to be adept on an instrument, just willing to approach it with attitude and energy. Also influential were the New York Dolls, whose outrageous, androgynous GLAM ROCK made them infamous.

In 1973 a bar in New York City's unsavory Bowery district opened called CBGB. The initials stood for "country, bluegrass, and blues," but owner Hilly Kristal was willing to try anything. He valued originality above all and gave a chance to fledgling rock bands who played for the door (the money that came from admission fees; the venue kept the money from alcohol sales). The first was Television, soon followed by the RAMONES. By 1976 CBGB was the main venue for New York's emerging punk scene (and a mecca for out-of-town bands). Other notables that played the club regularly were the Patti Smith Group, TALKING HEADS, BLONDIE, and the Heartbreakers (with two ex-members of the New York Dolls).

The Ramones and several other of the New York groups toured in England, connecting with the Sex Pistols and the Clash and fanning the flames already burning there for a punchy and minimalist form of rock. The Sex Pistols achieved notoriety through vulgarity and a brilliant publicity campaign but burned out after making only one album, a caustic and provocative statement that is still essential listening. The Clash continued to develop, expanding their sound over seven albums.

Punk rock emboldened people to take up guitars, start bands, and get out in front of an audience without waiting. All it took was some inspiration and the desire to say something. Thousands of bands recorded, and many more never did.

In wedging a fissure in popular music, punk opened new directions. Some of them were carried over into the style called NEW WAVE. Punk also influenced ALTERNATIVE ROCK and GRUNGE bands, including the Replacements, R.E.M., and NIRVANA. More than just being a bridge to new wave, alternative, or grunge, punk has continued as a vital style. After recording for several years, Bad Religion, from southern California, came to prominence in the late 1980s, becoming known for their intelligent lyrics.

Their guitarist Brett Gurewitz started his own label, Epitaph, which became one of punk's largest and best-known, featuring Bad Religion as well as second-generation punk bands like the Offspring and Rancid. From the volatile style of early British punk and the more diverse American bands of the time, punk has broadened into substyles, such as hardcore (more intense and sometimes politically charged), and offshoots such as psychobilly (a mix of punk and rockabilly). A more melodic form of punk, called pop punk, found market success with the likes of Green Day and Blink 182. There was a future after all.

Queen

Queen mixed the androgyny and spectacle of GLAM ROCK with the guitar riffing of early HEAVY METAL and the classical influences of PROGRESSIVE ROCK. More than merely rock stars, Queen became an institution in popular music, and, with their efforts for charity, a shining example of caring and helping.

They formed in 1971 with Freddie Mercury, a flamboyant, posturing vocalist who sometimes played piano, and Brian May, whose prowess on GUITAR was celebrated in guitar magazines, plus bassist John Deacon and drummer Roger Taylor. There were no changes in personnel throughout the band's existence. The name *Queen* is rich with connotations. One is that in making reference to the British monarch, Queen Elizabeth II, the band's country of origin—England—is implied. Another connotation, clearly intended, referred to Mercury's homosexuality.

Often called art-metal, they actually covered a wide range of styles, from the camp of old British music halls to the mysticism of prog rock, presented with a knack for pop hooks, a willingness to experiment, and a tongue-in-cheek sense of humor. They avoided being stereotyped because their hits were so varied, from the ROCKABILLY-inspired "Crazy Little Thing Called Love" to the crowd chant of "We Will Rock You" (which became a football stadium favorite), to the disco dance floor hit "Another One Bites the Dust" (parodied by Weird Al Yankovic as "Another One Rides the Bus"). Their vocals are particularly elaborate and the most famous of their multitude of hits is the semioperatic opus "Bohemian Rhapsody."

Though Queen were one of the most commercially successful of all rock bands in all their presentations—extravagant live shows, immaculately produced recordings, and innovative videos—critics dismissed them for being pretentious and annoying. The authors of *The Worst Rock and Roll Records of All Time,* naming two Queen albums in their "top 50," write: "Queen deteriorated into such an overblown spectacle that it's easy to forget that they were a truly malignant band from the start."[18] Other authors just ignored them: Queen is absent from the indexes of both *Rock of Ages: The Rolling Stone History of Rock & Roll* (1986), by Ed Ward, Geoffrey Stokes, and Ken Tucker, and *Rock and Roll: An Unruly History* (1995) by Robert Palmer. But fans know what they like.

Queen did its initial gigs in 1971, and the next year was signed to a management, publishing, and production contract, and then to the EMI label. Their debut album did not chart on its release in 1973, but did after the band had built its fan base by touring in the United Kingdom and United States, sometimes to support Mott the Hoople and sometimes as the headliner. Their first hit in America was "Killer Queen" in 1975.

"Bohemian Rhapsody," ludicrous and lovable in its exaggerated pomposity, was their next American hit. It came from Queen's fourth album, *A Night at the Opera* (1975), one of the most expensive records ever made. The album was named after a 1935 Marx Brothers film, considered to be their best and one of

Queen (Michael Ochs Archives.com)

the finest comedy movies ever made; the inspiration of the comedy team's madcap humor is evident. Not only were the members of Queen fans of the Marx Brothers—their next album, *A Day at the Races* (1976), was named after a 1937 Marx Brothers film—but they visited Groucho Marx, at his invitation, while on tour in Los Angeles. The album's hit was "Somebody to Love."

The ensuing years brought a dizzying succession of hit singles and albums, tours, soundtrack work, best-selling videos, and side projects, several quite successful. One of their top albums was *The Game* (1980). Produced in Germany, it made number one on both sides of the Atlantic. When "Radio Ga-Ga," written by Roger Taylor, became a hit in 1984, it marked a unique event: each of the four members had been individually responsible for composing at least one of their top 10 hits. The next year, Queen's performance at the Live Aid benefit concert was a sensation. The album *Innuendo* (1991) and its title song topped their respective charts in England.

In November 1991, the day after Mercury publicly announced that he had AIDS, he died peacefully at his home amid family and friends. As the most prominent figure in entertainment to die of AIDS, his death came as a shock, but also called attention to this devastating and still uncontrolled epidemic. In tribute, and in keeping with Mercury's last wishes, "Bohemian Rhapsody" was rereleased to raise money for charity. It entered the U.K. charts at number one (the first U.K. single to ever make number one twice) and stayed there for more than a month, while 10 of Queen's albums were in the U.K. top 100. The reissue raised more than £1 million for the Terence Higgins Trust, a London-based HIV and AIDS charity. Boosted by its use in the movie *Wayne's World* (1992), the song charted again in the United States.

The next year the three surviving band members hosted an emotional tribute to Mercury at London's Wembley Stadium. All 72,000 tickets were sold out within six hours, with no mention as to who the guest artists would be. They were a who's who of rock: DAVID BOWIE (who had collaborated with Queen on the hit single "Under Pressure"), Elton John, George Michael, Seal, Paul Young, Roger Daltrey of the WHO, Tony Iommi of Black Sabbath, Slash and Axl Rose of Guns n' Roses, Ian Hunter and Mick Ronson of Mott the Hoople, James Hetfield of METALLICA, Robert Plant of LED ZEPPELIN, Annie Lennox of Eurythmics, plus Liza Minnelli, who was one of Mercury's chief inspirations. The audience for the live television broadcast numbered more than 1 billion. A foundation, the Mercury Phoenix Trust, was set up to administer the monies generated by the concert, and it has distributed millions of dollars to charities.

In 1992 and 1993 the Brian May Band toured North and South America, Europe, and Japan, sometimes supporting Guns n' Roses, other times as the headliner. A final Queen album, called *Made in Heaven*, came out in 1995, made from Mercury's last recordings, which had been finished by the others.

In 2002 the Guinness World Records declared that "Bohemian Rhapsody" was the United Kingdom's all-time "favorite hit record," and that Queen has had more top 10 singles in the United Kingdom than anyone apart from the BEATLES.

The legacy of Queen is impressive. A stage musical, created in collaboration with May, Deacon, and Taylor, called *We Will Rock You* and based on Queen's songs, opened in London in 2002. There is also a surprising number of books, either biographies of Freddie Mercury or histories of the band, plus box sets, three volumes of greatest hits albums, video collections, and dozens of Web sites honoring them.

Radiohead

From Oxford, England, Radiohead came to prominence in the 1990s with an innovative and unique approach to ALTERNATIVE ROCK. In addressing the fear and wonder of modern life through constant creative development, Radiohead's nuanced work rewards repeated listenings and places them as one of rock's most important bands. Early hit singles "Creep" and "Street Spirit (Fade Out)" were standouts, and their breakthrough album was the challenging, enchanting, essential *OK Computer*. It received many awards and rave reviews and was hailed by critics and fans as a masterpiece.

In 1982, four school friends, aged 14 and 15, got together to play music: vocalist Thom Yorke (b. 1968), guitarist Ed O'Brien (b. 1968), bassist Colin Greenwood (b. 1968), and drummer Phil Selway (b. 1967). Colin's younger brother Jonny (b. 1971) hung around, wanting to join, and eventually did, playing keyboards, xylophone, and guitar. They played their first gig in a tavern in 1987. Each of them went on to higher education institutions but all dropped out to pursue music full time.

A demo tape they made in 1991 was taken by a friend to a recording studio, and the people there thought it showed a little promise, so they asked for more. A few months later, a new tape showed growth and the makings of an original identity. They received some publicity in the local press, and the band, then called On a Friday (their usual rehearsal day), began gigging regularly. Record labels expressed interest, and EMI signed them, though a reviewer noted that their sound reminded

him of the Pixies and the Jam. They changed their name to Radiohead after a TALKING HEADS' song.

Radiohead's first marketed recording came out in 1992, a four-song EP, which sold poorly but is now highly collectable. A subsequent session produced "Creep," about hopeless longing and self-deprecation, musically somewhat in the style of Scott Walker (of the Walker Brothers, whose 1960s hits were produced in a style reminiscent of PHIL SPECTOR's productions). Before it was included on their debut album, *Pablo Honey* (1993), it was released as a single. "Creep" did poorly, but months later was picked up by California radio stations and became a top-40 hit in the United States. Rereleased in the United Kingdom, it made the top 10 (one year after its first appearance).

The search for a follow-up single was stressful— the group had a modest hit from a live EP—but with the album still selling well and crossing into new markets, Radiohead continued to tour. Returning to the studio after playing in the Far East, the new songs were recorded quickly, having been honed in live performance. Several singles were released from the second album, *The Bends* (1995), and the fifth one, "Street Spirit (Fade Out)," a slow, minor-key song about desperation, featuring soothing 16th-note guitar arpeggios, put them back in the U.K. top 10. The album got good reviews but only moderate sales.

Recordings for their third album, *OK Computer*, were started at the band's own studio, a converted shed that had once stored apples. The rest of the recordings were made in a mansion in Bath previously occupied by film and television actress Jane Seymour. The isolation in this luxurious setting allowed for unpressured creativity. The band set up in the ballroom, and the control room was in the library, overlooking the gardens.

OK Computer (1997) is a bold and brilliant set of experimental modern rock music. It powerfully comments on the challenge of finding meaning, maintaining individuality, and experiencing beauty amidst the alienation, terror, and emptiness of modern, technologically advanced society. At times the album is reminiscent of PINK FLOYD's *Dark Side of the Moon.* Sonically dense, with haunting vocals and layers of unusual instrumentation—a mix of acoustic, electronic, and computer-generated sounds—this cohesive, thoughtful work of art affects the senses and the emotions. *OK Computer* has the power to thrill and transport listeners while shifting their conceptions not only of music but of the world itself.

Critics and fans went wild for it. It is seen as one of the most significant albums of the 1990s, even as one of the greatest ever made. In the United States it won the Grammy Award for Best Alternative Music Performance, went to number 21 on the album charts and earned platinum-level sales. In the United Kingdom it went right to number one and stayed on the charts for more than a year. Three singles went into the U.K. top 10: "Karma Police," "No Surprises," and "Paranoid Android," a six-minute epic of clashing styles. The video for "Paranoid Android" received extensive airplay on both sides of the Atlantic, and both the song and video were highly praised.

Radiohead then went on tour. Previously, in support of *The Bends,* they had toured Europe opening for R.E.M. Before *OK Computer* was made, they tried out some of the new material during a tour of the United States, opening for Alanis Morissette. Once the album was released, Radiohead toured Europe, the United States, and Japan as the headliner. A surrealistic documentary film of their life on the road, called *Meeting People Is Easy,* was made by Grant Gee, the director of their "No Surprises" video.

After some time off, with side projects and occasional performances such as for Amnesty International, Radiohead returned to recording. After much anticipation—there were no singles but new songs were premiered during three Internet webcasts—and a three-year wait, the next two albums came out only eight months apart: *Kid A* (2000) and *Amnesiac* (2001). Their themes were more nihilistic, and their new sound was almost unrecognizable: a mix of distorted vocals, guitar riffs, and electronic beats. They had been inspired by the musical experiments of Can, Kraftwerk, and jazz bassist and composer Charlie Mingus. *Kid A* hit number one and won a Grammy Award for Best Alternative Album. *Amnesiac* hit number two and sold even more than *Kid A.*

Before the release of their sixth album, *Hail to the Thief* (2003), unfinished recordings and preliminary mixes were stolen and presented on the Internet. Some tracks were even played on the radio. Then the finished album was leaked to on the Internet. Nonetheless, when it was released officially it was as successful and welcomed as its predecessors. Despite its themes of dread and confusion, it is less bleak than the previous two albums: within the sonic diversity and complicated arrangements are glimpses of humanity. Thom Yorke, tired of being cast as the angst-ridden spokesperson of a lost generation, has hinted that this album will be the last from the band known as Radiohead. He and his fellow band members have constantly moved forward. Legions of loyal fans are waiting to see what Radiohead, in whatever form it takes, will do next.

Ramones, The

In T-shirts and leather jackets and faded, ripped jeans they looked scruffy, with long hair falling in their faces. They all had the same last name: Ramone. Their music was simple, fast, and loud. The Ramones were never very successful: none of their 21 albums sold in great quantities, and in America only three singles brushed the charts, none higher than number 66. So why did they make it

The Ramones (Michael Ochs Archives.com)

into the Rock and Roll Hall of Fame? Because—at a time when rock seemed to have lost its way—they understood what real rock and roll was and they played it. They kept playing it, despite personnel changes and the frustrations of never making it big, doing more than 2,000 shows from their first in 1974 to their last in 1996.

They were inspired by 1960s rock, the kind heard on transistor radios on top-40 stations and bought by teenagers on 45rpm singles. In reaction to the orchestrated and indulgent corporate rock of the 1970s, the Ramones played raw and catchy two-minute songs stripped to the essentials: guitars, simple lyrics, and energy. Considered to be one of the first PUNK ROCK bands, they influenced countless others, both in America and Britain (where they toured often and had more hits), as well influencing HEAVY METAL and GRUNGE bands. A tribute album, called *We're a Happy Family,* includes Ramones songs as played by METALLICA, U2, KISS, the Red Hot Chili Peppers, Rancid, the Offspring, Marilyn Manson, the Pretenders, and Tom Waits.

The band members were in their early and mid-20s when they played their first gig in 1974 at a private party in the middle-class Forest Hills section of Queens, New York, where they all lived. That summer they developed their act as the house band at CBGB, the now-legendary bar in New York City that figures in the careers of BLONDIE, TALKING HEADS, Patti Smith, and Television. The next year, a few months after an unsuccessful audition that had them opening for Johnny Winter and an unimpressed audience of 20,000 people, they got a record contract. In 1976, to promote their debut album (which cost only about $6,000 to make and is now a classic), they played in London alongside the Flamin' Groovies, a San Francisco band with similar influences. Then, and the next year on a United Kingdom tour, with the intro to every song being a shouted "1-2-3-4" (as in the BEATLES' "I Saw Her Standing There") and their catchphrases "Hey ho, let's go!" (from their own "Blitzkrieg Bop") and "Gabba gabba hey!" (from their song "Pinhead," with lyrics derived from the 1932 movie *Freaks*), they made a big impression and influenced the emerging punk scene. "Sheena Is a Punk Rocker" went up the charts. In 1979 they appeared in the Roger Corman film *Rock 'n' Roll High School* and in 1982 they played at the US Festival to probably their largest audience: 500,000 people.

In 2002 the Rock and Roll Hall of Fame inducted the band, naming five of its members: lead vocalist Joey Ramone (b. Jeffrey Hyman, 1952–2001), who died of cancer the year before the induction, bassist Dee Dee Ramone (b. Douglas Coldin, 1952–2002), who left the band in the late 1980s but continued to write songs for it and who died two months after the induction; guitarist Johnny Ramone (b. John Cummings, 1951–2004); Tommy Ramone (b. Tommy Erdelyi, 1952), first their manager, then their drummer, then their producer; plus his replacement on drums, Marky Ramone (who joined in 1978). C. J. Ramone (b. 1965), Dee Dee's replacement, was not included in the honor.

Detractors accused the Ramones of stupidity, but supporters knew their lyrics could be witty and that there was depth behind the minimalism of their three-chord songs and tuneless vocals. With enthusiasm and determination they conveyed the joy and humanity of the early rock and garage music that inspired them at a time when most music fans either considered it irrelevant or weren't old enough to remember it. The Ramones not only acknowledged their influences but built on them, thus inserting themselves into rock and roll history.

Rascals, The

Known early in their career as the Young Rascals, the Rascals were a New York band that was very popular in the 1960s. Six of their 18 hits made the top 10. Their sound was based on black music—rhythm and blues, MOTOWN, soul, and gospel—but they also did pop ballads and psychedelia. The soul component was evident in their use of the Hammond organ, also common in gospel, and in the vocals, which were as soulful as those of the RIGHTEOUS BROTHERS, Steve Winwood, Mitch Ryder, or anyone else in the "blue-eyed soul" category.

Their three number-one hits each represent a different aspect of the band's evolution. At first they were known as the Young Rascals, a rhythm and blues band with punchy songs like the driving "Good Lovin' " (1966) that were covered by garage bands. With "Groovin' " (1967), their biggest hit, they shifted to more mellow songs of happiness, introspection, and appreciation. By 1968, calling themselves just the Rascals, they added gospel themes with "People Got to Be Free."

The uplifting intent of soul music, with its roots in church and its desire for racial harmony, was present in their lyric themes, expressed directly in "Glory Glory," "Heaven," "Ray of Hope," and "See," and indirectly in many others. The band explored a wide variety of sounds. For example, "It's Wonderful" has a psychedelic edge and uses tape-speed manipulations, and "How Can I Be Sure" is in waltz time, with upright bass and an accordion.

The name Young Rascals was a marketing gimmick—they wore outdated little-boy knickers and ties—and they shortened the name as soon as they could. Whatever they were called, the personnel remained mostly stable. Felix Cavaliere (b. 1944) sang lead and played organ and piano. He met Eddie Brigati (b. 1946), who sang backup and occasionally sang lead and played percussion, and Gene Cornish (b. 1945), who contributed to the vocals while playing bass or guitar, while they all were part of the backing band for Joey Dee of "Peppermint Twist" fame. Drummer Dino Danelli (b. 1945) also came from the New York club scene. After putting in rehearsal time they soon created a sensation at top nightclubs around the city. After their first two hits, which came from outside writers, all subsequent hits were composed by Cavaliere, usually with lyrics by Brigati.

This lineup remained stable from 1964 to 1971. They signed to the Atlantic label and had eight albums released, one a greatest-hits set. A final incarnation, with new recruits replacing two departed original members, lasted only a few months until the Rascals disbanded in 1972. Danelli and Cornish then worked together in Bulldog, which had one hit in 1972, and Fotomaker, which had two in 1978. Felix Cavaliere had a solo hit in 1980, and he reunited with Cornish and Danelli in 1988. In 1997 the original group was inducted into the Rock and Roll Hall of Fame.

reggae

Reggae is a vibrant style of Jamaican music that has an infectious groove. It was created in Jamaica, found its first international audience in Britain, invigorated rock and was invigorated by it, spread to America and Africa, and evolved, absorbing techno influences and inspiring hip-hop. Unique among popular music styles created in English-speaking countries, reggae is sensual dance music with a political and religious conscience.

Reggae developed in the 1960s and came to international notice in 1969 with Desmond Dekker's "Israelites," a number-one hit in the United Kingdom that also made the top 10 in the United States. The style was further popularized in the 1970s by Bob Marley and the Wailers and rock musicians who adopted its repertoire and characteristic beat. ERIC CLAPTON's version of Marley's composition "I Shot the Sheriff" was a number-one single in 1975 and boosted the mainstream acceptance of reggae. Reggae influenced NEW WAVE, especially in the music of the Police, (the title of *Reggatta De Blanc* from 1979 is said to mean "white reggae" in patois), and PUNK ROCK, especially in the music of the Clash.

Bob Marley (1945–81) is the icon of reggae, and since his death by cancer at the early age of 36, his popularity has only increased. He stands as a righteous prophetlike figure whose mystical side inspires and whose cries for justice still resonate. "Get Up Stand Up" is in the Grammy Hall of Fame. *Legend*, a greatest-hits album, has sold 10 million copies in the United States alone and is one of the top catalog records. In the January 4, 2000, edition of *Time* magazine, Bob Marley and the Wailers' *Exodus* (1977) was named "the album of the century." The article stated "Every song is a classic, from the messages of love to the anthems of revolution . . . the album is a political and cultural nexus, drawing inspiration from the Third World and then giving voice to it the world over." Marley's style of reggae—sometimes called roots rock reggae—has remained popular alongside variants and later developments.

Reggae, like its predecessors ska (also known as "blue beat") and rock steady, features syncopated rhythms with accented off-beats. All three styles mix elements of Afro-Caribbean folk music (such as calypso and mento) with the influence of American jazz, R&B, MOTOWN, folk, soul, and gospel. Historically, Jamaica and portions of the United States were at one time British colonies whose economies were built on slavery. Geographically, Jamaica is close enough to the United States that residents could hear radio stations in New Orleans and Miami. Reggae's use of horns, impassioned lead vocals, and gospel-style background vocals were influenced by soul. From R&B and Motown, reggae borrowed three-part harmonized lead vocals and the characteristic of tightly arranged ensembles with the players each contributing their set part to a rhythmically integrated whole. Reggae's use of keyboards may owe something to the admiration of the likes of FATS DOMINO. From folk, reggae took inspiration from BOB DYLAN's social comments and critiques. In its preaching and biblical quotations it was connected to gospel.

That the term *reggae* comes from slang is generally agreed upon, though what it refers to—"ragged," "struggle," a "loose woman," or perhaps just a short way of saying "regular"—is debated. If it comes from "ragged," raggedy clothes supposedly, then the derivation would be in keeping with the music's origins in the Trench Town ghetto of Kingston, Jamaica's capital city. Jamaica is a large island in the West Indies that was unknown to Europe until Columbus encountered it in 1494. It was ruled by Spain, which all but exterminated the indigenous people and imported African slaves. The British captured Jamaica in 1655 and made it a colony and a center for the American slave trade until Britain abolished slavery in the West Indies in 1833. In the 1940s Jamaica attained self-government. It achieved full independence in 1962.

American jazz was popular in Jamaica in the 1940s, and local musicians developed their skills in bands playing for tourists. In the 1950s American R&B was all the rage. Few people could afford record players, so they heard the songs on the radio or at outdoor weekend parties where a disc jockey (called a music selector) and a master of ceremonies (called a toaster) would play records on loud mobile discotheques (called sound systems). With the rise of recording studios in Jamaica, the competition between sound system owners shifted from the challenge of obtaining American R&B records to producing their own discs of local talent.

Reggae's predecessors were ska and rock steady. Ska, first popular around 1960, had faster tempos, bouncing bass lines, and made more use of horns. Perhaps the first example of white ska was the BEATLES' "Ob-La-Di, Ob-La-Da" (1968). Later, ska was revived by British "two-tone" (racially integrated) bands that emerged from the punk movement, such as the Specials, the English Beat, the Selector,

and Madness. A second revival occurred in North America in the 1990s. Rock steady, popular in the mid-1960s, used fewer horns, had the bass play clusters of notes rather than continuously, slowed the tempo, and was more sensual and inspired by soul vocalists. Songs with lyrics about "rude boys" (Trench Town delinquents) were common at the time. Reggae relaxed the tempo a little more and placed further emphasis on rhythm by putting the bass in the foreground.

Reggae's moral conscience comes from Christianity and a sect called Rastafarians. Ras Tafari was the original name of Haile Selassie, the former emperor of Ethiopia, to whom the sect is devoted. They believe him to be the Second Coming of Christ. Rastafarians conceive of Africa in heavenly terms. They wear their hair in ropelike strands known as dreadlocks, espouse love and peace, and believe that ganja (marijuana) is a sacred herb. Reggae music is an expression of Rastafarianism, and though only some of its practitioners belong to the sect, reggae lyrics are infused with its religious tenets and political stance.

The spreading of Jamaican sounds to the United Kingdom and the United States is marked by Millie Small's "My Boy Lollipop" (1964), a huge international hit and the first with the ska beat. Small, also known as the Blue Beat Girl, was a Jamaican who recorded in England. The record was produced by Chris Blackwell, an upper-class white man who spent his childhood in Jamaica, completed his education in England, and returned to Jamaica in 1955. He started a record label called Island, named in reference to the novel *Island in the Sun* (1956), by Alec Waugh. The story, set in the West Indies, concerns interracial relations.

Island issued its first album in 1959 but relocated its headquarters to London in 1962. Jamaican expatriates in London made for a more lucrative market than their impoverished homeland. Island became one of the most important independent record labels. It issued reggae records by Bob Marley, Toots and the Maytals (the first to use *reggae* in a song title), Burning Spear, Third World, and Black Uhuru. Island was also heavily involved with rock acts, from the Spencer Davis Group (whose debut hit "Keep On Running" in 1966 was written by Jackie Edwards, a Jamaican whom Blackwell brought to England) to U2 in the 1980s and the Cranberries in the 1990s. In 2001 Blackwell was inducted into the Rock and Roll Hall of Fame.

Chris Blackwell was involved in the careers of other singers who brought the Jamaican sound to the international pop charts. Jimmy Cliff had a big hit in 1970 with "Wonderful World, Beautiful People" and he starred in the movie *The Harder They Come* (1973), which Blackwell financed, about the rise and fall of a Trench Town rude boy. The popular film and its soundtrack album featured Cliff's music and some classic reggae singles. Another singer, Johnny Nash, had hits with "I Can See Clearly Now," on which he was backed by Bob Marley and the Wailers, and "Stir It Up," written by Marley.

Marley and his band, originally known as the Wailing Wailers, had been popular in Jamaica for more than a decade. The front line was a vocal trio of Marley, the reclusive Bunny Livingston (later known as Bunny Wailer and the one most involved with Rastafarianism), and the volatile Peter Tosh. They were together on early Island recordings, but Wailer and Tosh left for solo careers in 1974. Tosh was an associate of the ROLLING STONES and Mick Jagger sang on his 1978 hit "(You've Got to Walk and) Don't Look Back." Tosh was murdered during a robbery at his home in Jamaica in 1987.

There are several discs of reggae versions of rock and pop songs and whole albums devoted to those of the GRATEFUL DEAD and the Beatles. To this day, many rock bands have a reggae song or two in the repertoire. Typical choices are "I Shot the Sheriff" as done by Eric Clapton, Cat Stevens' "Wild World" as done by Maxi Priest, "Tide Is High" by BLONDIE (a cover of a song by the Paragons), "Red Red Wine" by UB40 (Neil Diamond's song), CHUCK BERRY's "Johnny B. Goode" (with place names changed to Jamaican locales) by Toots and the Maytals, or something off the *Harder They Come* soundtrack,

perhaps Jimmy Cliff's "You Can Get It If You Really Want" or the rude boy song "Johnny Too Bad" by the Slickers.

Reggae has been adapted into techno, had its vocals removed (a style called dub), and been rapped over. In the evolution of African–American popular styles, reggae—as played by Jamaicans and as adopted by rock bands—acts as a bridge between soul and hip-hop. Reggae continues, with festivals in Jamaica, the United States, Canada, and throughout Europe. Several reggae pioneers are still active and acclaimed, notably the group Culture and Toots Hibbert of Toots and the Maytals. African performers Alpha Blondy and Lucky Dube are international reggae stars. And the biological and musical siblings of Bob Marley do their part to carry the torch.

R.E.M.

The band formed in early 1980 in Athens, Georgia (where the B-52s preceded them in the city's thriving music scene). R.E.M. stands for "rapid eye movement," a phase of sleep. The name was appropriate, for they brought a dreamlike quality to much of their work. Their lineup of vocalist Michael Stipe (b. 1960), guitarist Peter Buck (b. 1956), bassist Mike Mills (b. 1958), and drummer Bill Berry (b. 1958) remained consistent for 17 years, until Berry retired from the band. Mills and Berry had played together since high school in Macon, Georgia, and had moved to Athens to attend the university, where they met the others, who were fellow students.

Their first album, *Murmur* (1983), on the independent I.R.S. label, is one of the defining records of ALTERNATIVE music, the kind embraced by college radio and also known as indie rock or college rock. Critically acclaimed at the time—*Rolling Stone* magazine named it Album of the Year—it is still regularly cited as one of the best records of the decade. Their status grew throughout the 1980s, and by the early 1990s they were one of rock's most popular, influential, and respected bands. They are also one of its most unpretentious and musically original. They provided a focal point for alternative's emerging subculture: young, educated people looking for music more socially responsible than mindlessly hedonistic, more artistic and profound than mainstream pop's blandness, and more tolerant and humane than the angry aggression found in more marginal music forms.

Their southern FOLK ROCK style changed and evolved: every album is different. All of them show the band's generally consistent good taste, with few missteps into dullness or self-indulgence. Though all members are equally important, their sound is characterized by Michael Stipe's obscure and abstract lyrics—associative rather than narrative—and sometimes unintelligible vocals. Stipe is a charismatic and eccentric front man, Peter Buck's inventive, angular GUITAR playing elevates the band, Mike Mills contributes melodic, at times funky, BASS playing and harmony (and occasionally lead) vocals, and Bill Berry (no longer a member) contributed muscular drumming. They are influenced by the BYRDS, the VELVET UNDERGROUND, the BAND, CREEDENCE CLEARWATER REVIVAL, the DOORS, CHUCK BERRY, the BRITISH INVASION, SURF, COUNTRY, PUNK ROCK, and hard rock. R.E.M.'s dark lyrics explore southern themes and mystique and avoid pop clichés. They sing about weather, drowning, nightmares, eccentric individuals, trains, and separation. Their later work has more explicitly political themes, and Stipe's enunciation is clearer. There are three main periods in their career: the beginning, when they built their following while recording for the thriving independent label I.R.S.; the middle, when they made more accessible music and reached stardom while recording for the major label Warner Bros.; and their current incarnation as a trio.

One of their first gigs was in an abandoned church where two of them resided. By summer 1980 they were playing dates in neighboring cities and states. All the band members dropped out of university. In 1981 R.E.M.'s debut single came out on a small independent label. The members were 21 to 24 years old at the time. The next year they signed with I.R.S. and started to tour nationally. Their first release was *Chronic Town* (1982), a five-song EP that showed their sound nearly fully realized: beautiful melodies, mumbled vocals, jangling guitars playing arpeggiated chords, and a good beat.

Murmur (1983) is an enigmatic, intimate masterpiece. It is mystical, haunting pop that combines musical self-confidence and a childlike innocence. With an earthy, organic feeling from the guitar, bass, drums combination that put it in stark contrast to the artificiality of the synthesizer bands so popular at the time, its warmth and ambiguous meanings engaged listeners' imaginations and rewarded repeated listenings. To support their next album, *Reckoning* (1984), a recording similar in tone to the previous one (for perhaps the only time in their career), they toured overseas and performed on national television in the United States, on *Late Night with David Letterman*. In a review of the album in his *Village Voice* column, the famous rock critic Robert Christgau wrote, "This charming band makes honestly reassuring music—those guitar chords ring out with a confidence in the underlying beauty of the world that's all but disappeared among rock-and-rollers who know what else is happening."[19]

Fables of the Reconstruction (1985), recorded in London with producer Joe Boyd (known for producing the Incredible String Band, Fairport Convention, and Nick Drake), was named Album of the Year by *College Media Journal*. Though most fans are generous in their estimation of it, the band members consider it one of their weaker albums. At that time they were on tenuous terms with each other and unsure of their direction, and the energy is muted. The result is richly textured, mysterious, impressionistic, and gloomy.

Lifes Rich Pageant (1986) (named after a line from a Peter Sellers film), and the single "Fall on Me," brought R.E.M. mainstream attention. On this LP, R.E.M. had a tougher, rocking, more infectious and direct sound. While Stipe's lyrics remained obscure, the words were more audible, and the music at a creative peak. It is a highlight in their career. *Dead Letter Office* (1987), collected demos, outtakes, and B sides, plus all of their *Chronic Town*

EP. Alongside sloppy originals were several cover songs: three by the Velvet Underground, and one each by AEROSMITH and Pylon (also from Athens, Georgia), plus Roger Miller's country novelty "King of the Road."

No. 5: Document (1987) was their first top-10 album and it gave them their first top-10 single: "The One I Love," a painful love song. "It's the End of the World As We Know It (And I Feel Fine)," with its rapid stream-of-consciousness lyrics reminiscent of BOB DYLAN's "Subterranean Homesick Blues," also made the charts. The album was recorded in Nashville and mixed in Los Angeles and shows the band's creative evolution. With the vocals clearer still, the band's aim to depict the chaotic time in which it was made had them writing a few politically conscious songs, including "Welcome to the Occupation" and "Exhuming McCarthy." A fan favorite (as are several other of their albums), it is absorbing and powerful and it was influential. After *Eponymous* (1988), a compilation album that fulfilled their obligations to I.R.S. Records, they signed a million-dollar contract with Warner Bros.

Their major-label debut, *Green* (1988), was more polished and more uneven. It included another top-10 hit: "Stand." R.E.M. were heavily promoted, and the venues they visited during their extensive tour were mostly stadiums. That year, *Rolling Stone* put them on its cover; the heading said "America's Best Rock 'n' Roll Band." *Out of Time* (1991) was their first number-one album, and it won three Grammy Awards, while the video for "Losing My Religion" (a southern phrase for being at wit's end) won six MTV Music Awards. It made the top 10 on the singles charts, as did "Shiny Happy People."

Automatic for the People (1992), named after a sign in front of a restaurant in their hometown, had less variety than the previous album. These songs are slow, reserved, and mournful. Themes of death, jealousy, and redemption were treated with melancholic yet beautiful music, and the public responded: it sold 4 million copies in the United States and generated three hit singles: "Drive," "Man on the Moon," and "Everybody Hurts."

Monster (1994) showed another side of the band. Its cacophonic, GRUNGE-influenced hard rock riffs disappointed many older fans and critics, but it contained four hit singles, including "What's the Frequency, Kenneth?". "Let Me In" was a beautiful yet harrowing tribute to the late Kurt Cobain of NIRVANA. *Monster* hit number one and sold 4 million copies in the United States. During the 1995 tour, drummer Bill Berry suffered a brain aneurism onstage in Switzerland. He was operated on and made a full and speedy recovery, but after recording their next album, he retired from the band in 1997. In 2003, he made a surprise appearance as a guest, joining his mates for two songs during an encore at a show in North Carolina.

They re-signed with Warner Bros. for $80 million; at the time it was the largest record contract in history. *New Adventures in Hi-fi* (1996) was still experimental, but in contrast to the noise of *Monster,* it was subdued. Many of the tracks are long and dark, and the overall mood is weariness. "E-Bow the Letter" is a collaboration with the legendary Patti Smith, an idol for the band members. It made the top 10 in the United Kingdom, where the band has a cult following.

As a trio R.E.M. released *Up* (1998), a compelling record that is deep and reflective and diverse, and that contained "Daysleeper," a moderate hit. *Reveal* (2001) was another strong album that, like *Up,* made the top 10. It featured "Imitation of Life." *In Time: The Best of R.E.M. 1988–2003* (2003), included two new songs plus "The Great Beyond," one of their best trio songs, previously only available on the *Man in the Moon* soundtrack. *Around the Sun* (2004) was an emotional and uplifting album that showed renewed confidence.

In an era when hair metal bands and NEW WAVE synthesizer bands were popular, R.E.M.'s music gave hope that new rock that drew from older models could still be valid, and that rock still prized art over commerce. In setting the pace for alternative music, they inspired a multitude of other musicians and their influence can be seen directly on bands such as Pavement and RADIOHEAD.

Righteous Brothers, The

In 1962, while in rival bands that were each recording for the Moonglow label of Los Angeles, Bill Medley (b. 1940), a bass singer, and Bobby Hatfield (1940–2003), a tenor, met and formed a singing duo. Their style was based on R&B, and became known as blue-eyed soul, a term for white singers who "sound black." Their name came about when a black marine in the audience at a nightclub show declared, "That was righteous, brothers."

Their biggest hits were slow, passionate declarations of love, desire, and loss sung with gospel-like fervor and accompanied by lush orchestration. However, not all of their songs were slow: their first hit, "Little Latin Lupe Lu" (1963), written by Medley, was an energetic rocker that charted again in versions by the Kingsmen as well as Mitch Ryder and the Detroit Wheels, and was a common song in the repertoires of garage bands.

Their biggest hits remained in the public consciousness through constant radio airplay and, since the 1980s, use on movie soundtracks. The dramatic "You've Lost That Lovin' Feelin'" (1964) was their third hit and first number one. According to Broadcast Music International (BMI), it is the most-played song on the radio, ever: almost 10 million times at last count (if the same recording was played over and over, it would take more than 50 years to play it that many times). It was written by the husband-and-wife team of Barry Mann and Cynthia Weil (who wrote many other hits), plus PHIL SPECTOR, who produced it. It is a superb example of his famous "wall of sound" technique. Two other Spector productions, released on his Philles label in 1965, were also huge: "Unchained Melody" and "Ebb Tide," both remakes of hits from the mid-1950s.

The Righteous Brothers' association with Spector dated from 1963, when he was the orchestra conductor for a package show in San Francisco and was impressed by the duo's performance. Parts of this show were released on an LP called *Memories of the Cow Palace;* on it the Righteous Brothers do their second hit, "My Babe." Another fortuitous moment came the next year when Jack Good, a British television producer who had moved to Los Angeles, saw the singers and put them on the popular *Shindig!* show. They also were regulars on a similar show called *Hullabaloo.*

Moonglow kept releasing old recordings, including the Righteous Brothers' version of "Georgia on My Mind" (a standard written by Hoagy Carmichael in 1930), which made the charts in 1966. That year, a shift to MGM's Verve label gave them another number-one hit with "(You're My) Soul and Inspiration" (also written by Mann and Weil, and produced in the Spector manner), plus another half-dozen chart entries. The duo split up

The Righteous Brothers (Michael Ochs Archives.com)

in 1967 when shifting styles in rock and pop began to favor a psychedelic sound and Bill Medley wanted to try a solo career. He did have some modest solo hits, but Bobby Hatfield and his new singing partner, Jimmy Walker, formerly of the beat group the Knickerbockers (popular in the mid-1960s with "Lies" and "One Track Mind"), had none. They called it quits in 1970.

Medley and Hatfield reunited briefly in 1974, gaining three final hits, including "Rock and Roll Heaven," which paid tribute to JIMI HENDRIX, JANIS JOPLIN, Otis Redding, and Jim Morrison, and other recently deceased stars. After that, Medley's ex-wife was raped and murdered, a case that remains unsolved. Distraught, Medley put his career on hold for five years. On his return in the early 1980s, he opened a nightclub in L.A. and had two more solo hits.

Another reunion for the duo was instigated by a 1982 TV special celebrating *American Bandstand,* and they performed together regularly in the ensuing years. The popularity of their old recordings in movie soundtracks boosted their attendances, while Medley had new soundtrack recordings that were successful, notably his duo with Jennifer Warnes on "(I've Had) The Time of My Life" (from *Dirty Dancing*), which reached number one in 1987.

Billy Joel cited them as an inspiration upon their induction to the Rock and Roll Hall of Fame in 2003. Later that year, Hatfield died of acute cocaine intoxication shortly before a scheduled performance in Michigan.

rockabilly

Record reviewers coined the term *rockabilly* in 1956 to describe a rhythmic, intense style of rock and roll from the American Mid-South, introduced by ELVIS PRESLEY's first records. Though the term *hillbilly* (implied in the style's name) was considered derogatory, *rockabilly* replaced other descriptions, such as "country and western rhythm and blues."

Of the thousands of rockabilly songs recorded in the 1950s, few made the charts. "Blue Suede Shoes" is the best known; composer CARL PERKINS' version is more rockabilly than Presley's. Rockabilly faded by 1960, lying dormant until a revival in the late 1970s.

Radio began to play blues, rhythm and blues, and gospel in the late 1940s, exciting listeners across North America. Young white musicians, especially in locales with black populations, blended country styles—western swing, hillbilly boogie, bluegrass, and honky-tonk—to eventually create rockabilly.

In July 1954, at Presley's first session (for SAM PHILLIPS' Sun label of Memphis, Tennessee), he recorded "That's All Right," a song written by Mississippi bluesman Arthur "Big Boy" Crudup. The other side was a hopped-up version of "Blue Moon of Kentucky" by bluegrass founder Bill Monroe, transformed from a medium-tempo waltz. These renditions laid the foundation for rockabilly that others emulated and developed. The band was just a trio—rockabilly's quintessential instrumentation. Accompanying Presley's strummed acoustic guitar was Scotty Moore's electric guitar providing fills and Bill Black's propulsive upright bass. Presley sang with more black inflections and emotional intensity than other country singers did at the time, and, as shown at his debut performance later that month, moved more onstage too.

The trio, adding drummer D. J. Fontana, toured almost continuously across the South in 1954 and 1955. They ignited audiences and caused musicians to change over from country to rockabilly, including BUDDY HOLLY and Marty Robbins, who was already an established star. Musicians who saw Presley perform made almost all the rockabilly recorded in these years. In 1956 Presley, now signed to RCA and recording in Nashville, performed on prime-time television and sold millions of records. Labels scrambled for similar performers, finding singers like Gene Vincent, whose "Be Bop A Lula" soon hit the charts.

The Sun label recorded rockabilly by Carl Perkins, JERRY LEE LEWIS, ROY ORBISON, Warren Smith, Billy Lee Riley, Sonny Burgess, and many others. Some of them, plus Charlie Feathers and

Johnny Burnette and the Rock 'n Roll Trio, received their biggest recognition in the rockabilly revival of the 1970s and 1980s. Nashville country stars jumped on the fad. So did young female singers, such as Wanda Jackson, BRENDA LEE, and Janis Martin. Regionally, strong rockabilly communities developed, including Texas (Buddy Knox, Sleepy Labeef, Ronnie Dawson, future country star George Jones) and California (RICKY NELSON, EDDIE COCHRAN, the Collins Kids). As rockabilly evolved, more sounds entered—piano, saxophone, harmony singing, background vocal groups—and diluted its sound. By the end of the 1950s, rockabilly was spent.

Several factors, including the death of Presley in 1977, led to a revival, first in Europe. Fans wore 1950s-style clothes, collected old records, and brought veteran rockabillies overseas to festivals. Younger bands formed, notably the Stray Cats from New York. Finding acceptance in England, they brought a hard, lean version of rockabilly back to America, where their caricature look made an impact during MTV's early days. Rockabilly became popular in such far-flung locales as Japan and Russia, and is going strong to this day.

rock festivals

Through the late 1960s and the 1970s, outdoor rock festivals were a phenomenon of immense proportions, not just in size but also in cultural significance. In more recent decades they have continued as important venues for rock musicians and as tribal gatherings for rock fans. Earlier festivals promoted music alone, some later ones served additionally to support a social cause.

Music festivals are nothing new in classical music. Folk festivals have been around since the 1930s, and jazz festivals almost as long. Rock festivals, however, began in the 1960s. The MONTEREY POP FESTIVAL, which took place in northern California in June 1967, is considered the first. It is one of a handful of events in rock and roll history, along with WOODSTOCK in upstate New York, and Altamont, in northern California (both in 1969),

that have an aura of legend about them. Each one was a moment of awareness for the counterculture movement. Monterey was beautiful and full of possibilities. Woodstock was massive and relatively free of problems; it came to symbolize the force of the youth movement so much that hippies were referred to as the Woodstock Nation. Altamont, mere months later, was so ugly that it is perceived as the end of the dreams of utopia that flourished in the 1960s.

The ill-fated Altamont festival took place in December 1969. On the suggestion of the manager of the GRATEFUL DEAD, the ROLLING STONES, criticized for the high ticket prices on their American tour, decided to do a free show in San Francisco with leading California bands. One day before the show, the site was changed to a speedway in Altamont, though the new site's food, toilet facilities, and even the stage itself were inadequate. The Altamont concert took place with a feeling of dread and doom easily felt by watching the documentary film *Gimme Shelter* (1970). At the concert, captured on film, the Hells Angels motorcycle gang, hired to provide security and paid with booze and drugs, beat people in the audience. At one point Marty Balin of JEFFERSON AIRPLANE jumped off the stage to provide a protective role and got knocked unconscious, and Grace Slick spoke to try to calm the crowd. An argument between a musician and an Angel was broadcast over the PA system. The Hells Angels killed a man in front of the stage during the Rolling Stones performance of "Under My Thumb."

Each of these three festivals have a secure place in rock history because they were filmed. One important addition to *Monterey Pop, Woodstock,* and *Gimme Shelter* is a film about a rock festival in England: *Message to Love: The Isle of Wight Festival 1970,* which was not released until the 1990s. Besides noteworthy performances by a host of top acts, including the DOORS, the WHO, and JIMI HENDRIX (his last stage show; he died a few days later), the Isle of Wight film shows confrontations between organizers and self-righteous attendees whose antiestablishment beliefs caused them to demand free admission. Many more festivals were recorded but not filmed, and others are just fading memories.

The largest gathering of people occurred at the Summer Jam held at Watkins Glen, New York, on July 28, 1973, which had a crowd of 600,000, four times what organizer Bill Graham anticipated. Only three bands were on the bill, but all were big draws: the Grateful Dead, the BAND, and the ALLMAN BROTHERS BAND. It was supposed to be just one day, but on the day before, when all bands did a sound check they played to the 250,000 or so people already on the site. As at Woodstock and many other festivals, a summer downpour inconvenienced all but did not dampen festive spirits. Other important events include the series of Knebworth festivals in England that began in the 1970s, and the US Festivals of 1982–83 in San Bernardino, California, which featured established rock groups and included younger bands playing PUNK ROCK, NEW WAVE, and HEAVY METAL. Charity events such as Live Aid became a phenomenon in the 1980s. Later rock festivals, like rock music itself, became more niche oriented, and there have been festivals of specific styles, such as JAM BANDS, CLASSIC ROCK, PROGRESSIVE ROCK, and the like.

Much organization is required for a festival and much is unpredictable, from the weather to the behavior of masses of people. To hold a festival, a location such as farmland or a stadium has to be found, permits obtained, and liaisons with the local authorities established. Artists have to be booked and accommodated, and publicity is essential. Provisions need to be made for parking, camping, sanitation, food, and vendors. Security staff and crews to do the sound and lights and to construct and tear down the stage must be hired. Medical teams have to be prepared to treat everything from minor cuts and sunburns to psychotic episodes and drug overdoses; there have been births and deaths at festivals.

Many festivals are underprepared and lose money for the promoters. Most concertgoers come with goodwill, but there are cases of aggression or just plain stupidity. Fights, thefts, forged or stolen tickets, and vandalized entrances where people enter for free are not uncommon. Food and water supplies may be inadequate, including toilet facilities. At the end of a festival, there is inevitably a disheartening amount of litter to clean up. As people learn from experience, running a festival can become almost a science.

Festivals are places where people can leave behind their daily routines and meet friends and make new ones. No matter what side attractions exist, they are mostly about the music. Fans are willing, in a spirit of adventure, to endure some hardships to get to a festival and stay while the music plays. Hearing a brilliant performance, finally getting to see a favorite act, or discovering a sensational new artist are some of the things that are cherished long after any ordeals are forgotten.

rock revival

Some time had to pass and new kinds of music had to develop before it was possible to look back to the 1950s as rock and roll's golden age. Looking back on early rock is often done as an act of nostalgia or parody.

By 1969 rock and roll started to experience a revival. Sha Na Na, students at Columbia University in New York City, performed that year at the WOODSTOCK festival. Though their stage show parodied some elements of 1950s fashion and the character stereotypes of the juvenile delinquents or the bobby soxers who danced around the jukebox at the malt shop, the music they recorded—new versions of old hits—was done in loving tribute. Their album *Rock and Roll Is Here to Stay!* includes spoken word passages by disc jockey Alan Freed. Also in 1969 a concert called the Toronto Rock 'n' Roll Revival featured, among others, CHUCK BERRY, BO DIDDLEY, JERRY LEE LEWIS, LITTLE RICHARD, and Gene Vincent (backed by ALICE COOPER). Also on the bill was John Lennon, fronting a unit called the Plastic Ono Band and playing some rock and roll classics. A 1969 parody was the FRANK ZAPPA album called *Cruising with Ruben and the Jets,* which poked fun at teenage concerns and simplistic music.

The movie *American Graffiti* (1973), directed by George Lucas (who later did the *Star Wars* films), is a coming-of-age story of teens on the last night of the summer of 1962. They cruise in their cars while listening to real-life disc jockey Wolfman Jack (who makes a cameo appearance), stop at the drive-in, and drag race. The film's success led to other films about the 1950s, including *American Hot Wax* (1976), about Alan Freed, *The Buddy Holly Story* (1978), and *La Bamba* (1987), about RITCHIE VALENS. All of these films share a sense of lost innocence, missed opportunities, or tragic circumstance that apply to the real and imaginary characters portrayed, but also to rock and roll itself.

American Graffiti and its double-album soundtrack widened the market for oldies acts so much that virtually every city had at least one or two. Some of them managed to have national hits, such as Flash Cadillac, formed by University of Colorado students.

The year after *American Graffiti,* 1974, was a big one for acknowledging earlier rock and roll. Bill Haley's "Rock around the Clock," recorded 20 years earlier, hit number one again. Established artists paid tribute also, such as the Guess Who with "Clap for the Wolfman" (which included bits of Wolfman Jack's dialogue), the ROLLING STONES with "It's Only Rock and Roll (But I Like It)," and Grand Funk Railroad with a remake of "The Loco-Motion" (which hit number one). A collection of early BEACH BOYS hits, called *Endless Summer,* also hit number one, the first time an oldies album had done so. A return to rock's roots revitalized the Beach Boys in *15 Big Ones* (1976), and their version of Chuck Berry's "Rock and Roll Music" hit the top 10.

Later songs include Bob Seger's "Old Time Rock and Roll" (1979), and Billy Joel's "It's Still Rock and Roll to Me" (a number-one in 1980). To this day, early rock and roll records are highly collectible, and old songs appear frequently on movie soundtracks while party bands everywhere play them. Rock and roll will never die.

Rolling Stones, The

They have been called "the greatest rock and roll band in the world," and few would deny it after attending one of their concerts or hearing the many gems in their huge catalog of recordings. They were inspired by American blues and R&B; their name comes from a song by Muddy Waters, "Rollin' Stone" (1950). In one of the verses of that song, a mother-to-be, in conversation with the future father, predicts that their child will be a boy and he will be a "rollin' stone," a person constantly on the move. The name was prophetic, because since the band's inception in London in 1962, they have been recording and touring regularly.

The core of the band is its most famous members: vocalist Mick Jagger (b. 1943) and rhythm guitarist Keith Richard (b. 1943), who changed his last name to Richards in 1977. They were friends as schoolchildren but lost contact with each other until meeting again as teenagers at a train station and discovering that they were both keen on American records. Brian Jones (1942–69), was an eclectic multi-instrumentalist who had a big influence on the band's early musical explorations. His drug use made him unreliable, and he was asked to leave the band in June 1969; he died the next month from drowning in his swimming pool under mysterious circumstances. His replacement was Mick Taylor (b. 1948), a superb blues guitarist who had played with John Mayall. Taylor left the band at the end of 1974 and was replaced by Ron Wood (b. 1947), formerly of the Faces, a later development of the Small Faces that featured Rod Stewart on vocals. Drummer Charlie Watts (b. 1941), a jazz fan who is the third original member still in the band, and Bill Wyman (b. 1936), the impassive bassist who retired from the Stones in 1993, formed the highly respected rhythm section. Pianist Ian Stewart (1938–85) was considered the "sixth Stone," though he was relegated to the background because his chunky physique and straight manner was out of keeping with the bad-boy image promoted by the band's manager Andrew Loog Oldham. Their image was consciously made in opposition to the wholesome one of the BEATLES,

The Rolling Stones (Michael Ochs Archives.com)

and it was cultivated through a marketing campaign and a series of publicity stunts.

In their early period the Rolling Stones, having been nurtured by Alexis Korner, one of the pillars of British blues, played R&B on the club circuit. For eight months they had a once-a-week gig at the Crawdaddy Club in Richmond, near London. When they became a recording act, they played only cover versions at first. Their debut single was "Come On," a lesser-known song by CHUCK BERRY, whom Richards would work and clash with during the filming of the 1987 documentary *Chuck Berry Hail! Hail! Rock 'n' Roll*. Manager Oldham had a connection to the Beatles, and John Lennon and Paul McCartney gave them "I Wanna Be Your Man" (before the Beatles recorded it).

They came to America in 1964 as part of the BRITISH INVASION, with an album that proclaimed them as *England's Newest Hit Makers*. Their first U.S. hit was "Not Fade Away," written by BUDDY HOLLY in the style of BO DIDDLEY, whom the Stones had toured with, along with the EVERLY BROTHERS, in the United Kingdom. That summer they recorded "It's All Over Now" (originally by Bobby Womack when he was in a band called the Valentinos) and "Time Is on My Side" (originally by Irma Thomas, known as the Soul Queen of New Orleans) and other songs at the famous Chess Studios in Chicago. There they got to meet some of their idols: Muddy Waters, Chuck Berry, and Willie Dixon, who wrote their second U.K. number one, "Little Red Rooster."

Challenged by their manager to write their own material, Jagger and Richards, working as a team, soon developed into two of the best writers of their generation. They gained momentum as writers with "The Last Time" and "As Tears Go By," a hit for Jagger's then-girlfriend Marianne Faithfull (and a hit for the Stones later). It was, however, the massive success (and cultural resonance) of "(I Can't Get No) Satisfaction" (1965), an original composition and their first number-one hit in the United States, that upgraded their status from just another interesting British invasion band to a major force. As with the Beatles, original songs came to dominate, and *Aftermath* (1966) was the first Stones album to contain all originals. In their FOLK ROCK phase (and afterward) they wrote songs that commented on social issues, like "Get off My Cloud," "19th Nervous Breakdown," and "Mother's Little Helper" (about pill taking). As with the KINKS, some of their music from the mid-1960s shows a particularly British touch, as in the Elizabethan-sounding "Lady Jane" and the music-hall influence heard on *Between the Buttons* (1967). On *Their Satanic Majesties Request* (1967), seen as a response to the Beatles' *Sgt. Pepper's Lonely Hearts Club Band*, they experimented with psychedelia.

In 1968 with the song "Jumpin' Jack Flash," produced by Jimmy Miller, who had worked with Traffic, they solidified a new sound, their own hard-rocking style, which would be the foundation of all later work. The riff-based "The Last Time" and "Satisfaction" were obvious forerunners of this sound, but the Stones developed it brilliantly from *Beggars Banquet* (1968), with "Sympathy for the Devil" and "Street Fighting Man," through *Let It Bleed* (1969), with "Gimme Shelter," and *Sticky Fingers* (1971), with "Brown Sugar," to *Exile on Main Street* (1972), with "Tumbling Dice." In later years they would dabble in other styles, such as disco ("Miss You," a number-one hit in 1978), REGGAE, and ROCKABILLY. *Steel Wheels* (1989), considered their best album in a decade, included "Continental Drift," which featured the Master Musicians of Joujouka, an ensemble that Brian Jones had discovered and

recorded in Morocco. However, the Stones always return to R&B for revitalization. They kept R&B songs in their live repertoire, and gained latter-day hits with some of them, such as two MOTOWN songs from 1966: "Ain't Too Proud to Beg" (1974), originally by the Temptations, and "Going to a Go-Go" (1982), by the Miracles. As of 2004, the Stones' last top-10 hit was "Harlem Shuffle" (1986), a cover of a 1963 Los Angeles recording by the duo Bob and Earl.

The Rolling Stones' tours and their drug arrests were more newsworthy than their hit records. Their appearance at the notorious Altamont festival in 1969 was documented in the movie *Gimme Shelter* (1970), and much additional concert footage has helped spread their fame. *The Rolling Stones at the Max*, filmed in Europe during their 1991 tour, was the first concert movie ever shot in the IMAX large-screen format. They never stopped being stars. In 1995 "Start Me Up," from *Tattoo You* (1981), was used by Microsoft to launch its Windows 95 computer operating system. In 2002, with much fanfare, the band and its millions of fans celebrated the Rolling Stones' 40th anniversary. Their 2002–03 tour grossed almost $300 million. In Toronto in 2003, they headlined a show in front of their largest audience to date, some 500,000 people. Their 2005 touring schedule was greeted with intense interest.

roots rock

Roots rock is a term for later music that builds on the traditions of 1950s and 1960s rock and roll and its sources. It underlines the continuing presence of guitar-based bands and the glory of live performance. Although roots rock existed before, since the late 1970s it has been a home to those who reject synthesizers, drum machines, samplers, and sequencers. Related and overlapping styles that build on country music traditions are known as alt-country (which draws from PUNK ROCK and COUNTRY ROCK) or Americana (which breathes new life into more traditional country and folk styles).

From the 1960s, musicians inspired by early rock have presented tributes, revivals, and new sounds that evoke and keep alive the values and spirit of rock's pioneers. Many terms have been used, none universally. *Roots rock* was originally used to describe a movement in the 1980s: country rock and cowpunk bands that were part of an alternative, or "indie," underground scene. It is still used in that way, but the term is gaining currency as a logical moniker for rock-based bands that eschew modern technology. (A similar but unrelated term is *roots-rock reggae,* used to describe 1970s Jamaican REGGAE.)

The foundation of roots rock is the BRITISH INVASION groups, the BEATLES, ROLLING STONES and others, whose covers of American rock and roll and R&B songs were first heard in North America in 1964. Another is BOB DYLAN, once he moved from acoustic folk to rock in 1965. Backed by musicians who were steeped in the blues (members of the Paul Butterfield Blues Band accompanied him at the Newport Folk Festival that year), and ROCKABILLY and R&B (the BAND), Dylan made music that fused them all. GARAGE ROCK is an additional foundation.

The proclamation phase of roots rock came with the release of the Band's first two albums, *Music from Big Pink* (1968) and *The Band* (1969). They, and the Band's performances, were inspirational in showing how early rock and roll and its roots could fertilize new creations. CREEDENCE CLEARWATER REVIVAL and ERIC CLAPTON (in his early solo career) carried on the momentum. In the same period the rise of country rock and the work of Gram Parsons, the BYRDS, and Bob Dylan with *Nashville Skyline* (1969) showed that country could be part of the mix. Another part was the concise, earthy music that occurred in San Francisco after the waning of psychedelia, as in the GRATEFUL DEAD's *Workingman's Dead* and *American Beauty* (both 1970).

In the 1970s early rock and roll was primarily presented as parody and tribute, with the movie *American Graffiti* and Sha Na Na. This gave way,

following the death of ELVIS PRESLEY in 1977, to the rockabilly revival as a return to basics (without parody) and a rejection of disco. Rockabilly shared the same stripped-down energy as PUNK ROCK, and a hybrid of the two became known as psychobilly. Punk itself, in bands like the RAMONES and the Clash, took influence from pre–British invasion styles, as did some in NEW WAVE. Elvis Costello's music had a sonic link to 1960s garage in the use of the organ.

In the 1980s the popularity of bands like the Blasters, R.E.M., and Los Lobos showed that artistic expression and sonic references to their inspirations were not incompatible. A revival, called the Paisley Underground, of the Los Angeles form of PSYCHEDELIC ROCK had a brief but intriguing flourishing. Van Morrison's affection for early rock has always informed his work. Roots rock can also include the so-called heartland rock of BRUCE SPRINGSTEEN, Tom Petty, John Mellencamp, and Bob Seger, the trad rock of the Georgia Satellites, the Black Crowes, and the JAM BANDS who played the H.O.R.D.E. festivals (started by John Popper of Blues Traveler). It can also describe bands who just like to play good old rock and roll: ROCK REVIVAL, retro, classic rock and roll, party and bar band rockers.

Many of the heroes of roots rock, like Jim Dickinson, never strayed beyond the margins of the mainstream. Some have reached cult status, such as Alejandro Escovedo, NRBQ, and Tav Falco's Panther Burns. While some notable acts are defunct, younger ones have arrived on the scene, like the North Mississippi All Stars. In virtually every city where rock and roll is loved, there are local musicians of stature and artistry doing roots rock, from those creating new works to those doing something closer to nostalgia. On high-profile tribute albums, major rock stars also acknowledge their forerunners with new versions of songs by such figures as Jimmie Rodgers, Leadbelly, Woody Guthrie, and Gram Parsons.

Santana (and Carlos Santana)

One of the most distinctive sounds in rock is the crying sustain that Carlos Santana (b. 1947) wrings from his electric guitar. It is particularly appealing when he solos, accompanied by his band, simply called Santana, over medium-tempo minor key pieces, such as three of their biggest hits: "Evil Ways," "Black Magic Woman," and "Smooth." Thirty years separate "Evil Ways" (1969) from "Smooth" (1999). In between was a period of intense activity, musical experimentation, and ups and downs.

Carlos Santana was born in Autlán de Navarro, west of Mexico City near the Pacific coast. His father was a mariachi violinist who taught him the basics of music, and Carlos began on the violin. Perhaps that is why his solo lines are so fluid and he favors a sustaining tone. By the time the family moved north to Tijuana, next to the California border, Carlos had switched to guitar. Another move north took them to San Francisco.

Upon leaving high school in 1966, inspired by seeing B. B. King perform, Carlos and some friends started the Santana Blues Band. When the name was shortened, in early 1968, to just Santana, keyboardist and vocalist Gregg Rolie and bassist David Brown stayed on, with new additions in drummer Michael Shrieve, and two percussionists, José "Chepito" Areas and Michael Carabello. The percussionists both played conga drums, and Areas also played timbales. Their presence gave a unique sound to the band, adding a Latin and Afro-Cuban flavor to the blues rock foundations. The band started making waves in San Francisco on the ballroom circuit.

Santana (1969), their debut LP, showed where these influences came from. "Evil Ways" was learned from a 1967 record by Latin jazz percussionist Willie Bobo; it was written by his guitarist Sonny Henry. "Jingo," Santana's first hit, was written by Nigerian drummer Michael Babatunde Olatunji, and recorded on his influential 1959 album *Drums of Passion,* which introduced African drumming to millions. The other songs were originals credited to "Santana Band." *Santana* was released just months after the band created a sensation at WOODSTOCK and two other major festivals, and their fiery performance of "Soul Sacrifice" in the *Woodstock* movie (and the album soundtrack) did wonders for their already growing reputation.

Abraxas (1970), Santana's second album, hit number one and featured "Black Magic Woman." FLEETWOOD MAC guitarist Peter Green wrote the song. The album also contained another of Santana's biggest hits, "Oye Como Va," written by Tito Puente (known as "the King of Latin Music") and the perennial favorite "Samba Pa Ti," a lyrical instrumental written by Carlos. Santana toured internationally.

For *Santana III* (1971), the band was augmented by guitarist Neal Schon and several guests. This album also topped the charts and brought two more hit singles, but was the last with the original lineup, as alcohol, drugs, and personal conflicts took their toll. With the breakup of this band, the sense of collectivity among the musicians who had worked together on their way to success was replaced by Carlos Santana's personal direction. Subsequently, he would be the only mainstay, though many very talented musicians would play in Santana, including several long-serving players. Most of the members of the original band would make return visits.

After Carlos made a live album with drummer Buddy Miles, the new Santana band moved more toward jazz rock, which they explored throughout the 1970s. The plentiful subsequent albums contain funk, disco, arena rock, soul, blues, jazz, mainstream pop, and gospel. Some of the music is great, some of it is bland, and some of the songwriting is weak, but Carlos' guitar solos usually provide stellar moments even in mediocre material and unstructured jams.

Carlos adopted the additional first name of Devadip (meaning "the light of the lamp of the Supreme") upon becoming a follower of the guru Sri Chinmoy. With fellow devotees, Devadip Carlos Santana made two albums: *Love Devotion Surrender* (1973), with jazz rock guitarist John McLaughlin, who had passed through Miles Davis' band and his own Mahavishnu Orchestra, and *Illuminations* (1974), with Alice Coltrane, the widow of John Coltrane. Over the years Carlos has enjoyed collaborating with such artists as John Lee Hooker, ERIC CLAPTON, Willie Nelson, and Wayne Shorter. *Santana Brothers* (1994) featured Carlos with his younger brother Jorge and their nephew Carlos Hernandez, all guitarists.

Carlos's 36th and the biggest-selling album to date was *Supernatural* (1999), featuring a large number of guests. Together, the album and its hit songs "Smooth," with Rob Thomas of Matchbox Twenty, and "Maria, Maria" with Wyclef Jean, won a total of nine Grammy Awards. Santana is one of the only bands to have albums in the *Billboard* top 10 in the 1960s, 1970s, 1980s, and 1990s.

Carlos Santana's music spans not just musical genres but cultures, languages, and generations. He has supported numerous charitable causes, including disaster relief, education, and human rights. He continues to make music that transmits spiritual affirmations of peace and understanding at concerts that stir the soul and celebrate life. Through the journey of following the source of his virtuosic ability on guitar, Santana has enriched himself and the rest of us.

Carlos Santana (Michael Ochs Archives. com)

Shannon, Del (1934–1990) *rock singer and guitarist*

With a unique voice and his own compositions, guitarist Shannon was one of the few notable rockers to emerge in the early 1960s, when POP ROCK and novelty songs were the vogue. His recording career started after a disc jockey spotted his band at a nightclub in Michigan, his home state. He had changed his name (from Charles Westover), and for early press releases he altered his birth date, pretending he was 21 at the time of his first hit.

Del Shannon (Michael Ochs Archives.com)

Actually, he was 26 then, a week and a half older than ELVIS PRESLEY.

That first hit was his biggest: "Runaway" made number one both in the United States and the United Kingdom in 1961. It was coauthored by the band's keyboardist, Max Crook, who, for the often-copied solo, switched from the piano to an electronic organ, one that he had altered to give it a "futuristic sound." Shannon's falsetto singing of "I wonder, I wa-wa-wa-wa-wonder" was unusual as well, as was the chord progression in the verse (Am/G/F/E), which proved very influential.

"Runaway" 's dramatic shift from its minor-key verse to its major-key chorus was inspired by Hank Williams' "Kaw-Liga." Shannon's version of "Kaw-Liga" appears on his album *Sings Hank Williams* (1964), and Williams' lovesick and fatalistic songs, like "Your Cheatin' Heart" and the others, perfectly suited him. As seen in his string of hits to the mid-1960s, the protagonists in Shannon's own songs are often desperate. They are overcome by miserable loneliness, as in "Runaway" and "Cry Myself to Sleep," wounded by a sadistic temptress, as in "Little Town Flirt," or looking for a place to hide, as in "Sue's Gotta Be Mine" (about eloping), and "Keep Searchin' (We'll Follow the Sun)" and its sequel, "Stranger in Town," where the lovers are being hunted. Other songs gloat over retaliation, namely "Hats off to Larry" and "So Long Baby." Yet, after heartbreak comes the possibility of new love ("Hey! Little Girl"), joy ("Two Kinds of Teardrops"), and repair (Shannon's cover of "Handyman").

Even after the BRITISH INVASION swept many U.S. artists off the charts, Shannon not only kept on having hits but he embraced the new music. A popular artist in Britain, where his songs generally charted higher than in America, he toured there in 1962. On his 1963 tour he met the BEATLES, and he was the first in America to have a hit with a Lennon-McCartney composition. His version of "From Me to You" charted in June 1963, more than six months before the Beatles themselves would have an American hit. Another British invasion act, Peter and Gordon, whom Shannon met in Australia, had a hit with his "I Go to Pieces."

Shannon influenced and was held in high regard by many musicians. Elton John's "Crocodile Rock" was modeled on his "Cry Myself to Sleep." Later Shannon recordings were produced by Jeff Lynne (of ELECTRIC LIGHT ORCHESTRA), Dave Edmunds, and Tom Petty. From Shannon's 1981 comeback album, produced by Tom Petty, Shannon had one last hit: "Sea of Love," a remake of a 1950s song.

The anguish expressed in many of his songs was an expression of his psychological condition. He suffered from bipolar disorder, and he committed suicide in 1990, after playing for years on the oldies circuit.

Shirelles, The

Of all the GIRL GROUPS who were active in the early 1960s, the Shirelles were the most successful and enduring. Their singing was sensuous and passionate, conveying a mix of innocence and experience. They formed in Passaic, New Jersey, while in junior high school, inspired by the Chantels (one of the first important girl groups), who were from the Bronx, less than 20 miles away. For their name, they wanted something similar to that of their heroes, something feminine. Shirelles was a combination of Shirley (from Shirley Owens, b. 1941, who did most of the lead singing), with *elle,* the French word for "she."

A classmate had them audition for her mother, Florence Greenberg, who owned a small label. She signed them, and their first record was "I Met Him on a Sunday," written by the group. When it started to sell, it was leased to Decca and became a hit.

The Shirelles (Michael Ochs Archives.com)

Decca took them on, but when follow-up records went nowhere, Greenberg brought the act back to her Scepter label, newly formed with songwriter Luther Dixon. She became their manager, and he became their producer. The Shirelles had 25 hits on Scepter.

"Will You Still Love Me Tomorrow" (1961) directly addressed the concerns around romance and passion, and its feelings of longing and vulnerability resonated with listeners everywhere. It was the first number-one for the Shirelles, for any girl group, and for the writing team of Carole King and Gerry Goffin. It has been revived numerous times by other acts. The BEATLES later covered its flip side, "Boys," and recorded another Shirelles hit, "Baby It's You." Further evidence of their influence on BRITISH INVASION bands is Manfred Mann's cover of "Sha La La." "Soldier Boy" (1962) was another number one for the Shirelles, and "Dedicated to the One I Love" (originally by the "5" Royales), was a top-5 hit for them and for the MAMAS AND THE PAPAS, who reworked it a few years later.

Disputes with their label over money slowed their momentum, as did changes in popular taste, but they returned after two dry years with one last hit in 1967. By 1975, when Shirley Owens left for a solo career—she now tours as Shirley Alston Reeves—the Shirelles were favorites on rock revival shows. The other members were Doris Coley (b. 1941), who left in 1968, returning in 1975; Addi "Micki" Harris (1940–82), who died of a heart attack after a group performance; and Beverly Lee (b. 1941), who has carried on the group into the 21st century.

Simon and Garfunkel (and Paul Simon)

Paul Simon (b. 1941) sang lead, wrote the songs, and played acoustic guitar. Art Garfunkel (b. 1941) sang a pure tenor harmony—and lead sometimes—and helped create the arrangements. From 1964 to 1970 they made some of their generation's most popular and cherished music, and afterward as solo acts and in occasional reunions they maintained

their status as gifted artists, capable not just of providing nostalgia but making resonant and important new work as well. Their concerts—at least in their first five years together—were simple: one guitar, two voices. Simon's poetic lyrics literately treated themes of loneliness and alienation, as well as whimsy and euphoria.

The two were born within a month of each other and grew up just three blocks apart in the Forest Hills section of Queens in New York City. Simon's parents were Hungarian Jews; his father was a bass-playing bandleader who later taught at college, and his mother had been a high school English teacher. Garfunkel's grandparents were from Romania and his father was a traveling salesman.

Paul Simon and Arthur Garfunkel got to know each other in grade school, and as adolescents sang in DOO-WOP groups. While high school students, as an EVERLY BROTHERS–type duo called Tom and Jerry, they had a hit record in "Hey Schoolgirl," which they cowrote and performed on *American Bandstand*. After graduation, they drifted apart, each pursuing further studies.

In 1964 Simon went to Great Britain to join the folk scene; Garfunkel joined him while on vacation for a few shows. They decided to reunite and, back in the United States, signed to Columbia and recorded an acoustic folk album: *Wednesday Morning, 3 AM*. Along with the folk repertoire of traditional songs and a Dylan song, was "The Sounds of Silence," a Paul Simon composition. The album did not sell well, and Simon returned to Britain. Without their knowledge, their producer, following the trend for FOLK ROCK music, overdubbed an electric band onto "The Sounds of Silence" and released it as a single. When it started to become a hit, Simon returned to the United States, and he and Garfunkel toured to promote it. The song ended up selling a million copies and going to number one. Both a new album, with the hit song on it, and the earlier album, with the acoustic version, then became hits.

Once the duo was established, many hit songs and albums followed. Among their best sellers were "Homeward Bound," written in England, which

Simon and Garfunkel (Michael Ochs Archives.com)

spoke of the loneliness of the traveling singer, and "I Am a Rock," about emotional pain. They toured constantly from 1966 to 1968, mostly on college campuses, but they also performed at the legendary 1967 MONTEREY POP FESTIVAL. Simon was part of the organization committee and contributed funds to make it happen. Their performance of "The 59th Street Bridge Song (Feelin' Groovy)" is in the *Monterey Pop* movie. In 1968 some of their songs were on the soundtrack of *The Graduate,* a film that starred Dustin Hoffman. "Mrs. Robinson," from the film, won two Grammy Awards.

The biggest album of their career was *Bridge over Troubled Water* (1970). The album and the title song not only won a total of six Grammy Awards but each topped the charts in both the United States and United Kingdom. The album sold more than 10 million copies and produced four major hits: the title song (also a big hit for Aretha Franklin),

"Cecelia," "The Boxer," and "El Condor Pasa," which, with its Peruvian melody and flute, presaged Simon's future explorations in ethnic music. The long process of making the album, disagreements over song selection, and Garfunkel's involvement as an actor in a movie put a strain on the duo, and by the time the album came out, they had split up. The break-up was amicable.

Garfunkel continued with acting and made many solo albums; he had several hits, including the million-selling "Bright Eyes" (1979). He also wrote a book of poetry. Simon has had tremendous successes and a few failures. A half-dozen of his solo hits have made the top 10, and some of his solo albums did well, but biggest of all was *Graceland* (1986), a cross-cultural mix that is landmark in the development of world beat music. It sold 8 million copies. He followed that direction with *Rhythm of the Saints* (1990), which sold about 4 million copies. His film *One Trick Pony* (1980), for which he wrote the music and the screenplay, and performed the lead role, a musician who had only one big hit, was a moderate success, but his musical *Capeman* (1998), about the life of Puerto Rican teenage murderer in the 1950s who was saved from the electric chair and became a respected poet, did poorly at the box office and was hated by critics.

Simon and Garfunkel reunions happened sporadically, and the public always received them well. A 1975 record made the top 10: "My Little Town." A 1981 reunion concert in New York City's Central Park drew an audience of 400,000 to 500,000 people. (Ten years later, a concert by Paul Simon in the same place had an estimated audience of 750,000). A tour in 1982 and 1983 took Simon and Garfunkel through Europe, North America, Asia, and Australia. In 1993 another reunion began with shows at New York's Paramount Theater; despite high ticket prices (the money went to charity), they sold out all 21 shows and then toured Japan. In 2003 their "Old Friends" tour had the Everly Brothers as special guests.

Simon received many awards for his recordings, songwriting, and fund-raising. The duo was inducted into the Rock and Roll Hall of Fame in

1990, and Simon as solo artist in 2001. Their impact is reflected in the many books, Web sites, documentaries, and cover versions of their songs in all types of genres, from Muzak to gospel, from country to HEAVY METAL.

singer-songwriters

Singer-songwriters, sometimes called song-poets, emerged in the late 1960s from the influence of BOB DYLAN. The style flourished in the early 1970s with the success of James Taylor, Jackson Browne, Joni Mitchell, NEIL YOUNG (his acoustic music), and numerous contemporary troubadours. As if to underline the personal approach inherent in the style, they all presented themselves by their names, even when they joined forces, as in Crosby, Stills and Nash.

Their often autobiographical lyrics and tuneful songs were supported by acoustic accompaniment that featured GUITAR, KEYBOARDS, and harmony vocals augmented at times by a rock rhythm section (usually subdued), perhaps adding harmonica, pedal steel guitar, strings, horns, or percussion. The singer-songwriter style was extremely popular in its heyday and it has never disappeared. Working at least in part in the same territory is a long list of talented artists. Ones who were active in its early days include Van Morrison, Leonard Cohen, John Prine, Laura Nyro, Bonnie Raitt, Harry Nilsson, Melanie, John Denver, Roberta Flack, Fred Neil, Jim Croce, Carly Simon, Billy Joel, Don McLean, Joan Armatrading, Dan Fogelberg, Carole King, Jonathan Edwards, Harry Chapin, and Tom Waits. Others, who emerged later, include Tracy Chapman, John Hiatt, Suzanne Vega, Shawn Colvin, and Jewel.

In marked contrast to other concurrent developments such as hard rock and PROGRESSIVE ROCK, the music of the singer-songwriters was quiet and soul-searching. They probed difficult emotions in confessional lyrics and set them to crafted arrangements. They explored the possibilities of the acoustic guitar with deft finger picking and unorthodox tunings, bringing the instrument to unprecedented prominence. In creating their own songs, singer-songwriters conveyed an immediacy that was echoed in performances that retained, even in a concert hall setting, the intimate atmosphere of a living room gathering. The performers, like their admirers, favored unpretentious clothing of a rustic and homespun look, like jeans and cotton shirts.

The roots of the style were in the folk revival of the 1950s and early 1960s, the point of entry into the music business for Bob Dylan, Joan Baez, Richie Havens, and a host of others. Most of the participants in the folk revival were content to rework existing songs—it was seen as a revival, after all—but Dylan's original compositions inspired people to write their own material. Much of that writing, in the early 1960s, was channeled into finger-pointing laments known as protest songs. With the arrival in 1965 of FOLK ROCK, heralded by the BYRDS' first hits, including "Mr. Tambourine Man" (a Dylan song), and by Dylan's move from solo act to fronting a rock band, not only did the folk revival fragment into smaller niches, but songwriters, following Dylan's lead, chose to explore more personal realms with contemplative, meaningful lyrics. While this was seen by some as a betrayal of folk's populist political agenda, it was a new door opening. Paul Simon's compositions were another model, and some of the output of SIMON AND GARFUNKEL belongs in the singer-songwriter category.

There are many other early examples. Van Morrison, from Belfast, Ireland, had recorded in London with the BRITISH INVASION group Them before moving to New York for his first solo records. After the pop hit "Brown-Eyed Girl" (1967) he made an astonishingly inventive mix of rock, folk, and jazz in the all-acoustic and semi-improvised *Astral Weeks* (1968), an enduring critical favorite if not a commercial success. Throughout his career he has followed his own muse, drawing on rhythm and blues, Celtic music, and the writings of mystical poets. The first album of Leonard Cohen, an established Canadian poet and novelist from Montreal, was *Songs of Leonard Cohen* (1968). It included "Suzanne," still his best-known song. Its lyrics had already been published as a poem in 1962, and the song had been covered by Judy Collins in 1966. His deadpan baritone delivered lyrics full of striking images that mixed the sacred and the profane, and his music had a droning, ethnic flavor (derived perhaps from his Jewish heritage and the period in the early 1960s when he lived in Greece) that has made him an icon in distant countries.

Another Canadian, Joni Mitchell, from Fort McLeod, Alberta, moved from New York to Los Angeles, where she recorded her first album, *Song to a Seagull* (1968), produced by David Crosby (formerly of the Byrds). The title of Mitchell's second album, *Clouds* (1969), came from her lyrics in "Both Sides Now," which Judy Collins had taken to the top 10 in 1968. Mitchell then made a series of highly acclaimed and mostly acoustic albums, namely *Ladies of the Canyon* (1970), *Blue* (1971), and *For the Roses* (1972), that featured revealing insights into her romantic liaisons and her meditations on the contradictions of fame. Her devoted audience adored *Court and Spark* (1974), in which Mitchell incorporated jazz into her style, and made it her biggest-selling record. However, her continued pursuit of a jazz-inflected vocabulary was less well accepted. In the 1990s, Joni Mitchell's recordings tended to recall her earlier style.

After the harrowing events of the late 1960s, which included political assassinations, race riots, and student revolutionary actions, a general feeling of disillusionment led to a search for a more simple, grounded, and individual way of life. This urge fueled a back-to-the-land movement that saw some young people leave the cities and suburbs to live on farms and rural communes. Whatever the setting, the feeling of the times was expressed in the rise of ecological awareness, environmental causes, natural foods, and an introspection that included spirituality. Many singer-songwriters would address these issues in their songs.

James Taylor's first hit, "Fire and Rain" (1970), which made the top five, was in part inspired by the death of a friend. It is a melancholy reflection on loss and the absence of certainty. He admits to despair and calls on Jesus for support. Joni Mitchell's first hit, "Big Yellow Taxi" (1970), refers to personal bereavement and environmental deterioration with such memorable lines as "You don't know what you've got 'til it's gone" and "They paved paradise and put up a parking lot." She wrote "Woodstock" (1970), a big hit for Crosby, Stills, Nash and Young. Though she had not attended the WOODSTOCK festival, her composition captured its spirit and the underlying mood of the singer-songwriters: "I feel to be a cog in something turning . . . I don't know who I am but life is for learning." As a solo artist, Neil Young's only number one hit, "Heart of Gold" (1972), with backing vocals by Linda Ronstadt and James Taylor, describes his lack of fulfillment and acknowledges that he is aging and still searching.

Despite the fact that the singer-songwriters' music was perceived at the time as a new direction in rock, their fans were from the general rock audience, they performed at rock festivals, and they saw themselves as part of rock's evolution, singer-songwriters have been somewhat painted out of rock history. They are, for example, virtually absent from Robert Palmer's *Rock & Roll: An Unruly History* (1995) and the series of PBS television documentaries that it accompanied.

There are many possible reasons why the importance of the singer-songwriters in rock's development tends to be overlooked. Their music falls in a grey area between folk and rock, and its sentiments and presentation are associated with feminine or adult qualities while most rock is portrayed as masculine and youthful. Many women did work within the style, and it was marketed as adult contemporary music. Much of rock history seems to equate validity with loud volume, wailing electric guitars, fast tempos, and social rebellion—qualities not associated with this style. The lyrics were meant to be heard. The electric guitar was present, though its use was tasteful rather than noisy. For example, David Lindley's electric lap steel guitar added a distinctive color to Jackson Browne records. The singer-songwriters' music was for listening, not dancing, and they favored slow and medium tempos. Their rebellion was in the form of considered social critique, and many participated in benefit shows such as the MUSE (Musicians United for Safe Energy) No Nukes concerts of 1979 to promote a non-nuclear future. Held in New York's Madison Square Garden for five nights, the event was documented on film and on a three-LP set of records. The lineup included James Taylor, Carly Simon, Jackson Browne, Bonnie Raitt, Crosby, Stills and Nash, BRUCE SPRINGSTEEN, the Doobie Brothers, and Tom Petty.

If rock historians have trouble seeing singer-songwriters fitting in, the artists knew they were part of it. Original compositions formed the bulk of their output, but they made an exception for fondly remembered rock and roll and R&B songs that had been hits when they were younger. From the mid-1970s to the mid-1980s James Taylor had hits with many cover versions: "Everyday" (by BUDDY HOLLY, from 1957), "Handy Man" (Jimmy Jones, 1960), "Up on the Roof" (the Drifters, 1963), and "How Sweet It Is (To Be Loved By You)" (Marvin Gaye, 1964). In a duet with his then-wife Carly Simon, he did "Mockingbird" (by Inez Foxx and Charlie Foxx, 1963), and along with Paul Simon he sang backup for Art Garfunkel's rendition of "Wonderful World" (Sam Cooke, 1960). Taylor was not alone. Jackson Browne redid "Stay" (Maurice Williams and the Zodiacs, 1960). Joni Mitchell had a hit with her version of "(You're So Square) Baby I Don't Care" which ELVIS PRESLEY had sung in his 1957 movie *Jailhouse Rock*.

It was one thing to cover old hits, but Carole King redid old hits that she had cowritten with her husband Gerry Goffin. On her classic *Tapestry* (1971), King redid "Will You Love Me Tomorrow" (the SHIRELLES, 1960) and "(You Make Me Feel Like) A Natural Woman" (Aretha Franklin, 1967). The *Tapestry* album, with King's gospel-style keyboards leading the session musicians, was catchy, rhythmic, and soulful in a mellow way. It broke sales records by selling 15 million copies worldwide, more than any album before it. King's "You've Got a Friend"

was covered by James Taylor (who had played acoustic guitar on the *Tapestry* version) and it was his only number-one single. In 1980 Carole King reprised "One Fine Day," which she and her husband had written for the Chiffons in 1963.

The singer-songwriter style was international. Canada's most prominent singer-songwriter was Gordon Lightfoot, whose breakthrough single "If You Could Read My Mind" (1971) came after many years during which his talent was appreciated by a cult following. England had Cat Stevens, whose music had a mystic streak and who converted to the Muslim faith, changed his name to Yusef Islam, and renounced his pop career; the tragic Nick Drake, who committed suicide; Richard Thompson, who with the band Fairport Convention inaugurated British folk rock and whose bleak lyrics were offset by spectacular guitar playing; and the West Indies–born Joan Armatrading. And, though Bernie Taupin wrote the lyrics, some of Elton John's music, such as "Daniel" (1973), fits the category.

Spector, Phil (b. 1940) *innovative record producer*

Eccentric, insecure, a manipulative genius, Spector invented the "wall of sound" technique in the 1960s. The technique became world famous, and he was a millionaire by age 21, a recluse by 30, a Hall of Fame member in the 1980s, and charged with murder in 2004. Aside from SAM PHILLIPS, who first recorded Elvis, and George Martin, who worked with the BEATLES, no other producer in rock is as famous or influential. Spector worked with the Beatles himself—they called on him to organize the tapes for the sprawling *Let It Be* sessions, and he produced solo recordings for both John Lennon and George Harrison.

As a teenager in a group called the Teddy Bears, named for the ELVIS PRESLEY song, Phil Spector wrote a number-one hit: "To Know Him Is to Love Him." His mother had placed the phrase on the tombstone of his father, who had committed suicide when Spector was eight. A few years later, he and his older sister and their protective mother moved from New York to Los Angeles. An unpopular and sickly loner in high school, Spector followed his love of R&B and jazz to the guitar and took some lessons from jazz guitar great Howard Roberts. Roberts told him that pop music was more lucrative and that he should get involved in publishing and maybe apprentice at a record company to learn how records were made.

Spector gigged around town with a variety of people and started hanging around studios and watching sessions until he felt he was ready to record. A Teddy Bears demo led to a contract for four songs. One of them was "To Know Him Is to Love Him," a hypnotic number with Annette Kleinbard's lead vocals conveying a yearning sadness. Spector played all the instruments except drums. It got a little airplay, but was big only in Minneapolis until Dick Clark played it on *American Bandstand*. When it hit, in 1958, Spector was 17. His confidence rose and so did his ego. He bought a Corvette. A switch to a bigger label resulted in only two minor hits, and the Teddy Bears soon parted acrimoniously.

By then he had met Lester Sill, who managed artists, produced records, owned labels, and was a publishing partner with Jerry Leiber and Mike Stoller, one of rock's great writing teams (See LEIBER AND STOLLER). Sill signed Spector to a contract, took him to observe sessions (including Lee Hazelwood recording guitarist Duane Eddy in Phoenix and forging magic out of one track, echo, tape delay, and reverb), and introduced him to industry figures. Spector took up residence with the Sill family and began making records.

Los Angeles was not yet the recording center it would become. At that time New York was where the action was, and Spector wanted to work there. Sill set him up with Leiber and Stoller, and soon he had impressed and annoyed enough people in the New York music writing and publishing scene to earn himself a place. The first of the songs he wrote there that mattered was "Spanish Harlem," coauthored with Jerry Leiber. It was a major hit for Ben E. King

in 1961. Spector's talent was not in lyric writing but in coming up with musical ideas. Even stronger was his talent for producing. In New York he produced hits for Ray Peterson ("Corrina, Corrina"), Curtis Lee ("Pretty Little Angel Eyes"), Gene Pitney ("Every Breath I Take"), and the Crystals ("Uptown"). The latter was on the newly formed Philles label, set up by Phil and Les (Lester Sill).

In summer 1962 Spector returned to Los Angeles. (He had come back the summer before to produce "I Love How You Love Me" for the Paris Sisters as a favor to Sill; it made number five.) There he perfected the wall of sound. It was achieved by layering multiple instrumentalists (a gang of session players) playing the same parts simultaneously and then overdubbing on top of that to create a blur, an auditory barrage. His first hit back in L.A. was another with the Crystals, "He's a Rebel"; this

Phil Spector (Michael Ochs Archives.com)

one made number one. The next year they hit big with "Da Doo Ron Ron (When He Walked Me Home)" and "Then He Kissed Me." Spector's run of hits—most of them his own compositions, with coauthors—continued with the Ronettes. Their first hit was their biggest, the superb "Be My Baby." Spector courted and eventually married their lead singer, Ronnie (Veronica Bennett). He had more hits with Bob B. Soxx and the Blue Jeans, Darlene Love, and the RIGHTEOUS BROTHERS, whose "You've Lost That Lovin' Feelin'," another one Spector cowrote, has reportedly been played more times on the radio than any other song.

His reign ended in 1966 with "River Deep—Mountain High," a song he wrote with the Brill Building team of Ellie Greenwich and Jeff Barry for Ike and Tina Turner. Tina's vocal was forceful. The lyrics and mood, as with other Spector records, encompassed tenderness and anguish in its declaration of love and devotion. The production, which cost more than $22,000, was typical Spector—in other words, majestic. He thought it was his masterpiece, but the public didn't go for it. Times had changed, and overblown orchestral pop was losing the competition to BRITISH INVASION, GARAGE ROCK, and FOLK ROCK. When "River Deep—Mountain High" did not become a hit (it went only to number 88), Spector was devastated. He retreated into seclusion and delusion in his fortified property, the windows covered, listening to the same records and watching *Citizen Kane* over and over, terrorizing the mansion's residents and guests, and drinking.

There were no Spector productions released in 1967 or 1968; during this time he dabbled in television and film projects. He and Ronnie had lived together since Spector divorced his first wife in 1965, and they married in 1968 (they had a nasty divorce in 1974). Phil Spector returned to production in 1969, and one song made the top 20. In the 1970s, following his involvement with the Beatles' *Let It Be* (released after they broke up), he produced hit singles and albums for John Lennon, including "Instant Karma" and "Imagine," and George Harrison, including *All Things Must Pass,* with "My Sweet Lord."

In the late 1970s he produced an album for Leonard Cohen and one for the RAMONES, whose remake of the Ronettes' "Baby I Love You" was a number-two hit in England. Since then he has remained reclusive, but was back in the news in 2003, implicated in the death of an actress at his mansion. At last hearing, the case was unresolved. Though he seems a troubled soul, Spector's contributions to rock and roll are immense, his influence widespread, from the BEACH BOYS to BRUCE SPRINGSTEEN and beyond.

Springsteen, Bruce (b. 1949) *singer and songwriter*

Bruce Springsteen, known as "the Boss" or just Bruce to his loyal fans, is a highly respected artist who follows his own muse rather than commercial trends. Some see him as the last true voice of rock and roll. He is a passionate singer, songwriter, and bandleader who projects integrity through a rebellious and independent, but caring, persona. Springsteen became a superstar in the 1980s by writing eloquent songs about the dreams, virtues, shortcomings, and frustrations of small-town dwellers and blue-collar workers, and singing them in marathon live shows backed by one of the best rock bands in the business.

His studio albums contain only his own compositions, but in his energetic and intense concerts, which seem like ceremonies of collective celebration and identification, he always adds other songs. They range from the early rock and roll songs that inspired him to covers of folk, blues, MOTOWN, soul, and NEW WAVE. In terms of album sales, he is one of the top 15 artists, regardless of musical genre, and his *Born in the U.S.A.* (1984) has sold 15 million copies in the United States alone. He has participated in numerous benefit concerts and guest appearances supporting political and social causes such as Amnesty International and USA For Africa, the famine relief project that produced the song and video "We Are the World." One of the cover songs he most often played was Edwin Starr's "War," with its famous refrain "What is it good for? Absolutely nothing!" Springsteen's version hit the top 10 in 1986.

He was born into a working-class family in New Jersey. In 1963, when he was in high school, Springsteen bought his first guitar in a pawnshop. Before long he was writing songs and joining local bands. He spent the next few years performing in New Jersey, meeting the musicians who would later make up the E Street Band. He signed a management contract with Mike Appel, who arranged an audition for him with John Hammond Sr., the legendary producer whose career stretched back to the 1930s, who signed him to Columbia Records.

Springsteen's first two albums were released in 1973: *Greetings from Asbury Park N.J.*, and *The Wild, The Innocent & The E Street Shuffle*. Springsteen's introspective and verbose lyrics caused critics to hail him as the "new Dylan," a difficult tag that a few other artists have had to endure. The records sold only in moderate quantities. Actually, the comparison to BOB DYLAN had some truth in it. Not only did they both record for Columbia thanks to Hammond, they both wrote literary lyrics that gave voice to the outsider and championed the underdog. Also, they both took inspiration from the music of Woody Guthrie.

A glowing review by rock critic Jon Landau, reporting on a 1974 show in Cambridge, Massachusetts, included the now-famous sentence: "I saw rock and roll future, and its name is Bruce Springsteen." The article also stated:

> [H]e made me feel like I was hearing music for the very first time. When his two-hour set ended I could only think, can anyone really be this good; can anyone say this much to me, can rock 'n' roll still speak with this kind of power and glory? . . . the answer was yes. Springsteen does it all. He is a rock 'n' roll punk, a Latin street poet, a ballet dancer, an actor, a joker, bar band leader, hot . . . rhythm guitar player, extraordinary singer, and a truly great rock 'n' roll composer. He leads

> a band like he has been doing it forever. I . . . can't think of a white artist who does so many things so superbly. There is no one I would rather watch on a stage today. . . . Every gesture, every syllable adds something to his ultimate goal—to liberate our spirit while he liberates his by baring his soul through his music. Many try, few succeed, none more than he today.[20]

Such praise motivated Columbia to mount a publicity campaign. Landau and Springsteen became friends, and Landau shared producing duties with Appel on the next album, *Born to Run* (1975). This album showed Springsteen's rock side (it was his first album with the E Street Band) and sonically hearkened back to PHIL SPECTOR's "wall of sound" approach. Springsteen had found his own style. The album was a best-seller, and he gained his first two radio hits with the title song and "Tenth Avenue Freeze-Out," a soul-influenced track complete with a horn section. The record and his extensive touring made Springsteen famous. He was on the cover of *Time* and *Newsweek* magazines in the United States and gained extensive publicity when in Europe. In many articles the press described him as a savior of rock and roll.

Legal disputes over money with his manager, who was unhappy with Landau's involvement, delayed further recordings. When things finally settled in 1977, Landau was in as producer and manager, and Mike Appel was out. Around this time, other artists had hits with Springsteen songs: Manfred Mann's Earth Band took "Blinded by the Light" to number one in 1977, the Pointer Sisters had a number-two hit with "Fire" (1978), and Patti Smith made the top 20 with "Because the Night" (1978), a song she and Springsteen wrote together.

Darkness on the Edge of Town (1978) showed some of the pain caused by the career difficulties mentioned above, but also evoked images of Americana. Two more radio hits came from *Darkness*: "Prove It All Night" and "Badlands." Springsteen again toured extensively, as he would do frequently in the years ahead. *The River* (1980), an assured double album and his first to make number

Bruce Springsteen (Michael Ochs Archives.com)

one, established him as major international star. "Hungry Heart" finally put him in the top 10 on the singles charts, and "Fade Away" made the top 20.

One of the songs Springsteen would often play as an encore was Gary U.S. Bonds' "A Quarter to Three," a fun party record (in a style later called frat rock) that hit number one in 1961. In the early 1980s the two men became friends, and Bonds' career was revived with two albums that contained some Springsteen compositions. The albums were produced by Springsteen and his guitarist Miami Steve Van Zandt (also known as Little Steven), and they and other band members played on the tracks. From these recordings, Bonds got three hits, including "This Little Girl," which made the top 20. In another homage to an earlier rock star,

Springsteen was one of many artists who backed up ROY ORBISON for a filmed concert just before Orbison's death.

Springsteen's next album was dramatic change in direction. *Nebraska* (1982) was a stark solo acoustic set that he recorded at home on a four-track cassette recorder. Its folk feel and sometimes painful topics gave it a raw and direct tone.

His peak, in terms of sales and popularity if not artistry, came two years later with *Born in the U.S.A.* It stayed on the international best-seller charts for more than two years. Seven of the 12 songs were released as singles and all seven were top-10 hits. Besides the title track, whose message was not grasped by many listeners, the others are: "Dancing in the Dark," "Cover Me," "I'm on Fire," "Glory Days," "I'm Goin' Down," and "My Hometown." Besides Steve Van Zandt, the rest of the E Street Band consisted of keyboardists Roy Bittan and Danny Federici, saxophonist Clarence Clemons, whose big sound is anchored in R&B, bassist Gary Tallent, and drummer Max Weinberg, well known as a TV bandleader and the author of a book profiling rock drummers. Other formations of the band also included guitarist Nils Lofgren.

Lengthy touring in sold-out arenas provided lots of material for bootleggers and an audience eager for illegally recorded copies of the concerts. To appease the desire, and to cut in to the bootlegger's profits, a live box set was released of songs selected by Springsteen himself from 21 concerts. On vinyl, *Live 1975–1985*, spanned five records; on CD it was a three-volume set. Released in 1986, it made number one on the album charts. So did the next studio album, *Tunnel of Love* (1987), with the hit "Brilliant Disguise" and a theme of faithless love. It seemed autobiographical, as Springsteen's marriage to Julianne Phillips soon ended in divorce. Around that time Springsteen broke up the E Street Band. In 1991 he married his backup singer Patti Scialfa.

In 1992 he released two new albums simultaneously, the courageous and mature *Human Touch* and *Lucky Town*. Also released that year was *In Concert— MTV Plugged*, which reprised some favorite songs.

Dates for the upcoming 1993 European tour were listed on the CD's back cover, an unusual but effective means of advertising. Springsteen's acoustic "Streets of Philadelphia," the emotional theme song to the Tom Hanks film *Philadelphia* (1993), was another top-10 hit and won several prestigious awards.

The Ghost of Tom Joad (1995), a second solo album, was more philosophical than *Nebraska*, and more in the folk tradition of Woody Guthrie and Bob Dylan. It was a strong work but made a weak showing in the marketplace. Over the next few years, Springsteen slowed the pace, settling into family life as he and his wife raised three children. During this time, a four-CD a box set of unreleased studio recordings, *Tracks* (1998), was released, containing more than five dozen songs. In 1999 he was inducted in the Rock and Roll Hall of Fame, and he reunited with the E Street Band for a long, triumphant tour. Some of that energy was documented on *The E Street Band Live in New York City* (2001).

The terrorist attack of September 11, 2001, on the World Trade Center in New York City was a devastating blow to the whole nation. In the aftermath, many people found outlet for their grief in the production of art and music. Springsteen's poignant and uplifting *The Rising* (2002), with the E Street Band in full glory, was his first new material in more than five years. It was widely praised for its honesty and compassion. The album earned a Grammy Award for Best Rock Album, and the title song won two more, for Best Rock Song and Best Male Rock Vocal Performance. *Devils & Dust* (2005) debuted at number one on the charts in the United States and nine other countries. His sparse production highlights the forlorn, haunting songs and Springsteen's acoustic guitar playing.

Springsteen's status as one of rock's greatest figures has been acknowledged in several tribute albums. *Cover Me: Songs by Springsteen* (1990) includes some of the hits that others have had with his songs. The double CD *One Step Up/Two Steps Back: The Songs of Bruce Springsteen* (1997) features

Joe Cocker, DAVID BOWIE, and many others, and *Light of Day: Tribute to Bruce Springsteen* (2003), another double-CD set, features DION and Elvis Costello among the participants.

Steely Dan

Steely Dan's smooth, quirky, sophisticated rock, often set to a relaxed but funky beat, made them one of the most popular, if most unusual, acts in the 1970s. The foundation of their jazz-inflected sound was KEYBOARDS: electric pianos and synthesizers, often overlaid with hot GUITAR solos.

Bassist Walter Becker (b. 1950) and keyboardist Donald Fagen (b. 1948), who also sang lead, were the songwriters; they penned all their hits and almost everything Steely Dan recorded. One notable exception was an acknowledgment of their interest in jazz: "East St. Louis Toodle-Oo" by Duke Ellington.

Becker and Fagen met while attending college in upstate New York. In 1971, while trying with limited success to sell their songs, they joined Jay and the Americans (a band with many hits in the 1960s), and subsequently met producer Gary Katz and guitarist Jeff "Skunk" Baxter. When Katz moved to Los Angeles to work as a record producer, he arranged a job for them as staff writers, so Becker and Fagen also moved there. They were soon given the chance to record their own songs, and to do so formed a six-piece band, which included Baxter. Steely Dan's first album, *Can't Buy a Thrill* (1973), generated two top-20 hits: "Do It Again" and "Reelin' in the Years." Katz produced that album and all subsequent ones.

The band performed some live shows in the United States and the United Kingdom, but split up in the mid-1970s, except for the songwriting duo—they made money from royalties and felt little need to tour, whereas the others relied on performing. Baxter joined the Doobie Brothers, while Becker and Fagen carried on as Steely Dan, now a studio-only unit augmented by top session musicians. They continued to have hits, including "Rikki Don't Lose That Number" (1974).

Steely Dan (Michael Ochs Archives.com)

Their lyrics were literary, influenced by the Beat writers, but tended to be pessimistic and obscure. Some critics found them pretentious. The lyrics were less concerned with emotions than with obsessions about relationships and drugs, presented through observing unsavory characters in enigmatic situations.

With unusual chord progressions and jazz musicians as session players, Steely Dan created complex yet accessible rock that was polished to a bright sheen. Their album *Aja,* which contained "Peg" and "Deacon Blues" (both top-20 hits), won a Grammy in 1978 for Best-Engineered Non-Classical Recording. The production values brought an impressive precision that at times was coldly antiseptic, but more often than not managed to convey personality. Their music was embraced by FM radio; fittingly, their song "FM (No Static at All)" was used in the soundtrack to the film *FM* (1978).

After the duo separated in 1981, Donald Fagen put out a successful solo album, *The Nightfly.* Then neither Becker nor Fagen put out a record for more than a decade. Becker was hit by a car and badly injured, and after his girlfriend committed suicide by drug overdose, he became addicted himself. He managed to overcome his substance abuse eventually, and in 1993 and 1994, the duo went on tour, documented on *Live in America*. In 2000, 20 years after the last Steely Dan album of new material, they reunited for the acclaimed and true-to-form *Two against Nature,* and then again for *Everything Must Go* (2003).

Steppenwolf

Steppenwolf's first and biggest hits were "Born to Be Wild," about the thrill of motorcycle riding, and "Magic Carpet Ride," about the transporting power of music. They have, for decades, been featured extensively on movie and television soundtracks because they evoke the spirit of their time: the late 1960s. Because "Born to Be Wild" and "The Pusher" (a put-down of hard drugs and those who profit by them) were used in the 1969 film *Easy Rider,* Steppenwolf gained international recognition but got labeled as a "biker band" due to the subject matter of the film. The perception stuck, as it fit their hard-rocking sound and rough look, with singer John Kay's sunglasses (he is sensitive to light, cannot see colors, and is legally blind) and black leather clothes, but it was not really accurate. If their music had been acoustic (and it was on occasion), they could easily have been called folk protest singers for the social and political issues addressed in many of their songs.

The story of Steppenwolf is one of persistence, survival, and support from their fans. Though John Kay (b. 1944), lead singer and the band's main writer, is the one consistent element in Steppenwolf, numerous other members have been essential to the band's success. Kay was born Joachim Krauledat in Germany. His father was killed in World War II, and at the war's end, Kay and his mother were living in East Germany. When he was five, his mother bribed some border guards and they made it past the Berlin Wall into West Germany, where Kay became enthralled with rock and roll from hearing it on the Armed Forces Radio Network. In the late 1950s they moved to Toronto, Ontario; a few years later to Buffalo, New York; then to Los Angeles. As an adolescent Kay got interested in blues, R&B, and country, and began playing folk music in coffee houses in New York's Greenwich Village and then back in Toronto in the Yorkville Village. There he joined the Sparrow (which would evolve into Steppenwolf), replacing original lead singer Jack London, and the band shifted from their BRITISH INVASION sound to BLUES ROCK.

Their goal of making it big may have seemed unrealistic, but their sense of brotherhood and willingness to work hard in rehearsal and performance allowed the Sparrow to avoid the top-40 repertoire that was the standard fare for club bands and still win over audiences with their original, blues-based sound that featured Kay's gruff voice, heavy organ, and electric guitar. From Toronto the Sparrow went to New York City, where they played clubs for a few months and recorded in 1966 for Columbia (this material was not issued until 1969, after Steppenwolf had its first hits). From New York the Sparrow drove to Los Angeles, where they played clubs on the Sunset Strip, and then to San Francisco, where they gigged in the psychedelic scene as the hippie movement was getting underway. A 1967 show at the Matrix in San Francisco was issued as *Early Steppenwolf* (1970). It shows not only the band's blues foundations but songs that extended those traditions into an individual expression.

The Sparrow broke up in San Francisco, but John Kay regrouped in Los Angeles with former members keyboardist Goldy McJohn (b. 1945), and drummer Jerry Edmonton (b. 1946), joined by new recruits guitarist Michael Monarch (b. 1950) and bassist Rushton Moreve. Edmonton's brother Dennis, a former Sparrow now calling himself Mars Bonfire, contributed "Born to Be Wild." Their producer suggested the name Steppenwolf, the title of a popular book by German novelist and poet Hermann Hesse (1877–1962), because of its aura of mystery and power. Their first album was recorded and mixed in four days, and contained both songs that were used in *Easy Rider* the next year. Contracted for two albums per year, for the next few years they came up with hit albums and hit singles—six of their first seven hits made the top 40 and another half dozen songs also charted—and toured extensively, weathering some personnel changes, including a temporary return of bassist Nick St. Nicholas from the Sparrow.

Steppenwolf broke up in 1972. Kay then recorded two solo albums. The band reunited in 1974 to tour Europe, and, buoyed by the response they received, they carried on and made three more albums until the momentum ran out in 1976. Kay then made another solo album. Angered by former members using the name Steppenwolf to play on the bar circuit, he decided in 1980 to raise the band's stature, and returned, with new musicians, under the name John Kay and Steppenwolf. That band has toured extensively, recording new albums, pleasing old fans and winning new ones. They have done it through their own initiative and the support of their fans, cultivated in part through the band-run Web site. In doing so, they are a model of a band having a successful career long after getting dropped from a major label.

As Kay has said (in an interview at the band's Web site), Steppenwolf is about "giving a damn." They cared about the quality of their music and worked relentlessly on it; they cared about what was happening in their world and in society and sang intensely about it. In doing so, they touched and empowered masses of people, and as of this writing are still doing so, mixing in the hits with the new songs that show the band is much more than a nostalgia act.

surf rock

In the early 1960s the Los Angeles area was the home of surf music, which appeared originally in an instrumental form (Dick Dale, the Chantays), then a vocal form (Jan and Dean, the BEACH BOYS). Surf music celebrates the experience of surfing and the surrounding lifestyle, especially hot rod cars and racing. Just like Hollywood or Disneyland, other Los Angeles–area creations, surf music offers a carefree fantasy land. The image of an easy life full of cars, surfboards, skateboards, waves, bikinis, sun, sand, and sex has sold millions of records.

Instrumental surf music was, in the early 1960s, the music of choice for many of the state's 100,000 surfers. It often used minor keys (especially the natural minor scale, as in "Pipeline" by the Chantays) and sometimes had an ethnic flavor, which comes from Dick Dale (known as "King of the Surf Guitar"). His "Miserlou" is an actual eastern European melody. Dale's tremolo picking technique (16th notes) is reminiscent of bouzouki-like instruments.

Horns were also part of surf music. Dale was also a strong trumpet player, and many surf instrumentals feature a saxophone. Many songs used sound effects, especially waves, and shouted out song titles, such as "Wipe Out" by the Surfaris, which opens with the sound of a surfboard splitting apart and someone laughing and saying the title.

Born at teen dances at large halls along the coastline, surf music became a sensational if short-lived fad. Its peak year was 1963, when it was dubbed the "biggest overnight sensation since the twist."[21] California instrumental groups, starting with Dick Dale's, tried to imitate the powerful feeling of surfing—awe, freedom, skill—in their songs by using trebly-toned amps with lots of reverb, and Fender guitars strung with medium- or heavy-gauge strings that provided rich tone while limiting note-bending to a half-step. The generally sunny outlook, humor, and rich musical textures were carried into the vocal version of the surf style.

Vocal surf at its peak used complex vocal harmonies and carefully crafted arrangements. Its lyrics dealt with the joys of the hedonistic, easygoing southern California beach culture in songs that referred to surfing techniques, odd characters, types of cars and their mechanical components, and romantic opportunities and relationships. Brian Wilson of the Beach Boys was a masterful writer who often managed to go into emotional territory, bringing far greater depth to surf music in songs such as "Don't Worry Baby" and "In My Room." His lyrics were often matched with highly sophisticated melodic and harmonic material borrowed from pop traditions. He wrote or cowrote most of the Beach Boys' hits (as well as coauthoring Jan and Dean's "Surf City"), which feature major diatonic harmonies, sometimes quite elaborate ones, and savvy modulations. Harmonizing groups from Los Angeles, from surf onward, defined post-DOO-WOP pop harmony singing and remain influential. However, surf music was swept aside by the BRITISH INVASION.

Instrumental surf was revived several times. One wave (to use an appropriate image) came from the impact of the soundtrack for the popular movie *Pulp Fiction* (1994). It popularized "Miserlou" by Dick Dale and His Del-Tones, and also featured songs by the Tornadoes, the Centurians, the Revels, and the Lively Ones.

Talking Heads

They were among the earliest of the NEW WAVE bands and a forerunner of ALTERNATIVE ROCK. Talking Heads were, along with the RAMONES, BLONDIE, Television, and Patti Smith, part of the early punk scene at the CBGB bar in New York in the mid-1970s. They had a sophisticated, eclectic approach that, from their first album in 1977, separated them from most practitioners of PUNK ROCK. Talking Heads recorded for Sire, a label that specialized in new wave acts, and they established themselves as a major band exploring an original course. They created a unique and influential body of music that was intellectual, emotional, and had a sense of humor. It had the bounce of pop dance music, yet was brooding and haunting. Their status grew with their continued musical evolution, which involved expanding their lineup of players and incorporating soul, funk, and ethnic rhythms into their sound. Notable solo albums and collaborations enhanced their profile.

With three members who had studied at the Rhode Island School of Design, Talking Heads formed in 1974 and moved to New York. Vocalist and guitarist David Byrne (b. 1952) was the principal songwriter. His insightful perceptions of life's ironies and complexities, addressing nihilism, paranoia, politics, and suburban banality, were presented through cryptic, cerebral lyrics that could be dark or whimsical. He sang in a tense, wavering voice, and his live-wire stage presence made him a charismatic focal point. Bassist Tina Weymouth (b. 1950) and drummer Chris Frantz (b. 1951),

inspired by vintage soul and hardcore funk, made for one of the most dynamic rhythm sections in rock. Keyboardist and guitarist Jerry Harrison (b. 1949), formerly of the Modern Lovers (led by Jonathan Richman), started playing with Talking Heads in 1976 after seeing them perform in Boston (where he was teaching design at Harvard). The next year, shortly after Harrison joined as a full-time member (after completing a degree in architecture), the band toured in Europe supporting the Ramones. Their future producer, Brian Eno (formerly a member of Roxy Music), caught one of their shows in London. Less than two weeks after their return to the United States, Frantz and Weymouth wed.

Their first record, *Talking Heads: 77,* presented the ideas that they would develop on subsequent records. To support it, the band toured across America and returned to Europe, this time as headliners. Dire Straits were their opening act in the United Kingdom; XTC in Europe. The album, which contains "Psycho Killer," one of the earliest originals in their repertoire—it would become one of their signature songs—stayed on the top-200 chart in *Billboard* for more than six months, though it never rose higher than number 97. *More Songs About Buildings and Food* (1978), their first album with Eno as producer, had more percussion and contained their hit version of "Take Me to the River," originally by soul singer Al Green. Their touring took them around the Pacific: New Zealand, Australia, Japan, and Hawaii, then to the continental United States. The album entered the top 30 in both the States and England, and *Fear of Music* (1979), with "Life During Wartime" did nearly as well.

Between Talking Heads albums, the members took time away from the band for side projects. David Byrne and Brian Eno's innovative *My Life in the Bush of Ghosts* (1980) added rhythm tracks to samples of singing and speech found on records and on the radio. Talking Heads' fourth album, *Remain in Light* (1980), was their most ambitious to date: more rhythmic, with an Afro-funk approach, a brass section, and chanted vocals. Five extra musicians, including guitarist Adrian Belew (who had played with FRANK ZAPPA and DAVID BOWIE and would become a member of King Crimson) and keyboardist Bernie Worrell (of Funkadelic) were added to the lineup for touring. At shows in London, U2 (then a new band) was the opening act. Songs recorded on tour were collected on *The Name of This Band Is Talking Heads* (1982). Frantz and Weymouth's band Tom Tom Club had a charting single and album. Harrison recorded a solo album, *The Red and the Black*. Byrne's *The Catherine Wheel* (1981), the first of several solo albums, was music for a ballet that was performed on Broadway and on television.

They regrouped in 1983. "Burning Down the House," from their self-produced *Speaking in Tongues,* was a top-10 single, their highest chart placement. *Stop Making Sense* (1984), one of the best of all rock concert movies, shows them at a peak moment in their career. *Little Creatures* (1985), *True Stories* (1986), and *Naked* (1988), their last album together, were supported by odd videos and all sold well. *True Stories* contained Talking Heads' versions of songs that had appeared in a movie by the same name that Byrne had directed. They disbanded in 1991, and the members stayed involved in the music business. David Byrne's solo career had the highest profile. Jerry Harrison fronted a band called Casual Gods that had two albums, in 1988 and 1990. The Tom Tom Club stayed active, releasing their fourth album in 1992.

In the mid-1990s, an attempt to reunite the band was foiled when Byrne refused. Weymouth, Frantz, and Harrison went out as the Heads, recording *No Talking Just Head* (1996) with an updated sound and a variety of lead singers. Though all the singers contributed their own lyrics, the common thematic tone, by accident or design, was realistic and somewhat disturbing. Participants were peers and friends from various bands: Debbie Harry (of Blondie), Michael Hutchence (INXS), Johnette Napolitano (Concrete Blonde), Ed Kowalczyk (Live), Maria McKee (Lone Justice), Andy Partridge (XTC), Richard Hell (Television, the Voidoids), Gordon Gano (Violent Femmes), and Shaun Ryder (Happy Mondays). The Heads toured with Johnette Napolitano as lead vocalist, mixing new songs with Talking Heads classics. Old fans, despite being disappointed that Byrne was absent, acclaimed her vocals and the lineup's prowess as a live act.

Talking Heads were inducted in the Rock and Roll Hall of Fame in 2002.

Turner, Big Joe (1911–1985) *singer*

A Kansas City, Missouri, blues shouter known as "the Boss of the Blues," Turner took part in John Hammond's landmark From Spirituals to Swing concert at Carnegie Hall in 1938. He made the first of hundreds of records the next year, and became a rock and roll star in the 1950s. His rock and roll songs, mostly recorded in New York City, crackle with excitement as Turner sings with great verve and joy in his powerful, resonant, and expressive voice to the backing of top session players such as Harry Vann "Piano Man" Walls, whom he calls by name in "Boogie Woogie Country Girl." While recording in Chicago, Turner was backed by Elmore James, and while in New Orleans, he was backed by FATS DOMINO.

Turner's biggest pop hit was a rock and roll version of "Corinna, Corinna" (1956), a blues song that dates back to the 1920s, credited to the Mississippi Sheiks. In Turner's version the use of a walking bass line (a new note on every beat) doubled in octaves by bass and guitar predates late-1960s BLUES ROCK, where the device was deployed in much heavier fashion. Some of the songs he introduced were more successful when done by others: "Shake Rattle and Roll" was a hit for BILL HALEY AND HIS COMETS (1954), and "Chains of Love" was a hit for Pat Boone (1956). "Honey Hush" was redone by Johnny Burnette and the Rock 'n Roll Trio (1956). "Flip Flop and Fly" became a standard, done by ELVIS PRESLEY, and revived by Downchild Blues Band and the Blues Brothers in the 1970s.

From the 1960s until just before his death from a heart attack in 1985, Turner kept on doing what he had always done: singing the blues, playing in clubs, and making records. Two years after he died he was inducted into the Rock and Roll Hall of Fame.

U2

They formed in Ireland in the 1970s and came to worldwide fame in the 1980s with an inspirational outlook and a unique ALTERNATIVE ROCK sound. They have continued to challenge themselves artistically. In their early career U2 elaborated on some of the elements of PUNK ROCK, then in midcareer they explored American influences, shifting to incorporate electronic and dance music before returning to their original sound at a higher level of artistic achievement. Along the way they retained their fans and gained new ones at each juncture.

From 1987, with their album *The Joshua Tree,* through the 1990s and to the present, they have consolidated their position as one of rock's most popular and critically acclaimed bands. The *Joshua Tree* tour was the top-grossing tour in 1987. The Zoo TV tour (supporting *Achtung Baby*) was the top grossing tour of 1992. In 1997 U2's PopMart tour (supporting *Pop*) was the second-highest-grossing tour in the United States, selling 1.7 million tickets and bringing in nearly $80 million. In 2001 their Elevation Tour (promoting *All That You Can't Leave Behind*) sold out all 113 shows throughout North America and Europe. It brought in $109.7 million, making it the highest-grossing tour of 2001 and the third highest ever: only BRUCE SPRINGSTEEN's *The Rising* tour of 2002–03 and the Rolling Stones' *Voodoo Lounge* tour of 1994 brought in more money ($115.9 and $121.2 million, respectively).

U2 has won countless awards for their albums, songs, singles, songwriting, performances, tours, videos, and album covers, as well as for their online fan site and for having the best male singer, best guitarist, best bass guitarist, best drummer, and best producer. They have won such accolades as "band of the year" and "artist of the year," and others too numerous to mention here.

Far beyond any account of statistics or awards, U2 have had an incredible impact, inside and outside of the field of music. They have been brave and outspoken, consistently standing for social justice and ecological responsibility, and have supported organizations such as Amnesty International and Greenpeace. Their stance contributed greatly to the movement of benefit concerts, and they were involved with Band Aid (1984) and Live Aid (1985). They headlined Amnesty International's Conspiracy of Hope Tour (1986), which also included Peter Gabriel, Lou Reed, Bryan Adams, the Neville Brothers, Joan Baez, and Sting.

The group was formed in 1976 in Dublin, Ireland, by five schoolmates: drummer Larry Mullen Jr. (b. 1961), bassist Adam Clayton (b. 1960), guitarist and vocalist Paul Hewson, better known as Bono (b. 1960), plus two brothers: guitarist, keyboardist, and vocalist David Evans, better known as the Edge (b. 1961), and guitarist Dick Evans. Originally a cover band, they played one gig under the name Feedback, then changed the name to Hype. The repertoire was songs by other groups, such as the BEATLES and ROLLING STONES. With the departure of Dick Evans, they adopted the name U2 and began to focus on original material. The name was chosen for its simplicity and strong graphic look, and the wealth of possible connotations, not the least of which was the inclusive "you too." Mullen, Clayton, Bono, and the Edge have stayed together ever since: none have ever left U2, and though they have associated themselves creatively with many other musicians, no one has been added to the band.

After playing around the Dublin area and building up a following, they gained a manager in 1978. Record companies took little interest in U2, however, until their first release, an EP, went to the top of the charts in Ireland, the only place it was available. After the single "Another Day" (1980) also hit number one in Ireland, they were signed to Island Records in England and teamed with producer Steve Lillywhite. He produced their first album, *Boy* (1980), as well as the next two albums, which brought them devoted audiences in Europe and North America. Touring to promote *Boy,* including opening for TALKING HEADS, pushed the album into the American charts. *October* (1981) was their breakthrough in Britain, entering the top 20; it did not have much success in the United States. Videos for "Gloria" (with Latin religious words) and "I Will Follow" (from *Boy*) were played on MTV, which, with their touring, boosted their American following.

War (1983), whose message called for an end to conflict, went to number one in the United Kingdom and into the top 20 in the United States, where "New Year's Day" became their first charting single. It and "Sunday Bloody Sunday" were much played on college radio and MTV, and the band was able to play large venues. The unconventional GUITAR playing of the Edge, which favored repetitive motives of ringing notes accompanied by droned open strings and was heavily processed with echo and other effects, gave them a signature sound. It has often been described as sweeping or ethereal. Clayton's insistent BASS and Mullen's hard rock DRUMS were forceful, if more conventional. All but Clayton were practicing Christians, and public declarations of their faith, for example in "40," an adaptation of Psalm 40 from the Bible, set them apart from contemporaries. In later years their faith would become more deeply personal. *Under a Blood Red Sky* (1983), recorded live and released as

an EP and a video, furthered their international popularity, and they were named Band of the Year in *Rolling Stone* magazine.

Around this time their manager negotiated a more lucrative deal with Island Records that also gave them complete creative control. They changed producers, bringing in the team of Brian Eno, who had worked with Roxy Music and Talking Heads, and Daniel Lanois, a Canadian musician and sound engineer. The two would produce most of U2's subsequent recordings. *The Unforgettable Fire* (1984), with a picture of an Irish castle on the cover, contained "Pride (In the Name of Love)," a tribute to the late Martin Luther King Jr. and his work in the Civil Rights movement. It was their biggest single yet in the United States. The album entered the British charts at number one, and made the top 20 in the United States. Its title refers to a collection of artwork made at the end of World War II by survivors of the bombing of Hiroshima that the band saw in a touring exhibit. They used some of the images as stage backdrops.

Their next five albums all went to number one in America. *The Joshua Tree* (1987), whose title referred to an ancient type of tree located in the California desert near Death Valley National Park, made them superstars. In the United Kingdom it was their third album in a row to enter the charts at number one and the fastest-selling album in history. It stayed on the charts almost two years in the United States and longer in the United Kingdom, charting two more times in subsequent years, and it topped the charts in 20 additional countries. The album gave them their only U.S. number one hits: "With or without You" and "I Still Haven't Found What I'm Looking For." The success of the album and the tour put them on the cover of *Time* magazine, with the headline "Rock's Hottest Ticket."

A camera crew documented their American tour and new recording sessions. *Rattle and Hum* (1988), a film and double album soundtrack (produced by Jimmy Iovine, who had done *Under a Blood Red Sky*), showed U2's fascination with American blues, soul, country, and folk. "Desire," a top-five hit, used the BO DIDDLEY beat. "Angel of Harlem," a tribute to jazz singer Billie Holiday, was recorded at the legendary Sun Studio in Memphis, where ELVIS PRESLEY got his start. "When Love Comes to Town" was a collaboration with the great blues guitarist B. B. King, who accompanied U2 on tour. Other examples of U2's appreciation for American music are their involvement in tribute albums for Jimmie Rodgers and Woody Guthrie. Bono has done duets with Frank Sinatra and with CARL PERKINS, and he and the Edge wrote "She's a Mystery to Me" for ROY ORBISON.

After time off, the band reconnected with producers Eno and Lanois in Berlin. *Achtung Baby* (1991) expanded the band's sound into electronic and dance music, giving them two more American top-10 hits with "Mysterious Ways" and "One." The Zoo TV world tour, which started in 1992 and continued for more than two years, was one of most ambitious ever staged. It satirized the bombardment of the media by presenting an innovative blend of multimedia electronics projected on a stage filled with televisions and decorated with suspended cars.

Over the course of the tour, Bono took on three different onstage personas. The Fly parodied the lewd and egotistical rock star. In shiny black clothes and bulging dark glasses, he posed for the cameras, spoofing rock's insincerity. Mirrorball Man was a television evangelist in a cowboy hat and sparkling clothes that flashed like a spinning disco ball. Mr. MacPhisto was a devil with red horns, white makeup, and a gold suit. During the show Bono would make calls on a cell phone: to the White House to urge the president to watch more TV, to sports figures, or to a local restaurant to order pizza for the audience.

During a break in the tour, U2 recorded *Zooropa* (1993). Though it contained a track sung by country icon Johnny Cash, the album further explored techno and dance styles, with loops and samples. *Zooropa*, which became the name for the rest of the tour, was influenced by the writings of William Gibson, who coined the term *cyberspace* in his novel *Neuromancer* (1984). The author traveled with the band and drew from his experiences in his 1996 novel, *Idoru*.

When the tour ended in 1993, the band took an extended break, temporarily reuniting in 1995 to record "Hold Me, Thrill Me, Kiss Me, Kill Me," for the soundtrack of the movie *Batman Forever*. They returned with *Pop* (1997), which was more diverse in sounds and influences and quite electronic, but still recognizable as U2 and very successful. It was a combination of satire and tribute to pop music, art, and culture. The PopMart tour, which visited North America, South America, Europe, Australia, and Japan, was another immense undertaking, with a huge video screen and massive props: a giant lemon, a giant olive and toothpick, and an arch reminiscent of a certain fast-food restaurant.

In 1999 and afterward Bono did humanitarian work, meeting with the pope and with U.S. officials, including the president, to help erase the public debt of dozens of the world's poorest countries, many of them in Africa. The next year, *All That You Can't Leave Behind* (2000) reunited U2 with Eno and Lanois as producers. This uplifting and award-winning album dropped the electronica influences for a return to their trademark sound of the later 1980s. "Beautiful Day" also won awards, including the Grammy for Record of the Year. "Walk On" was dedicated to Aung San Suu Kyi, a recipient of the Nobel Peace Prize and the leader of a nonviolent movement for human rights and the restoration of democracy in Myanmar (formerly Burma). Bono wrote the song "Stuck in a Moment You Can't Get Out Of" in memory of his friend Michael Hutchence, the singer in the Australian band INXS, who committed suicide in 1997. *How to Dismantle an Atomic Bomb* (2004), containing the hit "Vertigo," showed U2 maintaining its sonic identity while continuing to progress.

No other band has been so humanitarian in their beliefs and actions, and their passionate music has been infused with a rare integrity. U2 has taken the buoyant, rebellious spirit that has been in rock and roll since its inception and channeled it for good while creating some of the most beloved music of recent decades.

![v](musical notation showing the letter v)

Valens, Ritchie (1941–1959) *guitarist and singer*
At the time of his death in 1959 in the plane crash that also killed BUDDY HOLLY, the Big Bopper, and their pilot, Ritchie Valens was an up-and-coming rock star—the first such Latino. He was also only 17. Along with DION and the Belmonts and others, they had been performing in the Midwest on the Winter Dance Party tour. Valens had three hits on the charts, had shared stages around the country with stars like EDDIE COCHRAN and BO DIDDLEY, had been on TV on *American Bandstand,* and been in a movie: *Go Johnny Go,* where he mimed "Ooh My Head," modeled after a song by his idol LITTLE RICHARD.

Valens' first hit was the rousing "Come On, Let's Go," and his biggest hit was "Donna," a heartfelt song about a real girlfriend. However, he is most remembered for "La Bamba," a traditional Mexican wedding song played rock style and sung in Spanish. The simple sequence of chords used in "La Bamba" entered the vocabulary of rock, showing up in "Twist and Shout" by the Isley Brothers (1962, also covered by the BEATLES), "Hang on Sloopy" by the McCoys (1965), and many other songs. In 1987 a movie about Valens' life (which took some liberties with the facts) was called *La Bamba,* and the soundtrack version of the song by Los Lobos hit number one internationally.

Valens was born Richard Valenzuela in a Los Angeles suburb, and played guitar in high school, joining up with a local interracial band called the Silhouettes who played the hits of the day to great acclaim in the area. Spotted at one of their shows by Bob Keane, who had made hits with Sam Cooke, Valens soon was recording for Keane's Del-Fi label in Hollywood.

Valens was a fine guitarist who could play hot solos and instrumental features, a convincing singer of tender ballads and rock songs, and a

Ritchie Valens (Michael Ochs Archives.com)

talented songwriter. All of his recordings, both studio and live, including finished masters as well as fragments, can be heard on a three-CD box set on Del-Fi, revealing his stylistic versatility and underlining the tragedy of his death. A still extant memorial fan club, a festival held in his honor, and a legacy of influence—on Chicano rockers and rock in general—keeps Ritchie Valens' presence reverberating through the decades.

Velvet Underground, The

Their legendary lineup played together for only three years. Their final lineup contained no original members. They toured a lot, their intensity repelling or bewildering as many people as it excited. Most of their music was too raw for the radio; they never had a hit single. They made only four studio albums, and none of them sold well. The Velvet Underground is perhaps rock's quintessential cult band, certainly one of the most influential and perhaps one of the most misunderstood. The style they defined influenced Iggy Pop, Patti Smith, DAVID BOWIE and legions of PUNK ROCK, NEW WAVE, and ALTERNATIVE bands. After the band's demise, Lou Reed and John Cale continued to make important music in their solo careers.

As part of the New York scene in the 1960s, they were supported by pop artist Andy Warhol who, before and after their first record, presented them as part of a multimedia happening he called the Exploding Plastic Inevitable. In a similar way, in San Francisco around the same time, author Ken Kesey had the GRATEFUL DEAD as the house band for events known as "acid tests" that helped launch the hippie movement. The East Coast scene, as expressed by the Velvet Underground in songs like "I'm Waiting for the Man" (about trying to make a drug connection), and "Heroin" (which made it clear which drug), and even their name (taken from the title of a book on deviant sexuality), showed that they were far from the peace and love of the California hippies.

The Velvet Underground was basically a GARAGE ROCK band. They never explored musical finesse or exploited the possibilities of multitracking. They were the first band in rock to take on taboo themes, and their music depicted a sordid and disturbing inner-city world of drugs and kinky sex. Many found it sinister and frightening. Their sound on the harsh numbers was loud, chugging, dissonant, sloppy, menacing, abrasive, simplistic, repetitive, and hypnotic. On quieter songs, it could be pop and pretty, tender with harmonized choruses. Behind the provocative lyrics about heroin, bondage, transvestites, and oral sex was meaning, wit, irony, mischievous humor, compassion, and a yearning for salvation.

Theirs was a curious mix of talents and abilities. Lou Reed (b. 1942) was charming, egotistical, and abrasive. He had worked for a period as a contracted pop songwriter. His nasal, deadpan, almost atonal singing was sometimes reminiscent of BOB DYLAN; he also played lead guitar. John Cale (b. 1940) was clever and charismatic. He was born in Wales and had been a child prodigy on viola and piano in the United Kingdom. He came to America on a classical music scholarship, becoming part of New York's avant-garde music scene. Sterling Morrison (1942–95) was an intellectual. He played angular rhythms and leads on guitar and shared bass duties with Cale. Maureen (Moe) Tucker (b. 1945) was a musical primitive. She used no cymbals in her four-piece drum kit. Her self-taught style has been described by eyewitnesses as "beating," "flailing," and "smashing."

They played their first show at the end of 1965, and next year they played clubs in New York's Greenwich Village and started to tour. Touring on the East Coast, on the West Coast, and in Canada as part of the Exploding Plastic Inevitable—a sensory overload of music, dance, lights, and simultaneous images and movies—gave them publicity and notoriety. The events were hyped in advance, attended by those in the know and the curious, and analyzed afterward. The West Coast shows had their critics. When the program played in Los

The Velvet Underground (Michael Ochs Archives.com)

Angeles in May 1966 at the Trip, the opening band was the Mothers of Invention. (Both bands were signed to MGM/Verve but neither had their first album out yet; the Mothers' would be first.) Frank Zappa and Lou Reed took a mutual dislike to each other's music, and the snide remarks carried on for years. The same program was repeated later that month in San Francisco. Ralph J. Gleason, the eminent journalist who helped found *Rolling Stone* magazine the next year and who was the first music critic to identify and praise the emerging psychedelic scene, wrote in the *San Francisco Chronicle* in 1966: "If this is what America's waiting for, we are all going to die of boredom, because this is a celebration of the silliness of cafe society. . . . The Velvet Underground was really pretty lame. . . . Camp plus con equals nothing."

Their debut album was *The Velvet Underground and Nico* (1967). Nico (Christa Paffgen), a lanky, bored, and beautiful actress newly arrived in New York City from West Germany, was added at the urgings of Warhol, who was their manager. He produced the album and designed the cover: a painting of a banana on a sticker that could be removed (a play on peeling a banana). Nico's detached, haunting singing was featured on "Femme Fatale" and two other songs. Cale's electric viola brought a spooky mood to "Venus in Furs" and "Heroin." Following the album's release, the Velvet Underground parted from Warhol and carried on with Reed at the helm. Nico had already drifted away, involved in numerous romantic liaisons with rock stars. She did some solo work, sometimes assisted by Cale. She died in 1988, after years of heroin addiction. Her story is portrayed in the 1995 film *Nico Icon.*

Their second album, *White Light/White Heat,* recorded in a day, was released in January 1968 and went nowhere. The album was dominated by the sheer length (17 minutes) and audacity of "Sister Ray." Played live, as the band's last song in a concert it might be 40 minutes or more. One observer of a show in Pennsylvania called the song "an apocalyptic vision of eroticism, sadomasochism, and violence that is at once seductive and terrifying."[22]

Shortly after the release of *White Light/White Heat,* John Cale left the band over disagreements with Reed. Doug Yule came in on bass, from a Boston FOLK ROCK band. Some see this as the decline of the Velvet Underground, for they then pursued a more commercial direction, though they had no more success with their next, self-titled, record. Their label MGM then dropped them, but Atlantic picked them up for *Loaded* (1970). By the time it was released, Reed, fed up by pressure to come up with a hit and feeling uninspired, had departed. Tucker had already left, temporarily, to have a baby, and Morrison left the next year. He eventually earned a Ph.D. in medieval studies, taught literature at the University of Texas, worked on tugboats, and played in a garage band. Yule carried on for a while, using the name with other musicians.

Live albums and some previously unreleased material came out over the years. The earliest of the multitude of books on the Velvet Underground came out in 1973. The acclaimed *Up-Tight: The Story of the Velvet Underground* by Victor Bockris and Gerard Malanga, has, since its publication in 1983, been translated into German, Italian, Spanish, Greek, and Japanese. Bockris wrote many biographies, including ones on Lou Reed and Andy Warhol, and he collaborated with John Cale on Cale's autobiography, *What's Welsh for Zen* (1998).

As a solo artist Reed had a top-20 hit with "Walk on the Wild Side" (1973), about transvestites. His prolific solo output ranges from brilliant (*Berlin,* 1973) to unlistenable (1975's *Metal Machine Music,* an album of noisy feedback reportedly recorded to fulfill Reed's record contract). John Cale has maintained a following for his solo career. There have been various concerts and recordings that involved combinations of the original members, such as the collaboration of Reed and Cale on an album of songs dedicated to Warhol after his death in 1987. The Velvet Underground reunited for a European tour in 1993, but the old tensions ensured that the reunion was brief. Morrison died of lymphoma in 1995, the year before the trailblazing band was inducted into the Rock and Roll Hall of Fame.

Who, The

They created an aggressive, overamplified, original sound that was diverse and melodic. Their rebellious attitude, often leavened with humor, predated PUNK ROCK. The Who kept evolving, through their early mod style and psychedelia into hard rock and the rock opera, a form they helped pioneer with *Tommy.* Of the great 1960s British rock bands, only the BEATLES and ROLLING STONES (who were both a little older) have a higher stature.

The Who's hits include "My Generation" (1966), one of their early gems. During their middle period, from 1967 to 1973, they were at their peak, with innovative hits like "I Can See for Miles" (1967); "Pinball Wizard," and "See Me, Feel Me," from *Tommy* (1969); and "Won't Get Fooled Again" and "Behind Blue Eyes," from *Who's Next* (1971). They earned a reputation as one of rock's best live bands; a quintessential performance was captured on *Live at Leeds* (1970). Further proof is in the films and soundtracks of two legendary rock festivals, the MONTEREY POP FESTIVAL in 1967 and WOODSTOCK in 1969. After their second rock opera, *Quadrophenia* (1973), they began a long decline, exacerbated by self-destructive behavior. Nonetheless, the Who produced some classics in this phase, such as "Who Are You" (1978) and "You Better You Bet" (1981).

At center stage was macho vocalist Roger Daltrey (b. 1944) strutting and twirling his microphone at the end of its cable. Beside him was Pete Townshend (b. 1945), a high-strung, complex, creative genius and one of rock's underrated guitarists, leaping about or strumming his guitar, arm circling like a windmill. On the other side stood John Entwistle (1944–2002), calm and still, his flying fingers creating thunderous bass lines. Behind them was the manic energy of Keith Moon (1947–78), arms constantly in motion, making a musical racket on his drum kit.

The band was a contentious brotherhood of distinct personalities, each fiercely proud of their individual (and remarkable) talents and of their collective ambitions. There was no leader; friction propelled them. They worked, argued, created, criticized, feuded, joked, smashed hotel rooms, and smashed up their instruments at the close of their live shows. The first time Townshend destroyed his guitar is said to have been accidental: the ceiling of one nightclub was so low that he damaged his instrument, and in frustration he finished the job. Immediately it became part of their act and remained so for years. Audiences were mesmerized and shocked to see a band go berserk. Onstage the Who acted out and ritualized going crazy. Mental instability proved to be a common thread in their work and their lives: both of their rock operas dealt with it. Alcohol and drugs plagued the band and contributed to the death of Keith Moon and, much later, of John Entwistle.

Pete Townshend's mother was a singer and his father played saxophone in a dance band. He and Entwistle were schoolmates and started playing Dixieland jazz together in 1959, Townshend on banjo and Entwistle on trombone. By 1962 they were playing guitar and bass, respectively, and joined Roger Daltrey, then playing lead guitar, in a skiffle band called the Detours. The next year, the band shifted to R&B and rock and roll, with Daltrey now as lead vocalist. In 1964 they changed their name to the Who, and Keith Moon joined, coming from a SURF ROCK band. All members sang, sometimes in four-part harmony inspired by the BEACH BOYS.

They called their music "Maximum R&B," and like their compatriots in the BRITISH INVASION, took inspiration from American rhythm and blues. As with many of their peers, their music evolved into an individualistic sound that was developed through composing their own songs. In Townshend they had a unique and brilliant songwriter, a major, if erratic, talent. His search for meaning went beyond the band's celebration of the transcendent power of music; he delved into spirituality, finding

nourishment in the teachings of the guru Meher Baba. Entwistle's somewhat macabre compositions and French horn playing contributed to the band's diversity.

Unlike most British invasion acts, the Who took their time coming to America. Throughout 1964, the year Beatlemania swept the United States, they continued working in London clubs. They recorded under the temporary name the High Numbers, though only one single was issued. Both sides were written by Pete Meadon, their first manager, who shaped their image by connecting them to the mod movement. The mods were fashion-conscious, thrill-seeking British youths who drove scooters decorated with mirrors, danced to MOTOWN records, took amphetamines, and fought with the

The Who (Michael Ochs Archives.com)

rockers, tough fans of 1950s rock and roll. Though none of the Who were mods, Townshend empathized with their alienation. Their earliest hits articulated the mod subculture: "I Can't Explain," their first single as the Who; "Anyway, Anyhow, Anywhere," which contained the first extended use of feedback on record; and "My Generation," in which Daltrey's stuttered declaration of differentiation made them spokesmen for all inarticulate youth at war with authority. All three made the top-10 in the United Kingdom in 1965, but only two charted, modestly, in the United States.

The Who Sings My Generation (1965) contains, aside from two James Brown covers, all original songs by Townshend, except an instrumental written by the band. This debut album shows an evolved British invasion style: the pop hooks and Beatles inflections are there, but the Who's rhythm section is more punchy than that of other groups. The vitality of Moon's drumming and the locking power of Entwistle's bass provide an R&B-derived groove that had transformed into something typically English and, simultaneously, unique to the Who. A second album appeared in late 1966: *A Quick One*, containing Townshend's first extended piece, "A Quick One While He's Away." A few months later, the U.S. version came out, entitled *Happy Jack*.

Already veterans of U.K. and European tours, the Who finally came to America in early 1967 playing for 10 days in a package show in New York City. In June 1967 they played the Monterey Pop Festival, where JIMI HENDRIX and JANIS JOPLIN emerged as stars and the Who's violent stage act created a sensation. As seen in the *Monterey Pop* film, Townshend smashed his guitar and amp while Daltrey wrecked microphones and knocked down stands. With roadies lighting smoke bombs behind the gear, Moon kicked over the drums. While the others went wild, Entwistle stood out of the way, looking bemused and cradling his bass protectively in his arms.

The Who Sell Out (1967) was a brilliant, masterful concept album, a parody of pop taste in the form of a simulated radio broadcast, complete with hilarious fake ads that linked the songs. Townshend's writing was his most accomplished to date, Daltrey's singing was much improved, and the whole band was in fine form vocally and instrumentally. "I Can See for Miles" was the hit, their first big one in America, and the songs range from PSYCHEDELIC ROCK to acoustic folk.

In 1969 they played Woodstock, and the *Woodstock* film preserved their heavy version of EDDIE COCHRAN's "Summertime Blues" plus "See Me, Feel Me" from their just-released double album *Tommy*. One of the first, and certainly the most successful, of the rock operas, *Tommy* was the surrealistic story of a traumatized boy who became a pinball wizard despite being deaf, dumb, and blind. He gains followers who worship him but later turn against him. The underlying themes comment on the concerns of 1960s youth. Tommy's quest is a mystical journey, to find the true essence of reality beyond the world of the senses. Along the way there is the search for a spiritual guide and the rejection of organized religion as well as drugs. The music is accessible, beautifully sung and performed, full of original and melodic riffs on acoustic and electric guitars supported by bass, drums, and occasional keyboards and French horn. At their record launch and other shows, the Who performed the opera in its entirety. It made them famous. A dreadful film version came out in 1975, but *Tommy* was successfully revived as a Broadway show in 1993.

Their next album, *Who's Next* (1971), was a triumph. Everything worked, from the songwriting to the ensemble playing to the spectacular sonority of the production. Townshend's pioneering use of synthesizer loops gave the record an unusual timbre. Most of the tracks got heavy airplay on FM radio, including "Baba O'Riley," which begins with a nervous synthesizer and simple chords on piano, and ends, after the heavy rock main section, with an up-tempo country dance piece played gypsy style on violin.

The Who's second completed rock opera (one was abandoned) was *Quadrophenia* (1973). Like *Tommy*, it reflected on the meaning of life. The music, again brilliantly realized though perhaps less consistent, is more orchestrated than *Tommy,* which had comparatively sparse production. The protagonist, Jimmy, is a mod in the mid-1960s. He has multiple personalities, four in fact, each one representing a member of the Who, and their musical motives recur throughout. Jimmy is kicked out of the family home and rejected by his girlfriend. He becomes disillusioned about work, friends, the mod movement, and life itself. Selling out or suicide appear to be the only options. *Quadrophenia* ends ambiguously, with Jimmy stranded on a lonely rock in the ocean. Perhaps he has a revelation, that the sense of life is found in love, or perhaps he drowns himself.

The band then took a break, and the members pursued solo projects. The next two albums, though not without charm, are the last with Keith Moon and show his alcoholic deterioration. Townshend, too, experienced problems with alcohol and diminished inspiration. In 1978 Moon died at age 31 of an accidental drug overdose.

The Who carried on with a new drummer, Kenny Jones, formerly of the Small Faces. The 1979 release of the film of *Quadrophenia* revived interest in the band, and they soldiered on with two more albums, that were, aside from a couple of hits, lethargic and disappointingly generic. Fans felt that no one could or should replace Moon, but the real issue was more likely Townshend's exhaustion, depression, hearing problems (a severe ringing in the ears from exposure to excessive volume), and drug addiction.

Their 1982 tour was advertised as their farewell, but it was a premature gesture. The surviving three members re-formed (with various backup musicians) on several occasions, such as the charity concert Live Aid in 1985. They did tour again, first in 1989 to celebrate their 25th anniversary, and in the 1990s, to present *Quadrophenia* in concert, and then to play their greatest hits. In Las Vegas in 2002, on the night before the start of another tour, Entwistle died at age 57 of a cocaine-induced heart attack. As the eulogies poured in, Townshend and Daltrey canceled the remaining tour dates, but after consulting with Entwistle's family, decided to fulfill the schedule as a tribute to him.

All members of the Who, beginning in the early 1970s, released solo albums. Pete Townshend was the most prolific, while Keith Moon made only one (the light-hearted *Two Sides of the Moon,* 1975, featuring a cast of famous friends.) Roger Daltry had several solo hit songs and made eight solo albums. In his own series of albums, John Entwistle showed that he was a capable singer, and adept songwriter, and talented multi-instrumentalist.

Some of the solo album songs are close to the sound of the Who, while others show different musical sides of the band members. Not all of the albums are memorable, but most of them are at least entertaining for Who fans. A few albums are superior achievements, such as Townshend's *Rough Mix* (1977, a collaboration with Ronnie Lane, formerly of the Small Faces) and *Empty Glass* (1980), which sold a million copies in the United States. Others are middling efforts redeemed perhaps by a couple of charming or brilliant tracks among questionable creative experiments and occasional lapses in taste (including pretentious lyrics, predictable writing, overuse of synthesizers, and overdubbed narration). Additionally there are, of varying interest, live sets, collections of songwriting demos, and albums containing covers of older rock and roll songs. Contributing to these albums is a host of other musicians, including unsung studio players as well as cameos by such notables as ERIC CLAPTON, Ringo Starr, DAVID BOWIE, Joe Walsh, and John Lee Hooker.

Woodstock *music festival*

The legendary 1969 rock festival, officially called the Woodstock Music and Art Fair, was promoted as "Three Days of Peace and Music" on posters that showed the image of a dove on a guitar neck. The dove, a symbol of peace, was there to align the festival with the movement against the Vietnam war, and to promote a spirit of cooperation among the throngs that the organizers expected to come, attracted by the what the guitar represented: rock and roll as played by some of the hottest names in the business. It worked. The people came, united by a youth movement unprecedented in history, and they came in astonishing numbers, so many that the festival site was declared a disaster area. Despite the many hardships, there was a feeling of peace and cooperation, and the music, the best of it at least, was stellar.

Since the MONTEREY POP FESTIVAL in 1967, ROCK FESTIVALS had become common. But Woodstock was bigger in every way than any before it, and though more people gathered at later festivals, in cultural importance and impact Woodstock was paramount. The timing was a factor, more than just summer vacation, with young people looking for something to do. By 1969 the hippie movement had fanned out from its origins in San Francisco across the nation and internationally. The racial and political confrontations of 1968 had further polarized the population into "us and them" groups divided along generational lines, as well as by differences in ideology: over the war, over the use of drugs, over the foundations of society, including education, government, religion, and capitalism. The most potent force and expression of all of this was rock and roll. The music was the rallying point, and to be attracted to it, which to many young people began as a visceral response, was to become identified with it and what it stood for. Though the music, like the hippie movement itself, contained many variations and contradictions, it was the one factor that united millions of people.

In "The Times They Are A-Changin' " (1963), BOB DYLAN sang, addressing mothers and fathers, "Don't criticize what you can't understand, your sons and your daughters are beyond your command, your old road is rapidly aging." It was obvious that times were changing. For example, one month before Woodstock, a man, a U.S. citizen, walked on the Moon for the very first time. Space travel was a reality, and revolution was in the air.

Woodstock began in the evening of Friday, August 15, 1969, with the folk music of Richie Havens. It spilled over into the morning of Monday, August 18, ending with the heavy rock of JIMI HENDRIX. It was held on hundreds of acres of pasture land rented from a dairy farmer named Max Yasgur, near Bethel, New York, a town in the Catskills region with a population of fewer than 4,000 people. Many of the townspeople were opposed to the festival, afraid of the influx of hippies, whose long hair and ragged clothes represented leftist politics, drug use, and hedonism, all things that threatened society's order. In fact, a previously proposed site had been rejected by the local authorities when the promoters said the attendance could be as high as 50,000. They were being coy, because they figured the total would be closer to 150,000. Some say that number is how many actually did attend Woodstock, but the most commonly accepted attendance figure, based on police reports, is 450,000 (other estimates are even higher). Many who tried to attend were discouraged by the monstrous traffic jams that closed the New York State Thruway and clogged roads within a 20-mile radius. Previous music events had attracted, at most, one-tenth as many people.

However many there were, the facilities were woefully inadequate. People started arriving on the site as early as the Tuesday before, and one full day before the music began, traffic was backed up for 10 miles. People parked their cars and walked. The performers were brought in by helicopter. Tickets to Woodstock were $7 per day or $18 for all three, and about $1 million worth had been sold before the event began. The tickets were never collected, as the ticket booths were never installed. There were just too many people, and the organizers declared it a free festival. They lost a lot of money.

A total of 32 acts played. At least one act scheduled to play (Iron Butterfly) did not: their helicopter never came, so they could not get to the site. One unscheduled act did play. John Sebastian, the former leader of the recently disbanded Lovin' Spoonful, was pressed into performing during a gap in the proceedings. Country Joe McDonald, there with his band Country Joe and the Fish, was also pressed into service to play a solo set. Sebastian's and McDonald's sets were on Friday night, and fit the evening's musical theme of folk music, which also included Joan Baez, Arlo Guthrie, Melanie, and Tim Hardin. Ravi Shankar, the master Indian sitar player, also played Friday night. Saturday and Sunday were devoted to the rock bands.

The company that put on the festival was called Woodstock Ventures, Inc., named after the nearby town where Bob Dylan and other rock musicians lived. The company consisted of four men, none older than 26. John Roberts, from a family who had made a fortune in manufacturing, handled the finances and supplied the money. His friend Joel Rosenman, from a prominent family, was a guitar-playing graduate of Yale Law School. He handled administration and advertising. Artie Kornfeld, a successful songwriter, was the vice president of Capitol Records and had connections to the rock stars. He dealt with the publicity and subsidiary rights (for the film and the records). Michael Lang had produced the Miami Pop Festival in 1968, which drew 40,000 people. He was the executive producer. Lang had met Kornfeld when he tried to get a record deal for a group he managed, and they immediately became friends. The group of four talked about opening a recording studio, but by spring 1969, the plan was to make an extravagant rock festival that would highlight the youth culture. By May, advertisements were placed in underground and mainstream publications and on the radio.

To get the bands they wanted to sign, they offered large amounts of money. Once the JEFFERSON AIRPLANE, the most successful of the San Francisco psychedelic bands, signed for $12,000 (double their usual fee), the company gained credibility, and other acts soon signed as well. CREEDENCE CLEARWATER REVIVAL and the WHO got about the same amount. In all, $180,000 was spent to secure the talent. JIMI HENDRIX was considered the top star and received $32,000 (the other acts were told that for that amount he was to play two sets) and was guaranteed to close the festival. Hendrix had com-

manded bigger fees before, but by the time he was added, the festival already had the aura of being an important event. Other top artists on the bill included JANIS JOPLIN; the GRATEFUL DEAD; SANTANA; the BAND; Crosby, Stills, Nash, and Young; plus Canned Heat; Sly and the Family Stone; Mountain; Joe Cocker; Ten Years After; Johnny Winter; the Paul Butterfield Blues Band; and Sha Na Na. All but the Grateful Dead, whose set was plagued with electrical problems and was one of their worst performances ever, and Ravi Shankar, whose set came out on a separate album, appear on *Woodstock,* the 1970 film, the related record albums (a triple album and second volume that was a double), or both. (A couple of performers were not included on these until later, expanded versions were released.)

Other artists who performed at Woodstock but do not appear on the issued recordings are rarely associated with the event. Both the Incredible String Band and Blood, Sweat and Tears had lengthy careers and are nonetheless relatively well known, as is Keef Hartley, who had played drums in John Mayall's band before forming his own. Quill, however, remains obscure, as does Bert Sommer (who had been the guitarist in the Left Banke and was in the New York cast of the musical *Hair*). Because of a made-for-TV biography that was aired in 1999, alongside 30th anniversary observances and where-are-they-now features, Sweetwater is back on the map.

Woodstock's musical highlights were many, but the most notable include Jimi Hendrix's anguished "Star-Spangled Banner," Santana's sensational "Soul Sacrifice," Sly and the Family Stone's rousing "I Want to Take You Higher," Richie Havens' passionate "Freedom," Joe Cocker's intense reworking of the BEATLES' "With a Little Help from My Friends," and Country Joe McDonald leading the crowd in yelling the unprintable version of the "Fish cheer" and singing the antiwar anthem "I-Feel-Like-I'm-Fixin'-to-Die Rag."

For the festival itself, many of the pieces fell into place at the last minute. The stage was under construction until just before the music started. The deal with Warner Bros. for the film was finalized only two days before. Not everything on the stage was filmed because there was not enough film. The filmmakers' mandate was to document not just the music, but the event, complete with the stories of young people and the reactions of the locals. Food and security were handled by residents of the Hog Farm, a California commune lead by Wavy Gravy (Hugh Romney), and the Merry Pranksters, a group associated with author Ken Kesey, who were led at Woodstock by Ken Babbs, an experienced LSD user who had been in the marines. Many volunteers assisted with the constructing of kitchens and shelters and their operations. The basic meal made by the Hog Farmers was cooked grains with vegetables garnished with a few peanuts and served on a paper plate. When word got out that there was a lack of food, local people pitched in, and food was also flown in by helicopter. There was a medical ward for emergencies, including one called the "Freak Out Tent" for people who were experiencing bad drug trips, and another for the hundreds who cut their feet on broken glass. There were three deaths, two by drug overdose and one in a tractor accident.

A variety of people were there, who came from near and far: hippies, conservatives, Vietnam veterans, bikers, artisans, children and babies, high school and college students, people who fit several categories, and more. They wore tie-dyed tops, bell bottom pants, beads, jackets and hats sewn with American flags and peace symbols, and a few went naked, skinny-dipping in the nearby lake. Social responsibility and idealism mixed, sometimes within the same person, with selfish hedonism. The crowd sprawled over the hills on blankets and sleeping bags and folding chairs. They baked in the sun, got drenched in the rain, and shivered in the cool that followed. The mud was a foot or more deep in places, but some turned even that to spontaneous fun, sliding in it. The communal experience, while liberating, was not without its dark elements. There was no real violence, but enough problems and hassles to show that it took more than just numbers

and collective goodwill to make the future into something that approached the utopia dreamed up in reaction to horrifying social realities or glimpsed through marijuana smoke. After the festival, it took days to clean up the garbage.

Despite the travails of abandoning their vehicles, walking to the site, losing contact with friends, getting soaked in the thundershowers, and the lack of food and shelter, most attendees found the solidarity, the music, and the unbelievable numbers of people uplifting. The kindness of strangers—concertgoers and townspeople alike—was very touching. Perhaps most important, was the sense that the youth movement was so much larger than people had imagined. It was an unforgettable, eye-opening experience, much more than just a concert. The people gathered together for the music, but they were also pulled by larger, more intangible forces. For many, it was something like a religious experience. Eyewitnesses, describing the sight of sunlight shafting through the clouds after the rainstorm, and the masses of people spread out over the rolling hills in all directions, said it seemed like something out of the Bible.

Woodstock also inspired people who were not there, including Joni Mitchell, who wrote a song about it; "Woodstock" was a hit for Crosby, Stills and Nash. Even politicians and manufacturers henceforth paid more attention to the youth population. Woodstock has also inspired some people who were not even born when it occurred, who feel that the spirit of the event is worth remembering and carrying on.

Several events have aimed to evoke the spirit of the original festival. On the 25th anniversary, Woodstock '94 was held at Saugerties, New York, produced by most of the original partners of Woodstock Ventures. Tickets were $135 for the weekend and an international crowd estimated to be at least 235,000 attended. This Woodstock was well equipped in terms of food, sanitary facilities, and medical support. Before construction began, a prayer ceremony with a Tibetan monk and an American Indian chief blessed the grounds. The bill included some performers who had played in 1969: Crosby, Stills and Nash; Santana; Joe Cocker; Country Joe McDonald; and the Band (augmented by guests from Jefferson Airplane, the BYRDS, and the Grateful Dead). There were others from that era, including the ALLMAN BROTHERS BAND, Bob Dylan, and Traffic, as well as a host of newer acts, from country, blues, R&B, funk, pop, REGGAE, ALTERNATIVE, JAM BAND, PUNK ROCK, rap, and world beat. The show was enlivened by a mosh pit and crowd surfing and, after the rain came, a mud fight between the audience and the band and their crew during Green Day's set. Advanced technology permitted huge video screens, clear sound, and barely any time between bands. At the same time, 15,000 people gathered at the original Woodstock site for free shows by Melanie, Sha Na Na, and Arlo Guthrie, plus local performers.

Marking the 30th anniversary, Woodstock '99 was held in Rome, New York, 100 miles away from Bethel, on the site of a former air force base (the irony of holding a rock festival for peace on a former military complex was not lost on the organizers). The old hangars were used for a film festival and a rave, while nearby were extreme sports, a cybervillage, and vendors' tents. About 200,000 people attended, but the heat was unrelenting and no rain came to give relief to the thirsty and shade-deprived. Among those appearing at this event were James Brown, the DAVE MATTHEWS BAND, Alanis Morissette, and METALLICA. The media highlighted the amount of garbage, the exorbitant cost of food, the presence of bank machines and other signs of change from the 1969 festival, the differences in the generations represented, and the riot and arson that marred the close of the festival.

The original Woodstock festival has become a symbol, a celebration of life and the image of a generation empowered by its numbers in an era full of ideals and contradictions.

Yardbirds, The

Though they existed only from 1963 to 1968, and had hits only from 1965 to 1967, as pioneers of BLUES ROCK, PSYCHEDELIC ROCK, and hard rock, the Yardbirds' influence is immense. Passing through the ranks of this innovative band were three of the greatest guitarists of their generation: ERIC CLAPTON, Jeff Beck, and Jimmy Page, all raised within a few miles of each other.

This legendary band's name came from vocalist Keith Relf's reading of the books of Beat writer Jack Kerouac. *On the Road* and *Dharma Bums* often mention Charlie Parker, the great jazz saxophonist who was an architect of the bebop style; his nickname was Yardbird, a slang word for a railroad hobo. The Yardbirds, like the ROLLING STONES (who formed in 1962), and others on the London scene, were more influenced by blues and R&B than jazz, however. They learned from American records that were at the time obscure and hard to find, and studying this exotic music was an activity engaged in by a dedicated few who forged alliances based on their uncommon interest.

Shortly after they changed their name from the Metropolitan Blues Quartet to the Yardbirds, their first guitarist, Top Topham, returned to college. Eric Clapton took his place, joining Keith Relf, the frail, blond front man who also played harmonica; rhythm guitarist Chris Dreja; bassist Paul Samwell-Smith; and drummer Jim McCarty. The band was already on the gig circuit, and played every Sunday night at the Crawdaddy Club in the London suburb of Richmond, taking the place of the Rolling Stones,

who had gone on tour to promote their debut single. The club's manager, Giorgio Gomelsky, became the Yardbirds' first manager. Their brand of loud energetic R&B brought them a strong following. On their debut LP, *Five Live Yardbirds*, recorded at the Marquee club, the emcee described them as "most blueswailing."

Those days are represented by a glimpse of the band performing in a nightclub scene in the film *Blow Up* (1967), supposedly depicting the Swinging London of the 1960s. By then, Clapton had left the Yardbirds in disgust over their shift from blues to pop—a conflict, in his perception, between integrity and commercialism—after the recording of "For Your Love." That song certainly was commercial; it was their first big hit and their first in America. Instead of giving Clapton a prominent role, it featured Brian Auger guesting on the harpsichord, plus a bongo player and someone bowing a double bass. Jeff Beck then came in as lead guitarist, and his arrival ushered in a more experimental phase. He plays on the band's second American hit, "Heart Full of Soul," written, as was "For Your Love," by Graham Gouldman (who wrote hits for the Hollies and later was in the band 10cc).

They played live constantly: they toured in England, opening for the KINKS; they opened for the BEATLES in London and Paris. In 1965 they toured in the United States; "Shapes of Things" was recorded at the Chess studios in Chicago, and two songs were recorded at the Sun studios in Memphis. They toured again in America, in Europe, and in Australia.

The Yardbirds (with Jeff Beck, far left, and Jimmy Page, second from right) (Michael Ochs Archives.com)

Samwell-Smith, worn out from traveling, departed for a career as a producer (his credits would include Jethro Tull and Cat Stevens), and Jimmy Page, a top session guitarist who had played on records by Them, The Kinks, Tom Jones, DONOVAN, and The WHO, was brought in, first on bass but then back to guitar when Dreja took over the bass duties. For a brief period both Beck and Page played lead guitar; "Happenings Ten Years Time Ago," a classic of psychedelia, is one of only three songs that this formation recorded. Beck, feeling his role encroached upon, left partway through another U.S. tour, and soon formed the Jeff Beck Group, which included vocalist Rod Stewart and

future Rolling Stones guitarist Ron Wood on bass. The Yardbirds carried on as a quartet.

With pop producer Mickie Most trying to revive their chart career, they made one album, *Little Games,* their last. The title track and two other songs were hits, and their least successful. On this album are blues and folk songs from traditional and known sources whose authorship is erroneously credited to the band.

From their blues roots, acknowledged in numerous covers such as BO DIDDLEY's "I'm a Man," an early hit, and reinforced by backing up Sonny Boy Williamson II on tour in England in 1963, the Yardbirds grew into an eclectic rock band with an individual, moody sound. One of their initial inventions was the rave-up—a frenetic double-time passage towards the end of a song—added into blues jams. They expanded their sound canvas with finger cymbals, sitar-like drones ("Heart Full of Soul"), and monk-like chants ("Still I'm Sad"). Beck and Page used the guitar effects of fuzz tone, sustain, and feedback, and on two songs on their last album, Page played his guitar with a violin bow (a technique pioneered by Eddie Phillips of the Creation).

The Yardbirds disbanded in July 1968. Page immediately formed a new band who played their first gigs as the New Yardbirds, fulfilling contracted work in Sweden. On returning to England, they changed their name to LED ZEPPELIN. Dreja worked as a professional photographer (he took the group photo on the back cover of the first Led Zeppelin album). In 1969 Relf and McCarty formed a PROGRESSIVE ROCK band called Renaissance, which, for variety, put the emphasis not on guitars and blues but on keyboards and classical inspirations, and featured a female vocalist, Jane Relf, Keith's sister. The three of them left after one album and the rest of the band carried on without them. Relf did a heavy rock album with Armageddon in 1975, but died the next year at age 33, electrocuted at home while practicing on an improperly grounded guitar.

In the late 1970s McCarty and Jane Relf did three albums in a band called Illusion (later called Stairway). In 1984 Dreja, McCarty, and Samwell-Smith reunited in Box of Frogs, which never played live but released two albums; Jeff Beck guested on one and Jimmy Page on the other. Another recording project, the British Invasion All-Stars, saw McCarty with veterans of other notable bands. Inspired by their induction into the Rock and Roll Hall of Fame in 1992, McCarty and Dreja reformed the Yardbirds, with guitarist John "Gypie" Mayo, bassist and lead vocalist John Idan, and harp blower Alan Glen. They kept a low profile until 2003's acclaimed *Birdland*, the first Yardbirds album in 35 years. It included old and new songs, and many distinguished guitarists who eagerly guested with them: Jeff Beck, Slash (Guns n' Roses), Brian May

(QUEEN), Johnny Rzeznik (Goo Goo Dolls), Joe Satriani, Steve Lukather, and Jeff "Skunk" Baxter. To the delight of the fans, the band toured America and Europe to promote the album.

Young, Neil (b. 1945) *singer and songwriter*

Many of his fans consider him to be one of the mellow SINGER-SONGWRITERS and love his plaintive voice and the lilting, melancholic songs on his acoustic folk albums. Others see him as a forerunner of GRUNGE, citing his gutsy rock music and aggressive lead GUITAR accompanied by a band called Crazy Horse. Lots of people do not know what to make of him because he refuses to be pinned down, working in many different styles, from country to techno. One of his record labels once rejected an album's worth of recordings because they were not commercial and did not sound enough like Neil Young. He is gifted and productive, reckless and unpredictable, and while he is said to sometimes be overbearing and ruthless, he is one of the most fascinating and enigmatic characters in music, continuing to surprise, excite, and sometimes exasperate his fans. The best of his inconsistent work is brilliant.

Young was born in Toronto and grew up in a small town in northern Ontario (as he sang in "Helpless"). He was a sickly child who suffered from polio, diabetes, and epilepsy. His father was a famous sports broadcaster. After his parents divorced when he was 15, he and his mother moved to Winnipeg. Young took up folk music and played in garage bands. He was inspired by local guitarist Randy Bachman of the Guess Who (and later of Bachman-Turner Overdrive). Young's other main inspirations are BOB DYLAN, with whom he shares the first-take philosophy that values rough spontaneity over polish, and the ROLLING STONES, whose brash, hard-rocking exuberance is echoed in his own electric music.

Young then returned to Toronto, and with his group the Squires worked in the Yorkville district club scene. Another short-lived group, the Mynah

Birds, made one record. In 1965 Young and bassist Bruce Palmer (from the Mynah Birds) drove to Los Angeles to hook up with Stephen Stills, whom Young had met when Stills was touring Canada in a folk revival group. With two more musicians, the three of them formed the influential BUFFALO SPRINGFIELD, who broke up in 1968.

Young was signed to the Reprise label as a solo artist. His solo career began in 1969 with *Neil Young*, which was unsuccessful, and *Everybody Knows This Is Nowhere,* recorded with Crazy Horse, the ragged bar band with whom he would work on a occasional basis throughout his career. The second album contained the raw "Down by the River" and the catchy "Cinnamon Girl," his first solo hit. That summer he played his first concert with the newly formed Crosby, Stills and Nash. David Crosby had been in the BYRDS, Stephen Stills in

Neil Young (Michael Ochs Archives.com)

Buffalo Springfield, and Graham Nash in the Hollies, a successful BRITISH INVASION band from Manchester, England. Crosby, Stills and Nash performed at WOODSTOCK and released a self-titled debut album. Young joined as an official but part-time member, and their next album, *Déjà vu* (1970), was credited to Crosby, Stills, Nash and Young. It included their hit version of Joni Mitchell's "Woodstock" and was the first of three number-one albums in a row for the quartet; the other two were *4 Way Street* (1971) and *So Far* (1974). Young preferred to put his energies into his solo career, so the others carried on without him, but he worked with some or all of them on numerous occasions. They quartet reunited for *American Dream* (1988) and *Looking Forward* (1999).

After the two solo albums mentioned above, Young cemented the singer-songwriter part of his identity with two classic records. *After the Gold Rush* (1970) and *Harvest* (1972), his only number-one album, which included "Old Man" and "Heart of Gold" (his only number-one single), established him as a major singer-songwriter. The public prefers this side of his output, for Young's return to similar territory with *Harvest Moon* (1992) gave him the biggest-selling album in the 20 years since *Harvest.*

In 1979 he reconnected with Crazy Horse for two million-selling albums: *Rust Never Sleeps*, which acknowledged PUNK ROCK and the Sex Pistols in "Hey, Hey, My, My," and *Live Rust.* While few of Young's peers have shown much interest in new forms of music, he has done an album with PEARL JAM (*Mirror Ball*, 1995), and had ALTERNATIVE ROCK bands open for him, including Social Distortion and Sonic Youth, whose use of feedback as a cathartic element of their sound is similar to his own.

Young's membership in the rock community has resulted in many collaborations, including the BAND's Last Waltz concert and film. He has taken part in the ongoing annual benefit concerts, which started in 1986, for the Bridge School. The school is for children with learning disabilities, and was cofounded by his wife Pegi (their son Ben was one of its initial students). The mostly acoustic concerts have included a who's who of rock and folk musicians.

Young has covered a lot of ground with his lyrics and forays into various styles. He has attacked racism (in "Southern Man," which earned a response from Lynyrd Skynyrd in "Sweet Home Alabama"), violence (in "Ohio," concerning the notorious incident in which National Guardsmen killed four student antiwar protesters at Kent State University in 1970), the corporate sponsorship of music ("This Note's for You," which lampooned Michael Jackson's Pepsi commercial), and the use of drugs ("The Needle and the Damage Done"). He has looked at history ("Cortez the Killer," about Spain's marauding conquests in South America), and made his seemingly inconsistent views on politics heard on *Hawks and Doves* (1980) and other recordings. Stylistically, Young has explored country (with his version of Don Gibson's "Oh, Lonesome Me"), folk (his remake of Ian and Sylvia's "Four Strong Winds"), and ROCKABILLY (with 1983's *Everybody's Rockin'* credited to Neil Young and the Shocking Pinks). His dalliance with synthesizers on *Trans* (1983) was odd, but not without appeal. He has worked in film, but the eccentric experimental *Journey Through the Past* (1972), an autobiographical retrospective, remains obscure (though the soundtrack sold well enough). His acclaimed *Greendale* (2003), described as a "rock novel," is a social commentary presented through the story of a fictional California family. The first edition of the CD came with a bonus DVD of a live stage performance of actors playing the story's characters while Young and Crazy Horse play the music. A second CD edition (2004) has a different bonus DVD which shows Young and the band recording the songs in the studio. The actual *Greendale* film, released on DVD in 2004, was shot in the grainy super 8 format, which highlight the "family movie" feeling of the concept.

Whether in or out of the limelight, applying his muse to folk, R&B, rock and roll, country, techno, or any other style he is in the mood to play, Young has remained an uncompromisingly independent artist. His erratic and meandering career has yielded enough gems that his fans are willing to follow his development, bearing with the tedious to get to the transcendent.

Zappa, Frank (1940–1993) *composer and musician*

With and without his group the Mothers of Invention, Frank Zappa made music that was fun as well as weird and experimental. He could leave listeners in awe over his band's musical precision, in laughter over the targets lampooned in his satirical lyrics, or outraged by his forthright language and penchant for taboo topics. He was irreverent, iconoclastic, hard-working, and immensely talented as a guitarist, vocalist, bandleader, and composer. The most indelible visual trademark was his own face: a piercing gaze framed by long, black hair and a droopy mustache and goatee.

The two great musical touchstones of his life could not have been farther apart: 1950s DOO-WOP and 20th-century classical composers. His own creations managed an unlikely but fascinating bridge of lowbrow and highbrow culture. When asked to list his favorite music, Zappa included pieces by Maurice Ravel, Béla Bartók, Igor Stravinsky, Anton Webern, and Edgard Varèse. Throughout his life Zappa championed the work of Varèse, an innovative French-born composer who moved to United States in 1915. In Zappa's words, Varèse was "the idol of my youth"; they communicated briefly in 1957 but never met, despite an interest on both parties to do so. On the same list Zappa also named "Can I Come Over Tonight" by the Velours, a doo-wop group; "Three Hours Past Midnight" (which Zappa stated inspired him to play the guitar) by Johnny Guitar Watson, a rhythm and blues wizard who later embraced funk (and would perform on some of Zappa's albums); and "Stolen Moments," a jazz classic from 1961 by saxophonist and arranger Oliver Nelson. Jazz, REGGAE, classical, flamenco, blues, and his own rock GUITAR were part of Zappa's musical adventure, sometimes in the same piece.

Born in Baltimore, Maryland, in 1940, Frank Zappa grew up near Los Angeles. As a teenager he made music with Don Van Vliet, better known as Captain Beefheart, another iconoclastic artist with whom he reconnected when both were famous. At the start of Zappa's recording career, there were numerous unsuccessful singles, including one by the Penguins, a pioneering Los Angeles doo-wop group famous for "Earth Angel" (1954), who sang his song "Memories of El Monte."

He made approximately 60 albums during his lifetime. Zappa came to notice with *Freak Out!* (1966), one of rock's first double albums. Credited to the Mothers of Invention, much of it satirized aspects of American society, particularly rock culture and its fans. The satire continued on *Absolutely Free* (1967) and *We're Only in It for the Money* (1968), whose cover was a parody of the BEATLES' *Sgt. Pepper's Lonely Hearts Club Band* from the previous year. *Lumpy Gravy* (1968) was an instrumental album recorded with orchestra which made extensive use of tape collage techniques that Zappa had used earlier and would use again. *Uncle Meat* (1969), the last recording made with the original Mothers of Invention lineup, explored jazz rock fusion. Between them came *Cruising with Ruben and the Jets* (1968), a brilliant send-up of the harmony singing and romantic lyric clichés of doo-wop groups.

Issued under Frank Zappa's name only, *Hot Rats* (1969) was a jazz rock album that highlighted his formidable guitar playing. "Peaches en Regalia" and "Son of Mr. Green Genes" became widely played by jazz combos, partly due to their inclusion in *The Real Book,* a popular "fake book" (a repertoire source in which the pieces are presented in economical musical arrangements known as lead sheets). *Burnt Weeny Sandwich* and *Weasels Ripped My Flesh* (both 1970), like *Hot Rats,* mixed jazz, rock, and classical elements, and all placed higher on the British album charts than they did in the United States.

With *Chunga's Revenge,* Zappa brought in Mark Volman and Howard Kaylan (known then as Flo and Eddie) from the POP ROCK band the Turtles, whose biggest hit, "Happy Together" (1967), was reprised as the cynical punch line for the belabored story of groups and groupies that runs through *Mothers Live at the Fillmore East—June 1971* (1971). That record also featured a new lineup of the Mothers, documented as well on another live album, *Just Another Band From L.A.* (1972), and in the film *200 Motels* and its soundtrack (1972).

By this time, Zappa's eccentric persona, his prolific output, and the absurdly theatrical, humorous, and musically impressive live shows he and his musicians presented had connected with enough members of the rock audience to form a loyal fan base. With still quirky but less experimental mid-1970s albums, especially *Over-nite Sensation,* *Apostrophe ('),* which included former CREAM bassist Jack Bruce, and *One Size Fits All,* Zappa achieved a level of commercial success. Radio avoided him, but he did have three hit singles that gained popularity for their novelty: "Don't Eat the Yellow Snow" (1974), "Dancin' Fool" (1979), which skewered disco culture, and "Valley Girl" (1982), which featured the "totally awesome" suburban shopping mall slang of his teenage daughter Moon Unit Zappa. Frank Zappa was devoted to his wife Gail, who helped manage his business affairs, and they had three other children: another daughter,

named Diva Muffin, and two sons, Dweezil and Ahmet Rodan, both musicians.

Other items in Zappa's vast output include symphonic albums (such as *London Symphony Orchestra*), concept albums (including *Joe's Garage,* a three-act story of a future in which music is outlawed, and *Thing-Fish,* a musical that addresses AIDS and racism), albums that used the Synclavier synthesizer (*Francesco Zappa,* not Frank Zappa's music but that of a similarly named 18th-century composer, and *Jazz from Hell,* which won a Grammy Award for Best Rock Instrumental Performance), and multivolume retrospective collections of live

Frank Zappa (Michael Ochs Archives.com)

tracks (such as *Shut Up 'n' Play Yer Guitar* and *You Can't Do That on Stage Anymore*).

The music industry was always one of Frank Zappa's pet targets, and toward the end of his life he led the fight against censorship in music, articulately testifying in 1985 before a U.S. Senate committee in opposition to a campaign by the Parents' Music Resource Center (PMRC), founded by wives of Washington politicians and concerned about the perceived links between rock music and drug abuse, premarital sex, cults, and violence. The PMRC wanted to have records categorized, like movies, for what they saw as their offensive contents. Sound excerpts from the hearings were incorporated into *Frank Zappa Meets the Mothers of Prevention* (1985). These experiences, along with childhood memories and philosophical rants, are presented in *The Real Frank Zappa Book* (1989), an autobiography produced with the assistance of Peter Occhiogrosso.

Throughout his career, Zappa collaborated with, hired, produced recordings for, or promoted (through releasing records on his own label) a large number of artists. These include jazz fusion musicians Jean-Luc Ponty and George Duke; rock acts Grand Funk Railroad, Alice Cooper, and JEFFERSON AIRPLANE; other eccentric artists like Captain Beefheart, the GTO's, Wild Man Fischer, and hipster monologist Lord Buckley; as well as vocal harmony group the Persuasions and singer-songwriter Tim Buckley. Since his death from prostate cancer in 1993, symphony orchestras and his former band members have kept Frank Zappa's music alive. Numerous biographies have brought further attention to this singular man.

5

Appendixes

Appendix I

Discography of Recommended Listening

All are single CDs unless noted.

Aeromith *O, Yeah! Ultimate Aerosmith Hits* (Sony, 2002, two CDs)

Allman Brothers Band, The *Dreams* (Polygram, 1989, four CD box set)

Animals *Absolute Animals 1964–1968* (Raven, 2003)

Band, The *Best of the Band* (Capitol, 1990)

Beach Boys, The *Sounds of Summer: The Very Best of the Beach Boys* (Capitol, 2003)

Beatles, The *1* (Capitol, 2000)

Berry, Chuck *His Best, Vol. 1* (Chess, 1997)

Blondie *Greatest Hits* (Capitol/Chrysalis, 2002)

blues rock *John Mayall with Eric Clapton: Bluesbreakers* (Universal, 2001)

Bowie, David *Best of Bowie* (EMI, 2002)

British invasion *The British Invasion: 1963–1967* (Hip-O, 2004, three CDs)

Buffalo Springfield *Retrospective: The Best of Buffalo Springfield* (Atlantic, 1990)

Byrds, The *The Essential Byrds* (Columbia/Legacy, 2003, two CDs)

Clapton, Eric *The Cream of Clapton* (Polygram, 1995)

classic rock *Hard Rock Cafe: Classic Rock* (Rhino, 1997); *Power of Rock: 16 Classic Rock Hits* (Madacy, 1997)

Cochran, Eddie *Somethin' Else: The Fine Lookin' Hits of Eddie Cochran* (Razor and Tie, 1998)

Cooper, Alice *The Best of Alice Cooper: Mascara and Monsters* (Rhino, 2001)

country rock *Hillbilly Fever! Vol. 5: Legends of Country Rock* (Rhino, 1995)

Cream *The Very Best of Cream* (Polygram, 1995)

Creedence Clearwater Revival *Chronicle Vol. 1: The 20 Greatest Hits* (Fantasy, 1990)

Darin, Bobby *The Hit Singles Collection* (Rhino, 2002)

Dave Matthews Band *Under the Table and Dreaming* (RCA, 1994); *Crash* (RCA, 1996)

Diddley, Bo *His Best* (MCA, 1997)

Dion/Dion and the Belmonts *Dion and the Belmonts: Greatest Hits* (Repertoire, 2001)

Domino, Fats *Fats Domino Jukebox: 20 Greatest Hits* (Capitol, 2002)

Donovan *Donovan's Greatest Hits* (Sony, 1999)

Doors, The *Legacy: Absolute Best* (Elektra/Asylum, 2003, two CDs)

doo-wop *The Doo Wop Box* (Rhino, 1993, four CDs)

Dylan, Bob *Essential Bob Dylan* (Sony, 2000, two CDs)

Eagles, The *The Very Best of the Eagles* (Warner Strategic, 2003)

Electric Light Orchestra *Strange Magic: The Best of Electric Light Orchestra* (Sony, 1995)

Everly Brothers, The *All-Time Original Hits* (Rhino, 1999)

Fleetwood Mac *The Very Best of Fleetwood Mac* (WEA/Reprise, 2002)

folk rock *Spirit of the 60's: Folk Rock 1* (Time-Life, 2000)

Four Seasons, The *The Very Best of Frankie Valli and the Four Seasons* (Rhino, 2003)

garage rock *Nuggets: Original Artyfacts from the First Psychedelic Era, 1965–1968* (Rhino, 1998, four CDs) girl groups *The Best of the Girl Groups, Vol. 1* (Rhino, 1990)

glam rock *Glam Bam Thank You Ma'Am* (Buddha, 1999)

Grateful Dead, The *The Very Best of the Grateful Dead* (Rhino, 2003)

grunge *Singles: Original Motion Picture Soundtrack* (Sony, 1992)

Haley, Bill, and His Comets *20th Century Masters: The Best of Bill Haley and His Comets (Millennium Collection)* (MCA, 1999)

heavy metal *Monsters of Rock* (Razor and Tie, 1998)

Hendrix, Jimi *Experience Hendrix: The Best of Jimi Hendrix* (Experience Hendrix, 1998)

Holly, Buddy *The Buddy Holly Collection* (MCA, 1993, two CDs)

instrumental rock *Rock Instrumental Classics, Vols. 1–5* (Rhino, 1995)

jam bands *Into the Music: Jam Bands 1* (Red Line, 2001)

Jefferson Airplane/Starship *VH1 Behind the Music Collection* (RCA, 2000)

Joplin, Janis *Essential Janis Joplin* (Sony, 2003)

Kinks, The *The Ultimate Collection* (Import, 2002)

KISS *The Very Best of Kiss* (Universal, 2002)

Led Zeppelin *Early Days and Latter Days: The Best of Volumes 1 and 2* (Atlantic, 2002)

Lee, Brenda *Anthology, Vols. 1 & 2 (1956–1980)* (MCA, 1991, two CDs)

Leiber and Stoller *There's a Riot Goin' On: The Rock 'n' Roll Classics of Leiber and Stoller* (Rhino, 1991)

Lewis, Jerry Lee *25 All Time Greatest Sun Recordings* (Varese, 2000)

Little Richard *The Georgia Peach* (Specialty, 1991)

Mamas and the Papas, The *Greatest Hits* (MCA, 1998)

Metallica *Master of Puppets* (Elektra/Asylum, 1986); *. . . And Justice for All* (Elektra/Asylum, 1988); *Metallica* (Elektra/ Asylum, 1991)

Monkees, The *The Best of the Monkees* (Rhino, 2003)

Monterey Pop Festival *The Complete Monterey Pop Festival* (Criterion, 2002, 3 DVDs)

Motown *Hitsville USA: The Motown Singles Collection 1959–1971* (Motown, 1992, four CDs)

Nelson, Ricky *Greatest Hits* (Capitol, 2002)

new wave *New Wave Dance Hits: Just Can't Get Enough Vols. 1–15* (Rhino, 1994, 1995)

Nirvana *Nevermind* (DGC, 1991); *MTV Unplugged in New York* (Geffen, 1994)

Oasis *(What's the Story) Morning Glory?* (Sony, 1995)

Orbison, Roy *The All-Time Greatest Hits of Roy Orbison* (Sony, 1990)

Pearl Jam *10* (Epic, 1991); *Vs.* (Epic, 1993); *Vitalogy* (Epic, 1994)

Perkins, Carl *Blue Suede Shoes: The Very Best of Carl Perkins* (Collectables, 1999)

Pink Floyd *Echoes: The Best of Pink Floyd* (Capitol, 2001, two CDs)

Presley, Elvis *Elv1s 30 #1 Hits* (BMG, 2001)

progressive rock *The Best Prog Rock Album in the World . . . Ever!* (EMI International, 2003, three CDs)

psychedelic rock *Psychedelia: The Long Strange Trip* (Friedman/Fairfax, 1995)

punk rock *No Thanks: 70s Punk Rebellion* (Rhino, 2003, four CDs)

Queen *Greatest Hits, Vols. 1–2* (Hollywood, 1995)

Radiohead *The Bends* (Capitol, 1995); *OK Computer* (EMI, 1997); *Kid A* (Capitol, 2000)

Ramones, The *Loud, Fast Ramones: Their Toughest Hits* (Rhino, 2002)

Rascals, The *The Ultimate Rascals* (Warner Brothers, 1990)

reggae *Reggae Party* (Polygram, 1999)

R.E.M. *In Time: The Best of R.E.M. 1988–2003* (Warner Brothers, 2003)

Righteous Brothers, The *Unchained Melody: The Very Best of the Righteous Brothers* (Polygram, 1991)

rockabilly *Whistle Bait: 25 Rockabilly Rave-Ups* (Sony, 2000)

rock revival *Soundtrack of American Graffiti* (MCA, 1973, two CDs)

Rolling Stones, The *40 Licks* (Virgin, 2002)

Santana/Carlos Santana *The Best of Santana* (Sony, 1998)

Shannon, Del *Runaway: The Very Best of Del Shannon* (Collectables, 2002)

Shirelles, The *Greatest Hits* (Curb, 1995)

Simon and Garfunkel/Paul Simon *The Best of Simon and Garfunkel* (Sony, 1999); *The Paul Simon Collection: On My Way, Don't Know Where I'm Goin'* (Warner Brothers, 2002)

singer-songwriters *Songs: The Best of the Singer Songwriters* (WEA/Warner, 2001)

Spector, Phil *Phil Spector: Back to Mono (1958–1969)* (Abko, 1991, four CDs)

Springsteen, Bruce *The Essential Bruce Springsteen* (Sony, 2003, two CDs)

Steely Dan *A Decade of Steely Dan* (MCA, 1996)

Steppenwolf *All-Time Greatest Hits* (MCA, 1999)

surf rock *Cowabunga! The Surf Box* (Rhino, 1996, four CDs)

Talking Heads *Popular Favorites 1976–1992/ Sand in the Vaseline* (Warner Brothers, 1992, two CDs)

Turner, Big Joe *Big Joe Turner's Greatest Hits* (Atlantic, 1990)

U2 *The Best of 1980–1990* (Polygram, 1998); *The Best of 1990–2000* (Interscope, 2002)

Valens, Ritchie *The Very Best of Ritchie Valens* (Empire, 2000)

Velvet Underground, The *The Best of the Velvet Underground* (Verve, 1989)

Who, The *Meaty Beaty Big and Bouncy* (MCA, 1971) *My Generation: The Very Best of the Who* (MCA, 1997); *The Ultimate Collection* (MCA, 2002, two CDs)

Woodstock *Woodstock* (WEA, 1994, two CDs)

Yardbirds, The *Ultimate* (Rhino, 2001, two CDs)

Young, Neil *Decade* (1977, Warner Brothers, two CDs)

Zappa, Frank *Strictly Commercial: The Best of Frank Zappa* (Rykodic, 1995)

Appendix II

Chronology

1830s

Blackface performers (minstrel shows) are popular and remain so for more than 100 years. Their mix of white and black cultures is a predecessor of rock and roll.

1840s

Blackface minstrel shows proliferate. Stephen Foster (1826–64), America's first great songwriter, creates an enduring minstrel song in "Oh, Susanna!" (1848), which will be covered by the Byrds in the 1960s.

1850s

Stephen Foster writes more evergreens, including "Old Folks at Home" and "De Camptown Races." The former (also known as "Way Down upon the Swanee River") will become the biggest hit of 19th-century popular music, selling more than 20 million copies in sheet music.

1860s

American Civil War (1861–65).

1870s

Alexander Graham Bell invents the telephone (1876).

Buddy Bolden (1877–1931), the first great jazz musician, is born in New Orleans. He will never record.

Thomas Edison invents the phonograph (1877), and creates the first practical light bulb (1879).

1880s

Tin Pan Alley, a district of New York City, gains prominence as the center of the popular music industry in the United States.

Phonographs and recordings (wax cylinders) are manufactured for home use; the record industry begins (1888).

1890s

Jazz starts in New Orleans.

Ragtime starts in the Midwest and becomes widely popular by 1897. "Maple Leaf Rag" (1899) by Scott Joplin is reputed to be the first instrumental piece to sell a million sheet music copies.

Billboard, the authoritative publication of the music industry, begins publication (1894). Its charts come to be considered definitive.

1900s

Cylinder recordings have their peak of popularity in mid-decade, replaced by double-sided discs of various speeds.

Blues develops in the Mississippi River delta region.

1910s

The ocean liner *Titanic* sinks (1912).

"The Memphis Blues" (1912) written by W. C. Handy, the "Father of the Blues," is a sheet music hit. A recording of it by Morton Harvey (a white vaudevillian) and the New York Philharmonic Orchestra is the first vocal blues record (1915).

World War I (1914–1918). The United States enters the war in 1917.

First jazz record made, by the Original Dixieland Jazz Band: "The Dixieland Jazz Band One-Step" (1917).

1920

Prohibition starts in the United States (it will end in 1933).

"Crazy Blues" by Mamie Smith is the first blues recording by a black vocalist. Its immediate popularity catalyzes the record industry's involvement with African-American music.

1921

Radio that can transmit voices is introduced. It soon is immensely popular.

1922

"Ragtime Annie," a fiddle instrumental by Eck Robertson, is the first country record.

"My Man Rocks Me (With One Steady Roll)" by blues singer Trixie Smith is possibly the first appearance on record of the words *rock* and *roll*, euphemisms for sex.

1923

"Down Hearted Blues" is the first hit for Bessie Smith. She will be known as the "Empress of the Blues" and the "World's Greatest Blues Singer," and will influence later singers, including Janis Joplin.

Jazz and blues records proliferate.

1924

"The Prisoner's Song" by Vernon Dalhart is the first commercially successful country record.

1925

Big record labels begin using electric microphones for recording.

1927

The Jazz Singer starring Al Jolson is one of the first movies with sound. He performs in blackface.

1928

"Pine Top's Boogie Woogie" by Clarence "Pinetop" Smith is the record that gives the name to boogie woogie, a style of blues.

"West End Blues" by Louis Armstrong is the pivot between early jazz and swing.

Turntable speeds are finally standardized at 78 revolutions per minute.

1929

The stock market crashes in New York. The Great Depression begins, and one of its consequences is the near ruin of the record industry in the early 1930s.

1931

The first electric guitar, a lap steel guitar known as the Frying Pan, is invented by George Beauchamp.

1935

Swing jazz is popular: the big band era is underway.

1936

"Cross Road Blues," one of the first recordings by Robert Johnson, later known as the "King of the Delta Blues," is recorded. It will be revived in the 1960s, as "Crossroads," by Eric Clapton. Johnson dies in 1938.

The first electric guitar to be manufactured and offered for sale, the Gibson ES-150, is introduced.

1938

John Hammond presents his landmark From Spirituals to Swing concert at Carnegie Hall in New York City. The concert is a sensation and leads to a fad for boogie-woogie music.

1939

World War II begins.

Louis Jordan and his Tympany Five make their first record. Jordan is a pioneer of rhythm and blues; his style of jump blues will be extremely successful and influence many early rock and roll performers, including Bill Haley and Little Richard.

Charlie Christian, a great early player of the electric guitar, makes his first recordings, as a member of Benny Goodman's swing band.

1941

The United States enters World War II following Japan's attack on Pearl Harbor.

Muddy Waters is first recorded by folklorist Alan Lomax on a Mississippi plantation. The Rolling Stones will take their name from one of his songs.

1943

Hit Parader begins publication. In keeping with its title, it will follow popular trends, covering psychedelia in the 1960s and heavy metal in the 1980s. Until the mid-1970s, it published song lyrics.

King Records opens in Cincinnati, Ohio. It records hillbilly music, adding R&B in 1946, and becomes one of the most prominent independent labels, with many tracks that qualify as early rock and roll.

1945

World War II ends.

"Hillbilly Boogie" by the Delmore Brothers marks the start of a new country style: country boogie (or hillbilly boogie). A mix of blues and country, it is a prelude to rock and roll.

1946

"House of Blue Lights" is a hit for Freddie Slack and Ella Mae Morse, the earliest white R&B stars.

Independent labels are on the rise, like Imperial and Specialty which focus on black popular music, both in Los Angeles.

The use of tape for recording becomes more common.

With the return of servicemen from overseas, the baby boom begins.

1947

"Good Rockin' Tonight," a jump blues by Wynonie Harris, is recorded; it will be a hit the next year, popularizing the word *rock* in song lyrics. It is a strong candidate for the first rock and roll record. Elvis Presley will cover it in the 1950s.

"Old Man River" by the Ravens, with the lead vocals sung by the bass singer, is an important precursor of doo-wop.

Hank Williams, the future "King of Country Music," has his first hit with "Move It On Over," a prelude to rockabilly.

The Atlantic label, one of the most important independents in the history of R&B and rock and roll, is founded in New York City.

Jerry Wexler, a writer at *Billboard* magazine (and a future partner in Atlantic Records), invents the term *rhythm and blues*.

1948

"It's Too Soon to Know" by the Orioles is one of the first R&B vocal group hits. It is cited as the first doo-wop record and the first rock ballad.

"Boogie Chillen" by John Lee Hooker and "I Can't Be Satisfied" by Muddy Waters, both amplified delta blues, mark the rise of urban blues.

"Guitar Boogie" by Arthur Smith and the Crackerjacks popularizes boogie-woogie piano figures on the guitar, the forerunners of the rock riff.

The LP, the long-playing 12-inch vinyl record that spins at 33 ⅓ revolutions per minute, is introduced by the Columbia label.

Radio station WDIA in Memphis is the first to program black music fulltime. Other stations quickly follow, causing a greater demand for R&B and spreading its influence beyond its original audience. This is a key factor in the rise of rock and roll.

1949

RCA Victor introduces the 45 rpm record, a seven-inch disc that typically has one song per side. It is smaller, cheaper, and more durable than the 78 format.

Dewey Phillips, a white Memphis disc jockey, presents his first *Red Hot and Blue* program. It is an instant success. He will remain incredibly popular throughout the 1950s, with a nightly audience of about 100,000 listeners at his peak, spreading R&B and rock and roll throughout a wide area.

New Orleans–style rhythm & blues becomes popular due to musicians like Professor Longhair and Fats Domino. Domino's debut recording "The Fat Man" comes out this year.

Most record companies now use tape for recording.

Fender introduces the first mass-produced solid-body electric guitar.

1950

Patti Page's "Tennessee Waltz," a pop version of a country song, is a huge hit. Through tape overdubbing, she is able to sing harmony with herself. This influential technique changes how records are made.

"Hot Rod Race," a country boogie song by Arkie Shibley and His Mountain Dew Boys, introduces the topic of car racing into popular music. It will influence Chuck Berry's "Maybelline" and songs by the Beach Boys.

The Chess label (formerly Aristocrat) is founded in Chicago. It will launch the careers of Chuck Berry and Bo Diddley.

Cleveland disc jockey Alan Freed begins his *Moondog Show*, broadcasting rhythm and blues to a large and avid audience of blacks and whites.

1951

"Rocket 88" by Jackie Brenston and his Delta Cats (a pseudonym for Ike Turner's band) is recorded in Memphis by Sam Phillips. Later, some claim it is the first rock and roll record (but see 1947 for another candidate).

Les Paul and Mary Ford's "How High the Moon," a pop version of a jazz standard, is a number-one hit. It is the first hit to use extensive overdubbing, on the voice and on the guitar, and its influential electric guitar solo is the first solo with a rock and roll sound.

The Fender Precision Bass is the first electric bass guitar on the market.

1952

"Rock the Joint" by Bill Haley and the Saddlemen (soon to become the Comets) is the first rock song by a white performer and points the way to rockabilly.

"Lawdy Miss Clawdy" by Lloyd Price (with Fats Domino on piano) is a number-one R&B hit. It will be redone by Elvis Presley and others.

Alan Freed presents the Moondog Coronation Ball in Cleveland, an R&B concert. Tickets are oversold and the overflow crowd riots, generating much publicity and criticism.

The Sun record label is founded by Sam Phillips in Memphis. He records mostly blues and R&B at first.

1953

"Crazy Man Crazy" by Bill Haley and Haley's Comets is the first rock and roll song to enter the *Billboard* pop charts.

"Hound Dog" by Big Mama Thornton tops the R&B charts. It established Jerry Leiber and Mike Stoller's songwriting credentials, and will be a hit again in 1956 for Elvis Presley.

"Gee" by the Crows is a crossover hit on both the R&B and pop charts and the first doo-wop song to sell a million copies.

1954

Black vocal groups are popular with black and white record buyers. "Sh-Boom" by the Chords is one of the first hits to use doo-wop's nonsense lyrics. "Earth Angel (Will You Be Mine)" by the Penguins is the first of thousands of doo-wop songs to use the "Blue Moon" progression of chords. "Work with Me, Annie" by the Midnighters (later known as Hank Ballard and the Midnighters), a number-one R&B hit that spawns several sequel records, creates controversy over its suggestive lyrics.

"Shake, Rattle, and Roll" is a hit for Big Joe Turner and, in a sanitized cover version, for Bill Haley.

"That's All Right" by Elvis Presley, on the Sun label, is his first release and marks the start of rockabilly.

Alan Freed moves from Cleveland to New York and changes the name of his radio show to *Rock and Roll Party*. The music he plays is still R&B.

1955

Alan Freed's first dance concert in New York, Rock 'n' Roll Ball, presents an all-black roster of talent—Ruth Brown, Joe Turner, the Drifters, Fats Domino, the Moonglows, and the Harptones—to an audience nearly evenly split between black and white patrons. The two nights bring in almost $40,000.

Rock and roll hits the mainstream. "Rock around the Clock" by Bill Haley and His Comets is the first rock and roll number-one, its popularity boosted by its use in *Blackboard Jungle*, a film about juvenile delinquency. Fats Domino has his first top-10 hit, "Ain't It a Shame" (also known as "Ain't That a Shame").

Two rock and roll giants who record for the Chess label in Chicago have hits with their debut recordings: Chuck Berry with "Maybelline," which popularizes the guitar as a featured instrument, and Bo Diddley with "Bo Diddley," which popularizes the Bo Diddley beat, derived from African-American traditions.

"Rock Island Line," a song from the repertoire of black folk and blues singer Leadbelly, is an international hit as done by Lonnie Donegan from England. It launches a new folk style called skiffle that will be the training ground for a generation of U.K. musicians, including the Beatles.

Authorities in certain cities who are wary of rock and roll's power to excite young people cancel shows because of their fear of riots.

Cover versions of R&B hits are prevalent, typically, but not exclusively, by white singers on major labels.

Colonel Tom Parker becomes Elvis Presley's manager and arranges his signing to RCA.

1956

Rock and roll becomes huge. Elvis Presley creates a sensation with his television appearances and his hit records for RCA. Seventeen of his songs released this year will make the charts, including "Heartbreak Hotel," "Hound Dog," "Don't Be Cruel," and two other number-one hits. Both of his 1956 albums make number one, and his first film, *Love Me Tender,* scores at the box office. He is the biggest star that the field of entertainment has ever seen.

Rockabilly is popular with songs like "Blue Suede Shoes," a hit for both Carl Perkins and Elvis Presley, and "Be Bop A Lula" by Gene Vincent.

Many of the giants of early rock are having some of their best-known hits, including Fats Domino with "Blueberry Hill," Little Richard with "Tutti Frutti" and "Long Tall Sally," and Chuck Berry with "Roll over Beethoven."

Doo-wop is popular. For example, "Why Do Fools Fall in Love" by the Teenagers featuring Frankie Lymon (who at 13 is as young as his audience), and "In the Still of the Nite" by the Five Satins are both million-sellers. The Platters, the premier vocal group of the 1950s, have two number-one hits: "The Great Pretender" and "My Prayer."

Instrumental rock begins with Bill Doggett's "Honky Tonk."

The practice of white pop artists covering rock and roll songs by black artists starts to fade out after Little Richard's "Long Tall Sally" does slightly better than Pat Boone's cover, and Fats Domino's "I'm in Love Again" easily beats out the Fontane Sisters' cover.

The Girl Can't Help It, starring Jayne Mansfield and featuring performances by Little Richard, Fats Domino, and Eddie Cochran, is one of the first (and best) of numerous movies cashing in on rock and roll.

1957

Elvis Presley is still on top. He has four number-one hits, including "All Shook Up," the year's best-selling single.

Rock and roll is in full bloom. New stars of the highest caliber enter the scene: Jerry Lee Lewis, the Everly Brothers, and Buddy Holly have their first hits.

Rockabilly and doo-wop are going strong. Rockabilly hits include "That'll Be the Day" by Buddy Holly and "Party Doll" by Buddy Knox, and doo-wop successes include "Come Go with Me" by the Dell-Vikings and "Little Darlin' " by the Diamonds.

"La Bamba" by Ritchie Valens is the first rock hit in Spanish.

Rock and roll is in the media spotlight. Ricky Nelson, playing himself alongside his parents and older brother on *The Adventures of Ozzie and Harriet,* is the first TV star to become a rock star. *American Bandstand,* a television program from Philadelphia hosted by Dick Clark, is launched. It promotes a wholesome image of rock and roll as dance music for polite, well-groomed youth. The show popularizes the stroll, one of the first dance steps associated with rock. Rock and roll movies proliferate. *Jailhouse Rock,* Elvis Presley's third film, contains an elaborate and influential dance production sequence for the title song that is a precursor to the rock video.

Rock and roll spreads internationally. Bill Haley and His Comets tour the United Kingdom and Europe, and Little Richard, Gene Vincent, and Eddie Cochran headline a tour of Australia.

Little Richard decides to quit rock and roll and join the ministry.

1958

Rock and roll's first golden age continues, with many classic recordings such as "At the Hop" by Danny and the Juniors and "Johnny B. Goode" by Chuck Berry, but there is a backlash against it.

Doo-Wop is popular. "I Wonder Why" is the first hit for Dion and the Belmonts. "Get a Job" by the Silhouettes and "Little Star" by the Elegants are top singles. The Platters' revivals of old pop songs, such as "Twilight Time" (a hit for the Three Suns in 1944) and "Smoke Gets in Your Eyes" (a hit for Paul Whiteman's orchestra in 1934) represent a mellower side of the vocal group style that is also used for newly composed songs, such as Phil Spector's "To Know Him Is to Love Him" by his group the Teddy Bears.

Rockabilly is still popular, but many of its practitioners find that their most popular songs are the softer pop songs. Elvis Presley's rocking "Hard Headed Woman" is a number one and so is the ballad "Don't," but the latter sells more and stays at the top longer. Similarly, both the Everly Brothers' uptempo "Bird Dog" and the slow "All I Have to Do Is Dream" reach number one, but it is the dreamy one that generates more sales and has more longevity. Other examples are "Poor Little Fool" by Ricky Nelson and

"It's Only Make Believe" by Conway Twitty (who was an unsuccessful rockabilly when he recorded under his own name, Harold Jenkins, at Sun).

Instrumental rock is popular, such as "Tequila" by the Champs.

The Kingston Trio's "Tom Dooley" hits number one and marks the start of a folk revival so huge it is called the Folk Boom. Bob Dylan and many folk rock and psychedelic artists will take part in it early in their careers.

Rock and roll has attracted a young audience, and many songs cater to the sensibilities and concerns of adolescents. The lyrics of several hit songs describe teenagers' conflicts with parents, as in "Summertime Blues" by Eddie Cochran, "Sweet Little Sixteen" by Chuck Berry, and "Yakety Yak" by the Coasters.

Novelty songs do very well. David Seville's "Witch Doctor" features catchy nonsense lyrics and "The Chipmunk Song" has the sped-up voices of Alvin and the Chipmunks. Sheb Wooley scores with "The Purple People Eater." Bobby Darin scores his first hit with "Splish Splash," about a party starting while the protagonist is taking a bath.

16 Magazine, a fan magazine with a huge readership, begins publication.

Elvis Presley is inducted into the army and will serve two years in Germany.

Jerry Lee Lewis' first English tour is aborted after only three shows due to scandal when it is revealed that he is married to his 13-year-old second cousin. The American media shuns him on his return, and it will take years for his career to regain momentum.

Stereophonic records are introduced.

1959

Rock and roll has mellowed. Teen idols such as Frankie Avalon and Paul Anka are popular. Soft vocal groups like the Platters and the Fleetwoods have big hits.

Alan Freed is fired over the issue of payola, the practice of bribing disc jockeys to obtain airplay for records, and Congress soon begins an official investigation.

The most successful rock instrumental is the languorous "Sleep Walk" by Santo and Johnny.

The Drifters' "There Goes My Baby," produced by Jerry Leiber and Mike Stoller, introduces Latin rhythms and symphonic strings to pop music.

Buddy Holly, Ritchie Valens, and the Big Bopper die in a plane crash while on tour.

1960

After his stint in the army, Elvis Presley has a series of hit singles and albums. His image is now less menacing and more mature, and his songs are less rock and roll, like "It's Now or Never," adapted from an old Italian song.

Doo-wop is still popular, as in "Stay" by Maurice Williams and the Zodiacs.

Songs about dances become popular, none more so than "The Twist" by Chubby Checker, which inspires more twist records and new dance crazes.

Detroit's Motown label has its first million-seller with "Shop Around" by the Miracles.

Morbid songs about teenagers dying are popular, such as "Teen Angel" by Mark Dinning.

Novelty songs are popular, including the Hollywood Argyles' "Alley Oop" (about a caveman cartoon character), Larry Verne's "Mr. Custer" (about a cowardly Indian), and Bryan Hyland's "Itsy Bitsy Teenie Weenie Yellow Polka Dot Bikini" (about a child's self-consciousness).

The Shirelles' "Will You Love Me Tomorrow" launches the girl group era.

"Only the Lonely" is Roy Orbison's first major hit.

"Walk—Don't Run" is the Ventures' first and biggest hit. It will influence future surf rock instrumentals and inspire countless people to pick up the guitar.

"Let's Have a Party" by Wanda Jackson is a rockabilly hit, and will be the last until the 1980s revival.

Transistor radios are widely available.

Eddie Cochran dies at 21 in a car accident.

1961

The sound of 1950s rock and roll continues. Doo-wop is still popular, with "Blue Moon" by the Marcels and "The Lion Sleeps Tonight" by the Tokens both topping the charts. "Stand by Me" by Ben E. King is yet another hit written by Leiber and Stoller. Dion, Ricky Nelson, Pat Boone, and Elvis Presley keep having hits.

The folk revival is going strong.

"Running Scared" is Roy Orbison's first number one.

Surf rock music has its first hit with Dick Dale's "Let's Go Tripping."

Motown has its first number one with "Please Mr. Postman" by the Marvelettes.

Del Shannon's "Runaway" assures doubters that rock and roll has not gone soft.

1962

Dance songs are still popular. Chubby Checker's "The Twist," a number-one song from 1960, charts again at number one, the only rock record to do so. "Peppermint Twist" by Joey Dee and the Starlighters also hits number one.

Pop rock is popular, with many songs written at the Brill Building, in New York City, including "Breaking Up Is Hard to Do" by Neil Sedaka.

Girl groups are popular, such as the Shirelles and the Crystals.

The doo-wop sound continues, with Gene Chandler's "Duke of Earl" for example. Doo-wop is updated by the Four Seasons with "Big Girls Don't Cry" and two other number-one hits.

Motown gains popularity with hits by the Contours and Mary Wells.

Surf rock as a vocal style gets underway with the Beach Boys' "Surfin' " and "Surfin' Safari."

1963

Girl groups are popular, with the Chiffons ("He's So Fine"), the Angels ("My Boyfriend's Back"), the Ronettes ("Be My Baby"), and groups led by female singers.

Duos of a male and a female singer are popular: Dale and Grace, Paul and Paula, and Nino Tempo and April Stevens each have a number-one hit.

Surf rock is at its peak, with the Beach Boys having their first big year, Jan and Dean's "Surf City," the Trashmen's "Surfin' Bird," and the Surfaris' "Wipe Out."

Motown has big hits, including the first by Little Stevie Wonder.

The folk revival is strong. "Walk Right In" by the Rooftop Singers is a number-one hit. "Blowin' in the Wind" is a hit for Peter, Paul and Mary, bringing attention to its writer, Bob Dylan, an obscure folk singer at the time.

The FBI investigates "Louie Louie" by the Kingsmen, suspecting obscene lyrics.

Beatlemania begins in Britain.

1964

Beatlemania erupts with the Beatles' arrival in New York. They dominate the singles and album charts and lead the British invasion, which includes the Kinks, the Animals, the Rolling Stones, Manfred Mann, Peter and Gordon, and the Dave Clark Five.

Few American acts hold their own against the British invasion. Exceptions are the Beach Boys, Roy Orbison, and the Four Seasons, who score number-one hits with "I Get Around," "Oh, Pretty Woman," and "Rag Doll," respectively. Girl groups are still strong, such as the Shangri-Las ("Leader of the Pack") and the Dixie Cups ("Chapel of Love"). Teen idol Bobby Vinton has two number-one singles.

Motown has a peak year with hits by the Temptations, Four Tops, and their latest big act, the Supremes. In less than a year, the Supremes will have six number-one hits.

Dances like the watusi, the frug, the monkey, and the funky chicken are popular.

For the first time, albums (in the form of 12-inch vinyl LPs) by rock artists (other than Elvis Presley and Ricky Nelson), sell in great quantities.

Millie Small's "My Boy Lollipop," produced by Chris Blackwell in England, brings Jamaican music to the international pop scene and is a prelude to reggae.

1965

The British invasion has its second great year. The Beatles, the Rolling Stones, the Who, the Yardbirds, Herman's Hermits, Freddie and the Dreamers, the Dave Clark Five, and all the rest are at full force. The Stones' "(I Can't Get No) Satisfaction" is the year's best-selling single.

George Harrison's sitar playing on the Beatles' "Norwegian Wood" is the start of the influence of Indian music on rock.

In response to the British invasion, American garage bands form by the thousands.

The Beach Boys release three albums and all hit the top 10.

Motown is very popular, especially the Supremes and "My Girl" by the Temptations.

Folk rock gets underway with Bob Dylan's shift to electric music and "Mr. Tambourine Man" by the Byrds. Dylan's "Like a Rolling Stone," six minutes long, hits number two, breaking the unwritten rule that pop songs must be shorter than three minutes.

The Righteous Brothers' "You've Lost That Loving Feeling" boosts the popularity of blue-eyed soul (white singers who "sound black").

The foundations of psychedelic rock music—the communities, bands, multimedia shows, and venues—start to form.

Blues rock gains momentum with *Bluesbreakers* by John Mayall with Eric Clapton, and the Paul Butterfield Blues Band.

James Brown pioneers funk with "Papa's Got a Brand New Bag" and "I Got You."

The first rock concert movie, *The T.A.M.I. Show* (the initials stand for "teen-age music international"), filmed in Santa Monica, California, in 1964, is released. Featured performers include rock pioneer Chuck Berry; surf acts the Beach Boys and Jan and Dean; British invasion groups the Rolling Stones, Gerry and the Pacemakers, and Billy J. Kramer and the Dakotas; garage band the Barbarians; teen singer Lesley Gore; Motown acts the Supremes, the Miracles, and Marvin Gaye; and a spectacular finale by James Brown and His Famous Flames.

Tiger Beat, a West Coast competitor of *16 Magazine*, begins publication. Both survive by following the trends.

Alan Freed, the man who popularized the term *rock and roll*, dies at 43.

1966

The Beatles' *"Yesterday"... and Today, Rubber Soul*, and *Revolver* are commercial and artistic triumphs.

After a show in San Francisco, the Beatles retire from public performance.

Folk rock is strong. Simon and Garfunkel's "The Sounds of Silence" hits number one. The Lovin' Spoonful are very popular, with hit albums and singles, including "Summer in the City," "Daydream," and "Did You Ever Have to Make Up Your Mind?" The Mamas and the Papas debut and have the best year of their short career, with *If You Can Believe Your Eyes and Ears,* "California Dreamin' " and "Monday, Monday." Shortly after completing *Blonde on Blonde* (rock's first double album), Bob Dylan has a motorcycle accident and goes into seclusion.

Garage rock is at its peak. Of the 118 tracks on the *Nuggets* four-CD box set, the definitive anthology of garage music, 50 of them come from 1966, including "Talk Talk" by the Music Machine, "Little Girl" by the Syndicate of Sound, and songs by the Standells, Love, the Seeds, and the Shadows Of Knight. Several songs are forerunners of psychedelic music, such as "Psychotic Reaction" by the Count Five, "(We Ain't Got) Nothin' Yet" by the Blues Magoos, and "I Had Too Much to Dream (Last Night)" by the Electric Prunes.

Psychedelic rock emerges. "Eight Miles High" by the Byrds is the first hit in the style. Donovan has one of the biggest years of his career with "Sunshine Superman" and "Mellow Yellow," both of which have psychedelic undertones.

The Beach Boys are at their commercial and artistic peak, with the groundbreaking "Good Vibrations" and the celebrated *Pet Sounds.*

Blue-eyed soul is popular, with the Righteous Brothers, Mitch Ryder and the Detroit Wheels, the Rascals, and others.

The power trio format is launched by Cream and the Jimi Hendrix Experience.

The Monkees television show debuts in the fall and is a sensation. Both "Last Train to Clarksville" and "I'm a Believer" hit number one.

Hullabaloo magazine begins publication, changing its name to *Circus* in 1969. It attracts some top writers and follows the trends. Starting in the 1980s *Circus* will concentrate on heavy metal and hard rock.

Crawdaddy!, a serious magazine of rock and roll and contemporary radical viewpoints, begins publication in New York City. It will fold in 1979.

1967

Social and political strife is expressed in demonstrations against the war in Vietnam and in race riots in many big cities.

The Beatles release the immortal *Sgt. Pepper's Lonely Hearts Club Band,* as well as "Penny Lane," "Strawberry Fields Forever," "All You Need Is Love," and "Hello Goodbye."

Many major acts release their first albums, such as the Grateful Dead, the Doors, the Buffalo Springfield, the Jimi Hendrix Experience, Big Brother and the Holding Company (with Janis Joplin), the Mothers of Invention (led by Frank Zappa), the Velvet Underground, and Pink Floyd.

San Francisco's Summer of Love is preceded by the "Human Be-In," a musical gathering of hippies, poets, Hells Angels, and various others.

The Monterey Pop Festival in California is the first important rock festival. It makes stars out of Janis Joplin, Jimi Hendrix, and the Who.

Psychedelic music is at its peak. The Jefferson Airplane release *Surrealistic Pillow* and *After Bathing at Baxter's* and have their biggest hits: "Somebody to Love" and "White Rabbit." "Light My Fire" by the Doors, "Incense and Peppermints" by the Strawberry Alarm Clock, and "Green Tambourine" by the Lemon Pipers all go to number one. The Rolling Stones release *Their Satanic Majesties Request.* Cream releases *Disraeli Gears* with "Sunshine of Your Love."

The Monkees have their peak year. Of the seven albums that make number-one in 1967, three are theirs, including *More of the Monkees,* the year's best-selling album.

"Respect" is a number-one hit for Aretha Franklin, helping to make her the top singer in soul music.

Eight-track recording becomes standard.

Ralph J. Gleason and Jann Wenner start *Rolling Stone* magazine in San Francisco, covering music and youth culture and attracting some of the most prestigious writers and photographers in the field.

1968

Martin Luther King Jr. and Robert Kennedy are assassinated. There are numerous race riots, demonstrations, conflicts, and clashes in the United States and internationally. Students riot in Paris. Some people become more militant, others withdraw.

"Hey Jude" is the Beatles' biggest single ever, and *Magical Mystery Tour* and *The Beatles* (the so-called *White Album*) both hit number one.

Hard rock is popular. Much of it has a bluesy, psychedelic edge. *Electric Ladyland* by the Jimi Hendrix Experience, *Wheels of Fire* by Cream (who will disband at the end of the year), *Waiting for the Sun* by the Doors, and *Cheap Thrills* by Big Brother and the Holding Company are all number-one albums. The Rolling Stones solidify their style with "Jumpin' Jack Flash." Also important are the Who, Vanilla Fudge, Deep Purple, Iron Butterfly (who popularize the drum solo), Steppenwolf, and Blue Cheer.

Psychedelic music is very vibrant, with highlights including the Jefferson Airplane's *Crown of Creation* and the Grateful Dead's *Anthem of the Sun,* the first album to blend together live and studio tracks.

Bubblegum music, a style of blatantly commercial pop rock aimed at adolescents and with roots in garage music, is popular on AM radio. Bubblegum is fabricated by writing and production teams and studio singers and musicians. "Simon Says" and "1, 2, 3 Red Light" by the 1910 Fruitgum Company, and "Yummy, Yummy, Yummy" and "Chewy Chewy" by the Ohio Express are among the style's biggest hits. Bubblegum will influence the Ramones, the Cars, Talking Heads, and Blondie.

FM radio becomes an outlet for underground music. An alternative to commercial AM radio, FM stations play longer and more controversial material in a wide range of styles.

Days of Future Passed by the Moody Blues with the London Festival Orchestra is a forerunner of progressive rock.

Country rock emerges with the International Submarine Band led by Gram Parsons, and picks up momentum with the Byrds' *Sweetheart of the Rodeo.*

The singer-songwriter style develops with Joni Mitchell's debut album and Van Morrison's multifaceted *Astral Weeks.* Simon and Garfunkel's *Bookends* and the soundtrack of *The Graduate* (which features them) both hit number one.

Roots rock emerges with the Band and Creedence Clearwater Revival.

After years of avoiding public performance and starring in numerous movies of questionable merit, Elvis Presley makes a dramatic comeback with a television special that reunites him with his 1950s backup musicians.

Creem magazine begins publication in Detroit. It will feature some of the top rock critics, including Lester Bangs, Greil Marcus, Dave Marsh, Richard Meltzer, Nick Tosches, and Robert Christgau (the first to rate records from A to F). It will fold in 1994.

1969

Rock predominates and is evolving in every direction. Santana makes its recording debut and David Bowie's "Space Oddity" is released.

Psychedelic rock is evolving with the Jefferson Airplane's *Volunteers* and *Bless Its Pointed Little Head.* The Grateful Dead use 16-track equipment to record *Aoxomoxoa* and *Live/Dead;* the latter is the first live album to use it.

The top-selling album of the year is the original cast recording of *Hair,* the first rock musical.

Blues rock is developing. The Allman Brothers Band's first album is released. Fleetwood Mac records with blues veterans in Chicago at the Chess studios.

Hard rock is developing. Led Zeppelin's first two albums are released to immediate popular acclaim. Steppenwolf's *Monster* has a political message.

Roots rock is developing, with the Band's celebrated untitled second album and Creedence Clearwater Revival's *Green River.*

The Beatles make their last recordings together. *Abbey Road* is released.

Progressive rock gets underway with King Crimson's debut *In The Court of the Crimson King.*

Tommy by the Who is the first commercially successful rock opera.

Captain Beefheart's *Trout Mask Replica* is a pinnacle of idiosyncratic rock creativity.

Rock festivals Woodstock and Altamont are in the news.

The rock revival movement gets underway with events such as the Toronto Rock 'n' Roll Revival concert.

The film *Easy Rider* and its rock soundtrack make a big impression.

FM radio continues to grow, but with stations specializing in specific, limited formats, it has the effect of dividing the audience for popular music into niches, unlike AM radio's all-encompassing approach.

Brian Jones of the Rolling Stones drowns under mysterious circumstances, at age 27.

1970

The Beatles break up. *Let It Be* is their last album and "The Long and Winding Road" their last number-one hit. Paul McCartney releases his first solo album, *McCartney*, and George Harrison releases the successful triple album *All Things Must Pass* with "My Sweet Lord."

Classic rock is strong, with Derek and the Dominos' *Layla*, Led Zeppelin's *III*, Santana's *Abraxas*, Creedence Clearwater Revival's *Cosmo's Factory*, the Who's *Live at Leeds*, the *Woodstock* soundtrack, the Guess Who's "American Woman," the Shocking Blue's "Venus," and Three Dog Night's "Mama Told Me (Not to Come)."

Singer-songwriters become very popular with James Taylor's "Fire and Rain," Joni Mitchell's "Big Yellow Taxi," Neil Young's *After the Gold Rush*, Crosby, Stills, Nash and Young's *Déjà Vu*, and Simon and Garfunkel's *Bridge over Troubled Water*.

Motown, R&B, funk, and commercial pop ballads are popular.

Psychedelic music wanes; many bands have broken up. The Grateful Dead, with *Workingman's Dead* and *American Beauty*, take a more earthy, acoustic approach though they still include psychedelic music in their live shows.

Jazz rock fusion gets underway with *Bitches Brew* by Miles Davis.

Rock festivals are common.

Cassettes become popular.

Guitar Player magazine debuts, helping to start the rock music education industry.

Jimi Hendrix and Janis Joplin both die of drug overdoses at age 27.

1971

Singer-songwriters are popular, for example Joni Mitchell *(Blue)*, Carole King (*Tapestry*), Melanie, James Taylor, and Rod Stewart ("Maggie May").

The late Janis Joplin's *Pearl* includes "Me and Bobby McGee."

Progressive rock is popular.

Classic rock is popular, with the Allman Brothers Band's *At Fillmore East*, the Rolling Stones *Sticky Fingers* (with "Brown Sugar"), Santana *III*, Led Zeppelin *IV* (with "Stairway to Heaven"), the Who's *Who's Next*, Rod Stewart's *Every Picture Tells a Story*, and Three Dog Night's *Golden Biscuits* (a greatest hits set) and *Harmony*.

Motown is winding down, except for a few thriving solo careers.

One of the first rock concerts for charity is George Harrison's Concert for Bangladesh, at New York's Madison Square Garden. Ravi Shankar, Ringo Starr, Bob Dylan, Eric Clapton, and many others perform. The concert also results in a successful triple album and film.

Heavy metal emerges with Black Sabbath's *Paranoid*.

Jim Morrison of the Doors dies at age 27 of mysterious causes; Duane Allman of the Allman Brothers Band dies at age 24 in a motorcycle crash.

1972

Classic rock is popular, such as Deep Purple's "Smoke on the Water," the Allman Brothers Band's *Eat a Peach*, the Grateful Dead's *Europe '72*, the Band's *Rock of Ages*, the Faces' (with Rod Stewart) *A Nod Is as Good as a Wink . . . To a Blind Horse*, the Rolling Stones' *Exile on Main Street*, Jethro Tull's *Thick as a Brick*, Chicago *V*, and the Moody Blues' *Seventh Sojourn*.

Grand Funk Railroad breaks the Beatles' record by selling out New York's Shea Stadium in three days. The ticket gross is more than $300,000.

Progressive rock is popular, with *Close to the Edge* by Yes.

Singer-songwriters are popular, such as Don McLean ("American Pie"), Neil Young ("Heart of Gold" and *Harvest*), Cat Stevens (*Catch Bull at Four*), Carole King, and Roberta Flack.

Glam rock is popular, with David Bowie's *The Rise and Fall of Ziggy Stardust and the Spiders from Mars,* Mott the Hoople's "All the Young Dudes," and Lou Reed's *Transformer* (with "Walk on the Wild Side").

Chuck Berry's "My-Ding-A-Ling" is his only number-one hit.

Rick Nelson's "Garden Party" views the rock revival with some distaste.

Nuggets: Original Artyfacts from the First Psychedelic Era, a double album anthology of mid-1960s garage band singles, is released. It will inspire punk and revivals of garage.

Berry Oakley of the Allman Brothers Band dies at age 24 in a motorcycle crash.

1973

Classic rock is strong, with the Rolling Stones, the Allman Brothers (*Brothers and Sisters*), Led Zeppelin (*Houses of the Holy*), the Who (*Quadrophenia*), Steely Dan (*Can't Buy a Thrill*), the Edgar Winter Group ("Frankenstein"), the Doobie Brothers ("Long Train Runnin'" and "China Grove"), and Grand Funk ("We're an American Band"). Three of the Beatles (Paul McCartney, Ringo Starr, and George Harrison) have solo hits.

Singer-songwriters are popular (Jim Croce, Roberta Flack, Carly Simon).

Progressive rock is popular, with Jethro Tull, Electric Light Orchestra's "Roll over Beethoven," and Pink Floyd's *Dark Side of the Moon,* which will stay on the *Billboard* album charts for 741 weeks.

Glam rock gets more macabre with Alice Cooper (*Billion Dollar Babies*).

While George Harrison and Paul McCartney are having great solo success, *The Beatles/1967–1970,* a double album, goes to number one.

Elvis Presley has his last number-one album while he is alive, *Aloha from Hawaii via Satellite,* though he will continue having chart success.

Funk, R&B, and country ballads are popular.

Reggae spreads with *The Harder They Come* soundtrack, featuring Jimmy Cliff, the first reggae album to be commercially successful outside of Jamaica, and the Wailers' *Catch a Fire* (their first international recording).

The largest rock festival of all is held in Watkins Glen, New York, with a lineup of only three bands: the Band, the Grateful Dead, and the Allman Brothers Band. An estimated 600,000 people attend.

The film *American Graffiti* and its soundtrack boost the rock revival movement. Elton John acknowledges the trend with the nostalgic "Crocodile Rock."

Elton John's keyboard-based pop rock is popular. His *Don't Shoot Me I'm Only the Piano Player* and *Goodbye Yellow Brick Road* are number-one albums. Between 1972 and 1975, he will see five additional albums hit number one.

Bruce Springsteen's first two albums are released.

Gram Parsons, formerly of the Byrds and the Flying Burrito Brothers dies at 26 of a drug overdose; Clarence White of the Byrds dies at 29, hit by a car; Rod "Pig Pen" McKernan of the Grateful Dead dies at 27 of a liver ailment; and Bobby Darin dies at 37 of heart failure.

1974

Classic rock is strong, with the Steve Miller Band ("The Joker"), Wings led by Paul McCartney, ("Band on the Run"), John Lennon, Eric Clapton (*461 Ocean Boulevard*), the Rolling Stones (*It's Only Rock and Roll*), Bad Company, and Bachman-Turner Overdrive.

Looking to the past is successful for Ringo Starr, who remakes Johnny Burnette's "You're 16," and Grand Funk, who remake Little Eva's "The Loco-Motion." The Beach Boys' *Endless Summer,* a compilation of earlier material, hits number one.

Singer-songwriters are popular and creating some of their best work, such as Jackson Browne's *Late for the Sky* and Joni Mitchell's *Court and Spark,* though John Denver's hits drain most of the style's emotional depth.

Eric Clapton's version of "I Shot the Sheriff" brings mainstream attention to reggae and the song's composer, Bob Marley.

Disco appears with a few initial hits.

The Ramones and other punk and new wave groups start performing at New York's CBGB.

Trouser Press magazine, covering alternative music, begins publication in New York City. It reports on the British scene and new wave and punk and is the first rock magazine with a section for record collectors. It will cease publication in 1984, but a series of record guidebooks will later be published. Later still, their contents and many updates and additions will be available online at www.trouserpress.com.

Cass Elliot of the Mamas and the Papas dies at 32 of a heart attack.

1975

The year's best-selling records are a mix of singer-songwriters (Janis Ian, John Denver, Paul Simon), classic rock (Led Zeppelin, Wings, the Eagles, Jefferson Starship, Fleetwood Mac, Pink Floyd, Chicago), pop rock (Linda Ronstadt, Elton John, Olivia Newton-John), folk rock (Bob Dylan, America), and funk (Average White Band, Ohio Players, the Isley Brothers, and Earth, Wind, and Fire).

John Lennon's *Rock 'n' Roll,* a set of 1950s songs, is released. He assists David Bowie by coauthoring and playing guitar on "Fame," and Elton John by singing backup on his remake of the Beatles' "Lucy in the Sky with Diamonds." Elton John assists Neil Sedaka's comeback by singing backup on "Bad Blood."

Funk is popular and contributes to the disco style.

Bob Dylan releases *Blood on the Tracks,* one of his most acclaimed records, and takes his Rolling Thunder Revue on tour.

Led Zeppelin breaks box office records. They have six albums on the U.S. charts.

Bruce Springsteen hits the mainstream with *Born to Run* and makes the front cover of both *Time* and *Newsweek* magazines in the same week, unprecedented for a rock artist.

"Bohemian Rhapsody" is Queen's first million-selling single.

Toys in the Attic is the commercial breakthrough for Aerosmith.

Alive! is the commercial breakthrough for KISS.

Progressive rock has its last big year.

Punk gets underway in the United Kingdom; the Sex Pistols play their first gig.

Goldmine, the authoritative magazine for record collectors, begins publication. It features extensive articles on a wide range of collectible artists.

1976

Classic rock is popular. Artists with the year's number-one albums and singles include the Eagles,

Wings, Led Zeppelin, the Rolling Stones, Fleetwood Mac, Rod Stewart, Paul Simon, and Peter Frampton, with *Frampton Comes Alive!*

The Four Seasons have a comeback hit with "December, 1963 (Oh, What a Night)," their first number one since 1964. John Sebastian, formerly of the Lovin' Spoonful, sees his career boosted with "Welcome Back," the theme from *Welcome Back, Kotter,* a popular TV show.

The Band throws a farewell party called the Last Waltz. Director Martin Scorsese films the concert and interviews with the Band, and will release the documentary *The Last Waltz* in 1978.

Disco gains momentum.

Punk is on the rise. The first Ramones album is released and they tour in Britain. The Sex Pistols' controversial "Anarchy in the UK" is released.

Reggae is popular internationally. *Rastaman Vibration* is Bob Marley and the Wailers' top-selling album in America while Marley is alive.

Musician, a *Billboard* publication, begins. With intelligent and well-written articles and in-depth interviews, it covers rock, jazz, rap, and other genres.

1977

Classic rock is at a peak with Fleetwood Mac's *Rumours,* Wings' *Wings over America,* the Eagles' *Hotel California,* and Electric Light Orchestra's *Out of the Blue.* At the top of the singles chart are Manfred Mann's Earth Band and the rock and soul of Hall and Oates.

Grateful Dead live performances reach a zenith, according to a majority of Deadhead connoisseurs who trade live tapes.

Disco is very popular. Donna Summer's "I Feel Love" shows the direction for electronic dance music.

Punk is a phenomenon, with the Sex Pistols' "God Save the Queen" and *Never Mind the Bollocks, Here's the Sex Pistols.* Elvis Costello's first album, *My Aim Is True,* shows that punk's energy is compatible with a variety of styles. Talking Heads' *77* shows an arty side of punk.

Bob Marley and the Wailers release the acclaimed *Exodus.*

Vinyl sales peak in the United States.

Elvis Presley dies at 42. Millions grieve.

1978

Heavy metal moves into the mainstream. Van Halen's untitled debut album makes the top 20. Eddie Van Halen's guitar solo in "Eruption" inspires other players, popularizes the tapping technique, and adds a classical influence to hard rock.

Disco is at a peak, as shown by the success of the film *Saturday Night Fever.* Its soundtrack, featuring the Bee Gees, is the year's top album. Even the Rolling Stones join in with "Miss You."

New wave emerges. Blondie's *Parallel Lines* is their commercial breakthrough.

The movie *The Buddy Holly Story* invigorates the rock revival movement.

Digital synthesizers are introduced, to replace voltage-controlled (analog) synthesizers.

The first mass-marketed sequencer, the Roland MC-4, is introduced.

Keith Moon of the Who dies at 31 after overdosing on a prescription drug for alcohol withdrawal.

1979

Classic rock is popular. *The Long Run* by the Eagles is the year's top album. Other number-one albums are by the Doobie Brothers, Rod Stewart, Supertramp, and Led Zeppelin.

New wave is popular. "Heart of Glass" is Blondie's first number one.

Disco is very popular.

The top single of the year is power pop: "My Sharona" by the Knack.

A revival of ska, a musical style predating reggae, is popular in Britain.

The Clash's *London Calling* expands punk's musical vocabulary.

Goth rock emerges out of punk.

Rap emerges with the Sugarhill Gang's "Rapper's Delight."

Ry Cooder's *Bop Till You Drop* is the first digitally recorded rock album.

Vinyl sales decline worldwide as the popularity of cassettes increases.

Sony launches the Walkman portable cassette player.

Sex Pistols bassist Sid Vicious dies at 21 of a heroin overdose.

1980

The year's top album is Pink Floyd's *The Wall*, released in late 1979, a pinnacle of rock concept albums. Other top rock albums are by Bob Seger, Billy Joel, Jackson Browne, Queen, the Rolling Stones, the Bee Gees, and Bruce Springsteen (*The River*, his first number one).

John Lennon releases "Just Like (Starting Over)," his first record in five years, and *Double Fantasy* (with Yoko Ono). Days after the album's release, Lennon, at age 40, is murdered by an obsessed fan. The world mourns.

Punk, new wave, and disco are popular.

The Talking Heads' *Remain in Light* is a pioneering work in the development of worldbeat music.

The Sony Walkman sells 5 million units in the United States.

Led Zeppelin disbands after drummer John Bonham dies at 33 after a drinking binge.

Bon Scott of AC/DC dies at 25, reportedly after an all-night drinking binge.

1981

Classic rock dominates the charts. All of the number-one albums are by rock acts: REO Speedwagon, Styx, Journey, Pat Benatar, Kim Carnes, Foreigner, AC/DC, the Rolling Stones, Stevie Nicks, and the Moody Blues.

Blondie's new wave sound expands to include reggae and rap.

MTV debuts.

Academic acceptance of popular music grows with the formation of the International Association for the Study of Popular Music (IASPM) and the debut issue of *Popular Music,* an academic journal published by Cambridge University Press.

Simon and Garfunkel reunite for a live concert in New York's Central Park and draw an audience of 400,000 to 500,000.

Bill Haley dies at 55 of a heart attack; Bob Marley dies at 36 of cancer.

1982

New wave is popular. Men at Work's *Business As Usual* is the year's top album, and *Beauty and the Beat* by the Go-Go's is also a number one. The Human League and Toni Basil have top singles.

Mainstream rock is well represented with top albums by the J. Geils Band, Asia, John Mellencamp (as John Cougar), Paul McCartney (*Tug of War*), and Fleetwood Mac (*Mirage*). The best-selling single of the year is Joan Jett's "I Love Rock 'n' Roll."

Other top singles are by Survivor, Chicago, the Steve Miller Band, and Hall and Oates.

The popularity of the Stray Cats' *Built for Speed* and "Rock This Town" boost the rockabilly revival.

Rock critic Lester Bangs dies at 33 of an overdose of painkillers.

1983

New wave is popular. Eurythmics' "Sweet Dreams (Are Made of This)," Men At Work's "Down Under," and the Police's "Every Breath You Take" and their album *Synchronicity* all hit number one.

Heavy metal is popular, for example Quiet Riot's *Metal Health*, Mötley Crüe's *Shout at the Devil*, and Def Leppard's *Pyromania*. A variant called speed metal is introduced by Metallica on *Kill 'Em All*.

David Bowie has a number-one hit with "Let's Dance," his biggest since 1975.

Alternative rock is emerging. R.E.M.'s *Murmur* is a defining record of the style.

The year's top album by far is Michael Jackson's *Thriller*. It will break sales records and make him a global icon. Eddie Van Halen's guitar solo on "Beat It" gives Jackson wider appeal, as does his duet with Paul McCartney on the single "Say Say Say."

The Kinks' career gets a boost with "Come Dancing," their first top-10 hit in more than a decade.

While cassettes sell more than vinyl LPs worldwide, the CD format begins to sell.

Developed by manufacturers working together, MIDI (Musical Instrument Digital Interface), which connects musical instruments to computers, is introduced.

Yamaha's DX-7 synthesizer is introduced, the first to sell in quantity (180,000 units).

Dennis Wilson, drummer of the Beach Boys, drowns at 39.

1984

Mainstream rock predominates, with Van Halen ("Jump"), Kenny Loggins ("Footloose"), Hall and Oates, Phil Collins, and Bruce Springsteen's *Born in the U.S.A.* (his biggest album to date).

New wave is popular, with Culture Club, Duran Duran, the Cars, Cyndi Lauper ("Girls Just Want to Have Fun"), and Wham! all having hits.

The movie soundtrack *Purple Rain* by Prince is the year's top album. It includes "When Doves Cry."

"Like A Virgin" is Madonna's first number-one hit.

Yes, re-formed the year before, have a resurgence with "Owner of a Lonely Heart," their only number-one hit and their first charting single since 1972.

The reunited Everly Brothers have a comeback hit with a song written by Paul McCartney, "On the Wings of a Nightingale."

The movie *This Is Spinal Tap* parodies heavy metal.

1985

Mainstream rock predominates. The top artists are Bryan Adams, Phil Collins, Heart, REO Speedwagon, Huey Lewis and the News, Mr. Mister, Starship, and Foreigner. Dire Straits' *Brothers in Arms* (with "Money for Nothing," a top song with a popular video) helps boost the popularity of the CD format.

New wave is popular, with Wham!, Tears For Fears, Duran Duran, a-ha, and Simple Minds having number-one songs, albums, or both. ZZ Top's boogie rock shows some new wave influence on "Sleeping Bag."

Alternative rock is popular.

John Fogerty has success with his roots rock comeback, *Centerfield.*

The Live Aid charity concert raises funds for African famine relief and starts a trend for charity festivals and records.

Spin magazine begins publication. Similar to *Rolling Stone,* it covers rock and political and social issues with impressive contributors.

Rick Nelson dies at 45 with members of his band in a plane crash; Big Joe Turner dies of natural causes at 74.

1986

Mainstream rock predominates. Starship, Heart, Robert Palmer, Huey Lewis and the News, Boston, Van Halen, and Bon Jovi are among those with number-one songs, albums, or both.

New wave continues. The Human League, the Pet Shop Boys, Cyndi Lauper, and the Bangles all have number-one hits.

Bruce Springsteen and the E Street Band's *Live 1975–85* debuts at number one.

The Rock and Roll Hall of Fame begins inductions.

Graceland by Paul Simon is a landmark in worldbeat, incorporating African music into folk and rock.

Richard Manuel of the Band dies at 43 by suicide.

1987

Alternative rock is popular, with *Document* by R.E.M. and *The Joshua Tree* by U2. U2 have two number-one singles.

Bruce Springsteen's *Tunnel of Love* is a number-one album.

Classic rock is represented by top singles from Heart, Bon Jovi, Huey Lewis and the News, Starship,

Bob Seger, Whitesnake, and Billy Idol. Aerosmith's *Permanent Vacation* returns them to the big time.

The rock revival has a strong year, with several oldies featured on the *Dirty Dancing* soundtrack, 1987's best-selling album. *La Bamba,* a movie about Ritchie Valens, and a number-one hit version of the title song by Los Lobos, puts Valens' memory back in public consciousness. Chuck Berry's autobiography and the documentary film *Chuck Berry: Hail! Hail! Rock 'n' Roll* are released.

1988

Heavy metal is strong. Van Halen, Def Leppard, and Guns n' Roses all have number-one albums. Other top albums are by Bon Jovi and U2 (*Rattle and Hum*).

Worldwide CD sales overtake those of vinyl LPs.

The jam band scene gets a boost: Phish release their first album and start touring.

The Pixies' *Surfer Rosa* is a pinnacle of alternative music.

Grunge emerges in Seattle.

The Beach Boys' "Kokomo" is their first number-one hit in more than 20 years.

George Harrison's "Got My Mind Set on You" is his first number-one hit since 1973, and he and the other members of the Traveling Wilburys release their debut.

Roy Orbison dies at 52 of a heart attack.

1989

Mötley Crüe, Richard Marx, and Fine Young Cannibals have top albums.

The Rolling Stones' *Steel Wheels* is released.

The Grateful Dead release the live *Dylan and the Dead,* and their final studio album, *Built to Last.*

Buddy, a musical about Buddy Holly, opens in London.

The Jefferson Airplane reunites.

The Allman Brothers Band reforms.

1990

Pop rock with a singer-songwriter sensibility is popular, such as Phil Collins' . . . *But Seriously*, Bonnie Raitt's *Nick of Time*, and Sinéad O'Connor's *I Do Not Want What I Haven't Got*, all number-one albums. The success story of the year, however, is a rap album by M.C. Hammer. Of the number-one singles, Alannah Myles and Roxette are rock representatives amongst the pop ballads, rap, and R&B.

Tom Fogerty of Creedence Clearwater Revival dies at 48 of AIDS, believed to have been transmitted via blood transfusions.

1991

Grunge hits the mainstream with Nirvana's *Nevermind* and "Smells Like Teen Spirit," Pearl Jam's debut, *Ten,* and the film *Singles.* Among the number-one albums, alternative is present with R.E.M.'s *Out of Time* and U2's *Achtung Baby.* Heavy metal is prominent with albums by Skid Row, Van Halen, Metallica (the "black album"), and Guns n' Roses. However, the biggest album of the year, by far, is country, *Ropin' the Wind* by Garth Brooks. The only rock among the pop and R&B in the list of number-one singles is Roxette's pop rock "Joyride" and a Bryan Adams ballad.

The first Lollapalooza festival is held. It will become an important display of alternative rock.

Oliver Stone's movie *The Doors* brings new interest in the band.

Freddie Mercury of Queen dies at 45 of AIDS; Gene Clark of the Byrds dies at 46 of natural causes.

1992

Nirvana's *Nevermind* continues to sell in great quantities. Classic rock makes up much of the *Wayne's World* soundtrack. Heavy metal is represented by Def Leppard (*Adrenalize*), and southern rock by the Black Crowes (*The Southern Harmony and Musical Companion*). All of these albums hit number one.

Rage Against the Machine's first album fuses funk, rap, and heavy metal.

The mp3 format is invented to store music in computers.

1993

Among the number-one albums are grunge (Nirvana's *In Utero* and Pearl Jam's *Vs.*), classic rock (Meat Loaf, Aerosmith), alternative (U2's *Zooropa*), new wave (Depeche Mode), and pop rock (Billy Joel's *River of Dreams*). Eric Clapton's acoustic *Unplugged* album, with blues classics, new songs, and a reworked "Layla," is a surprise success.

Frank Zappa dies at 52 of cancer; Michael Clarke of the Byrds dies at 49 of liver failure.

1994

Grunge remains popular: Alice in Chains, Soundgarden, Stone Temple Pilots, Nirvana, and Pearl Jam all have number-one albums, and their influence is apparent on R.E.M.'s *Monster.* Classic rock veterans the Eagles reunite (*Hell Freezes Over*) and Pink Floyd returns to the top with *Division Bell.* Eric Clapton pays homage to his blues roots (*From the Cradle*). Bonnie Raitt's mix of blues, funk, and singer-songwriter traditions gives her another million seller in *Longing in Their Hearts.*

Pop punk breaks into the mainstream, with the Offspring, and Green Day (*Dookie*), among others.

The Vans Warped Tour, an annual punk festival, begins.

The soundtrack to *Pulp Fiction* inspires a revival of surf music.

Some 100 million personal stereos, like the Sony Walkman, have been sold worldwide to date.

CDs are outselling cassettes.

Paul McCartney is knighted, becoming Sir Paul McCartney.

Kurt Cobain of Nirvana dies at 27 by suicide.

1995

The number-one albums of the year show that grunge is popular, with the presence of the Smashing Pumpkins and Alice in Chains; that fame endures for the Beatles (with *Anthology I*) and Bruce Springsteen (*Greatest Hits*); and that Pink Floyd's latest is welcome (*Pulse*). The year's top album is Alanis Morissette's *Jagged Little Pill*, which has some of the self-absorption of the singer-songwriters, the emotional intensity of punk, and the sound of hard rock.

Britpop dominates the British scene and spills over to North America. Notables include Oasis, Elastica, and Blur.

Rock and roll officially becomes history. The Rock and Roll Hall of Fame and Museum opens in Cleveland, and two 10-part documentaries air on television: *Rock 'n' Roll* on PBS, and *History of Rock 'n' Roll*, produced by Time-Life, in syndication.

Jerry Garcia dies at 53 of a heart attack; the Grateful Dead disband.

1996

The Beatles' *Anthology* project continues to be successful with volumes two and three both hitting number one. The other number-one albums show

that rock is quite vibrant. Grunge is still popular, with archival recordings of Nirvana, *From the Muddy Banks of the Wishkah*, and Pearl Jam's *No Code*, as is heavy metal, with Metallica's *Load* and a greatest hits album by Van Halen. Rage Against the Machine, Hootie and the Blowfish, Bush, and Counting Crows also hit number one. No Doubt's ska rock *Tragic Kingdom* is the top-selling album of the year.

Jam bands are popular. *Crash* by the Dave Matthews Band is released and will be their biggest seller to date.

The original lineup of KISS reunites and returns to wearing makeup.

The surviving Sex Pistols reunite with original bassist Glen Matlock for the Filthy Lucre tour.

The DVD is introduced in Japan.

1997

The year's number-one albums are a mix of rock, country, rap, R&B, pop, and soundtracks. The two top albums are by the Spice Girls, a British pop vocal group assembled by a producer, and Garth Brooks, a country superstar. Rock veterans are well represented, with Fleetwood Mac's reunion *The Dance*, U2's *Pop*, Aerosmith's *Nine Lives*, and Metallica's *Reload*. Newer rock is represented by Live. The *Private Parts* soundtrack is loaded with old and new rock.

Blondie reunites.

Radiohead's *OK Computer* makes most critics' best-of-the-year lists.

1998

Most of the number-one albums are pop, rap, R&B, or country, but rock makes up much of the *City of Angels* soundtrack, and Korn, the controversial Marilyn Manson, and Alanis Morissette represent current rock. The *Titanic* soundtrack, featuring pop icon Celine Dion, is the year's top album. Among the top singles is Aerosmith's ballad "I Don't Want to Miss a Thing" and the Goo Goo Dolls' "Iris."

Portable mp3 devices are introduced.

1999

Pop, rap, R&B, and country are popular, but the top album of the year is Santana's *Supernatural* and the top single is Santana's "Smooth," featuring the vocals of Rob Thomas of Matchbox Twenty. Among artists with number-one albums, the continued presence of rock is seen in the hard rock of Rage Against the Machine and Creed, and rock hybrids: the techno rock of Korn, the industrial rock of Nine Inch Nails, and the hard rock and hip-hop mix of Limp Bizkit. Among the number-one singles is Cher's comeback "Believe."

Shawn Fanning founds the Napster online music service.

Rick Danko of the Band dies of unknown causes at 56.

2000

Hip-hop, R&B, and pop artists (Madonna, Britney Spears, Christina Aguilera) have most of the number-one hits. The Beatles' *1*, a collection of their number-one songs, is tied with albums by vocal group *NSYNC and rapper Eminem for the position of top album of the year. The only current artists with a number-one album and a strong connection to rock traditions are Radiohead (with *Kid A*) and Limp Bizkit. Rock artists with number-one singles are Creed, Matchbox Twenty, and Santana.

Napster is launched. It is a file-sharing Web site that allows users to exchange songs in the mp3 format for free. An estimated 100 million users take advantage of it.

2001

The year's 23 number-one albums are mostly by R&B, rap, and pop artists, though rock is represented by Dave Matthews Band (*Everyday*), Staind, Tool, and Blink 182. Of the number-one singles, only Nickelback's is rock.

Napster's popularity peaks while sales of CDs and other recording formats decline.

John Phillips of the Mamas and the Papas dies at 65 of heart failure; Joey Ramone dies at 49 of cancer.

2002

Rap and R&B are the most popular types of music.

A new version of garage rock and a new form of country, called alternative country is popular. Breaking into the mainstream, are such artists as the Vines, the Strokes, the White Stripes, and the Hives (garage), and Wilco and Ryan Adams (alt-country).

CD sales decline nearly 10 percent.

Dee Dee Ramone of the Ramones dies at 49 of a drug overdose; Joe Strummer of the Clash dies at 50 of a heart attack; John Entwistle of the Who dies at 57 of a drug overdose.

The Rolling Stones begin their 40th anniversary tour. It lasts over a year and takes them to the United States, Canada, Australia, the Far East, and Europe.

2003

Though rap and R&B are the most popular kinds of music, rock is vibrant. Metallica's *St. Anger* debuts at number one in 30 countries.

The Rolling Stones interrupt the European leg of their ongoing 40th anniversary tour to headline an 11-hour concert in Toronto, Ontario, in front of 500,000 people, their largest audience to date. The bill also includes AC/DC, Rush, the Guess Who, the

Isley Brothers, and Sam Roberts. The event, dubbed SARSstock, is intended to give Toronto a boost after an outbreak of the disease SARS had tarnished the city's reputation and affected its economy.

David Bowie previews *Reality,* his 26th album, with a live performance and a question and answer session broadcast into movie theatres by satellite.

Apple introduces iTunes, an online music service, which will sell 25 million song files by year's end.

Sam Phillips, the man who launched Elvis Presley's career, dies at 80 of respiratory failure; Noel Redding, bassist of the Jimi Hendrix Experience, dies at 57 of natural causes.

2004

Rap and R&B are the most popular kinds of music.

The Darkness, from England, are received rapturously while touring internationally in support of *Permission to Land.* Their sound updates the hard rock music and flamboyant stage posturing of Thin Lizzy, Van Halen, and Queen.

Evanescence continue to tour in support of their first album.

Veterans on tour include the Doors of the 21st Century, Deep Purple, the Moody Blues, Aerosmith, Yes, David Byrne (formerly of Talking Heads), Cyndi Lauper, Slayer, Metallica, the Beach Boys, Creedence Clearwater Revisited, Bobby Vee, rockabilly queen Wanda Jackson, Shirley Alston Reeves of the Shirelles, the Crickets, and John Kay of Steppenwolf.

The Vans Warped Tour, often referred to as "punk rock summer camp," has its 10th summer; 125 bands take part, with about 50 performing at each stop.

The documentary *Metallica: Some Kind of Monster* shows the band's near-breakup and renewal.

Tribute shows are more upscale than ever, with "Beatles" acts and two competing Pink Floyd tribute bands performing with full production at arenas and large concert halls.

Mick Jagger is knighted.

Phish's farewell shows and the Pixies reunion tour are major events.

Ramones guitarist Johnny Ramone dies at 55 of prostate cancer.

Buffalo Springfield bassist Bruce Palmer dies at 58 of a heart attack.

"Dimebag" Darrell Abbott, former guitarist of the heavy metal band Pantera, is fatally shot during a performance by a deranged fan. Abbott was 38.

2005

Spencer Dryden, former drummer of Jefferson Airplane, dies at 66 of cancer.

Jim Capaldi, former drummer of the British band Traffic, dies at 60 of cancer.

Rereleases of Elvis Presley hits "Jailhouse Rock" (1957), "One Night" (1959), and "It's Now or Never" (1960) top the British pop charts as RCA vigorously promotes his early hits before the expiration of the 50-year copyright protection laws on sound recordings in place in most European countries.

A welcome surprise is the reunion of Cream for a four-night run of shows at Cordon's Royal Albert Hall, site of their 1968 farewell.

Rockin' '50s Fest II presents, in Green Bay, Wisconsin, a mammoth six-day festival featuring an international cast of more than 100 acts, proving that rock and roll 1950s style is vibrant worldwide. Headliners include Bill Haley's Comets, Jerry Lee Lewis, the Crickets, and Frankie Lymon's teenagers.

Glossary of Music Terms

a cappella Literally "in the chapel." Used generally to describe unaccompanied vocal music.

accent Extra emphasis given to a note in a musical composition.

alto (1) The lowest female voice, below mezzo-soprano and SOPRANO. (2) In musical instruments, an instrument with a range of either a fourth or fifth below the standard range; the viola is tuned a fifth below the violin, for example. (3) The alto CLEF (also known as the C clef) used for notating music for alto instruments and voices.

arpeggio A broken CHORD; the notes of the chord played in succession, rather than simultaneously.

ballad (1) In folk traditions, a multiversed song that tells a narrative story, often based on historic or mythological figures. (2) In popular music, a slow lament, usually on the subject of lost love.

bar See MEASURE.

baritone (1) The male voice situated between the BASS (lowest) and TENOR (highest). (2) Baritone is sometimes used to describe musical instruments that play an octave below the ordinary range.

barrelhouse An aggressive two-handed piano style suitable for a piano player working in a noisy room, a bar, or a brothel. The same word is used to describe such a venue.

bass (1) The lowest male vocal range. (2) The deepest-sounding musical instrument within a family of instruments, such as the bass violin. (3) The lowest instrumental part.

beat The basic rhythmic unit of a musical composition. In common time (most frequently used in popular music), there are two basic beats to the measure; the first is given more emphasis, and therefore is called the *strong* beat, the second is less emphasized and thus is called the *weak* beat.

bebop A form of jazz that developed in the late 1940s and 1950s played by small ensembles or combos, which emphasized rapid playing and unusual rhythmic accents. Many bebop musicians took common CHORD PROGRESSIONS of popular songs and composed new melodies for them, allowing the accompanying instruments (piano-bass-drums) a form that could be easily followed while the melody parts (trumpet, saxophone) improvised.

bending notes Technique used on stringed instruments where the musician pushes against a string with the left hand, causing the note to rise in pitch. On an electric guitar, which has light gauge strings, the pitch may rise as much as a whole tone (two frets).

big band jazz A popular jazz style of the 1930s and 1940s featuring larger ensembles divided into parts (brass, reeds, rhythm). Riffs, or short melodic phrases, were traded back and forth between the melody instruments.

"Blue Moon" progression A sequence of four chords associated with the song "Blue Moon," popularized in 1935 by Benny Goodman and others. The chords are I, VI minor, IV (or II minor), and V. In the key of C, they would be: C, A minor, F (or D minor), and G. Each chord might be held for two, four, or eight beats, but they appear in sequence. The progression is very common in doo-wop music.

blues An African-American vocal and instrumental style that developed in the late 19th to early 20th centuries. The "blues scale" usually features a flattened third and seventh, giving the music a recognizable sound. The classic 12-bar blues features three repeated lines of four bars each, with the first two lines of lyrics repeated, followed by a contrasting line. The chord progression is also fairly standardized, although many blues musicians have found ways to extend and improvise around these rules.

boogie-woogie Boogie-woogie is a way of playing BLUES on the piano that was first recorded in the 1920s. Its chief characteristic is the left-hand pattern, known as eight-to-the-bar (a note is played on every one of the eight possible eighth notes in a measure of four beats), which provides a propulsive rhythm that seems to have been influenced by the sound of trains. Boogie-woogie became a fad after the 1938 and 1939 From Spirituals to Swing concerts, and was adapted into big band swing, pop, and country music. From there it became part of ROCK 'N' ROLL. To boogie in general slang (as in "I've got to boogie now") means to leave somewhere in a hurry. In musical slang, to boogie means to maintain a repetitive blues-based rhythmic foundation, particularly one associated with the style of John Lee Hooker, similar to the figure in his song, "Boogie Chillen."

brass Traditionally, musical instruments whose bodies are made out of brass (although sometimes today they are made out of other metals). Usually used to refer to members of the horn family, including trumpets and trombones.

British invasion Popular groups of the 1960s that dominated the American pop charts. The Beatles led the charge in 1964, but were quickly followed by many soundalike bands, as well as more distinctive groups like the Rolling Stones, The Who, the Kinks, and many others.

cadence A melodic or harmonic phrase usually used to indicate the ending of a PHRASE or a complete musical composition.

capo A metal or elastic clamp placed across all of the strings of a guitar that enables players to change key, while still using the same chord fingerings as they would use without the capo.

CD (compact disc) A recording medium developed in the mid-1980s that enables music to be encoded as digital information on a small disc, and that is "read" by a laser. Various forms of CDs have been developed since to contain higher sound quality and/or other materials (photographs, moving images, etc.)

chord The basic building block of HARMONY, chords usually feature three or more notes played simultaneously.

chord progression A sequence of chords, for example in the key of C: C, F, and G7.

chorus Most commonly used in popular songs to indicate a repeated STANZA that features the same melody and lyrics that falls between each verse. Perhaps because members of the audience might "sing-along" with this part of the song, it came to be known as the chorus (a chorus literally being more than one voice singing at the same time). See VERSE.

clef The symbol at the beginning of a notated piece of music indicating the note values assigned to each line of the STAFF. The three most common clefs used in popular music are the G clef (or treble clef), usually used to notate the melody; the F clef (or bass clef), usually used for harmony parts; and the less-frequently seen C clef (or tenor clef), used for notating instruments with special ranges, most usually the viola.

country and western (C&W) A category developed by the music industry in the late 1940s to distinguish folk, cowboy, and other musical styles aimed at the white, rural, working-class listener (as opposed to R&B, aimed at black audiences, and pop, aimed at urban whites). Later, the *western* was dropped.

cover versions The music business has always been competitive, and even before recordings were possible, many artists would do the same song, as can be seen by the multiple editions of the sheet music for certain hits, each with a different artists' photo on the front. In the 1950s the practice of copying records was rampant, particularly by bigger companies, which had more resources (publicity, distribution, influence) and which used their artists to cover songs from independent labels that had started to show promise in the marketplace. A true cover version is one that attempts to stay close to the song on which it is based. Interpretations of existing songs are often called covers, but when artistry is involved in giving an individual treatment to an existing song, that effort is worthy of being considered more than a cover version.

crescendo A gradual increase in volume indicated in music notation by a triangle placed on its side below the STAFF, like this <.

crossover record A record that starts in one musical category, but has a broader appeal and becomes popular in another category. For example B. B. King's "The Thrill Is Gone" started out as an R&B record, but crossed over to the pop category.

cut a record Recording a record.

decrescendo A gradual decrease in volume indicated in music notation by a triangle placed on its side below the STAFF, as in >.

Delta blues Blues music originating in the Mississippi Delta and typically featuring the use of a slide, intense vocal performances, an aggressive, sometimes strummed guitar style with bass notes "popped" by the thumb for a snapping sound.

diatonic harmony The CHORDS implicit in the major scale. The sequence of triads is I major, II minor, III minor, IV major, V major, VI minor, and VII diminished. Because the diminished chord is unstable, it is virtually never used in this context. Because major chords are more common, many songs use only them: I, IV, and V.

disco A dance form of the 1970s developed in urban dance clubs, consisting of a heavily accented, repeated rhythmic part.

Dixieland jazz Jazz style popularized in New Orleans at the beginning of the 20th century by small combos, usually including three horns: a clarinet, a trumpet, and a trombone. The rhythm section includes a banjo, a tuba, a simple drum set, and a piano, and occasionally a saxophone, string bass, or guitar is added.

DIY (Do-It-Yourself) An emphasis on homemade music and recordings, which began with the PUNK movement but outlived it. The message was that everyone could make their own music, and record and market it on their own, using simple, inexpensive instruments and technology.

DJ (deejay) The person who plays records at a dance club or on a radio station. DJs began to create musical compositions by stringing together long sequences of records, and then further manipulated them using techniques such as backspinning (rapidly spinning a turntable backward while a record is being played) and scratching (moving the turntable back and forth rapidly to emphasize a single note or word).

DVD (digital video disc) A form of optical disc designed to hold video or film, but also sometimes used for higher-quality music reproduction. See CD (COMPACT DISC).

easy listening See MOR (MIDDLE-OF-THE-ROAD).

eighth note See NOTE VALUES.

electronic music Music created using electronic means, including SYNTHESIZERS, SEQUENCERS, tape recorders, and other nontraditional instruments.

falsetto A high register vocal sound producing a light texture. Often used in soul music.

finger-picking A style of guitar playing that keeps a steady bass with the thumb while playing melody on the treble strings.

flat A symbol in music NOTATION indicating that the note should be dropped one-half step in PITCH. Compare SHARP.

flat pick A pick held between the thumb and first finger of the right hand that is very effective for playing rapid single note passages or heavy rhythm guitar.

flip side   The other side of a 45 rpm record, typically the nonhit song.

folk music   Traditional music that is passed down from one person to another within a family or a community. Often the original composer or songwriter is unknown.

45   A record that plays at 45 revolutions per minute (rpm). Developed in the 1950s by RCA, the 45 or "single" was the main way of promoting individual songs on the pop and R&B charts through the CD era.

gospel music   Composed black religious music.

half note   See NOTE VALUES.

harmony   Any musical composition with more than one part played simultaneously. In popular music the harmony is usually the accompanying part, made up of CHORDs, that complement the MELODY.

heavy metal   Rock style of the mid-1970s and later that emphasized a thunderous sound, simplified chord progressions, subject matter aimed to appeal to teenage boys (primarily), and flamboyant stage routines. Other variants (death metal, speed metal) developed over the coming decades.

hip-hop   The music (rap), dance (breakdancing), and visual expression (graffiti art) originating in urban areas in the mid-1970s.

holy blues   Songs that combine religious words with blues melodies and accompaniments.

hook   A recurrent musical or lyric phrase that is designed to "hook" the listener into a particular song or record. It is often also the title of a song.

interval   The space between two PITCHES. The first note of a SCALE is considered the first interval; the next note, the second; and so on. Thus, in a C major scale, an "E" is considered a third, and a G a "fifth." The I-III-V combination makes up a major CHORD.

jukebox   A machine designed to play records. Commonly found in bars (known as "juke joints" in the South), these replaced live music by

the mid-1950s, and were a major means of promoting hit records. Customers dropped a "nickel in the jukebox" to hear their favorite song.

key   Indicates the range of notes (or SCALE) on which a composition is based.

key signature   The symbol at the beginning of a piece of notation that indicates the basic KEY of the work.

looping   Repeating a short musical PHRASE or RHYTHM. SEQUENCERs can be programmed to "loop" or repeat these parts indefinitely.

LP   A "long-playing" record, playing at 33 revolutions per minute (rpm). Developed in the late 1940s, the LP enabled record companies to present more or longer compositions on a single disc (the previous time limit of 78s was 3 to 5 minutes, while an LP could hold 20 to 25 minutes per side).

major   One of the two primary SCALEs used in popular music. The relation between the seven notes in the major scale is whole step (WS)-WS-half step (HS)-WS-WS-WS-HS. Each scale step has a related CHORD defining major harmony. Compare MINOR.

measure   A unit of musical time in a composition defined by the time signature. In 4/4 time, for example, each measure consists of four beats (and a quarter note is equal to one beat). The bar line (a vertical line across all five lines of the STAFF) indicates the beginning and end of a measure.

melody   Two or more musical tones played in succession, called the "horizontal" part of a musical composition because the notes move horizontally across the staff (as opposed to the HARMONY which is called the "vertical" part because the harmony notes are stacked vertically on the staff). In popular music the melody of a song is the most memorable part of the composition.

meter   The repeated pattern of strong and weak rhythmic pulses in a piece of music. For example, in a waltz, the oom-pah-pah meter is the defining part of the music's style.

MIDI (Musical Instrument Digital Interface)   A common programming language that enables SYNTHESIZERS, computers, and SEQUENCERS to communicate with one another.

minor   One of the two primary SCALES used in popular music. The relation between the seven notes in the major scale is whole step (WS)-half step (HS)-WS-HS-WS-WS. (There are two variations of this basic pattern found in scales known as the "harmonic" and "melodic" minor.) Each scale step has a related CHORD defining major harmony. Compare MAJOR.

minstrel   Performance of African-American songs and dances by white performers in blackface, burnt cork rubbed on their faces beginning in the mid-19th century. Later, black minstrels appeared. Minstrel shows included songs, dances, and humorous skits. Many of these skits and songs made fun of African Americans.

modes   A type of SCALE. The two common scales used today (the MAJOR and MINOR) are two types of mode. In the Middle Ages, a system of eight different modes was developed, each with the same intervals but beginning on a different note. The modes are sometimes still heard in folk music, some forms of jazz, and some forms of contemporary classical music.

MOR (middle-of-the-road)   Pop music aimed at a wide audience, designed to be as inoffensive and nondisturbing as possible. This term is often used pejoratively by critics. Also sometimes called "easy listening."

movement   A section of a longer musical composition.

notation   A system developed over many centuries to write down musical compositions using specific symbols to represent PITCH and RHYTHM.

note values   The time values of the notes in a musical composition are relational, usually based on the idea of a quarter note equaling one beat (as in 4/4 time). In this time signature, a quarter note fills a quarter of the time in the measure; a half-note equals two beats (is twice as long) and a whole note equals four beats (a full measure). Conversely, shorter time values include an eighth-note (half a single beat), a sixteenth (¼ of a single beat), a thirty-second (⅛ of a single beat), etc.

octave   An INTERVAL of eight notes, considered the "perfect" consonance. If a string is divided perfectly in half, each half will sound an octave above the full string, so that the ratio between the two notes is expressed as 1:2.

opus   A numbering system used in classical composition to indicate the order in which pieces were composed. Some composers only give opus numbers to works they feel are strong enough to be part of their "official" canon.

percussion   Instruments used to play the rhythmic part of a composition, which may be "unpitched" (such as drums or cymbals) or "pitched" (such as bells, chimes, and marimbas).

phonograph   A mechanical instrument used to reproduce sound recordings. A phonograph consists of some form of turntable, needle, tone arm, amplifier, and speaker. A record is placed on a turntable, a disc that is set to revolve at specific speeds. The needle "reads" the grooves cut into the record itself. The vibrations then are communicated through the tone arm (in which the needle is mounted) into an amplifier (which increases the volume of the sound). A speaker projects the sound out so that it can be heard.

phrase   A subsection of the MELODY that expresses a complete musical thought.

Piedmont blues   A form of blues from the Carolinas, Georgia, Florida, and Alabama that uses a restrained style of fingerpicking and soft vocal performances. It also often uses ragtime CHORD PROGRESSIONS.

pitch   The note defined by its sound; literally, the number of vibrations per second (of a string, air column, bar, or some other vibrating object) that results in a given tone. Pitch is relative; in most tuning systems, a specific note is chosen as the pitch against which others are tuned. In modern music, this is usually A above middle C, defined as vibrating at 440 vps.

pop music   Any music that appeals to a large audience. Originally, the pop charts featured records aimed at white, urban listeners (as opposed to R&B, aimed at blacks, and C&W or country, aimed at rural, lower-class whites). Today, "pop" is applied to any recording that appeals across a wide range of listeners, so that Michael Jackson or Shania Twain could equally be defined as "pop" stars.

power chords   Played on the low strings of an electric guitar, power chords use only the root and the fifth (and often a repeat of the root an octave higher) of a triad, leaving out the third of the CHORD. With no third, the chord is neither MAJOR or MINOR. With only two notes, it is technically not even a chord, but an interval. The use of power chords was pioneered by Link Wray ("Rumble") and the Kinks ("You Really Got Me"), and used extensively in hard rock (Deep Purple's "Smoke on the Water"), heavy metal (Metallica), and grunge (Nirvana's "Smells Like Teen Spirit").

power trio   Three instruments—guitar, bass, and drums—played at loud volumes.

psychedelic   Popular ROCK style of the late 1960s-early 1970s that featured extended musical forms, "spacey" lyrics, and unusual musical timbres often produced by synthesizers. Psychedelic music was supposed to be the "aural equivalent" of the drug experience. See also SYNTHESIZER; TIMBRE.

punk   A movement that began in England and travelled to the United States in the mid-1970s emphasizing a return to simpler musical forms, in response to the growing commercialization of ROCK. Punk also encompassed fashion (including spiked hair, safety pins used as body ornaments, etc.) and sometimes a violent, antiestablishment message.

quarter note   See NOTE VALUES.

race records   Music industry name for African-American popular music recorded in the 1920s until around 1945.

ragtime   Music dating from around the 1890s and usually composed in three or four different sections. The most famous ragtime pieces were for piano, but the style was also adapted in a simplified form for the banjo and the guitar.

record producer   The person in charge of a recording session.

register   The range in notes of a specific part of a musical composition. Also used to define the range of an individual musical instrument or vocal part.

resonator guitar   Guitars with a metal front and back, often used in playing slide guitar, and prized during the 1930s for their volume.

rhythm   The basic pulse of a musical composition. In ⁴⁄₄ time, the 4 beats per measure provide the pulse that propels the piece. Compare METER.

rhythm and blues (R&B)   Black popular music that emerged around 1945 and peaked in popularity in the 1960s. It usually included gospel-influenced vocal performances, and a rhythm section of piano, bass, and drums. The lead instruments were often guitar and saxophone.

riff   A short, recognizable melodic phrase used repeatedly in a piece of music. Commonly heard in big band jazz or in electric guitar solos.

rock   An outgrowth of ROCK 'N' ROLL in the 1960s that featured more sophisticated arrangements, lyrics, and subject matter. The BRITISH INVASION groups—notably the Beatles and the Rolling Stones—are sometimes credited with extending the style and subjects treated by rock 'n' roll. Rock itself has developed into many different substyles.

rockabilly   Mid-1950s popular music that combined BLUES and COUNTRY music.

rock 'n' roll   The popular music of the mid-1950s aimed at teenage listeners. Popular rock 'n' roll artists included Elvis Presley, Chuck Berry, Little Richard, and Carl Perkins. Compare ROCK.

royalties   Payments to recording artists based on the sales of their records.

salsa   Literally "spice." A form of Latin dance music popularized in the 1970s and 1980s.

scale   A succession of seven notes. The most common scales are the MAJOR and MINOR.

score   The complete notation of a musical composition.

sequencer   An electronic instrument that can record a series of pitches or rhythms and play them back on command.

78   The first form of recorded disc, that revolved on a turntable at 78 revolutions per minute (rpm). The first 78s were 10 inches in diameter and could play for approximately three minutes per side; later, 12-inch 78s were introduced with slightly longer playing times.

sharp   A symbol in a piece of music indicating that a pitch should be raised one half-step in PITCH. Compare FLAT.

side   One side of a recording disc.

slide guitar   Style of guitar in which the player wears a metal or glass tube on one finger or uses a bottle neck to play notes. It creates a distinctive crying sound. Also called bottleneck guitar.

songster   A turn-of-the-20th-century musician with a varied repertoire that included different styles of music.

soprano   The highest female voice, or the highest pitched instrument in a family of instruments.

soul   A black musical style developed in the 1960s that combined elements of GOSPEL MUSIC with RHYTHM AND BLUES.

spirituals   Traditional religious music found in both white and African-American traditions.

staff   The five parallel lines on which the symbols for notes are placed in a notated piece of music. The CLEF at the beginning of the staff indicates the pitch of each note on the staff.

stanza   In poetry, the basic lyrical unit, often consisting of four or six lines. The lyrics to both the VERSE and CHORUS of a popular song follow the stanza form.

strings   Instruments that produce musical sound through the vibration of strings, made out of animal gut or metal. Violins and guitars are stringed instruments.

suite   In classical music, a group of dances played in succession to form a larger musical composition.

symphony   In classical music, a defined form usually consisting of three parts, played Fast-Slow-Fast.

syncopation   Accenting the unexpected or weaker BEAT. Often used in RAGTIME, jazz, and related styles.

synthesizer   An electronic instrument that is capable of creating different musical pitches and timbres.

tempo   The speed at which a piece of music is performed.

tenor   The highest male voice.

theme   A recognizable MELODY that is often repeated within a musical composition.

thumb picks and finger picks   Guitar picks made of metal or plastic worn on the player's right hand fingers and thumb in order to play louder.

timbre   The quality of a PITCH produced by a musical instrument or voice that makes it distinctive. The timbre of a guitar is quite different from that of a flute, for example.

time signature   In notation, the symbol at the beginning of each STAFF that indicates the basic metric pulse and how many beats are contained in a measure. For example, in 4/4 time, a quarter-note is given one beat, and there are four beats per measure; in 6/8 time, an eighth-note is given one beat, and there are six beats in a measure.

Tin Pan Alley   The center of music publishing on West 28th Street in New York City from the late 19th century through the 1930s (so-called because the clatter from competing pianists working in different buildings sounded to passersby like rattling tin pans). Used generally to describe the popular songs of this period.

tone   See PITCH.

tremolo   The rapid repetition of a single note to give a "quivering" or "shaking" sound. Compare VIBRATO.

turnaround   A musical phrase at the end of a verse that briefly outlines the CHORDS of the song before the start of the next verse.

12-bar blues   A 12-bar BLUES has 12 measures of music, or bars, and is the most common blues format, though eight bars and 16 bars are also used.

vamp   A short segment of music that repeats, usually two or four CHORDS. Two chord vamps are common in GOSPEL and ROCK, especially the I and IV chords (C and F in the key of C).

vanity records   Recordings that are conceived and financed by the artists involved. They are called "vanity records" because the motivation comes from the person or group themselves, not from a record company. The reason is to realize a creative project, to promote a career, or just to boost the ego. Previously, singers and musicians would pay to go into a studio and to cover the costs of backup musicians, mixing, mastering, and manufacturing. This continues, but with the rise of home studios, these steps can be done at home, with computerized recording and CD burning. Vanity records now represent perhaps the majority of recordings being made and are more likely to be called independent productions.

verse   The part of a song that features a changing lyric set to a fixed MELODY. The verse is usually performed in alternation with the CHORUS.

vibrato   A rapid moving up and down slightly in PITCH while performing a single note as an ornament. Compare TREMOLO.

walking bass   A style of bass playing that originated in jazz on the upright bass. The bassist plays a new note on every beat, outlining the CHORDS as they pass by in a CHORD PROGRESSION. Chord notes are primary, but passing notes and other decorations enliven the bass line, as well as brief rhythmic variations enliven the bass line. A rock example is Paul McCartney's bass part in the Beatles' "All My Loving" (1964).

whole note   See NOTE VALUES.

woodwinds   A class of instruments traditionally made of wood, although the term is now used for instruments made of brass or metal as well. Clarinets, flutes, and saxophones are usually classified as woodwinds.

Endnotes

1. Brian Wilson quoted in *Rolling Stone* 225, November 4, 1976.

2. Country music had introduced that theme with "Hot Rod Race," a 1950 hit for Arkie Shibley and His Mountain Dew Boys; the song was so popular that three other cover versions were also hits, and multiple versions and sequels were recorded.

3. Bowie, quoted in "The Best 100 Albums of the Last Twenty Years #6: The Rise and Fall of Ziggy Stardust and the Spiders from Mars." *Rolling Stone* 507, August 27, 1987, p. 45+.

4. Columbia Records contracted the band for one single. To expedite the recording process for the two songs, Columbia allowed only McGuinn to play on the session, while studio musicians played the rest. Once it was a hit, the Byrds themselves played on the other album tracks.

5. The initials stand for "Horizons of Rock Developing East Coast." This traveling festival, instigated by members of Blues Traveler, ran annually from 1992 to 1998.

6. Fornatale, Pete. "Doors' Organist Ray Manzarek." *Musician* 35, August 1981, 46–51, 60.

7. Dylan's Grammy awards were for Album of the Year, Best Contemporary Folk Album, and Best Male Rock Vocal Performance (for "Cold Irons Bound").

8. Bruce Jackson's article "The Myth of Newport '65: It wasn't Bob Dylan They Were Booing" is on his Web site "The Buffalo Report," at http://buffaloreport.com/020826dylan.html.

9. Don Waller, from the liner notes of the first volume of the Nuggets series, issued by the Rhino label in 1984.

10. It was covered by the Rolling Stones in 1965, and in 1967 Hendrix used it, along with other R&B classics, during auditions for the Experience. It remained in the repertoire during their early shows.

11. Roxon, 47.

12. Like several other acts, Big Brother and the Holding Company had balked at being asked to sign a release to be filmed for no compensation when they were already, because the festival was a benefit, performing for free.

13. Altman, 217.

14. Quoted in "The Making of Nevermind" by Alan di Perna, *Guitar World,* October 1996, 18.

15. *Generation X* generally refers to people born in the 1960s and 1970s. The term was picked up by the media from *Generation X: Tales for an Accelerated Culture* by Douglas Coupland, published in 1991.

16. This is according to Joel Whitburn and his Record Research company, which publish books that compile information from the sales charts of *Billboard* magazine and other music trade publications. They have made a science of tabulating and ranking the achievements of recording artists.

17. Mohawk is the name of an American Indian tribe, but punk's adoption of the mohawk cut is thought to have been inspired by Robert De Niro's character in the 1976 movie *Taxi Driver.*

18 Guterman and O'Donnell, 195

19 Robert Christgau in "Christgau's Consumer Guide," *Village Voice,* May 29, 1984. Available online. URL:http://www.robertchristgau.com. Downloaded on October 21, 2004.

20 Landau, Jon. "Growing Young with Rock and Roll." *The Real Paper* (Boston), May 22, 1974, n. p.

21 Shaw, 107.

22 Quote attributed to Charles O'Hara's unpublished manuscript "The Velvet Underground: Pittsburgh, PA 1968" (1984), from a 1989 sociology thesis by Tricia Henry: *Break All the Rules! Punk Rock and the Making of a Style,* excerpted on "The Velvet Underground Web Page," http://members.aol.com/olandem2/pert68.html.

Bibliography

Altman, Billy. "Led Zeppelin." *The Rolling Stone Record Guide.* Dave Marsh with John Swenson, eds. New York: Random House/Rolling Stone Press, 1979.

Amburn, Ellis. *Buddy Holly: A Biography.* New York: St. Martin's Press, 1995.

———. *Pearl: The Obsessions and Passions of Janis Joplin: A Biography.* New York: Warner Books, 1992.

Berry, Chuck. *Chuck Berry: The Autobiography.* New York: Simon and Schuster, 1987.

Betrock, Alan. *Girl Groups: The Story of a Sound.* New York: Delilah, 1982.

Black, Johnny. *Eyewitness Hendrix.* London: Carlton, 1999.

Chapple, Steve, and Reebee Garofalo. *Rock 'n' Roll Is Here to Pay: The History and Politics of the Music Industry.* Chicago: Nelson-Hall, 1978.

Clark, Dick, and Richard Robinson. *Rock, Roll and Remember.* New York: Thomas Y. Crowell, 1976.

Clarke, Donald, ed. *The Penguin Encyclopedia of Popular Music, 2nd edition.* London: Penguin, 1998.

Clemente, John. *Girl Groups: Fabulous Females That Rocked the World.* Iola, Wis.: Krause Publications, 2001.

Clifford, Mike, ed. *The Harmony Illustrated Encyclopedia of Rock.* New York: Harmony, 1992.

Crosby, David, and Carl Gottlieb. *Long Time Gone: The Autobiography of David Crosby.* New York: Doubleday, 1988.

Dalton, David. *Piece of My Heart: The Life, Times and Legend of Janis Joplin.* London: Sidgwick and Jackson, 1986.

Davies, Dave. *Kink: An Autobiography.* New York: Hyperion Books, 1996.

Davies, Ray. *X-Ray: The Unauthorized Autobiography.* New York: Overlook Press, 1994.

Dawson, Jim, and Steve Propes. *What Was the First Rock 'n' Roll Record?* Boston: Faber and Faber, 1992.

Dolenz, Mickey, and Mark Bego. *I'm a Believer: My Life of Monkees, Music, and Madness.* New York: Hyperion, 1993.

Einarson, John. *Desperados: The Roots of Country Rock.* New York: Cooper Square Press, 2001.

Einarson, John, and Richie Furay. *For What It's Worth: The Story of Buffalo Springfield.* Kingston, Ont.: Quarry Press, 1997.

Escott, Colin, with Martin Hawkins. *Good Rockin' Tonight: Sun Records and the Birth of Rock 'n' Roll.* New York: St. Martin's Press, 1991.

Fleetwood, Mick. *My Twenty-Five Years in Fleetwood Mac.* London: Weidenfeld and Nicholson, 1992.

Fornatale, Pete. "Doors' organist Ray Manzarek." *Musician* 35, August 1981: 46–51, 60.

Frame, Pete. *The Complete Rock Family Trees.* London: Omnibus Press, 1993.

Gaines, Steven. *Heroes & Villains: The True Story of the Beach Boys.* New York: New American Library, 1986.

Gans, David. *Conversations with the Dead.* New York: Citadel Press, 1991.

Gill, Andy. *Classic Bob Dylan 1962–69: My Back Pages.* London: Carlton, 1998.

301

Gillett, Charlie. *The Sound of the City: The Rise of Rock and Roll, Revised Edition*. London: Souvenir Press, 1983.

Gleason, Ralph J. *Jefferson Airplane and the San Francisco Sound*. New York: Ballantine, 1969.

Goldman, Herbert G. *Jolson: The Legend Comes to Life*. New York: Oxford University Press, 1988.

Goldrosen, John, and John Beecher. *Remembering Buddy: The Definitive Biography*. London: GPR1/Pavillion, 1987.

Goodman, Fred. *The Mansion on the Hill: Dylan, Young, Geffen, Springsteen and the Head-On Collision of Rock and Commerce*. London: Jonathan Cape, 1997.

Guralnick, Peter. *Last Train to Memphis: The Rise of Elvis Presley*. Boston: Little, Brown, and Company, 1994.

Hale, Jonathan. *Radiohead: From a Great Height*. Toronto: ECW Press, 1999.

Hardy, Phil, and Dave Laing. *The Faber Companion to 20th-Century Popular Music*. London: Faber and Faber, 1995.

Henke, James, with Parke Puterbaugh, ed. Essays by Charles Perry, Barry Miles, and Jon Savage. *I Want to Take You Higher: The Psychedelic Era 1965–1969*. San Francisco: Chronicle Books, 1997.

Hicks, Michael. *Sixties Rock: Garage, Psychedelic, and Other Satisfactions*. Urbana: University of Illinois Press, 1999.

Hoskyns, Barney. *Across the Great Divide: The Band in America*. New York: Hyperion, 1993.

Lazell, Barry, ed., with Dafydd Rees and Luke Crampton. *Rock Movers and Shakers*. New York: Billboard, 1989.

Lee, Brenda, with Robert K. Oermann and Julie Clay. *Little Miss Dynamite: The Life and Times of Brenda Lee*. New York: Hyperion Books, 2002.

Lewis, Myra, with Murray Silver. *Great Balls of Fire: The Uncensored Story of Jerry Lee Lewis*. New York: Quill, 1982.

Mantovina, Dan. *Without You: The Tragic Story of Badfinger*. San Mateo, Calif.: Frances Glover Books, 2000.

Manzarek, Ray. *Light My Fire: My Life with the Doors*. New York: G.P. Putnam's Sons, 1998.

Marsh, Dave. *The Heart of Rock and Soul: The 1001 Greatest Singles Ever Made*. New York: Plume, 1989.

———. *Louie Louie: The History and Mythology of the World's Most Famous Rock 'N' Roll Song; Including the Full Details of Its Torture and Persecution at the Hands of the Kingsmen, J. Edgar Hoover's FBI, and a Cast of Millions; and Introducing, for the First Time Anywhere, the Actual Dirty Lyrics*. New York: Hyperion, 1993.

Miller, James. *Flowers in the Dustbin: The Rise of Rock and Roll, 1947–1977*. New York: Simon and Schuster, 1999.

Morrison, Craig. *Go Cat Go! Rockabilly Music and Its Makers*. Urbana: University of Illinois Press, 1996.

O'Hara, Charles. "The Velvet Underground: Pittsburgh, PA 1968" (1984), unpublished manuscript cited in Tricia Henry: *Break All The Rules!: Punk Rock and the Making of a Style*, a 1989 sociology thesis excerpted on "The Velvet Underground Web Page."

Palmer, Robert. *Rock and Roll: An Unruly History*. New York: Harmony Books, 1995.

Perkins, Carl, and David McGee. *Go, Cat, Go! The Life and Times of Carl Perkins, the King of Rockabilly*. New York: Hyperion, 1996.

Phillips, Michelle. *California Dreamin': The True Story of the Mamas and the Papas*. New York: Warner Books, 1986.

Ponds, Steve. "A Biased History of UK Glam Rock." Available online: http://www.doremi.co.uk/glam/hist.html. Downloaded on August 8, 2004.

Ribowsky, Mark. *He's a Rebel: Phil Spector, Rock and Roll's Legendary Producer*. New York: Cooper Square Press, 1989.

Roxon, Lillian. *Lillian Roxon's Rock Encyclopedia*. New York: Grosset's Universal Library, 1971.

Ruhlmann, William. *The History of the Grateful Dead*. London: Bison Books, 1990.

Savage, Jon. *The Kinks: The Official Biography*. London: Faber and Faber, 1984.

Scott, John W., Mike Dolgushkin, and Stu Nixon. *Dead Base X: The Complete Guide to Grateful Dead Song Lists.* Cornish, N.H.: Dead Base, 1997.

Selvin, Joel. *Summer of Love: The Inside Story of LSD, Rock and Roll, Free Love and High Times in the Wild West.* New York: Plume, 1995.

Shaw, Greg. "The Instrumental Groups." *The Rolling Stone Illustrated History of Rock & Roll.* Jim Miller, ed. New York: Random House/Rolling Stone Press, 1980.

Slick, Grace, with Andrea Cagan. *Somebody to Love? A Rock-and-Roll Memoir.* New York: Warner, 1998.

Spector, Ronnie, with Vince Waldron. *Be My Baby: How I Survived Mascara, Miniskirts, and Madness, or My Life as a Fabulous Ronette.* New York: Harmony Books, 1990.

Stebbins, Jon. *Dennis Wilson: The Real Beach Boy.* Toronto: ECW Press, 1999.

Sullivan, Henry W. *The Beatles with Lacan: Rock 'n' Roll as Requiem for the Modern Age.* New York: Peter Lang, 1995.

Szatmary, David P. *Rockin' in Time: A Social History of Rock-and-Roll, Fifth Edition.* Upper Saddle River, N.J.: Prentice Hall, 2004.

Thompson, Dave. "Prisoner of Love." *50 Years of Rock 'n' Roll: 1954–2004, Part One '50s + '60s.* London: Q Special Edition, 2004.

Tobler, John, ed. *Who's Who in Rock and Roll.* Toronto: B. Mitchell, 1991.

Tosches, Nick. *Hellfire: The Jerry Lee Lewis Story.* New York: Delacorte, 1982.

———."20 Top Music Magazine Histories" Available online: http://www.cbub.com/history.htm. Downloaded on August 1, 2004.

Unterberger, Richie. *Turn! Turn! Turn! The '60s Folk-Rock Revolution.* San Francisco: Backbeat Books, 2002.

Ward, Ed, Geoffry Stokes, and Ken Tucker. *Rock of Ages: The Rolling Stone History of Rock & Roll.* Englewood Cliffs, N.J.: Rolling Stone Press/Prentice Hall, 1986.

Weinberg, Max. *The Big Beat: Conversations with Rock's Greatest Drummers.* Chicago: Contemporary Books, 1984.

Whitburn, Joel. *Pop Memories 1890–1954: The History of American Popular Music.* Menomonee Falls, Wis.: Record Research, 1986.

———. *Top Pop Albums 1955–2001.* Menomonee Falls, Wis.: Record Research, 2001.

———. *Top Pop Singles 1955–2002.* Menomonee Falls, Wis.: Record Research, 2003.

White, Timothy. *The Nearest Faraway Place: Brian Wilson, the Beach Boys, and the Southern California Experience.* New York: Henry Holt, 1994.

Zappa, Frank, and Peter Occhiogrosso. *The Real Frank Zappa Book.* New York: Poseidon Press, 1989.

Editorial Board of Advisers

Duckworth is currently a professor of music at Bucknell University in Pennsylvania.

Kevin Holm-Hudson, Ph.D., received his doctorate of musical arts (composition with ethnomusicology concentration) from the University of Illinois at Urbana-Champaign. He is an assistant professor of music at the University of Kentucky and is an editor/contributor to *Progressive Rock Reconsidered* (Routledge). Dr. Holm-Hudson is also the author of numerous articles that have appeared in such publications as *Genre* and *Ex Tempore* and has presented papers on a wide variety of topics at conferences, including "'Come Sail Away' and the Commodification of Prog Lite," at the inaugural Conference on Popular Music and American Culture in 2002.

Nadine Hubbs, Ph.D., is associate professor of music and women's studies at the University of Michigan (Ann Arbor). She has written extensively on classical and popular music, particularly in relation to gender and sexuality. Dr. Hubbs is the author of *The Queer Composition of America's Sound: Gay Modernists, American Music, and National Identity* (University of California Press) and various essays, including "The Imagination of Pop-Rock Criticism" in *Expression in Pop-Rock Music* (Garland Publications) and "Music of the 'Fourth Gender': Morrissey and the Sexual Politics of Melodic Contour," featured in the journal *Genders*.

Craig Morrison, Ph.D., holds a doctorate in humanities with a concentration in music from Concordia University (Montreal, Quebec). He is currently a professor of music at Concordia, where he teaches a course titled "Rock and Roll and Its Roots." Dr. Morrison is the author of *Go Cat Go! Rockabilly Music and Its Makers* (University of Illinois Press) and contributed to *The Encyclopedia of the Blues* (Routledge). He has presented many papers on elements of rock and roll.

Albin J. Zak III, Ph.D., earned a doctorate in musicology from the Graduate Center of the City University of New York and is currently chairman of the music department at the University at Albany (SUNY). His publications include *The Velvet Underground Companion* (Schirmer Books) and *The Poetics of Rock: Cutting Tracks, Making Records* (University of California Press). Dr. Zak is also a songwriter, recording engineer, and record producer.

Index